WERTHEIM PUBLICATIONS IN INDUSTRIAL RELATIONS

Established in 1923 by the family of the late Jacob Wertheim "for the support of original research in the field of industrial cooperation . . ."

Wertheim Publications in Industrial Relations

J. D. Houser, *What the Employer Thinks,* 1927

Wertheim Lectures on Industrial Relations, 1929

William Haber, *Industrial Relations in the Building Industry,* 1930

Johnson O'Connor, *Psychometrics,* 1934

Paul H. Norgren, *The Swedish Collective Bargaining System,* 1941

Leo C. Brown, S.J., *Union Policies in the Leather Industry,* 1947

Walter Galenson, *Labor in Norway,* 1949

Dorothea de Schweinitz, *Labor and Management in a Common Enterprise,* 1949

Ralph Altman, *Availability for Work: A Study in Unemployment Compensation,* 1950

John T. Dunlop and Arthur D. Hill, *The Wage Adjustment Board: Wartime Stabilization in the Building and Construction Industry,* 1950

Walter Galenson, *The Danish System of Labor Relations: A Study in Industrial Peace,* 1952

Lloyd H. Fisher, *The Harvest Labor Market in California,* 1953

Theodore V. Purcell, S.J., *The Worker Speaks His Mind on Company and Union,* 1953

Donald J. White, *The New England Fishing Industry,* 1954

Val R. Lorwin, *The French Labor Movement,* 1954

Philip Taft, *The Structure and Government of Labor Unions,* 1954

George B. Baldwin, *Beyond Nationalization: The Labor Problems of British Coal,* 1955

Kenneth F. Walker, *Industrial Relations in Australia,* 1956

Charles A. Myers, *Labor Problems in the Industrialization of India,* 1958

Herbert J. Spiro, *The Politics of German Codetermination,* 1958

Mark W. Leiserson, *Wages and Economic Control in Norway, 1945–1947,* 1959

J. Pen, *The Wage Rate under Collective Bargaining,* 1959

Jack Stieber, *The Steel Industry Wage Structure,* 1959

Theodore V. Purcell, S.J., *Blue Collar Man: Patterns of Dual Allegiance in Industry,* 1960

Carl Erik Knoellinger, *Labor in Finland,* 1960

Sumner H. Slichter, *Potentials of the American Economy: Selected Essays,* edited by John T. Dunlop, 1961

STUDIES IN LABOR-MANAGEMENT HISTORY

Lloyd Ulman, *The Rise of the National Trade Union: The Development and Significance of Its Structure, Governing Institutions and Economic Policies,* 1955

Joseph P. Goldberg, *The Maritime Story: A Study in Labor-Management Relations,* 1957, 1958

Walter Galenson, *The CIO Challenge to the AFL: A History of the American Labor Movement, 1935–1941,* 1960

Morris A. Horowitz, *The New York Hotel Industry: A Labor Relations Study,* 1960

Mark Perlman, *The Machinists: A New Study in American Trade Unionism,* 1961

Order of United Machinists and Mechanical Engineers of America.

Office of Executive Committee,
Atlanta, Ga., September 10th, 1888.

Dear Sir—The machinists of this place have for some time past had under consideration the general condition of our trade in comparison with that of other trades and professions, and we concluded after deliberate consultation and inquiry that the machinist trade, as it is termed, ranks among the highest, and we find that the unlimited number of machinists in this and other countries are made up of the most skilled and intelligent people among the mechanics of the land. We find in our shops men of the highest families, and a large majority of them are men of honorable, industrious and sober habits, while the minority are quite the reverse; and the conclusion is that this minority has, to a great extent, damaged the grand reputation that the better ones deserve. We also find that machinists, generally, are a healthy and long-living people, and that in the beneficial and life insurance societies we pay heavily for some of the other trades that are detrimental to health and old age. And again we find that the required amount of labor is greatly increasing, while compensation decreases gradually, thereby causing many unemployed men in our ranks; and we find that at most places we are poorly instructed in the general changes and improvements in the trade as well as of our advantages and dangers. And there the question arises, why should we be deprived of the good name we deserve, and why suffer all these disadvantages mindless of the great advantages in arms length of us? It is simply because we are living in an unusually selfish age—an age of strict sectionalism. You will find to-day everybody organized from the man that shovels sand upon the railroad track to the railroad president; from the street sweeper to the manufacturer, and even to the bloated bondholder is organized, each having their own organization so arranged as to carry their own personal ends, no matter who suffers. We, the machinists, are the only branch of trades that have no organization adapted to our immediate requirements, and why is it? Not because we have not got the intelligence; not because we do not need organizations, for numbers are organized against us, and set in secret session month after month, and year after year, planning and scheming to lower us to a point where we would be ashamed to arise and say, my time is my money and my money is my living for myself and my family. No, friend, it is because we need push and energy; we need to reflect upon these matters and consider where or what will we be ten years from to-day if we do not awake to our condition and danger. And in consideration of these facts, we, on the 5th day of last May, organized a lodge under the name and title above mentioned, under a code of laws stipulating that it should be a beneficial society, paying an indemnity to the sick and disabled—an endowment to the families of the deceased; that we should seek to keep ours employed and keep up the reputation of our trade and ourselves, and be better prepared to keep up an opposition to the burdensome and stringent requirements that are heaped upon us from time to time; and there is no reason why we should not have the strongest and most reputable order in the country—not one to create disorder and strikes, or to antagonize capital and enterprise, but one that will build up a friendliness between us and capital; one to abolish and make strikes a thing of the past. One, through which we can find employment for our unemployed without his tramping the country, leaving distress and want behind him; and through which we can make our superanuated brothers happy and content without dying under the sound of a bell or a whistle. Why can't we publish and circulate among ourselves a journal through wh[illegible] can convey the intellect of one to another? By the [illegible]hange of ideas great results accrue, and while a machinist is not a journalist, he h[illegible] and can give some of the best ideas known to science. So we hereby ask, let each one of us come to the front, combine our energies and make ourselves and our Order the pride of the country.

DESCRIPTION OF THE ORDER.

In answer to the many inquiries that have been received we give below a description of the order:

It is strictly a secret society, in nowise conflicting with one's Religious or Political opinion, holding meetings at least twice per month, admitting none but qualified members which must be (according to Article IV of Constitution) a white, free born male citizen of some civilized country, 21 years old, and must be a practical machinist capable of commanding the average rate of wages given in some well regulated machine shop, and must be working at his trade at the time of his election.

Each member pays a monthly contribution of not less that 50 cents per month, and after being in good standing six months gets, in case of sickness or disability, a benefit of $5.00 per week.

The Order seeks to find employment for its unemployed members and to protect them as well as employers against the burdens of unqualified men calling themselves machinists.

We propose, when thoroughly organized, to create a life insurance for our members, leaving it optional for them to insure, and for what amount, paying half of policies if permanently disabled.

We propose to publish a monthly journal through which we can get a statistical report of the different parts enabling members seeking employment to know where their services are in most demand and through which each one can convey his ideas to all concerned, no matter how limited he may be in education or journalistic qualification.

The order is at present governed by a general executive committee, which was elected May 5th, for a term of one year, or until a sufficient number of subordinate lodges were in operation, at which time a Supreme Grand Lodge will be organized, which will be composed of delegates from each local lodge, and its officers will then have full control and management of the Order, and at the same time all objectionable laws and usages of the Order can be fitted to the many.

We now have lodges in four states of the Union, viz: North Carolina, South Carolina, Georgia and Alabama, and expect before this year expires to call a meeting of delegates from each local lodge to organize a Supreme Lodge, and would be glad to have as many places represented as possible; therefore we ask that some machinist at each town or city take hold of the matter and put his energies to work for the formation of a lodge. Get eight or more machinists, picking the best, each one contributing equally to make the required sum which will be, for charter and supplies, seven dollars, which includes all printed blanks, rituals, constitution, &c., necessary for operating a lodge. Send in names with seven dollars to Executive Committe, and the charter and supplies will be forwarded to the member nearest you, who will organize and instruct you in the work, you paying his necessary expenses, and as we have about two hundred members scattered in different states, almost any place can be reached without any great traveling expenses.

By corresponding with the chairman or secretary of the executive committee they can instruct you as to the whole cost of organizing.

Hoping to hear from you, we remain yours,

WILLIAM DAWLY, Secretary,
68 Foundry St., Atlanta, Ga.

T. W. TALBOT, Chairman,
78 McDaniel St., Atlanta, Ga.

The original circular

THE MACHINISTS:

A New Study in American Trade Unionism

Mark Perlman

HARVARD UNIVERSITY PRESS
Cambridge, Massachusetts 1962

Second printing

Distributed in Great Britain by Oxford University Press, London

Library of Congress Catalog Card Number 61-16695

Printed in the United States of America

7

During the period when I was preparing this study, three of the senior scholars in the field of industrial relations history offered considerable advice and encouragement to me. All three were sons of the University of Wisconsin, having been trained by Professor John R. Commons. They all worked on the staff of the United States Commission on Industrial Relations.

I had thought to dedicate this book to these three men as representatives of a great generation of scholars. Between August 1959 and May 1960, all three died. Now I dedicate this work to their memories.

Selig Perlman, 1888–1959
Sumner Huber Slichter, 1892–1959
Edwin Emil Witte, 1887–1960

Foreword

The neglect of labor history has seriously distorted labor policy in the American community. The dependence of union growth on legislation has been exaggerated; the labor movement did not begin in the 1930's. The limits to which men and organizations can be molded by the fiat of legislative or administrative paper are not well appreciated. There is too little recognition that union government depends on the qualities of the members, on their environment and traditions, on the hard problems of the work place and the market, and on the policies selected to meet these problems rather than upon caprice or intrigue. There is almost no understanding of the rich experimentation in the past in union structure and government — the referendum and initiative, forms of financial control, limitations on local strike activity, powers of the union executive, and the internal judicial system.

The labor movement often reflects an inadequate recognition of its own past. The union member, and the officer particularly, is entitled to know more of his rich heritage. Just as good citizenship in the community depends upon a sense of the traditions, values and the choices of the past, so citizenship in the union community requires an appreciation of the union history.

The International Association of Machinists is one of our great national unions. It includes members in the widest range of industries. With almost a million members, it is the fourth largest national union. The machinists ranked fifth in membership in the American Federation of Labor in 1900, fourth in 1915, and eighth in 1935. Only one or two other national unions that ranked in the first ten sixty years ago are today on that list.

The adaptability of the machinists is, indeed, one of its most distinguishing characteristics. It started in 1888 as a pure craft union on the railroads. It is now both an industrial and craft union, and there is scarcely a major industry in which it is not represented. Moreover, the union has shown great imagination in inventing new forms of internal structure and in balancing the interests of members with varying degrees of skill. At the outset the union was limited to white workers, but its internal processes developed the policy of nondiscrimination. The union which originally opposed piecework and other aspects of the scientific management movement of the early 1900's has come to bargain over a variety of methods of wage payment and to use the most modern staff experts. Despite such vast changes, the machinists have maintained a distinctive spirit and unity.

The transformation of union government and policies in the face of changing technology, market competition, legislation and public policies, is an exciting and instructive story. The change was not always a simple or easy process, and it often involved much debate and experimentation. The costs and conflicts inherent in adaptation to change under democratic procedures, in labor organizations as well as more generally, need to be more widely understood in the American community.

Professor Perlman's study centers upon the international union, the grand lodge. It reports and analyzes the adaptations of the grand lodge in its internal government first, and then in its relations with the rest of the labor movement, with its employers, and finally with the community more generally. This method of organization has the merit that it shows the wide range of forces which have interacted to shape the government and policies of the machinists. The words which Professor George E. Barnett used in 1909 to describe his classic study of the printers are appropriate: "The present monograph differs from previous studies in that it aims to give a complete description of an American Trade Union. It has been undertaken in the belief that a study which included in connected form an account of the history, structure, and activities, even of a single union, would serve to supplement previous contributions by indicating the relations between the different parts of the subject."

The present volume is part of a larger research project on labor-management history at Harvard University announced on November 2, 1954. After conferences with President A. J. Hayes, General Vice-President Elmer E. Walker advised on July 8, 1955 that the executive council of the International Association of Machinists had approved the compilation of a history of the machinists and had voted to make a financial contribution to the labor-management history project. It was understood that "the standards of scholarship and the interpretation of events would be the responsibility of the scholar making the study." The union has cooperated fully in making available its historical records of all types, and its officers have generously taken time from their heavy schedules for interviews and discussion. While the union read the manuscript for factual accuracy, the interpretation of events is solely the responsibility of the author.

I know of no labor or management organization that has cooperated more fully with a scholarly study of its history. It is a measure of the stature and maturity of the machinists that they have been willing to lead in this area.

This study will be of immense value to all interested in labor-management relations. It is imperative that the American public generally, and policy makers particularly, better understand the decision-making processes of our labor organizations.

John T. Dunlop

May 14, 1961

Illustrations

Contents

Tables

Graph

Introduction by the International President

The International Association of Machinists will be 75 years old on May 5, 1963. It is appropriate that the members and officers of the I.A.M. should look back over the struggles, the experiments, and the progress of their own labor organization. It is urgent that they should develop a greater sense of appreciation of its history and internal government, its relations over the years with other unions and with their employers, and its increasing role and contribution to the country in peace and war.

Good citizenship in the American community depends upon an understanding of our traditions, values, and rich heritage. No less does good citizenship in a union require an appreciation of the contributions, sacrifices, and dedication of our union forefathers.

This volume is also designed to tell the story of the I.A.M. to those outside the union — to public officials, employers, reporters and press officials, students and scholars, and to citizens generally. The American community needs better to understand the role of free and democratic trade unions in our society; it needs to appreciate more the function that elected officers perform in accommodating the needs and aspirations of workers with the possibilities of the market and the interests of the community.

This history of the I.A.M. has been written by an established scholar under the auspices of a great university. The author was given full access to documents and records and the interpretations are his alone. The union does not agree with all of them. It is natural that events through which we have lived always seem different when they are recounted on paper. Nonetheless, this history is a scholarly and objective account of the development of our great union.

It is not enough to look back upon the past. The unwritten chapters of the future will depend upon the dedication and wisdom of the members and officers of the I.A.M. as they confront ever-changing problems and opportunities.

A. J. Hayes
INTERNATIONAL PRESIDENT

Washington, D.C.
May 5, 1962

Author's Preface

While there have been in the past many excellent narrative histories of particular unions and of the American labor movement, generally, there have been relatively few analytical examinations of the evolution of a union's policies. Several years ago Professor Dunlop noted this paucity in the study of American labor unionism and proposed the study of several selected organizations with the purpose of concentrating on some major policies in time depth. He took care to note that each study must be, in itself, the history of a complex institution, and that each should show the response to changing circumstances in order to emphasize the determinants of policy. Meaningful comparisons could then be made among unions, and the relative importance or even presence of determinant factors could be seen.

Because the grand lodge of the International Association of Machinists has long enjoyed the reputation of being one of the most efficiently and ethically run organizations in the labor movement, it was agreed that it would be appropriate to select it as one of the first organizations to be studied. Professor Dunlop approached the executive officers of the IAM, and their response exceeded all expectations. They agreed to open their files to me and to give me any other research aid which seemed to me to be desirable.

I sought first to get an over-all view of the union's "personality" over the years. Then, I examined its specific attitude toward other unions, toward employers and that economic system which we call (having turned an old Marxian epithet on its head) capitalism, and finally toward certain general social problems. The order of my examination seemed to me to be logical and it serves as the basis, with some obvious revisions, of the plan of the book.

My sources were mostly original or primary. The IAM has an excellent set of internal records, particularly for the period after 1926, and the *Machinists' Monthly Journal,* which in the early years was one of the first comprehensive records of thought and deed, served as one reliable source for the beginning period. The convention proceedings provided an excellent understanding of some issues. And the union's collection of its circulars proved most useful.

However excellent were these sources, the most helpful material came from the typed and penciled minutes of the old general executive board (later, the executive council). The IAM grand lodge has kept a marvelous record of the discussions and votes incident to the making of decisions by the executive. In fact, this source made it possible to interpret and reinterpret file materials, particularly correspondence, and to comprehend not only the actions that were taken, but also why others were not. Thus, although I was free to use the back files as much as I wanted (and they are traditionally considered the happiest hunting ground for historians), I soon learned that they were meaningful only in terms of the decision-making process itself, made evident in the minutes of the executive council.

I have tried to develop both a sense of the organization's *élan vital* and an analytical method for examining its motivations. I feel I have come close to my objective because of the great help extended me by Professor Dunlop and because of the cooperation of the IAM's elected and appointed officials. International President Hayes is certainly one whose interest should be acknowledged first. General Secretary Treasurers Eric Peterson and Elmer Walker (then resident general vice-president) gave much of their time and counsel. General Vice-President George Watkins, too, was most willing to try to answer an endless list of questions. Other elected officers as well as staff members in the international president's and the general secretary treasurer's departments pursued all avenues to get information for me.

In expressing appreciation, I would like to say that my greatest debt is owed to Harvard University, which financed all the necessary research activity. I wish also to acknowledge the helpful criticism from scholars connected with that and other academic institutions. The late Professor Sumner Slichter very kindly turned an attentive ear and gave me the benefit of his lifetime of study of union operations. My father, Selig Perlman, before his death in 1959, also gave me such counsel as his fifty-year association with the history of the American labor movement provided. Professor Dunlop read several drafts of the manuscript and spent many hours in discussion and speculation of the meaning of particular incidents and records. Mr. David Kaplan also read the manuscript and made some suggestions based on his long associations with the IAM. My wife, Naomi, not only helped me to gather data, but she also worked with me in its analysis. Mrs. Ruth Houghton and Mrs. June Hill edited the manuscript. The thanks due them are the special ones which an author reserves for those who read his words with particular care. One of my Johns Hopkins students, Mr. Alan Wilner, supported by a grant from the Ford Foundation to the Department of Political Economy of the Hopkins, also helped gather and analyze data found in Chapter VIII.

The book consists of three parts. The first is a narrative history and is focused on the administrations of the various international presidents. The second part discusses the governmental process, first qualitatively and then quantitatively, in order to indicate in a formal way how the union has grown. Part three is intended to be more analytical than historical and, as I noted earlier, deals with three sets of relationships — other unions, the employers, and the community at large.

In the course of studying any organic institution intensively, one always develops some over-all generalizations. I have come away from this study with a conviction that while the IAM has become large, very large, it has been able to retain a responsive or dynamic quality. It has made what seem to me some major errors in policy — some, revealed in the light of the present, were very unwise; but considering all things, I think its record up to my cut-off date, 1952, is an excellent one. I can think of few institutions of its size and political nature able to present a record morally or efficiently its superior.

Mark Perlman

Baltimore, Maryland
May 1960

PART ONE

The History

CHAPTER I

The Early Years

An institution's birth and development must be traced through an examination of its times, its local environment or place, and the previous experiences of its founders. The International Association of Machinists was started in Atlanta, Georgia, by nineteen railroad machinists on May 5, 1888. These men almost immediately established a monthly journal which, after a year, appeared regularly enough to provide contemporary students with an excellent source for tracing the problems of the union's growth.

In the early years, 1888–1893, three major influences affected the organization. First came the "Knights-of-Labor tradition" and the "Southern influence." In time, the third influence emerged to become almost completely dominant. This may be called, perhaps ambiguously, the "pure and simple trade-union principle." Besides these three generally systematic influences, there were, of course, happenstance occurrences which had an important impact. But these three can be used to explain the major lines of the union's development during the first five years of its existence.

The impact of the "Knights-of-Labor tradition" upon the machinists' union was primarily upon its formal constitution and laws. The positive characteristics which the legacy from the Knights contributed included a commitment to individual moral improvement, a hope for the eventual regeneration of society along cooperative lines, an interest in political programs, and above all, some of the trappings and traditions of a secret society or fraternal order. The constitution of the IAM to this day retains many characteristics attributable to the Knights.

The "Southern influence," nonegalitarian in nature, emphasized the superiority of a particular type of white, fully trained craftsmen. In effect, it was a striving for quality — using the word with more reference to its social than to its economic ramifications. However, it did have at least one important economic consequence.

Becoming personally known in a new town was a necessity for that fraction of railroad machinists who were itinerant (the boomers). The resident railroad machinist was also concerned with the problem of newcomers not only because he often lent money to the boomer, but because the local merchants' resentment toward bill-skipping itinerants often affected him. The machinists' union hoped by restricting membership to "honest, sober men," it could rid its membership of the unstable, unreliable itinerants. On the whole, however, this emphasized a mutuality of interest of the machinists as good men rather than a mutuality of interest as craftsmen. In the beginning this influence was particularly strong; in fact, its echoes are still heard regularly at conventions.

The "pure and simple trade-union principle" refers to a concentration on the problems of effective job control, although the term is broad enough to incorporate internal union-security devices. The significant thing about this principle is its emphasis on the mutuality of economic interest of all machinists regardless of their personal attitudes toward morals, mores, or men, in contrast with the Southern influence.

From the earliest period, the relative strength of each of these three influences has varied. Our interest lies in the enduring pattern of their development as well as the temporary conflicts among them. To trace this growth and the changes that came about, we now turn to a narrative of the earliest period.

Most of the nineteen men who formed the new union had been members of the Knights of Labor. This organization, in some senses the greatest achievement of American labor until that time, was then falling on evil days. It was no longer winning strikes—an action it professed to abhor, but one which it could easily tolerate in the face of success. Membership in the Knights by 1888, it also may be recalled, had fallen off two-thirds from its high of 700,000 in 1886.[1] In short, the Order had acquired a bad name. Even the brotherhood's shibboleth "One for all, all for one" was being used against it to conjure the specter of violent boycotts, labor-class uprisings, and unlimited (possibly corrupted) power. Within the Order itself, there was a prevalent desire to break away from the past. For example, the general officers of the Knights' own National Trade Assembly 198 (which included machinists) announced, "The odium which the Order [of the Knights of Labor] has gained is damaging to us. We will have to cut loose from [it] before the employers will meet us or respect us in any way." [2] Thus it is not surprising that the Atlanta machinists also sought to disassociate themselves from the Knights.

The guiding spirit in the new machinists' organization was Thomas W. Talbot, a man of strong personal convictions as well as a felicitous manner of presentation.

Born on a South Carolina farm on April 17, 1845, Talbot first went to work at ten years of age in a shoe factory. In 1865 he apprenticed himself in the North Carolina Railroad machine shops in Florence, South Carolina. He completed this training and also worked for the same railroad as an engineer until 1874, when he opened his own machine shop in Sumpter, South Carolina. Later he returned to Florence to work in the Wilmington, Columbia, and Augusta Railroad shops, and became active in the Knights of Labor, serving as master workman and state organizer. In these capacities he organized eleven assemblies. These experiences led him to conclude that the machinists should have their own organization, which he unsuccessfully tried to start in Florence. In 1887 he took a job in the Eastern Tennessee, Virginia and Georgia Railroad in Atlanta and used the opportunity afforded him there to organize on May 5, 1888, with eighteen others, the first local of what now is the IAM.[3] Talbot's purposes in forming the new union were several—some of which indicated a desire to get away from the Knights' ways of doing things, while others accepted many of its established practices. He believed that a new union was necessary to resist wage cuts (brought about by the current business recession), and he wanted to provide insurance against unemployment, illness, accidents, and needs of the superannuated. Beyond these, however, he wanted membership in his new organization to be a public identification of craft skill and reputable character. This last purpose was in marked contrast to that of the Knights who would accept all who "lived by the sweat of the brow."

Accordingly, on September 10, 1888, Talbot sent out a circular announcing the founding of the "Order of United Machinists and Mechanical Engineers of America." It called upon machinists of "honorable, industrious and sober habits," who were being adversely affected by that ever-present minority "which has destroyed the good reputation of the majority," to form a benevolent society especially designed to meet their needs.

Talbot's dream for the new union was a fraternity of like-minded, as much as high-minded, practicing machinists, each of whom was committed to preserving the new body's separateness from lesser men, that is, those without equal social standing and equal craft skill. "Don't think for one moment," wrote Talbot, "that the writer is one of the so-called labor agitators, for I believe that the only right way of obtaining greater consideration is by persistently showing that we are more worthy men and better mechanics than formerly, thereby proving to our employers and the world at large that we are justly entitled to standing and distinction."

The emphasis on quality precluded the acceptance of alleged "social inferiors" such as Negroes. It also excluded those who were not full citizens.

An early circular limited membership to "none but white, free born citizen[s] . . . who must be practical machinist[s] capable of commanding the average rate of wages given in some regulated machine shop and [the] trade at the time of election [to the Order]."

Talbot and his associates borrowed the formal organizational aspects of their new union from the Knights. The union was presided over by a grand master machinist (instead of a grand master workman); the second officer was called the grand foreman (instead of a worthy foreman). The officialdom consisted of a grand guard, a grand inside sentinel, and so on. Local units were termed local lodges; the parent or roof organization the grand lodge. The founders devised a secret ritual and invented secret passwords. No regalia was adopted, however, because although the Order of United Machinists and Mechanical Engineers was "strictly a secret society, [it was] in nowise [to conflict] with one's Religious or Political opinion." [4] Though the Knights' ritual was originally derived from the Masons and was thus repugnant to Catholics, by the 1880's it had lost its anti-Catholic connotations. Several of the nineteen founders of the machinists' union were Irish Catholics. The Masonic-like character of the ritual did not seem to be a problem to them, transmuted as it had been by its association with the Knights.

As with the Knights, the need for individual self-improvement was stressed. In the original circular a journal was proposed "through which we can convey the intellect of one to another"; its columns to be filled with well-written debates on all topics.

The pure and simple trade-union influence was also present, but not emphasized. The earliest circular noted that machinist participation in the usual workingmen's beneficial or friendly societies was not desirable because machinists tended to live longer and therefore did not enjoy advantages in benefits. What was needed was a society for machinists alone which could use the actuarial advantage to provide extra benefits for illness, disability, and superannuation. It was an age of organization, the circular added, and machinists with their own problems and their own set of resources needed their own association if they were to cope successfully with the organized world about them.

The new union was to all intents and purposes purely a railroad organization at first. It may also have included job machinists, but it was primarily oriented to the railroad aspects of the craft. As can be seen on the map, it spread rapidly, absorbing disaffected Knights-of-Labor groups. Its locus of growth followed the path of the "boomers" along southern, midwestern and later, western lines. Within a single year it numbered 40 lodges, 26 of which were in the south and 12 in the midwest. Two years later, in 1890, there were

101 lodges, of which 41 were in the south, and 40 in the midwest, while 17 were in the far west, and 1 had been organized in Canada. By 1891 there were 189 lodges (whether all were active, there is no way of knowing) — of these, 54 were in the south, 76, in the midwest, and 3, in New England.[5]

But the price of growth was the loss of the cultural homogeneity contributed by the Knights-of-Labor and Southern influences. About this time (1889–1890) Talbot and his colleagues became aware of the establishment and growth of rival machinists' unions in the north. One, in particular, seemed to be a distinct threat because it was affiliated with the AFL and could use this relationship to advantage when trying to pirate members. Called the International Machinists' Union, it was led by Thomas J. Morgan, a Socialist and a leading opponent of Samuel Gompers.[6] Talbot and the others did not realize that Gompers would never have favored Morgan's IMU, — since it was aggressively industrial in nature and led by a politically ambitious Socialist — either one of the two characteristics being sufficient enough to rouse all of Gompers suspicions. But Talbot's group, lacking such information, decided to "play it safe" and sent an organizer into Pennsylvania and later into New Jersey and New England railroad and job shops, to proselytize and forestall the growth of their rival.

His efforts were only too well rewarded with success. As the organization took in more and more northern machinists, the type and tone of membership changed. The union had been founded by southern railroad men and had spread to small railroad centers in the south and west. In these areas there were few machine shops, and when a man was laid off or blacklisted he usually moved on to a new center. When the union went north, however, there were job machine shops; that is, small firms which did machine work under small contracts. Thus, an unemployed railroad machinist could take a nonrailroad job in the same town. In this way, the union came to have job machinists as well as railroad men. During this period, however, the predominant membership was still railroad in character, but the type began to change, as did the tone of membership. The self-described "honorable, sober, and industrious" workman, the southern prototype of quality, found himself increasingly in the company of aggressive northerners (many of whom were unassimilated Irishmen to whom the adjective "quality" was, through several decades of painful association with Scottish and English craftsmen, repugnant). This change signals the union's first divisive experience. Ceasing to be culturally homogeneous, the binding factors became economic rather than social. In other words, the identity of interest among all the membership centered on topics directly connected with the administration of jobs and work opportunity. It was this change which signaled the rise of the trade-union influence and indicated the relative decline of the other two forces, the Southern influence and the Knights-of-Labor tradition. It should be added that all these changes did not occur simultaneously; we note them at this point simply to indicate the general shape of unfolding events.

The prestige of the new organization was great enough to merit an address by United States Senator Hope Smith at the first anniversary meeting of the Atlanta Lodge on May 6, 1889. Senator Smith gave a typically Populist address in which he noted that the concentration of wealth in the United States was in the hands of 10 per cent of the people. He then went on, in the words of the journal's reporter, to direct: "attention to the fact that however much labor may dislike to admit it, supply and demand will regulate the price and treatment of labor, and the line of thought which encourages great enterprises, monopolies and trusts, lessens the number of employers and thereby destroys the competition on the part of those who demand labor." [7]

The senator ended his remarks by referring to an episode in which a (monopolistic) railroad had abused its power by discharging an employee because he had spoken out in conscience against the railroad's interests. Smith said he was not in favor of strikes, but that he would have been glad if the laborers had been strong enough to have forced the corporation to rehire the man.

The Order held its first convention shortly afterward in the state of Georgia Senate Chamber. At this convention the major order of business was to adopt a constitution. It gave stated powers both to the grand lodge and to the local lodges. It also included a formal trial procedure for dealing with charges against members alleged to have violated the rules and customs of the Order. A ritual was devised and carefully explained in detail. Talbot was unanimously named to the post of grand master machinist, and W. L. Dawley of Atlanta (Local Lodge 1) became grand secretary. After lengthy discussion and two votes, the name of the organization was shortened and changed to the National Association of Machinists. A monthly journal, to consist of not less than sixteen pages, was established. One other decision, particularly worth noting, was the adoption of a five-point Aims and Objects manifesto, which concluded with the statement, "that we are opposed to strikes and favor the settlement of all grievances by arbitration [in this context, collective bargaining], and we shall endeavor to create and maintain harmonious relations between employees and employers, and that we denounce any attempt to antagonize the interests of labor and capital." This was hardly a clarion call for union militancy. The convention was held in an atmosphere of friendship and peace.

This antistrike plank with its eschewal of militancy, characterizes the sentiment of the first convention at a time when the Southern influence was strong. The trade-union influence, necessary for the union's growth, came later. At the second convention, held in Louisville in 1890, the requirement of being a "citizen" was dropped from the constitution because it implied attainment of twenty-one years of age. A mandatory monthly per capita tax of 25 cents was levied; previously the first convention had established the same rate, but left its collection to the discretion of the general executive board. Talbot was reelected after the two opposing candidates withdrew. J. J. Creamer [8] of Richmond became grand foreman, and W. L. Dawley of Atlanta [9] was reelected secretary. J. R. Miles of Marshall,[10] Texas, was named treasurer.

Soon after the convention, Talbot resigned as grand master machinist, giving "matters of personal concern" as his excuse. The record indicates that shortly afterwards he was murdered by two young men, one of whom he had horsewhipped for insulting a member of his family. He was succeeded by J. J. Creamer, whose place as grand foreman was taken by C. C. Busbee, the man whom Creamer had defeated for the post at the Louisville convention. Busbee came from Mobile, and therefore the southern hegemony remained dominant.

After Creamer became grand master machinist, the spread of the organization to the north became increasingly important. In addition to employing organizers, the union sent out 10,000 circulars. As a result, an increasing number of job machine-shop men joined, and with the growth of membership, relationships with employers became more complex. More effort was required for handling the interests of the machinists in job shops. The proliferation of contacts with job shops, particularly where there were competition-conscious employers, made the existence of the antistrike plank in the platform worse than useless. It is not surprising, therefore, that Creamer, ignoring the union's own laws, began to write editorials in the journal threatening a resort to strikes if other methods were ignored or failed.[11] One non-IAM big city local, in particular, refused to consider affiliation until the no-strike plank was dropped. This was done in 1891, although the platform continued to urge arbitration "when possible to do so." When convinced that peaceful means would not avail, the local lodge could hold a strike vote. If 75 per cent present in secret ballot so voted, the local could petition the general executive board for strike authorization. Strikes could be undertaken only with general executive board approval. It was now necessary to establish provision for strike benefits.

But absorption of the new membership required considerably more than the abandonment of the no-strike clause. The new members had different mores and values. They did not draw the color line, an attitude which bothered many of the older members. For instance, when the Erie Machinists' Union 4081 affiliated, fear began to develop in the south that Negroes might be joining. One southern correspondent even sent to the journal a crude dialect letter, ostensibly coming from an old Negro in Sebannah (*sic*) asking for acceptance into the Erie local. And Talbot, shortly before his death, addressed a strong appeal to the membership on the question. Writing in what now could be considered a highly intemperate, if not inflammatory, way, he urged the membership not to open its ranks to Negroes, a race he considered morally unfit and economically untrustworthy. On the other hand, the important New York City Machinists' Union No. 1 refused to affiliate unless, and until, the color bar was removed from the constitution.

Clearly the situation was not easy. Tension resulting from employer recalcitrance was combining with tension from the different attitudes toward membership qualifications. Creamer was asked to rule whether a local master machinist could singlehandedly blackball an individual applying for membership, and ruled that he could not. His decision was appealed and the general executive board, reflecting the tension, refused to support Creamer's position, but avoided the issue by censuring the ruling on a procedural technicality.[12] In brief, what was occurring was a challenge of the Southern or quality influence, directly affected by the growth of regional factionalism.

Exactly what occurred at the 1891 Pittsburgh convention is unknown because no copy of the minutes exists. We do know that the name of the organization was changed from the National to the International Association of Machinists, thus indicating the existence of a growing number of Canadian and Mexican local lodges. Creamer and Dawley, both from Richmond, were reelected; new men were selected. John O'Day of Indianapolis became grand treasurer, two full-time organizers (coming from the midwest) were chosen,[13] and a completely new general executive board was named, all but one coming from northern or midwestern locals. It is not the selection of this set of officers alone which marks the end of the southern hegemony, but rather the decision to continue and to expand the organizing effort in the north.

This was the period when the machinists' concern about the weakness of their organization in the northeast was at its peak. Therefore Creamer and the general executive board sent the two organizers to Pennsylvania, New York City, and New England. There they found prospective members, who were unwilling to pay a quarterly per capita tax of 25 cents. Moreover, some northern local organizations saw no reason to pay charter fees, since, as they were eager to point out, many of them predated the Atlanta founding.[14]

Creamer was not satisfied with the efforts of the two organizers. The expense of maintaining them was so great, he feared it would bankrupt the treasury. He dismissed one of them after a few months, and the general executive board assented to the action. In the meantime the remaining organizer complained of his scant salary and expense allowance. Creamer's reaction was to conclude that "the appointment of paid organizers was a bad step"; instead, he urged the appointment of district organizers who would work at the trade most of the time in order to support themselves, but who would take occasional days off to do the union's business. In particular, he pointed to the work of one Harry Easton, who was active on the Union Pacific and other railways in the west.

One assignment of the two paid organizers was to a meeting with Samuel Gompers and a group of machinists and blacksmiths who were planning to form a new union within the AFL. The IAM representatives were to "use their utmost endeavor to try to induce them to not form another union in as much [*sic*] as there were at present National bodies of the Machinists and Blacksmiths, but for them to join their forces to those already formed thereby saving any divission [*sic*] of the two crafts." Whether as a result of their efforts, or otherwise, no new union was formed.

At this time there were two views on organizational structure. Both were concerned primarily with railroad machinists. Easton, who later proved to be something of a personal empire builder, advocated a different type of organizational structure from the simple one theretofore established. Taking his cue from the Knights, he organized a "district grand lodge" (namely, district assembly) comprising all the IAM locals on the Union Pacific Railroad.[15] Easton was militant and preached "pure and simple" trade unionism, which amounted to concentrating upon wages, hours, working conditions, and above all, the policing of work opportunity. He established in this first district grand lodge both a data collection system, including a crude local cost-of-living index, and a coordinated grievance-committee process.

In contrast to Easton's "pure and simple" plans, there was a move to merge the IAM with other similar railroad-shop craftsmen's unions, into a common organization. This was a renascent Knights-of-Labor influence—it did not get far, although it was discussed fully. Later a loose-knit federation, permitting full autonomy, was created. During the early nineties, however, there was no more than a continual vocal pressure to move in the indicated direction.

Because the early nineties were not prosperous, IAM membership ebbed. Locals repeatedly sought permission to strike—permission which the general executive board was loath to grant because of the danger of depleting the treasury by the payment of strike benefits. In a few instances, notably on the Pennsylvania–Panhandle Railroad system, the Richmond (Virginia) Locomotive Works, the Union Pacific, and at a small motor works in Indianapolis, strikes were authorized.

The first of these, called because of the introduction of a piecework system, ran from February until June, 1892. It was unsuccessful. The failure resulted in a great deal of local antagonism directed toward the national officers, based on a belief that the grand lodge had not played an active enough role in the effort. From the first, Creamer had been doubtful of a successful outcome and for that reason had hesitated in granting strike sanction. But it was O'Day, who by June had become the grand master machinist, upon whom the brunt of the men's displeasure fell. With the general executive board's assent, he ordered the suspension of strike benefits when he believed the strike to be a lost cause. He probably expected that the general executive board would stand by him when local dissatisfaction exploded. But the general board sought, with its own political motivations, to take refuge as best it could. "In view of the fact," it announced to the membership, "that a majority [of the general executive board] voted to declare the strike off, we indorse the action of the grand master machinist in this matter acknowledging [at the same time that] he was too hasty, and [we] recommend that in cases of a similar kind in the future, more time be taken before a fixed date be made to declare a strike off." [16]

The Richmond Locomotive Works' strike is particularly interesting because of two aspects which became evident for the first time. A common laborer was assigned to watch a lathe during the latter's routine operation. Traditionally this was machinists' work and was done by one in the craft — that is, a journeyman or an apprentice. One of the apprentices objected, the journeymen machinists formulated a grievance, but the general manager refused to negotiate. The journeymen of all the other craft unions, except patternmakers and boilermakers, then went on strike. Two issues were involved: the rights of skilled labor, and indirectly, common action between different unions. About the first issue, the journal was quite explicit: "The strike is one in support of skilled labor against unskilled labor. It is a fight in behalf of the apprenticeship system, a custom established by our forefathers, and against the cheap labor or scab system . . . A mechanic's skill is to him what the capitalist's money is to the capitalist." As for the second issue — because the molders, blacksmiths, and carpenters also struck, there was some belief that the machinists could get the support of other labor, and through the use of the boycott, force the management to negotiate. To this end, one local lodge wrote to the general executive board asking that the locomotive engineers be asked to boycott Richmond steam engines. The general executive board was under no illusion about the extent of Chief Engineer

Arthur's interests, and replied that the likelihood of success did not warrant the effort. The management eventually starved the men into returning to work — and this strike, too, ended in complete failure. In this case, the incident had occurred in the home city of the grand master machinist, the city in which the headquarters was located.[17]

The strike on the Union Pacific is also significant for two reasons. One issue involved relationships with the Knights of Labor. It may be recalled that District Assembly 82 of the Knights had been recognized in 1884 — but, subsequently, the railroad management had overlooked the agreement. The district, quite naturally, wanted the old agreement reinitialed and sought to get the management to recognize it as the employee's sole organization. This stand quite naturally was antithetical to the IAM's desire to represent the machinists. As a result, the district assembly and Easton's IAM district grand lodge were at loggerheads, with neither side the victor. The other issue was the division of work opportunity — the employer wanted to reduce the total quantity of work, either by fewer hours per man or a smaller work force. The Knights wanted to cut the hours per man; the IAM, the size of the labor force. The result was success in principle for the IAM, but since seniority was not protected, and key IAM men were laid off, it was an empty victory.[18]

The issue of skilled versus unskilled men was also raised in the (Indianapolis) Janney Motor Company strike. There, the employer, embracing what is known as the chunker system, put the journeymen machinists on jobs only after some less skilled individual had done the rough shaping operations, thereby taking from the journeymen some work opportunity. In this case the IAM was successful. The employer agreed to cease the practice and to hold frequent consultations with the union. Unfortunately, this was the smallest of the four strikes. Contrasted with the failure elsewhere, the officers' success here did not contribute much to their reputation.

The Indianapolis strike has another significance. It indicates quite clearly that the IAM was not entirely a railroad man's union — the union's claim to job machine-shop representation was recognized by practice. Further evidence of the same development was a decision in 1892 to organize a special geographical district lodge, comprising the local lodges in the Chicago area. Thus, the structure of the union was responding to certain economic pressures — locals dealing with the same employer had their own district lodges, and locals dealing with different employers, who were "competitive" with each other, had their own district lodges too.

The fourth convention was held in Chicago in 1892. Records regarding its sessions are all but nonexistent. Several new officers were elected. O'Day succeeded Creamer — Creamer probably could not afford to remain grand master machinist, an ill-compensated job requiring much travel. H. E. Easton was elected grand foreman, a position to which were added the duties and title of organizer. A new treasurer was named — one J. J. Lamb, of whom more will be said later. And the general executive board was expanded from five to seven practicing machinists.

Although Easton continued his organizing efforts in New England and the mid-Atlantic states to the extent that Grand Master Machinist O'Day could write with pride that "[he] was putting up lodges right under the nose of Mr. Morse, the organizer of the Machinists' National Union, and Mr. Gompers, his aider and abettor," the situation within the IAM was not good.[19] The union, now truly an international organization, was spread wide and thin. The Knights-of-Labor influence was never terribly important — and in no sense did it contribute much internal strength. The Southern influence had lost most of its positive character — in fact, it was becoming a source of dissension as more and more northern locals joined. By default, the trade influence was becoming the most important, but the officers were either unable or unwilling to reshape the organization in accord with the principles of trade unionism. Therefore, by the end of 1892, the prospects were discouraging and were accentuated by business depression. A rejuvenation was needed. To accomplish this, a strong grand master machinist was required. Fortunately for the IAM, such a man appeared. He was James O'Connell, a railroad machinist from Oil City, Pennsylvania, who had served on the general executive board from 1891 to 1893.

CHAPTER II

Toward Bargaining Unionism: The O'Connell Administration

THE INITIAL PERIOD: 1893–1899

By 1893 it was evident that things had changed. The membership was no longer primarily southern, leadership was coming from the north and the midwest, and the domination of trade-union influence was impending.

James O'Connell, the new grand master machinist was born in Minersville, Pennsylvania, August 22, 1858, and went through his apprenticeship at the engine works. He worked off and on as a railroad machinist, leaving the trade for two years (1882–1884) to enter the oil business. He was active in the Knights, having been a delegate to the Richmond convention (1886), and served that organization as a lobbyist at Harrisburg, Pennsylvania, in 1889 and again in 1891. He became a member of the IAM in 1890 and a member of the IAM general executive board in 1891. Although his home was in Oil City, Pennsylvania, his ties were not geographically limited. He was a close friend of J. J. Creamer, and had lived with Creamer in Richmond.

O'Connell sought to propel the IAM into a job-oriented trade union. He wanted it to be an efficient organization, which would proceed in a realistic manner to the achievement of such material objectives as higher wages and shorter hours. His program, in the first years of his administration, was certainly straightforward and simple. He wanted the union to assert control over all jobs filled by skilled machinists, and he wanted the organization to include all men competent to fill the jobs. Initially, he defined competence as four years' experience or apprenticeship. He believed his union should work closely with other unions, which meant affiliation with the AFL. He believed it desirable to develop comprehensive, stable, and formal agreements with employers. He believed in a strong union treasury; first, to impress employers during negotiations; and second, in the event of a strike to provide necessary benefits to those, who, without such benefits, might be obliged to sabotage union policies. These were the main lines of his program.[1] It took him about seven years to work out the details.

Affiliation with the AFL was an important first objective because it would give the IAM allies in strike situations and boycotts. The major obstacle to affiliation was Gompers' refusal to accept any union with an avowed "whites only" policy. Thus O'Connell had a double task — to convince the IAM membership of the desirability of affiliation, and second, to convince them that the affiliation was worth their sacrificing the offending clause.

O'Connell's long-range campaign predated his election as grand master machinist. In 1893, while still on the general executive board, he was instrumental in getting Samuel Gompers to attend and address the Indianapolis convention, in an effort to sway the delegates and to convince them to affiliate with the AFL. Gompers recognized that the major block to affiliation was his own insistence on the deletion of the "whites only" clause. He held true to his principles; while urging the delegates to vote affiliation, he told them that the "whites only" qualification was wrong and would have to be dropped before he would consent to taking the IAM into the AFL. The delegates refused to remove the offending phrase at that time.[2]

After his election, O'Connell increased his efforts. He toured the country, visiting many of the active lodges and had a hand in reactivating quite a large number (including Local Lodge 1 in Atlanta). In these efforts he reiterated the necessity for making membership an economic rather than a social distinction. "Think of this, I say," wrote one correspondent in the journal echoing the same line, "remember that we are a trades' union, not a social organization, and as such we should reject none who are competent to take our place in time of trouble."

O'Connell's philosophy of unionism was probably popular with most of the nonsoutherners in the organization. He symbolized the emergence of northern influence in the union. However, there were critics who did not want the IAM to lose its general fraternal order quality, earlier termed the Southern influence. For better or worse the critics chose to take their stand on the "whites only" clause, and wrote numerous bitter letters in the journal about mongrelization of the job. One of the Mexican locals (composed entirely of machinists from north of the border), even predicted a wave of secessions were O'Connell's proposal to be accepted. There were also many moderates who, though personally unhappy about the change, were able to appreciate the necessity for the step.

The spectacular failure of the American Railway Union's Pullman strike in 1894 reemphasized the difficulties of "going it" alone. This failure was attributed in part to the fact that the American Railway Union was not a member of the AFL; thus, it had been unable to get other unions to support its strike effort.

Additional interest in AFL affiliation grew out of the fight for control between Gompers and the Socialists within the AFL. The climax of this struggle was at the 1894 Denver AFL convention. Within the IAM there were two factions — the O'Connell or Gompers group and the pro-Socialists. Both sides wished to affiliate with the AFL in order to participate in deciding the issue.

From the short-run point of view, it may have been fortunate that a showdown over the offending clause was avoided. Acting AFL President Duncan agreed to withdraw official objections to issuing an AFL charter to the IAM if the "white" qualification were removed from the constitution, regardless of its inclusion elsewhere. This minimal change was accomplished at the 1895 IAM convention, the southern locals having been pacified by the incorporation of the "whites only" clause into the secret ritual, and the IAM was then ready to apply for an AFL charter. It was speedily granted.[3]

To O'Connell, the affiliation meant a great deal. "It meant," he wrote in the journal, "that we have come to that stage in our organization's existence where both swaddling clothes and childish ideas of trade unionism are left behind . . . We are closely allied now with the leading minds in the labor movement." It signified to him the final triumph of job-oriented unionism over the Southern quality tradition. "[We] must forget all petty jealousies . . . solidify ourselves by education; educate ourselves by fair-minded discussion, irrespective of who furnishes the subject for debate, whether he be a popular brother or not."[4]

Naturally O'Connell went as a delegate to the 1895 AFL convention in New York. There he managed to have the charter of the rival IMU withdrawn. Two years later, he was also elected a vice-president of the federation, a position he occupied for over two decades.[5]

At about this time the issues of Socialism and industrial unionism versus craft unionism first came to the fore. O'Connell conceived of the IAM as a craft union. His eagerness for AFL affiliation was based on a belief in Gompers' continued dominance. Illustrative of his opposition to industrial unionism are some of his comments on the American Railway Union: "we are at a loss to see the advantage to be derived by our members joining [the ARU], because it is confined . . . to *one branch* of industry solely, and less than one fourth of the machinists of any country are employed on railroads."[6] Those within the IAM favoring industrial unionism were largely Socialists. Several of them charged O'Connell with having contributed to the failure of the Pullman strike. Although he admitted that he did not personally favor the

ARU, and that some members of the Richmond lodge (where IAM headquarters were located) had acted as strikebreakers, he denied the charge. The bitterness of this allegation is the first intimation of a new force or influence in the IAM–Socialism. From the first, it was critical of O'Connell; many years later, as will be noted, it grew strong enough to drive him from the leadership of the IAM and attempted to drive him from his AFL office. But the origins of this conflict, to a great degree, were associated with the Pullman strike.

O'Connell's administration of the IAM encountered some difficulties from the first. At the 1893 convention the defeated Treasurer, J. J. Lamb, defaulted with the treasury, and through a technicality, the bonding company disclaimed responsibility.[7]

O'Connell's control was threatened by Harry Easton, who had scored great success earlier on the Union Pacific. In April, 1894, the general executive board, led by O'Connell, audited Easton's accounts and examined his administrative procedures. After inquiry, the general executive board voted that he resign from his office as grand organizer, because there was evidence that he had "during his entire term of office given out statements, oral and written, of an untruthful nature regarding other grand lodge officers."[8] Easton refused and the general executive board then removed him. Easton resorted to the courts, and after much litigation involving among other things an injunctive order forbidding the general executive board to mention the case in the journal or elsewhere, Easton lost. Repercussions sounded after the court's decision, and in the words of the journal, Easton's case "in some instances has caused lodges to boldly [*sic*] rebel against the grand lodge." The importance of the affair rests in the grand lodge's attempt to suppress the expressions of local autonomy which it aroused. That Easton was an empire-builder appears to be evident; but even more significant was O'Connell's decision that there was not room in the organization for two strong leaders.

During this period, sentiment developed in the IAM, as in other unions, favoring direct membership control of the union.[9] The impetus for the reform appears to have had mixed origins, ranging from those who had disagreed with the grand master machinist to those who believed in popular democracy *per se*. In any event the short-run price paid by O'Connell for eliminating his most outspoken rival was loss of popularity. In 1895 the first referendum rule was instituted over the opposition of the administration-appointed Committee on Law.[10] O'Connell did not oppose it, but warned against its being used as the basis for electing officers. Initially, it was limited to constitutional changes between conventions of the grand lodge. Later it was broadened to include all the matters originally handled at conventions as well as such issues as the calling of a convention. In practice, it was an attempt to take questions out of the hands of the administration and to put them squarely before the membership. At first, there was a requirement that at least 5 per cent of the lodges and 50 per cent of the membership had to vote in order to make the results binding. Later this rule had to be modified, because the number voting was very small — generally in the neighborhood of 20 per cent.

Other important decisions, aside from the technical elimination of the "whites only" clause and the establishment of the mandatory referendum, were taken at the sixth (1895) convention. The grand lodge reorganized the membership roll-keeping process. It assumed the responsibility of maintaining a master list of all members as well as the names of those having been rejected for, or expelled from, membership. To finance the organizing drives, the per capita tax was increased from 25 cents per quarter to 15 cents monthly. The amount was to be collected by the local lodges and forwarded to headquarters. The lodges were instructed to stamp the cards of paid-up members.

Admission requirements were further liberalized to permit the acceptance of "any machinist of good moral reputation who receives the average wages paid in his locality." This change eliminated all reference to the applicant's previous apprenticeship or time spent in the trade.

The grand lodge also abolished the constitutional provision which directed all local lodges, regardless of their own preference, to join district lodges. In other words, the option of joining was left free. This decision was probably reached as a direct consequence of the Easton affair. Its significance leads to the conclusion that the grand lodge probably sought to weaken the district lodges by making their continued existence a result of a concurrent majority sentiment, thereby limiting the number of focal points of resistance to grand lodge policies.

After the events of 1895, it was only reasonable that a period of consolidation should take place. The period, however, is of interest because tremendous philosophical differences became evident. As noted above, O'Connell's philosophy of unionism was oriented to job control. He believed that unionism, alone among all the methods tried, helped workers to gain social status and increased real wages. Moreover, he believed that the process of unionism was educationally and morally desirable — it demonstrated meaningfully that the price of important liberties was the sacrifice of certain less important individualistic qualities. His beliefs were shared by one member in particular of the general executive board, Robert Ashe.[11]

The Socialist challenge to O'Connell's philosophy appeared originally not as criticism of the grand master machinist, but in a series of polemics directed against some views expressed by Ashe. The protagonist for the Socialists was P. J. Conlon, at the time a railroad machinist working in the midwest. He, like the Socialists generally, was not a Marxian. His "Socialism" had a strong Populist coloration. Nonetheless, he and the others like him referred to their doctrine as Socialism.

The specific points of difference involved three principal topics: convention — or "direct membership" — control of the IAM; use of political action and the method of legal enactment; and the importance of high per capita taxes. Conlon charged that Ashe was opposed in principle to the referendum and that Ashe preferred the convention system whereby the administration could more easily put through its policies. Implicit in Conlon's position was the assertion that the IAM could not only be run by referendum, but that it would be better and more democratically run that way.

On the question of governmental intervention Conlon stressed two things. He favored blanket endorsement of political parties and he was sympathetic to the Erdman Act (which sought to encourage compulsory arbitration on the railroads). His position on the first was partly accepted. The IAM did issue a circular urging support of the Democratic Party against the "money power," the Republicans. But on the second question, there was disagreement and he was unable to secure IAM support for the Erdman Act. Ashe, undoubtedly supported by O'Connell, would not give ground; to him "the damnable so-called arbitration bill" was too broad in scope and covered employee groups who by direct negotiation with the employers had achieved more than they would ever be able to secure through arbitration. In taking this position, Ashe was also supporting Gompers' view. Ashe pointed to the difficulties the IAM was having with the navy department in the naval yards, as indicative of what unions could expect from the government. Ashe was quite certain that little material good came out of putting one's trust in princes, or their bureaucratic functional descendants. As a Socialist–Populist of the grass roots American variety, Conlon could not disagree more violently.

Ashe's view on dues had to do with strengthening the grand lodge's position. He urged an increase in the per capita tax to $1.00 per month. With it, he wanted the grand lodge to assume responsibility for sick benefits, out-of-work benefits, funeral benefits for each member and his wife, and accident benefits. It would, he argued, tie the membership to the union just as similar policies had done in England. Conlon did not disagree with Ashe's proposal for increased per capita taxes and benefits, but he was opposed to the grand lodge's holding considerable cash. He wanted the grand lodge to "bank" most of its money with the local lodges and to call for it only when a specific need could be demonstrated. His proposal, of course, was designed to weaken the grand lodge's control and increase local union autonomy. It seems obvious that Ashe was the Hamiltonian, Conlon the Jeffersonian. Here it is sufficient to add that, like Jefferson, Conlon changed his views about the prerogatives of the executive when he later became part of the organization's administration. At this point it is important to note the beginning of a new split. In place of the Southern vs. the trade-union dichotomy, the division was now between the Socialists, stressing local autonomy partly because they were strong only on that level, and the "pure and simple Gompersians," advocating the dominance of the grand lodge, largely for a similar reason.

In 1896 the first "professional" full-time business agents (as distinct from lay members hired on a temporary basis) were hired to handle local union affairs and to aid in organizing in Chicago, New York, Cleveland, and Lynn, Massachusetts. In addition, a regular practice of putting on local men for limited periods during organizing drives was instituted for a short time. Generally these drives were run by outsiders, officers or appointees of the grand lodge.

During this period the IAM became involved in some developments within the AFL. There was what proved to be an endemic struggle with the International Typographical Union regarding which of the two unions had jurisdiction over the machinists' installing linotypes.[12] O'Connell enjoyed Gompers' support in the AFL executive council and, quite naturally, felt confident about putting pressure on the ITU there. The ITU, on the other hand, had the strongest closed shop contracts in America and, obviously, did not choose to let the matter be resolved in the AFL executive council. The dispute continued for years. The fact that the ITU not only refused to surrender jurisdiction, but actually raided IAM locals between 1896 and 1900 despite Gompers' orders to the contrary, was ample evidence that affiliation with the AFL was not a substitute for militancy and constant organizing efforts.

Two other developments should be mentioned — both illustrating O'Connell's approach. At this time he was instrumental in organizing the Federated Metal Trades Association. Consisting of the boilermakers, the molders, the blacksmiths, the brassworkers, and the machinists, this association was a loosely-knit organization, useful for defining common objectives. It could not enforce these "agreements," however — which was O'Connell's preference. For, unlike the Socialists, O'Connell was jealous of the IAM's independence of action. Its first goal was to secure ten hours' pay for a nine-hour day, time and a half for overtime, and half holidays on Saturdays.[13] Its first major test of strength was in 1896 when it struck the Brown Hoisting Works in Cleveland. The company's eventual response, which the union ultimately accepted, was to refuse to accept the nine-hour proposal, but to accept a 50 per cent premium on work in excess of ten hours per day. It also agreed to the Saturday half holiday, but it would not consider negotiating with either the federated crafts or the craft unions singly.

The other development involved the method of negotiation with employers. O'Connell believed that preliminary negotiations should, whenever possible, be carried on at the top level. For instance, he intervened in the Brown Hoisting Works strike, and brought along Samuel Gompers. They suggested arbitration of the issues to no avail. The company ran the plant with strikebreakers. Violence occurred, and at least two men were killed. Notwithstanding this failure, O'Connell continued to advocate active co-operation with other metal trades unions and negotiations with employers at the top.

At the 1897 convention the shape of O'Connell's plans became fully evident. He sought to expand further the IAM's conversion to the "pure" trade-union principle. This change involved a radical reconsideration of the basis for admission and the basis for discipline of the organization. He wanted to admit anyone — man, woman, or youth — whose job brought him or her into the normal area of union activity. He told the delegates:

> Every day our trade is becoming more and more specialized, and if we hope to . . . protect our craft it is necessary that our qualifications for membership be radically changed. The multifarious industries in which our membership are employed warrants . . . steps that will bring [in] . . . thousands of new men, who, under our former laws, would not come up to the qualifications required. Women are being rapidly introduced into the trade, and we should change our laws so that we can take them in when . . . qualified.[14]

Since O'Connell was well aware of the dangers of attracting "industrial transients," he advocated two devices. The first was a rule requiring four years' work experience at the trade. The second was a policy of having each membership card designate the class of machinist: (1) general [machinist], (2) competent floor hand, (3) competent lathe hand, (4) competent vise hand, (5) competent planer hand, (6) competent milling machine hand, (7) competent slotting machine hand, (8) competent die-sinker, tool maker, and boring mill hand, and (9) competent linotype machinist. O'Connell also urged that apprentices be taken into the IAM after two years for education as unionists.

The convention accepted O'Connell's recommendations, and authorized a $1.00 to $5.00 fine for any member claiming a level of general competence to which he was not entitled. Its decision to limit the punishment for falsification to a small enforceable amount was an explicit reflection of O'Connell's views toward discipline. He believed the strength of a union lay in its appeal to workmen. He further believed that any workman in the trade who remained outside the organization represented a constant threat. For the union to expel a man without the most dire provocation was, in his eyes, tantamount to suicidal madness. He observed:

> Since the birth of our association there have been hundreds of members expelled, and in many cases on very questionable ground [*sic*]. Some of our local lodges have endeavored to start a debt-collecting agency for those outside of our movement; other lodges have set up a standard of temperance and morality far beyond the dignity of a labor organization . . . it is far better, unless in extreme cases, that men be reprimanded or fined rather than expelled . . . I . . . recommend further protection . . . to prevent this great number of expulsions.

Two other developments occurred at the 1897 convention. The delegates agreed to waive their right to select the IAM representatives to the AFL convention, turning the selection over to referendum vote. They also voted to establish a death benefit of $50.00 for any member having six months' continuous membership at time of death.

During this initial period of O'Connell's administration, great changes were occurring in industrial engineering. Mechanization of industrial processes was becoming the rule at increasingly greater rate. Standardization of parts and specialization of labor function were supplanting the traditional practices of the craft. What later came to be called "Taylorism" or "scientific management" was being introduced gradually in plants throughout the country. Payment by piece, incentive schemes, and operation of two machines by one man were everywhere gaining employer advocates. Not only did these changes mean the admission of specialists to the union, they also required a thorough reexamination of the organization's working rules. At most, they foreshadowed industrial dislocation and strife. Their appearance, along with the development of the incipient Socialist–Gompers hiatus, were the two specks "no larger than a man's hand," which eventually brought an end to O'Connell's control.

The Apogee of O'Connellism: 1899–1901

In 1899 membership was approximately seventeen thousand; by the middle of 1901 it had more than trebled. This was the period of O'Connell's greatest success. He built up membership, he worked closely with the AFL, he negotiated successfully with the leaders of industry, and he further developed his plan of turning the grand lodge into an effective bargaining agent.

The 1899 convention was held in Buffalo. It was an efficient session, and was clearly dominated by O'Connell. There, the importance of the ritual was again reduced. As if to lay the ghost of the Knights of Labor, the eloquent titles of the grand lodge officers were eliminated. In place of grand master machinist, the title, international president, was adopted, the grand vice-president became the international vice-president, and so forth.

The convention, guided by the international president, cut back the use of the referendum and reallocated to itself the authority for selecting the IAM representatives to the AFL.

The convention also decided to encourage grand lodge authority over the local business agents by authorizing the grand lodge to pay 50 per cent of the salaries and expenses of those whose selection it approved. Moreover, the grand lodge officers were directed to refuse strike benefits to any local taking strike action without previous grand lodge authorization. And no member was eligible to receive any benefits unless his dues payments were in order, or were not delinquent in excess of three months.

The convention considered the whole question of benefits and their costs. It was agreed that a strike fund was necessary, for which purpose a $1.00 monthly special assessment was levied. A new death-benefit program was considered and turned over to the officers for technical development. It was eventually submitted to referendum vote and passed. It provided for varying amounts depending upon length of membership. The revised scheme increased the benefits to $75.00 after one year's continuous membership; $100 after two years; $150 after three years; up to a maximum of $200 after four years.

O'Connell reported to the delegates on his negotiations with the ITU. He noted that the friction on the issue was not at the top, but on the local level — in many instances encouraged by the employers. O'Connell's optimism — that the differences could be amicably settled — proved to be an error in judgment.[15]

Undoubtedly the most important issue considered at the convention was O'Connell's treatment of the question of relations with employers. O'Connell and the IAM had been chosen by the AFL to lead the fight for the nine-hour day. O'Connell reminded the delegates that to win victories, concessions might have to be made. What he had in mind was the IAM's traditional opposition to piecework. To him piecework was an iniquitous system, but one which could not be successfully opposed.[16] Therefore he suggested that the

IAM select the best system, agree to work under it, but in return demand some standard concessions. In this way, O'Connell recommended emulation of the ITU experience with the linotype, where technological advance had been accepted by the union simultaneously with the employers' acceptance of the closed shop.

This piecework proposal was not acceptable to the convention. O'Connell then lost no time in disavowing it.[17] Its suggestion illustrates that he recognized the futility of blind opposition to piecework.

Without any doubt, the signal achievement of O'Connell's administration was the negotiation of the famous Murray Hill Agreement.[18] As already noted, O'Connell, Gompers, and those forming the dominant enclave in the AFL believed that the aims of labor would be best served if basic agreement could be secured from the dominant figures in industry. Their view was not unfounded; they had tasted at Homestead and again at Pullman the fruits of vigorous, unreasoning employer opposition. Moreover, among the employers, there were strong voices preaching cooperation with the unions. Chief among the latter was U. S. Senator Marcus A. Hanna, a wealthy Ohio industrialist and major power behind President McKinley. Hanna's brand of Republicanism was far from being generally popular. So long as Hanna retained national political power, however, it was a force to be reckoned with.

The vehicle for transmitting Hanna's views regarding labor and management was the National Civic Federation.[19] The federation, an outgrowth of the Civic Federation of Chicago, was formed in 1900. Early in its life the labor figures associated with it, namely Gompers and John Mitchell (then president of the United Mineworkers' Union), sought to bring Senator Hanna into the organization so that he could "[send] some telegrams 'at the right time to the right people.'" And within a few months he was its president.

Hanna's philosophy, in many important ways similar to O'Connell's, was to "talk, rather than fight, things out." He advocated the acceptance of unionism, always noting when the opportunity arose, that rational workmen were unionists because unionism was the workers' main protective device.

At the height of his power — during and immediately after McKinley's successful second campaign — Hanna's views carried great political weight. His influence was particularly strong among the leading manufacturers of metal supplies and goods. Having formed a more or less temporary bargaining association in response to a patternmakers' strike in Brooklyn in 1899, they institutionalized the organization a very few months later, naming it the National Metal Trades Association.[20]

Early in 1900 the IAM authorized strikes in three centers, Chicago, Cleveland, and Paterson, New Jersey, to secure the nine-hour day, the closed shop, a minimum rate of 28 cents per hour, time and a half for overtime and double time for Sundays and holidays, as well as some less important points. The Chicago strike was particularly well organized and commenced on March 1. By March 3 the manufacturers were negotiating directly with O'Connell; the latter, however, was adamant on all points, particularly the nine-hour day. The negotiations broke off until March 17, when the NMTA, representing a significant faction of the employers, suggested resumption of work and then arbitration of the outstanding issues. Once again, O'Connell refused, insisting on arbitration before the resumption of work.

After further delay and intermittent negotiations, the employers made some significant concessions. They agreed to give up the use of the blacklist and all other discriminatory antiunion practices, they agreed to the arbitration of grievances, they agreed to the principle of the fifty-four hour week (provisionally allowing a transitional period), and they agreed to bargain on wages (with resort to arbitration if agreement were not otherwise forthcoming) in New York on May 12. The Chicago strikers voted 3028 to 396 to accept this proposal, labeled "the Chicago Agreement." The outstanding strikes, in Cleveland and Paterson, New Jersey, were called off.

O'Connell was very enthusiastic about the success. In the words of the journal:

> Too much stress can not be put on the importance of the Chicago agreement. It is national in its scope . . . If [the] idea [of this type of negotiation] is carried out in a spirit of fairness and equity, mutual concessions being made, and everything done with honesty and truthfulness, there need never be any more strikes or lockouts as far as the machinist trade is concerned . . . [and allowing for a period of adjustment and education], everything will run smoothly without a discord.[21]

O'Connell, Douglas Wilson (the vice-president and editor), and Hugh Doran (of the general executive board) met with three representatives of the NMTA at the Murray Hill Hotel in New York City on May 10–18. From these sessions a national agreement was issued, including (a) an agreement by the IAM that the NMTA would bargain for all the metal trades firms, whether NMTA members or not, (b) acceptance by each organization of responsibility for the acts of its constituent members, (c) a broad definition of what constituted the machinists' trade, (d) an agreement regarding overtime — namely time and a quarter until 10 P.M., time and a half from 10 P.M. until midnight, and double time thereafter, as well as on Sundays and holidays, (e) agreement to accept at least one apprentice in every shop and an apprentice ratio of one to five journeymen; and most important of all, (g) the nine-hour day after one year.

To O'Connell, this Murray Hill Agreement meant success. "The International Association of Machinists had at last, and at once, become a factor of national importance, and considered worthy of consultation and conference." It looked as though the fight for recognition had been won.

Unfortunately for the IAM this did not prove to be the case. When in May, 1901, the nine-hour day was scheduled to go into effect, the IAM officials, who were asking for a 12½ per cent wage increase in hourly rates, learned to their dismay that the NMTA had every intention of maintaining the same hourly rates, thus reducing take-home pay by 10 per cent. Remonstrances were useless, and the union, relying upon its relatively plentiful treasury, authorized strike action, if necessary, to achieve that which it thought it had won the previous year. The strike was called for May 20, 1901, when more than forty thousand machinists went out. Since the union membership was only approximately fifty thousand, many of whom were railroad machinists, it is evident that many nonmembers were among the strikers.

By mid-June, the IAM claimed that two-thirds of the firms had signed, although it admitted that the acquiescent firms were the smaller ones in the trade. The NMTA, on the other hand, when confronted with the strike, held that the IAM violation of the no-strike provision of the 1900 Murray Hill Agreement was cause enough to cancel that agreement. The NMTA then pledged war to the end. It reorganized itself and made the open-shop policy the cornerstone of its program. It organized a strikebreaker service, and it made plans to pool its constituents' financial resources to ensure victory.

By mid-summer, the IAM realized that its own financial resources were no match for those of the NMTA. It appealed to the National Civic Federation to use its good offices to end the dispute. The federation, after making an avowedly pro-IAM effort, was unable to negotiate a compromise. By then President McKinley had been assassinated, and Hanna's personal influence was on the wane. In October, O'Connell even appealed personally to President Roosevelt to order all government work being held up by the strike transferred to naval yards.

The NMTA was adamant in its refusal to negotiate with the IAM. All efforts to redirect its policy failed. In two years prior to the big strike the IAM had paid a total of $64,643 in strike benefits; in 1901, alone, it paid $154,128. In all, the NMTA fight was expensive, it defied negotiation and in the long run could not be won.

What is possibly even more significant than the loss of the strike was the failure of O'Connell's plans. As indicated earlier, his program embraced cooperation with the AFL and negotiation with the leaders of industry. Within the AFL he had not been successful in the ITU fight. And even the combined efforts put forth in the NCF proved useless in the NMTA struggle.[22] The union, financially pressed as well as dismayed by the turn of events, began to reject his leadership. But took ten years to dethrone him.

The Slow Decline of O'Connellism: 1902–1911

In retrospect it is clear that the nine-hour strike of 1901 marked the turn of the O'Connell administration's fortunes. The open-shop campaign, aggressively waged by the NMTA as well as by many kindred organizations, put all unions on the defensive. It also made the Gompers–Mitchell–O'Connell plan of negotiating with top management no more than a dream. That O'Connell's administration managed to remain in power for ten years in the face of organized opposition, is the remarkable thing.

Strikes and Strike Policy

Four issues, all recognized earlier, dominated the IAM's relationship with employers. The first, wage rates, was of course directly related to business conditions, with depressions occurring from 1903 to 1904, 1907 to 1908, and again in 1910 until 1911.

The second was union recognition and was the thorniest of the four. With the development of the antiboycott league, the open-shop federation, as well as such militantly antiunion organizations as the NMTA and the NAM, it was only to be expected that any progress would be slow. Strike after strike occurred to prevent victimization, and time after time ended in failure. The decade was in great part one of reaction, where even the educators, particularly President Charles William Eliot of Harvard, were vehemently antiunion.[23] In brief, the former dream of negotiating for basic agreement at the top was completely at variance with the situation. Top management, highly influenced by the J. P. Morgan attitude expressed in U. S. Steel, was completely antagonistic.

The third issue was piecework and involved the introduction of work rationalization. Piecework was not merely "payment by results"; it was predominantly a new concept of the job. It transferred many decisions, based on skilled judgment, from the individual craftsman to the industrial engineer. In the transfer process, the artisan lost not only his real sense of personal significance (not to be minimized), but he was also forced to give up whatever shreds of bargaining power he had once enjoyed in dealing with his employer. The fight against piecework was more than a blind fight against technological development; to the unionists, it was a fight for preservation of the dignity of the craftsman and such economic bargaining as he possessed.[24]

The remaining issue was the one which had precipitated the NMTA showdown, namely, shorter hours. The IAM was committed to the eight-hour day, and whatever may have been the exigencies of a given moment, the long-range aim was never forgotten. At times, as in 1901, it might have been willing to settle temporarily for the fifty-four hour week; but concessions such as this were only halfway stations on the road to the ultimate goal.

Strikes over these four issues occurred against both the railroads and industrial employers, the latter including what came to be known as the "contract shops" after 1904.[25] On the railroads there was almost continual militancy, with recognition and piecework the usual issues.

Although numerous agreements, generally covering wage issues and prevention of victimization, were concluded from time to time, what stands out were the big strikes, lasting many months and frequently resulting in violence on both sides.

In July, 1902, the Union Pacific machinists struck to eliminate the piecework system which had been introduced shortly before. The strike lasted over eleven months and when finally "settled," most of the men received their old jobs back and the right to refuse piecework on an individual basis. The principle of the nine-hour day was included in the agreement.[26] The significance of the victory lies in the willingness of the Harriman lines (of which the Union Pacific was a major part) to negotiate with the IAM, and in their acceptance of the nine-hour day. The piecework issue was in reality lost, however, since it was patently obvious that the union could eliminate or retard piecework only by an outright prohibition of the system — anything less could only result in its gradual adoption insofar as it encouraged each worker to compete against other workers to ensure himself work opportunity and earnings. And there were many abuses of the pay scale associated with the piecework system, the arbitrary setting and then unilateral raising of work standards, and the callousness of personnel policies toward veteran employees who were unable to meet the pressure of production-oriented thinking, or able to find jobs comparable to the ones to which they had grown accustomed.

In 1909 a similar strike was called on the Baltimore and Ohio Railroad system.[27] Initially, the issue was the introduction of piecework, although as is often the case in long strikes, other issues were added. This strike lasted from June 3, 1909, until a final "settlement" was negotiated on December 30,

1910. During its course, IAM Vice-President Walter Ames, who was supervising the strike for the union, and four other members were indicted for conspiring to dynamite Baltimore and Ohio property. The four were brought to trial and acquitted. Charges against Ames were dropped. Again, as in the earlier Union Pacific instance, the IAM secured the right of each striker to return to work with protection of his seniority. But on the major issue, piecework, there was no victory. Here, too, the "settlement" in reality represented a loss for the union. Where piecework had been established previous to June, 1909, it was to be continued; elsewhere the company agreed not to force its introduction, but to let each member decide for himself. In effect, the company agreed to permit the system to propagate itself — which was just what happened.

The railroads at this time came to employ a master personnel record system; in practice, an effective blacklisting apparatus. This, together with an elaborate system of industrial espionage (planting spies in unions), represented the employers' offensive. To counter it, the unions began to consider federation of all unions in the shops and the coordination of their policies. A decision to strike was reached in 1911 to force the Harriman lines and the Illinois Central to recognize the federation of shop craft unions as the exclusive, legitimate bargaining representative of their workers. The idea of federation seemed so obvious and logical to the men that they refused to heed the warnings voiced by O'Connell who literally begged the IAM not to engage in an effort he foresaw to be doomed.

O'Connell's unorthodox attitude toward piecework, so evident at the 1899 convention, was not expressed again for several years. Where he could, he tried to have the system abolished; elsewhere, there was no negotiable position which he could take. At the 1903 convention in Milwaukee, the delegates unanimously decided that after July 1 of that year no member could operate more than one machine at a time or accept the introduction of the piecework system; where the system was already in practice, it would have to be abolished by July 1, 1904. The question of enforcing the new rule was put to referendum vote and was rejected by the membership 8693 to 1610; in O'Connell's words the latter decision "was a wise one . . . because trade conditions would not warrant . . . striking . . . [and because the union] had on [its] hands as much trouble as one organization might be expected to successfully and scientifically look after."

This pious policy, without possibility of enforcement, was continued year after year. It is clear, however, that many, if not most, members could not afford to refuse to work under the piecework system where it existed. Nonetheless, from time to time, action was taken to stop its spread. In 1909

O'Connell estimated that 50 per cent of the strikes and 60 per cent of the strike benefits paid out were associated with the issue. He asked again for greater latitude for himself and the general executive board to regulate the system where it existed—particularly where new contracts could be obtained. Strangely enough, he was given this permission and in at least one instance, an agreement with a major employer (American Locomotive) was reached. The law, however, was tightened at the 1911 Davenport convention.

The IAM was adamant about Taylorism in government arsenals and brought what political pressure it could on Congress to prohibit time and motion studies. Only at first were the attempts successful in this area.

The war with the NMTA grew more bitter. The NMTA, setting out systematically to break the union, employed any and all tactics to secure its ends. By 1907 the yellow-dog contract had become the standard practice in many sectors. Toledo was one of the few places where the IAM managed to hold on to the original terms of its contract with the Pope Motor Car Company, but only after a bitter strike.[28] Elsewhere the reverse was more often the case, and by 1909 it was estimated that there were about 750 NMTA shops where IAM members were working not only without contracts, but frequently were forced to hide their union membership.[29] By 1907 the nine-hour day, fifty-four hour week was the general practice; in a few shops, agitation had secured the eight-hour day. But such situations were rare, particularly after 1907, when a depression occurred. Where the IAM could, it sought recognition—elsewhere the men settled for shorter working hours.

Table 1. *Strike benefits, 1900–1911.*
(in dollars)

Year	Amount	Amount raised by strike assessment
1900	44,040	18,219
1901	154,128	62,513
1902	128,177	22,084
1903	103,765	48,232
1904	245,914	19,012
1905	253,222	29,869
1906	162,104	59,106
1907	341,204	60,591
1908	318,250	109,165
1909	135,484	117,630
1910	339,484	155,398
1911	414,712	164,455

The whole period was marked by strikes, which severely strained the strike-accumulated resources of the union. Special strike levies were required.[30] These were invariably unpopular, their unpopularity being associated with O'Connell's policies. Thus, by 1911 the membership was tired of both, quite irrespective of the fact that both O'Connell's position and the necessity for extra revenue were unquestionably necessary. More than any other factor, this caused the dissatisfaction which led to his defeat. It was ironic that his last effort as international president was directed at stopping the Illinois Central and Harriman lines strikes, the most expensive of all strikes; his efforts for peace were frustrated by the very members who had hitherto been the loudest in their denunciations of his expensive strike policy.

Table 1 gives a clear picture of the actual cost of strike benefits from 1900 through 1911.

Relations with Other Unions

O'Connell's policy of close cooperation with the AFL was of some assistance in the big NMTA 1901 strike insofar as financial aid and Gompers' moral help were concerned. But because the result was defeat, not victory, all the assistance given by the AFL was soon overlooked by the IAM members. Moreover, Gompers' impotence in the ITU–IAM struggle involving jurisdiction over linotype mechanics was remembered long after the 1901 episode had been forgotten.

Besides following the original policy of close cooperation with the AFL top leadership, O'Connell put renewed emphasis on integration with the other unions in the metal trades to gain unity in time of strikes. In 1903 O'Connell took a major part in resuscitating the old Metal Trades Federation, and was elected its president.[31] In time, it became the metal trades department within the AFL. But from the first, it was a formless organization, having neither the fact nor the shadow of power. In particular, it lacked funds.

Disputes with various unions developed and increased in intensity. There was the unresolved conflict with the ITU over the repair of linotypes. There was also a seemingly irreconciliable conflict with the British Amalgamated Society of Engineers, which had a North American membership of eighteen hundred loyal men. The ASE forbade dual membership and refused to support the IAM in the latter's strikes. Eventually open conflict between the two unions developed, and the IAM persuaded the AFL to rescind its recognition of the ASE.[32]

One other important conflict should be mentioned. A group of mechanics engaged in the installation of elevators formed their own union in 1903, getting an AFL charter. The IAM immediately asserted its claim to this job territory, but without success. The elevator constructors were building tradesmen, who worked closely with employer–contractors and the other unions in the construction industry and used their friendship with the latter in the AFL executive council. O'Connell was unsuccessful in his efforts to encourage their amalgamation with the IAM. While he remained president, an open breach was avoided, and the two unions at least lived together. The elevator constructors and the IAM both finally joined the Building Trades Department, but only after the IAM had protested the other's admission.[33] By 1912 the two unions were approaching a showdown.

At this point, one amalgamation deserves notice. In 1904 after a referendum vote, the fifteen hundred members of the International Association of Allied Metal Mechanics were admitted to the IAM with protection of their former beneficiary rights.[34] This action is usually referred to as the first admission of specialists, while, in fact, O'Connell had brought specialists in earlier.[35]

The Internal Policies of the IAM

The administration of the IAM grew steadily more complex as its problems multiplied. Accurate membership figures do not exist, but approximations were as follows: [36]

1895	8,000	1901	57,000	1907	57,000
1896	9,000	1902	40,000	1908	61,000
1897	15,000	1903	50,000	1909	45,000
1898	16,000	1904	44,000	1910	54,000
1899	17,000	1905	45,000	1911	64,000
1900	22,000	1906	50,000		

The trend, begun earlier by O'Connell to control the union from the top as much as possible, continued. In 1901 the convention created five vice-presidents, each of whom was to assist O'Connell in organizing and controlling strikes. Two years later, in 1903, the number was increased to seven, and salaries were raised. In 1905 an assistant general secretary-treasurer was appointed, a further indication of the pressures of increased centralization—in this instance, of record keeping. Details on the evolution of the governmental instrument are treated in Chapter VII; here, it is relevant only in pointing out O'Connell's creation of a corps of paid officials, upon whom he relied to keep a tenuous hold on the union.

The policy relating to admissions went through several refinements during this third period of O'Connell's administration. O'Connell's devotion to the trade-union principle has been amply noted. He wanted the organization to include all those who had a direct economic interest in the machinists' job. Furthermore, he realized that the job existed in a particularly dynamic industrial context—thus, he was eager to broaden the definition of machinist whenever it seemed wise. On the other hand, he was deeply conscious of the necessity of maintaining a tightly knit, well-disciplined organization, capable of making decisions and living by them. He thus drew the line between semi-trained machinists (specialists) and helpers or handymen.[37] He accepted the former, while consistently rejecting the latter groups. He favored admitting apprentices into the IAM. They actually had their own lodges, but he later urged their inclusion in the regular lodges.[38] O'Connell's critics stressed what they believed to be a major inconsistency in his approach. He encouraged the affiliation of mere stripling apprentices, while opposing the affiliation of mature men, albeit unskilled helpers. To this, O'Connell had no ready answer. He was willing to grant considerable autonomy within the IAM to nongeneral machinist groups, but he did not want to get involved with the unskilled. What he did suggest was the use of the man's wage rate as the criterion—if a man's rate of pay was the approximate average for machinists, he was eligible. As an administrative rule of thumb, this suggestion had merit; as a doctrine enunciated in the presence of "underdog-minded" Socialists, it sounded vindictive.

By 1911 O'Connell's influence was practically gone. At the Davenport convention, held that year, the helpers were formally declared eligible for admission, albeit only to their own locals. Their dues books were to be stamped "machinist's helper," and it remained a cardinal offense for any qualified machinist to teach a helper any of the skilled practices of the trade. O'Connell, throughout the period, was actually aware of the discriminatory features of his policy, as well as the inevitable technological developments which would make it outdated. But he had no better answer.

The 1911 convention was also noteworthy because it authorized the admission of women. The first constitution of 1889 had actually limited membership to males; all others had omitted the subject. In 1911, however, the reform spirit ran high and the presence of women in the trade was acknowledged.[39]

The IAM was a low-dues organization and unfortunately, the objectives of its members needed money to be realized. The 1903 convention authorized the payment of superannuation benefits, but provided no funds to finance it. Naturally the authorization was observed in the breach, to be removed in 1909. Throughout the period, a high death-benefit program was operating. To finance the union's strikes as well as its growing bureaucracy, more money was needed.[40] Assessments of $1.00 were levied from time to time; in 1904 there were two assessments, and in 1905, one. At the Denver convention of 1909 a special assessment of "one day's pay" for each of the succeeding three years was voted. The amount was finally set at $2.50. Special assessments always annoyed the members and were hard to collect. On the other hand, raising per capita tax was no easier. In 1901, it was 40 cents monthly for all except apprentices, for whom it was 20 cents. In 1905 the amounts were increased to 55 cents and 25 cents respectively, with a special arrangement of 20 cents for those out of work.

The remaining topic within the category of internal policies particularly worthy of notice is the role of personalities. Several incidents occurred revealing the general secretary-treasurer's personal ambition. Once, he was formally censured by the general executive board and forced to apologize.[41] The episode has importance only in relation to later developments; in 1916 he was defeated in a special election.

Two local business agents were disciplined by O'Connell. One, Nathan A. Cole, had been a candidate for delegate to the AFL. O'Connell determined that he was not eligible for membership and, obtaining general executive-board concurrence, expelled him.[42] The other was George Warner who had been a delegate to the AFL and had accepted a bribe from the Erie Railroad. O'Connell had been charged by the railroad officials with countenancing corruption, and when the situation became clear to him, he demanded Warner's expulsion. Warner's lodge (District Lodge 15) gave him an honorary withdrawal card, which O'Connell insisted it rescind. O'Connell successfully carried the matter to the Denver convention and later to a referendum vote.[43] Warner's many partisans turned vehemently against O'Connell and later joined with the Socialists to oust him.

The Socialist Issue

The failure of the agreement with the NMTA after 1901 was an additional factor in the growth of Socialist feeling in the IAM. By 1903 there was a sizable minority within the IAM who were convinced of the soundness as well as the inevitability of Socialism. It should be made clear, however, that to them Socialism meant no more than anti-Gompersism, industrial unionism, Populism, and increased political action. At the Milwaukee convention, they sought to persuade the IAM delegates to the AFL to vote against the reelection of Gompers and for the endorsement of Socialism. The issues went to referendum vote where the Socialists did not prevail and lost the first question, but won on the second. Nevertheless, there was no change in AFL policy.

The Socialists' two greatest *coups* prior to 1911 were expressions of the Populist side of their doctrine. In 1905 they succeeded in amending the constitution to provide for the popular election of all grand lodge officers (except the assistant general secretary-treasurer). In addition, it was decided to submit the question of holding a convention to referendum vote every two years. (After 1895, in the absence of, or in addition to, conventions, issues could be popularly handled by referendum at the option of a stated number of local lodges.) In this way, the Socialists managed to remove the election of officers as well as legislative determination of policy from O'Connell's grasp. By 1907, moreover, the union had gone referendum-wild — all issues, big and small, came to require action by all the members. Incidentally, only a relatively small fraction of the members bothered to vote.[44] Thus the referendum mirrored the larger struggle between O'Connell's administration and the Socialists. Each side won battles, but the Socialists won the war in 1911.

The 1911 convention, controlled by the Socialists, carried the referendum campaign to its dizziest heights. It enacted an "initiative and recall provision," which made it a simple matter for as few as eighty dissatisfied local lodges (providing not more than ten were in any single state, province, or territory) to compel any offending officer to stop his activities and run again for office. Even if he were to be reelected, his influence would have been lessened by the experience of the campaign. At the very best, the practice helped maintain conformity among the elected officers.

The Socialist vs. O'Connell issue involved a great deal of personal libel and slander. At the Boston convention (1905), the constitution was changed to fine or expel any member guilty of "circulating or causing to be circulated . . . malicious or untrue statements reflecting upon the standing or character, private or public, of any officer or member." Enforcement was left to the local lodges, although the general executive board would get cases on appeal.

In 1909 a further section was added to the constitution. It provided for the punishment of those advocating secession — referring in particular to members affiliated or seeking to be affiliated with the Industrial Workers of the World. Some IWW sentiment had appeared as early as 1906. In one instance, the anti-Catholicism of the IWW caused a local to expel a member.[45] In another instance, the IAM paid a death benefit to a member of a local lodge which had transferred (immediately after his death) to the IWW. What stands out in relation to the secession clause, however, was a provision giving the international president and the general executive board original jurisdiction in the event that a local lodge failed to act. In 1913, after O'Connell's defeat, this enforcement procedure also was applied to the slander clause.

O'Connell's influence had waned considerably by 1911. He claimed that he had decided not to run, but that the charges made against him made seeking reelection the sole honorable course. In a privately printed election circular prepared for that campaign, there is a review of his long association with the union and his lengthy career as an officer. In it he noted the organization's early financial difficulties and his own personal sacrifices to provide it with working capital. He referred to the wage increases which had occurred during his stewardship; he also noted that necessary increases in per capita tax had unfortunately not occurred. But he insisted, "Our financial affairs have been conducted as well, as economically and as profitably as those of any bank or commercial house [*sic*]in this country." [46]

Right or wrong, to the majority of those voting in the 1911 election, his claims were not enough. In the first case, too many strikes had been lost; the union treasury was low; the members were opposed both to further special assessments and radically increased per capita taxes. In brief, by 1911 the IAM was in anything but a good economic state.

But another reason for O'Connell's drop in favor was that he did not offer the workers "a dream." W. H. Johnston, his Socialist-supported opponent, did. And given a choice between a few hopeful crumbs and "pie in the sky," the majority chose the latter. Johnston won, 15,300 to 13,321.

O'Connell's defeat came prior to the Davenport (1911) convention. He presided as a "lame-duck" official and was rudely treated by the delegates. He begged the convention not to strike against the Harriman lines and the Illinois Central Railroad, but his words fell on deaf ears. At the end of the convention no one even rose to give him formal thanks for his long service to the association. In fact, the only mention of his efforts were in some of his own bitter, concluding remarks. He left the presidency deeply disappointed.[47] Because his friends in the AFL, notably Samuel Gompers and the AFL executive council, chose to stand by him (supporting his election to the presidency of the Metal Trades Department), the Socialists' low regard for him later came home to haunt them. This is elaborated on in Chapter III.

O'Connell had retained too much power in the labor movement (including a vice-presidency of the AFL) for anyone — particularly his successors — to have treated his feelings so callously. His was the administration in which the IAM developed its basic stability. O'Connell's philosphy was "job-conscious" unionism. His weakness was the inability to inspire membership in the face of a groundswell of anti-O'Connell Socialism. To say he was only a "business unionist" — a much misunderstood term — is erroneous. He had a vision of successful unionism, involving the admission of specialists and cooperation with the leaders of industry. His views on piecework were far more realistic than the union would concede at the time. And his dues policy was unmistakably correct. His friends and allies were not all wisely chosen. But his defeat was more a product of the times — of the antiunionism of the NMTA, and the railroads, as well as the emotional enthusiasm stirred up by the Socialists — than the result of his own conscious errors. For all the words spoken against him, his administration was honest and unassuming.

CHAPTER III

The Declining Momentum of Reform: The Johnston Administration

William H. Johnston was born in Nova Scotia in 1874. He served his apprenticeship at the Rhode Island Locomotive Works in Providence and worked for a few years thereafter as a railroad machinist. Later, he worked at a job shop where he organized a local lodge (Local Lodge 379). He returned to railroad work for a time, and then joined the Hoe Printing Press Company. He became business agent for Local 147 in 1906 and in 1909 president of District Lodge 44. In January, 1912, he became international president. Fourteen and a half troubled years later, broken in health and spirit, he resigned.[1] By all accounts he was an honorable man. The record of his administration is marred by the fact that the union was bitterly divided. From the outset, when Johnston assumed the leadership of this financially decrepit organization, the union was critically divided between a "Progressive" or Socialist faction and a "pure and simple" or O'Connell faction. As head of the former group, he enjoyed only a narrow majority. Toward the end, even his grip on that faction had slipped.

In considering the development of this administration, several significant facts should be kept in mind. First, Johnston's great appeal was an idealistic quality which O'Connell lacked. This was an amalgam of Progressivism, Populism, and grass roots American Socialism. Second, he favored, at least in the beginning, industrial unionism, which he and a majority of the membership believed would give the advantages of collective bargaining to those who were not craftsmen. Third, his personal hold as titular leader of his faction was never very strong. And fourth, he was unable, or perhaps even unwilling, to convert the opposition to some form of support for his administration.

One interesting aspect of this period was the existence and the breakdown of what was in effect a two-party system. Every election was a struggle between the "ins" and the "outs," although neither was ever really in or ever completely out. Each had great reservoirs of strength in local and district lodges, and each had ambitious leaders, full of plans for establishing hegemony. By 1922, however, Johnston had come over to the old O'Connell position — but by then the wounds were too deep, the hatreds too violent to permit a peaceful two-party system (one based on consensus) to work effectively. Thus the history of Johnston's regime is one full of friction and quarrels. It gives a picture of the Socialists' loss of a dream, and Johnston's eventual endorsement of the type of efficient "pure and simplism" which earlier he so loathed in James O'Connell. This chapter could well have been entitled "The Failure of a Two-Party System." In Chapter IV there is extended discussion of this.

This section is divided into three periods of time; 1912–1916, 1917–1919, and 1920–1926. In general, the first was a period of employer antiunion activity, during which Johnston attempted to consolidate his hold on the organization. The second includes the years of war prosperity when membership swelled to unprecedented proportions. And the third is the postwar period of union decline when the practical and necessary bases of unionism were reexamined.

Attempted Consolidation: 1912–1916

When Johnston took office in 1912, the treasury was empty.[2] For several of the previous years the IAM had been paying out more than it took in. The reasons for this were the paying of strike benefits throughout many long, bitter strikes, plus an unwillingness to raise the per capita tax significantly. From a business viewpoint, this was not the preferred way to run a union. But Johnston was not elected for his business approach. His supporters wanted militancy, and they talked, thought, and planned strike action.

Strikes

During O'Connell's last year as international president, the union overrode his objections and struck both the Illinois Central and Harriman railroad lines. The nominal issue was the refusal of the railroad managements to bargain with the newly formed shop-craft system federations, committees made up of representatives of the machinists, railway carmen, blacksmiths, boilermakers, and sheet metal workers' unions. The managements claimed to be willing to talk to each craft union separately, but were unwilling to meet the crafts in a group.[3]

These system federations were actually a major step in reorganizing unionism on the railroads, an important alternative to industrial unionism, and one which permitted the crafts to retain their identities. Thus the issue of recognition of the system federations was ideologically important. It is not surprising that many members of the IAM — particularly those who had condemned O'Connell's craft exclusivism — were prepared to fight hard to prove their point. Each railroad was to have its own federation of crafts, called a system federation.

O'Connell and the lame-duck general executive board were articulately opposed both to the federation system and to the two proposed strikes. They were opposed to the federation system because they were reluctant to yield even partial control of the IAM membership to any other organization, comprised mostly of non-IAM members. They also did not believe that the IAM was in a financial position to undertake what they correctly assumed to be long strikes. The Davenport IAM convention, taking the matter into its own hands, passed a special strike assessment of $2.50 for journeymen and $1.25 for apprentices.

On September 30, 1911, about forty thousand men (including three thousand machinists eligible for strike benefits) began the strike.[4] The railroad managements, adamant in their refusal to make concessions, secured injunctions, fired the strikers and refused all proffered offers for mediation or arbitration. By the beginning of 1912, when Johnston formally became international president, the strikes had become endurance contests.

By the spring of 1912 it was obvious that the two strikes could not succeed unless something dramatic occurred. The decision to organize the Federation of (System) Federations was a response to this situation, largely resulting from the pressure of the machinists; its first president was Arthur O. Wharton (a member and later international president of the IAM). This Federation of Federations, consisting of the same five unions which made up the AFL Railway Employees' Department, was organized along truly federal lines.[5] Each union was represented equally in each system federation, and each system federation, regardless of size, was represented equally in the Federation of Federations. In other words, it gave the IAM, which was making the largest contribution in strike benefits, relatively less than its expected share in the determination of policies.

In the spring of 1912 the newly formed Federation of Federations ordered a vote for a general strike on all the western railroads to support the Harriman lines men. Forty per cent of the members of the Federation of Federations did not participate in the vote, and those who did, voted by a small majority against authorizing any general extension of the strike. Whether the Federation of Federations officials actually expected to use the general strike weapon (or merely to threaten its use), the failure of the members to respond to their leader was all too apparent.

By May, 1913, the IAM had paid $400,000 to the strikers. In December, 1914, International President Johnston reported that the IAM, having paid out $700,000, which exhausted its financial resources, had to cease paying strike benefits. All during this time the railroads ran and if their profits were seriously impaired, it was not evident. Nonetheless, the men still refused to call off the strike, voting 1601 to 1052 (the IAM vote was 750 to 461) to continue it. Despite this opposition, Johnston and the general executive board withdrew IAM participation in the strike on June 28, 1915.[6]

Bitterness against the leadership was only natural, and there were many charges that Johnston mishandled funds. In time, the allegations became so embarrassing that Johnston brought charges against James Kline, president of the boilermakers, charging libel, citing a letter by Kline to the IAM membership.[7] The charges were heard at the 1916 convention of the Railway Employees' Department, and Kline was formally censured. But by that time the issue was an old one and the matter was dropped.

One of the IAM firebrands was a young machinist from Clinton, Illinois, named Carl Persons, who throughout the strike published the *Strike Bulletin*.[8] For this he was indicted by the state and charged with circulating materially defamatory information about the Illinois Central Railroad. While out on bond he was lured into a meeting with the leader of the IC strikebreakers, a former Clinton police chief, and beaten up. At the height of the beating he shot and killed his assailant. The unions, particularly the IAM, collected money for his defense. After a trial (including a jury deliberation of nearly twenty-four straight hours), he was acquitted. Despite the aid he received from the IAM, Persons was vehement in his denunciation of Johnston and several of the IAM leaders for calling off the strike. He appeared at the Kansas City convention of the Railway Employees' Department and presented his view of Johnston's "treachery and chicanery." For this he was summarily expelled from the IAM. His trial is historically important in the development of the presidency as a power, and will be analyzed later in this chapter as well as elsewhere in this study.[9] It is enough now to note that Johnston came away from the strike with his popularity dimmed, and that the IAM's leading martyr was thrown out of the union. The Federation of Federations was later supplanted by the old Railway Employees' Department of the AFL, and by 1915 the Federation's leader, Arthur O. Wharton, became president of the Railway Employees' Department. He was one of the officials connected with the affair who succeeded in maintaining (if not actually enhancing) his personal reputation.

During this period there were other railroad strikes as well. As mentioned before, frequent issues both on the railroads and in the other sectors of the metal trades industry were piecework and the institution of Taylorism or scientific management. The brunt of the piecework struggle, however, was borne by those in the army arsenals, which could be made to respond to congressional pressure. Repeatedly the IAM and the other metal trades unions lobbied for prohibition of the use of federal appropriations for time and motion studies. O'Connell, by this time president of the AFL Metal Trades Department, was appointed to the U. S. Commission on Industrial Relations and took advantage of the opportunities offered him to attack Taylorism.[10] These efforts were nominally successful; riders were attached to appropriation bills forbidding the disputed techniques. Yet, in some of the arsenals where the union's influence was not strongly felt, the union was unable to prevent the changes. General Crozier, the commandant of the Watertown (Massachusetts) Arsenal, was one, in particular, who ignored the prohibitions, and there, piecework increased each year.[11] In the private sectors of the economy, the union's resistance to the change was, if anything, less successful. Johnston, like O'Connell before him, was skeptical of victory, but in the union ranks there were many who urged active opposition to these changes.

The eight-hour day was becoming the general rule in American industry. In 1916, for instance, Congress, taking notice of this development (as well as the immediacy of a strike of the operating crews on railroads), granted the eight-hour day to the operating railroad brotherhoods. The IAM's activities in industry reflected this trend and gained many eight-hour agreements.

Dr. Thomas Holland, in an unpublished manuscript dealing with the significant labor events of 1915, discusses the IAM experience in Bridgeport, Connecticut. His study provides an excellent view of what was transpiring. Early in 1915 over 30 per cent of the local machinists were unemployed; by the end of that year it was a seller's market. In order to hold on to its labor (as well as to keep out the union), Remington Arms, the major employer, suddenly cut its work week from fifty-five to forty-eight hours (spread over six days). Other firms in the area were obliged to follow suit. Then to appeal further to the workers, Remington Arms raised wages $1.00 per day. In response to the same economic pressure, similar developments occurred in Boston and New York. Only in Cincinnati, where the NMTA influence was strong, were employers slow to grant these concessions, and even there, they were granted after a year or two. The relevant point is that the union's successes were intimately associated with tight labor markets, not with the results of effective organization. In general, the period 1912 through 1916 was not a good one for the union as a bargaining institution.

Relations with Other Unions.

One of the most critical problems faced by Johnston in 1912 was the guiding of the IAM's relationship with other unions. He was not only the man who had defeated James O'Connell (whose closeness to Gompers and the others on the AFL executive council remained unchanged by defeat), but his Socialism was an unwelcome and repugnant philosophy to most of the AFL unions' leaders.[12]

Johnston may have thought it logical that he replace O'Connell on the AFL executive council. At any rate, in 1916 both the IAM convention and the membership voted (the latter 7732 to 1429) to instruct the AFL delegates to press for the change. The AFL, pointedly ignoring Johnston, retained O'Connell as an official until 1918. In that year Johnston succeeded in having him defeated as a delegate to the AFL convention.

Thus the IAM, and Johnston in particular, had a powerful adversary in the AFL. There is evidence that this situation bothered Johnston, but there was nothing he could do about it. As noted earlier, O'Connell became president of the Metal Trades Department after his defeat. The one thing Johnston could do was to form alliances within the union movement in some sector other than the metal trades. And that is what he did.

In early 1914, for instance, the IAM paid per capita assessments to the AFL and its departments as follows: (1) to the AFL, on two thirds of the membership, (2) to the Metal Trades Department (O'Connell's stronghold), on one quarter of the membership, (3) to the Building Trades Department, on one third of the membership, and, (4) to the Railway Employees' Department (reflecting the focus of IAM interests), on one half the membership. At its 1914 convention the AFL reorganized its affiliation fees; the IAM responded by reorganizing its per capita representation. It increased its basic representation in the AFL to 100 per cent, in the Metal Trades Department to 50 per cent, in the newly organized Mining Department to 50 per cent, and in the Railway Employees' Department to 100 per cent. It cut its basic in the Building Trade Department to 20 per cent. But these were makeshift arrangements. Johnston and the IAM did not enjoy rapport with the AFL leadership, with the possible exception of the Railway Employees' Department, and frequently considered whether the expenditures on per capita affiliation fees were arranged in an optimum manner. The important conclusion is that he did not wish to disaffiliate, but sought to use the IAM's affiliation fees to the maximum advantage. In some instances he paid a nominal sum in order to permit the IAM to voice its opinions; in others, he paid more because that gave the IAM a more powerful vote.

In 1915 the IAM planned to broaden its membership requirements to allow all metal tradesmen (including boilermakers, sheet metal workers and others) to join the IAM. Johnston, switching from an earlier pro-industrial union stand, urged the general executive board not to sanction the change which, he thought, would "cause unlimited [jurisdictional] trouble."[13] The change had been authorized by the membership. General Secretary-Treasurer Preston refused to go along with Johnston's instructions unless so ordered by the general executive board; the general executive board then followed Johnston's lead. In this instance O'Connell came out in full support of Johnston, one of the very few times he did so.[14]

Jurisdictional disputes developed with several AFL unions. A few were amicably settled. These include a dispute with the pressmen — it was settled by giving them the right to operate "all printing and lithographing machinery," and the IAM the right to manufacture all presses and accessories. One novel feature of the accord was a plan for joint strike benefits to members of both unions paid by the union calling the strike.[15]

A major conflict developed with the flint glass and bottle blowers. The IAM objected to Gompers' issuing a charter to them before their differences with the IAM had been settled. This dispute continued for years, with the IAM getting no satisfaction.[16]

But the most serious fight occurred within the Building Trades Department.[17] It involved the IAM on two fronts — a dispute with the carpenters over the millwrights, and one with the elevator constructors. The former was the more serious, since the two unions involved were major organizations. In 1908 the carpenters took in the millwrights. In theory, the millwrights were supposed to arrange shafts and belts for power transmission, work assumed to be less skillful than machinists' work. In practice, the difference in the order of skill was not great, and both unions wanted the job opportunity and were prepared to fight for it.

In 1914 the IAM secured passage of a resolution at the AFL convention assigning to it the disputed territory. The carpenters responded by withdrawing temporarily from the Building Trades Department. Even at the time no one in the IAM (least of all Johnston) felt that "victory" had been secured. And it had not.

The dispute with the elevator constructors was with a smaller union which the IAM wished to absorb through amalgamation. The elevator constructors, however, wished to remain apart because their principal ties were with the building trades. Johnston, in 1914, tried to get the AFL convention to direct amalgamation, but Duncan of the granite cutters stopped him short.[18] In 1915 the carpenters made a deal with the elevator constructors. If the elevator constructors would support their readmission to the Building

Trades Department, the carpenters would support an elevator constructors' proposal to expel the IAM from the Building Trades Department. This is what occurred. From 1915 on, in spite of repeated efforts, the IAM was unable to regain admission. The basic causes of the conflict are discussed in Chapter IX.

Internal Affairs

There were four chief developments in this area. The first was the continued antagonism among the officers and instability resulting from liberal use of the recall provision. The second was the growth of the power of the international president. The third involved changes in the relationship between the grand lodge and the subordinate lodges. And the fourth stemmed from the grand lodge's shaky financial situation during the period.

The recall provision. The initiative and recall constitutional provision became effective in 1911. Shortly afterward, it was invoked against J. J. Keegan, who had been elected a delegate to the AFL.[19] The crux of the matter was Keegan's earlier (pre-1911) affiliation with the National Civic Federation, and a resulting charge that he was proemployer. (In 1911 the union voted in a referendum to forbid any IAM member from holding membership in the NCF.) Keegan was successfully recalled, and Arthur O. Wharton, then leader of the Federation of Federations, was elected in his place. The vote was 6565 to 3344 (with a membership of about 63,000 eligible to vote).

In 1915 there was a second attempt to unseat an officer. In this instance it was an attack on Vice-President J. J. Keppler by Local Lodge 126 (Chicago) which charged that he had sabotaged its strike against the Otis Elevator Company.[20] Moreover, it charged him with being reactionary and with attacking the progressivism of Johnston and the latter's associates. Keppler successfully defended himself, winning by a vote of 8369 to 6403; union membership at the time was approximately 75,000.

The major recall attempt, however, involved a long and tortuous attempt to unseat General Secretary-Treasurer George Preston.[21] Preston had first been elected in 1895, when he defeated one of the founders, William Dawley. An unusually proud and sensitive man, Preston had a penchant for becoming involved in personality fights. In 1907 he had been reprimanded by the general executive board for exceeding his authority — a public action taken because of personal frictions.

One of Preston's more formidable antagonists on the general executive board was William Somerville, a Canadian, who, while in the field, was greatly angered both by the poor cooperation he received from headquarters and reports of similar cavalier treatment accorded to local secretaries. In 1912 a St. Paul local became so provoked with Preston that they initiated a recall action against him. Preston then asked the general executive board to permit him to go to Minnesota to quiet the protest. The general executive board agreed to his request, but told him to pay his own way.

Two years later Preston was again engaged in a dispute. This time it involved a minor procedural question. Vice-President Conlon (to whom the matter had been mistakenly sent) had certified a victimization pay roll of a St. Louis local — a matter rightfully Preston's concern. Preston refused to pay the money and told the local that they would have to reinitiate the whole matter. The case was carried to the general executive board which, while acknowledging that Conlon had been technically in error, censured Preston for his attitude and for delaying payment.

In 1916 dissatisfaction with Preston reached the point of no return. After much hesitation, the general executive board had decided to sponsor a referendum vote for a convention. The membership agreed 7776 to 3336 to call the convention (there were approximately 100,000 members at the time). The general executive board then had to name the convention city. After some discussion, it narrowed down to Toledo and Baltimore. Two general executive board members voted for each and Somerville wired Preston from Moosejaw, Saskatchewan, saying, "I am inclined to favor Baltimore, but before voting would like to know the views of other members." Preston assumed this message to be a positive vote for Baltimore, and when Somerville insisted otherwise, Preston preferred charges against him for "gross neglect of duty in failing to vote [properly]."

The question was then resubmitted to the general executive board on Johnston's instructions and for unexplained reasons Preston was away from headquarters when the second ballot came in. The constitution specifically forbade the general secretary-treasurer's leaving headquarters without prior general executive board sanction. Preston's trip, it was implied, was a pleasure jaunt. Moreover, Preston had written an article for the journal, blaming the general executive board for the delay in selecting the convention site.

On May 11, 1916, the holdover general executive board (in response to Johnston's urging) voted to remove Preston for malfeasance. This unauthorized absence was said to have caused delay in naming the convention city. He was charged with arrogance for his refusal to answer communications because they were inaccurately addressed. He was also charged with having written an untruthful article in the May 1916 journal, blaming the general executive board for the delay. The indictment noted that he had "been repeatedly warned, censured and reprimanded for his unjustifiable and arbitrary conduct, in dealing with not only grand lodge, but also local lodge affairs, without . . . any effect whatsoever."

Preston was not without friends. Of the five members comprising the new general executive board elected in 1916, three were for him. Moreover, Somerville had been defeated. Preston, taking advantage of the general feeling against the old general executive board (and to a degree against Johnston), appealed to the convention, which acted as a committee-of-the-whole on the matter. The convention went into executive session for three days and after much bitter debate in which Preston's personality, the intensely personal nature of his feuds, and his incompatibility, were much discussed, it first voted to sustain the old general executive board as having acted within its power and then voted to return Preston to office until a formal recall vote could be held.

It should be added that Preston had just been reelected general secretary-treasurer with 18,871 votes to 10,351 for Fechner (one of his chief critics and a great friend of Johnston). It is obvious that the convention was reluctant to depose him—particularly if it meant putting Fechner in his place. Preston ran against Emmet Davison in the recall election, losing with 16,235 votes to 19,006 for Davison. With a faintly praising letter from the general executive board, he left the IAM after twenty-one years of full service. Unlike O'Connell, Preston had no friends in high places to look after him, and he died a simple chicken farmer.[22]

The Preston recall illustrates the continued turmoil during Johnston's administration. One of Preston's supporters had described him as "absolutely honest, trustworthy, efficient, [but] a disagreeable little crab."[23] In spite of Johnston's protestations to the contrary, ridding himself of Preston was neither necessary nor desirable. True, he was difficult; but in a job which required integrity, Preston's integrity was more important than his overwhelming ambition. Preston's friends were largely unfriendly to Johnston; Preston's enemies were virtually all personal allies of the international president. When the showdown finally came, Preston was forced out, but when the Preston fight was over, little accord remained in the IAM. There were no victors—Preston lost his job and Johnston lost a chance for consolidating his position.

Growth of international president's power. Johnston's partisanship in the Preston affair was not an isolated episode. While it is true that the constitution gave him broad powers to intervene in the judicial process, the remarkable fact was his willingness to use them, considering the number of enemies he made. Four cases stand out. The first, occurring in 1914, dealt with the refusal of Local Lodge 112 (St. Paul) to accept a member's payment of a $50.00 fine for unbecoming conduct and its subsequent refusal to issue a membership book to him. Johnston and the general executive board accepted the fine themselves and ordered the local lodge to reinstate him.[24] This was one of the first times that the grand lodge and an international president took the necessary countermoves to force local lodge compliance when the constitution was being defied.

A second case that same year in Binghamton, New York, is of similar importance. Two members wrote to their employer to call his attention to their superior work in the shop. The local charged them with "showing fellow members in a bad light," and they were fined $50.00 each.[25] They appealed to Johnston who not only upheld the fines but indicated that he would countenance more severe penalties. Their local lodge then expelled them. This illustrates the assumption of responsibility by the international president. He felt he could not only review passed sentences and reduce them, but that he could recommend harsher terms.

The third case was in many respects the most sensational. It involved Carl Persons, the "martyr" of the Illinois Central strike. Persons' membership was suspended by Johnston's direct order, because of the scurrilous nature of his attack on Johnston at the Kansas City convention of the Railway Employees' Department. Persons appealed Johnston's action to the 1916 Baltimore convention, alleging that the international president had no authority to suspend a member without a trial. The convention upheld Johnston, but directed Johnston to readmit Persons if he would admit his error and seek forgiveness, but Persons never did.

The fourth, a case against H. W. Kingston and Local Lodge 468 (Salem, Massachusetts), was the most far reaching. Kingston had published a circular, bearing the seal of the Local Lodge 468, containing personal allegations against Johnston. It included charges that he was a despot who had usurped powers beyond those granted in the constitution; that he had caused the IAM to be expelled from the Building Trades Department; that he was a spendthrift; that he had misused his influence in the matter of the IC and Harriman strikes, and so on. Johnston then directed Local Lodge 468 to discipline Kingston, but the trial was never held. (Johnston was represented by Fechner, who insisted upon the observance of technicalities — Kingston then refused to be tried and was upheld by the local.) Johnston prevailed at the general executive board hearing when it decided to expel Kingston and to revoke the local's charter.[26] While there can be no doubt that Johnston and the general executive board were within their rights, it is no less true that their action brooked no later compromise. And compromise is the essence of strength in the normal operation of democratic organizations.

These four cases constitute a chapter in the growth of the powers of the international presidency and also illustrate Johnston's lack of skill in handling relationships. For a man elected as a Populist-Socialist, he was far from adept in consolidating popular support.

Grand lodge and local lodge relationships. The grand lodge asserted new degrees of control over locals in other ways. It should be recalled that the Socialist complaint against the O'Connell administration was that it had interfered in local affairs. However, during Johnston's first year in office, he came to realize that the grand lodge had to hold tight reins on the locals. In 1912 he and the general executive board established rules "as would afford the grand lodge reasonable protection in the supervision of the bookkeeping of local lodges under which we could alone feel justified in assuming the responsibility of furnishing bonds." [27] In 1914 the grand lodge directed the local lodges not to advance money to grand lodge representatives until they were specifically ordered to do so.[28]

Grand lodge finances. The most critical internal aspect of Johnston's first four years had to do with finances. He had pledged himself against both special assessments and higher per capita taxes during the 1911 campaign. Considering the membership's proclivity to strike, Johnston's words soon echoed back at him. Thus in 1912, only three and a half months after taking office, he was forced to seek additional funds, in the form of voluntary contributions, for the two big railroad strikes which had begun six months earlier. Over $54,000 was contributed in response to this appeal. In all, he raised almost $71,000 in 1912 and $57,000 in 1913 by voluntary donations.

Impressive as these amounts were, they were not enough. In 1913 Preston sent out a circular asking for a return to the previous assessment practice.[29] Noting that the grand lodge was without cash, he asked that "wherever possible every lodge levy an assessment equivalent to one month's dues, say for a month, as a loan to the grand lodge." He hoped that his appeal would bring between $50,000 and $60,000 to the grand lodge within thirty days.

The critical financial condition caused some additional changes in the per capita tax and dues and benefits schedules. In 1913 the union by referendum vote raised the per capita tax for journeymen from 55 cents to 60 cents per month. At the same time, it lowered the tax on specialists from 55 cents to 45 cents. In 1905 it had set $1.00 per month as the minimum local lodge dues to be paid by journeymen, but in 1913 it established a sliding scale of benefits for specialists — those earning 25 cents per hour or less would pay a minimum of 75 cents per month, but would receive only three-fourths of the journeyman's strike-victimization and death benefits. Thus, strange as it may seem, the Socialists sponsored a discriminatory dues and benefits policy — "from each according to his ability and to each according to his status."

Organizing in 1915 was handicapped because of a lack of funds. Consequently the administration attempted to raise the per capita tax (its major source of income) in 1916. It proposed an across-the-board increase of 10 cents per month, and sought to raise minimum local lodge dues to $1.25 and

$1.00 for the two major classes of members (journeymen and specialists). It hoped, in this way, to increase grand lodge yearly revenue no less than $100,000. The proposal of course was submitted to referendum. With less than 15 per cent of the membership voting, it was defeated 5897 to 8998.

Running the union with little money required ingenuity. In order to assure meeting overhead expenses, it became obvious that funds would have to be segregated. Consequently Johnston proposed that all grand lodge income be allocated in the following manner:

For strike fund purposes	40%
For general expenses	40%
For death benefits payments	11%
For the journal	7%
For convention expenses	2%

The general executive board was to be allowed to reallocate funds in times of emergency. This proposal passed the referendum 11,106 to 3594.

The chaotic conditions relating to the calling of the 1916 convention and the bitterness at the sessions have already been described briefly. In addition to the Preston matter, the Persons case, the establishment of a line item budget, and the abortive per capita tax increase, the convention undertook some other major internal changes. The delegates voted to have a regularly scheduled quadrennial convention, instead of irregular ones called by referendum. After 1916, officers were elected for four- rather than two-year terms. The convention voted to deny death benefits (effective January 1, 1917) to any member joining or rejoining the union after his fiftieth birthday. It also specified that the editor should run the journal subject to the advice of the general executive board, thereby taking away his plenary power over the publication. The 1916 referendum rejected, in addition to the per capita tax increases, salary increases for the officers and increased expense allowances for the AFL delegates.

The Green Years: 1917–1919

The union expanded rapidly during the First World War. Membership rose from 107,444 in 1916 to a high of 331,449 in 1919. Wartime prosperity and the concomitant shortage of labor made the antiunion campaign of the various employer organizations less effective than previously. Indeed, where the union felt that a blacklisting system was operating, it often complained to sympathetic government officials, who in some cases used their influence to stop this production-hindering practice.

The IAM in company with many other unions used the labor shortage of the First World War to obtain the eight-hour day. When the war was over, Johnston was intent on preserving the gain. He told the members, "our slogan shall be — '8 hours of labor and no more in a period of 24.' This does not mean a basic 8-hour day, neither does it mean a period of time after 8 hours for which time and one-half is paid, but to discourage the working of overtime in every instance." [30]

During this period, the railroads were under direct governmental control. By and large the IAM was happy with the arrangement. It was given far more recognition than under private management. Therefore, it was only natural that the IAM should support the Plumb Plan for the nationalization of the railroads. Under this plan management of the railroads would be by a tripartite committee, composed of representatives of labor, management, and the government. Half the net earnings would be put into a sinking fund to retire the debt incurred in the nationalization; the other half would be paid to wage and salary employees of the railroads in the form of dividends. Despite the pressure for the adoption of the plan brought by the IAM as well as by the railway brotherhoods and the Railway Employees' Department, Congress rejected it and turned the railroads back to private ownership in 1920. The manager of the Plumb Plan League, former Congressman Edward Keating, made fruitful use of this disappointment by becoming the editor of *Labor,* the Washington weekly publication which best expressed the positions taken by the railway unions. More will be said of *Labor* later.

In a few instances where jurisdictional strikes flared, particularly with the carpenters, Gompers used his influence to soothe the situation. One example involved a jurisdictional strike between the two unions in a plant of the American Can Company. The unions, encouraged by Gompers, decided to let the management choose between them. It chose the IAM, agreed to rehire the strikers, fire the "scabs," pay 55 cents per hour to regular machinists, pay a 6 cents differential to tool makers, grant the eight-hour day, and pay double time for overtime. It refused, however, to recognize the diesetters as a part of the bargaining unit, but it agreed to rehire them.[31]

Within the IAM the frictions of the earlier period continued. The Johnston administration was far from secure. On the other hand, there was no concerted, well-organized opposition with the power to overthrow it. In the 1918 election Johnston defeated J. A. Taylor 36,000 to 23,000 votes, but J. F. Anderson defeated Johnston's "candidate" for vice-president, Conlon, 36,000 to 22,000. Anderson, a Mormon, was an independent. Conlon, whom he replaced, was both a devout Roman Catholic and a supporter of the Populist or Socialist views held by Johnston.[32]

In 1919 a recall was initiated to remove Anderson from his position, but it failed.[33] He had been charged with not exerting sufficient effort in pressing IAM demands on the federal railroad administration. He replied that one could not strike against a government-operated utility — regardless of how much a local might want to do so. Moreover, he did not think that the local's claims had merit and voiced this belief, again illustrating the lack of tact and political know-how in the organization's politics.

The grand lodge entered the war period with an empty treasury but relatively few outstanding debts. It had borrowed approximately $17,000 at 4½ per cent interest; in addition it owed $8000 to some local lodges. It felt that its expenditures were not wisely allocated. In February 1917, for example, the general executive board became concerned because so much money was being spent on organizing. It should be remembered that the 1917 general executive board was not sympathetic to Johnston, anyway, and attack on this front served as a good way to try to discredit him, or diminish his influence.

The general executive board named the eighteen organizers it wanted dismissed, including Robert Fechner, who had been one of the leaders in the fight against Preston. Johnston believed that the general executive board was usurping his powers as international president in dismissing any men, and that he, as general organizer, had the authority to choose his own men. He appealed to the grand lodge legal counsel for an opinion but then capitulated. He sent out eighteen letters of dismissal. Even the letter had been composed by the general executive board.[34]

How the membership responded to the wrangling is not clear. In the 1918 elections it elected a pro-Johnston general executive board (by three to two). But the new general executive board along with Johnston proceeded to ask for a per capita tax increase — raising the monthly assessment to $2.00 for journeymen and specialists, $1.50 for helpers, and $1.00 for apprentices and women. The issue had, of course, to go to referendum. It was defeated by 22,818 to 21,769 (with about 300,000 eligible to vote). Thus, it is not clear whether the close defeat measures the relatively equal drawing power of the pro-Johnston parties, or whether the relatively small vote indicates profound apathy.

In the July referendum a similar situation existed. The IAM endorsed Gompers' candidacy for reelection by 13,944 to 12,111; again a close vote and again a relatively small turnout. In November, 1919, when it became blatantly obvious that the costs of the postwar strikes could not be met by the cash reserves, the membership did endorse a special emergency assessment of $6.00 each to be paid in monthly installments during the first half of 1920. The vote was 34,987 to 21,123. Johnston had been forced to swing the complete circle regarding his earlier criticisms of O'Connell. He had tried to change the low per capita tax tradition, which earlier he had done much to establish, and in the end was forced to finance the grand lodge strike-benefit program by special assessments. By November, 1919, the grand lodge was overdrawn to the extent of $20,000 and was paying weekly strike benefits of $50,000. Its normal weekly income intended to cover all expenses, was $47,000. In the months of November and December it borrowed $200,000. Once more the grand lodge was insolvent.

Finances were not the only crises which developed during the second period of Johnston's administration. He was involved in serious conflict with several local and district lodges, which in some instances, had been O'Connell strongholds. Others resented the extension of grand lodge authority quite apart from any previous "political" commitments. Former Grand Master Machinist Creamer, for one, became infuriated with Johnston's sloppy handling of a discipline appeal.[35] Local Lodge 10 had fined Creamer's client. Upon appeal, Johnston reversed the finding. Then the lodge sent in additional evidence, and after an *ex parte* proceeding, Johnston changed his decision.

In Bridgeport, Connecticut, there was a particularly unpleasant incident.[36] A business agent, Samuel Lavit, was accused by a local newspaper of immoral behavior. Johnston was angry with Lavit because he had taken twenty-two thousand men out on strike without grand lodge sanction. But he ordered Lavit to sue the newspaper for printing the story, or to resign as business agent. Lavit refused to sue and refused to resign. The general executive board was unwilling to give Johnston its support without its own investigation. Johnston argued that the local business agent's job was covered by the grand lodge constitution; consequently two years' membership was a prerequisite for the office. The local lodge replied that these were local officials, and their choice was the business of the lodge alone.

But the publicity of Lavit's escapades proved to be a weapon which Johnston could use to advantage. Davison, the new general secretary-treasurer, found upon investigation that many Local Lodge 30 members were IWW and WIIU (the De Leon faction) radicals and, in some instances, not even machinists. The general executive board finally decided to support Johnston, and the local's charter was rescinded. At this point, Local 30 backtracked quickly, threw out Lavit, and stopped its agitation against the grand lodge. In time the charter was reissued. Johnston's success was complete, although it may have provoked some resentment in other autonomy-minded locals.

Another troublesome situation occurred in the Boston district lodge.[37] Here, Johnston attempted to redraw the district boundaries. George B. Loring, the district lodge secretary, refused to comply with Johnston's order. Johnston then went to court and got a writ against him, and Loring was expelled from the union. In this case O'Connell did not remain silent in the wings. He wrote a letter to Loring's attorney, attacking Johnston. The general executive board split evenly when the case came to a vote: Hannon, Kepler, and Ames voting in favor of Loring, with Savage (Johnston's "heir apparent"), Nicholson, and the new general secretary-treasurer, Davison, voting in favor of Johnston's position. In such cases, the international president casts the deciding vote—consequently Johnston was victorious, but at a high price.

Perhaps the Sonnabend case vies with the Persons case as being the most spectacular of the period.[38] Joseph Sonnabend was a member of Local Lodge 330 (Buffalo, New York), who ran a Trade Union Defense League in Buffalo and participated in union affairs in other areas as well. There was considerable suspicion, however, that Sonnabend played both sides. While he had exposed at least one labor spy, his willingness to act as a free lance business agent outside his home territory made his position unclear. Consequently Local Lodge 340 (Newark) asked Local Lodge 330 (Buffalo) to try Sonnabend for conduct detrimental to the IAM's cause. Local Lodge 330 found him not guilty, and the case was appealed by the plaintiff, Local Lodge 340 (Newark), to Johnston. In due course, both Johnston and the general executive board found him guilty and expelled him. Naturally Local Lodge 330 resisted the judgment; not only did it seem that Johnston had decided to favor a local friendly to him over one in the other camp, but it seemed to them that a verdict of not guilty should not be reversible.[39] Notwithstanding their objection, Sonnabend was expelled. There can be no doubt that Johnston's ability to reverse a "not guilty verdict" contributed to a growing conviction that he was power-hungry.

Johnston's greatest problem came, as might be expected by anyone conversant with left-wing politics, from the radicals. Once his supporters against O'Connell, they quickly dropped him when it became clear that he would not do their bidding. In 1919 Johnston ordered the suspension of four One Big Union enthusiasts from Local Lodge 159 (Philadelphia). The men had attacked Johnston's cooperation with the AFL leadership. They were suspended because, as Johnston put it:

> One cannot serve two masters, and if we are to preserve our integrity as a craft organization [*sic*], we cannot afford to have in our membership persons who devote the greater part of their time and effort to preaching the doctrines of such other organizations as will spell ruin for us if such other organizations become successful.

He ended this same address saying:

our Constitution specifically prohibits the discussion of "partisan politics" in the meetings of local lodges. [neither] The IWW, the Socialist [*sic*], the Communist, the Republican, the Democrat . . . nor any other political partisan can lawfully use our meetings to spread its propaganda. We endeavour to promote the industrial welfare of our members by the use of means recognized by the American Federation of Labor . . . No argument can be advanced which would convince us that it is necessary to attempt the overthrow of our present form of government to promote the industrial welfare of our members. *Those of opposite views are traitors TO THEIR COUNTRY and traitors to the labor movement.*[40] [Italics added.]

In this issue, he was upheld by the full general executive board. Three members were Johnstonites, and the other two were in full agreement because he had obviously come over to the O'Connell position.

Other developments during this period of Johnston's tenure include a decision to build a seven-story office building in Washington, part of which would be used as headquarters. The general executive board also investigated the economic advantages of owning and operating a printing plant. Both developments reflected a desire to invest the unions' funds wisely, and at the same time reduce expenses.

Forced Reappraisal of Means and Ends: 1920–1926

The year 1919 was one of industrial restlessness. Besides layoffs attributable to postwar reconversion, there were numerous strikes resulting from the workers' short-run willingness to live on wartime savings, while they prepared to hold their wartime gains against what they assumed to be the employers' desire to return to the former *status quo*. The piecework fight had been lost — both incentive systems and motion-and-time studies were the general practice in both the manufacturing and the railroad shop sectors of the economy.

Strikes

The 1919 strikes had met with varying degrees of success. Where wage and hour matters were involved, labor shortages had worked to the union's advantage. Wages were raised and the eight-hour day was becoming generally accepted. But many manufacturers and railroad managements refused to sign formal joint agreements with unions. Congress' failure to adopt the Plumb Plan and its subsequent enactment of the Esch–Cummins Law indicated that there would probably be an early return to antiunion tactics on the railroads. And the American Plan,[41] combining the earlier antiboycott and open-shop movements, emerged as the leading expression of the rights-of-management movement.

The general executive board decided in 1920 to make its American Can Company campaign an all-out effort against the American Plan. It authorized a strike at each of the company's fifty-six plants and agreed to pay strike benefits to all strikers, whether members of the IAM or not. The strike occurred in September 1920.[42] The principal issues were union recognition and a wage increase, although extension of the company's incentive system was also a factor. The union realized that it had set itself a formidable task, because the company was closely connected with the violently antiunion U. S. Steel Corporation. Strike action was authorized only after it had been recommended by the Rochester convention.

The IAM neglected no opportunity in this campaign. It listed the food firms that used American's cans, suggesting a secondary boycott; at the same time, it published a list of the customers of the Container Can Company, urging purchase of their products. It even suggested that American Can Company's products were toxic. This type of propaganda only contributes to long-run loss of jobs and is self-defeating. Its use by the IAM reveals the hatreds that were being generated.

Despite the depth of its efforts, within a few weeks the strike was clearly doomed. In August, 1921, the general executive board authorized the striking locals to negotiate directly with local plant managers to reach local agreements regarding the rehiring of the strikers. These efforts were not, on the whole, successful. And by the end of January, 1922, the general executive board decided to inform the local lodges that the grand lodge's serious financial situation made mandatory the reduction of the American Can Company's strike payroll. Finally in May of that year the strike was called off. It had been a major effort, and it had been disastrous. The IAM was unable to storm the type of citadel which had been established after the 1901 NMTA strike. However, it should be noted that the American Can Company strike was not the only one in which the union was involved. The union also tried with equal lack of success to break the resistance of antiunion employers in Cincinnati, one of the major area strongholds of the open-shop movement. The failure of these strikes approximately reduced the union to its prewar position. A possible exception was the situation on the railroads, where the unions had had a three-year opportunity during the period of governmental operation to entrench themselves.

The events leading up to the shopmen's strike of July, 1922, are well chronicled elsewhere.[43] Briefly, the facts are these. The Transportation Act of

1920 returned the railroads to private ownership. It also established a tripartite, nine-man Railroad Labor Board, which was to have the power to set wages and control working rules. The board raised wages 13 cents per hour in July, 1920, on the eve of a business recession. Marked unemployment, up to 40 per cent, resulted. During the period, March to June, 1921, wage reductions requested by the employers, which ranged from 5 to 18 cents per hour, were granted. Later in 1921 the board abandoned premium (overtime) rates for Sunday and legal holiday work as well as other work rule changes.

The Railway Employees' Department agreed to all the work-rule changes except the elimination of overtime rates. On that issue it sought further discussion. Then the member unions brought to the board's attention the recent management practice of sending work out on contract, in order to extend the piecework system. The board ordered the elimination of this practice in May, 1922, but the railroad managements refused to accept the order. Employees who protested were fired.

At the same time several railroads, notably the Pennsylvania system, started to organize company unions. The board ordered the railroad to stop these efforts, but the railroad succeeded in securing an injunctive order, which prohibited the board from interfering. Simultaneously, the board authorized a new wage cut. The confluence of these several events toward the end of June precipitated a strike of all the railroad shop craftsmen, in which the maintenance-of-way men did not participate. The issues were three: (1) the elimination of premium pay for Sundays and holidays, (2) the contracting-out system, and (3) the latest wage cuts. The unions emphasized managements' refusal to accept any unfavorable board rulings, and their own reasonable suspicion that the railroads were returning to their antiunion status.

After presenting the question to the membership of all the unions involved, each of the shop crafts struck, despite opposite advice from their leaders.[44] The maintenance-of-way men and the operating brotherhoods did not, since at that time they were not part of the Railroad Employees' Department. The strike was about 90 per cent effective. It was attacked by Chairman Hooper of the Railway Labor Board. When the public members joined the employer members in threatening the strikers with loss of seniority if they did not return to work, the labor members (notably A. O. Wharton) denounced Hooper.

Except for the Baltimore and Ohio Railroad, the railroad executives refused all offers of mediation, proffered both by the operating brotherhoods and by public officials. These executives insisted upon a full resumption of work before any talks began. They were out to break the power of the unions, and by the end of August, two months after the strike was called, their objective was nearly achieved. For some inexplicable reason, Harding's attorney general, Harry Daugherty, chose that moment to ask for a sweeping injunctive order from Federal Judge James Wilkerson forbidding the Railway Employees' Department, the 6 shop craft unions, or the 120 system federations from engaging in any activities at all connected with the strike effort. The order was granted adding insult to injury, but its blatancy only evoked popular sympathy, giving new encouragement to the strikers.

Early in July, 1922, within a week of the strike's beginning, Justice Brandeis and Interstate Commerce Commissioner Potter arranged a meeting between Johnston and Daniel Willard (President of the Baltimore and Ohio), and Captain Otto S. Beyer, an industrial engineer, who had evolved a joint union–management shop plan intended to serve both the cost-cutting purposes of management and the security-seeking needs of the union. A similar meeting was arranged with the president of the New York Central Railroad, but it foundered on the piecework principle.

Beyer's plan was enthusiastically accepted by Willard — less enthusiastically by the striking Baltimore and Ohio men.[45] Beyer envisioned a system in which the unions would be given responsibility, recognition, and authority. The plan was first tried at shops in Glenwood, Maryland, with only limited success. Far from disheartened, Beyer and Willard renewed their efforts.

Thus it was that settlements began to occur. By mid-October, 98 railroads with 75,000 miles of track and over 25,000 locomotives agreed to make tentative peace with the unions. These included, besides the Baltimore and Ohio, the Milwaukee, the North Western, the Seaboard, the Southern, the New York Central, and even the Erie, whose practice of contracting-out had earlier been one of the irritants. As already implied, the settlements were pretty nearly on the terms dictated by management. What the unions managed to salvage was protection of the strikers' seniority. Perlman and Taft argue that, in addition, the union's abortive effort did have the general effect of arresting a wage deflation movement. The settlements rescued the seniority of 225,000 striking shopmen. An additional 175,000 were not so fortunate. No settlements were forthcoming on the Pennsylvania, the Missouri Pacific, the Frisco, the Wabash, the New Haven, and a few others. On May 14, 1924, after trying for almost two years, the IAM formally called off its effort. It continued to express bitterness toward the Pennsylvania and the Long Island, however, since both railroads were indomitable in advancing the cause of company unionism.

Benefits were paid during the early months of the strike. The IAM called for a voluntary assessment in 1922, which yielded only $5528. The Railway

Employees' Department gave the IAM $1994 per month. In addition, the IAM officers went on half pay. In 1922 the IAM paid over $600,000 in strike benefits; in 1923, over $84,000. Full strike benefits could not be paid because the union lacked resources. After two months of strike the general executive board decided to appropriate $9000 per month to keep up the strikers' IAM insurance, an innovation dating from the 1920 convention, which is treated later in this chapter.

Membership declined drastically as a direct result of the failure of strikes in such key firms as the American Can Company and the railroads: 1921, 225,857; 1922, 155,372; 1923, 111,677; 1924, 81,678; 1925, 73,372. In 1925 the IAM tried to lure back some of its former members by offering a thirty-day reinstatement privilege for $7.50, with former status unimpaired and no demand for back dues or per capita tax.[46] However, membership continued to fall, becoming 71,689 in 1926.

The leadership of the IAM pinned its hopes in the railroad sector on the Baltimore and Ohio Plan. Somerville, the Canadian general vice-president, succeeded in having a variant form of it introduced on the Canadian National Railways.[47] At the 1924 convention, Johnston's advocacy of the plan was at first attacked, but in the end, supported.[48] The plan was actually small consolation. It is no wonder that the railroad machinists were far from happy with it or with him. Their man was A. O. Wharton, who in 1911, had engineered the Federation of Federations, and who in 1922 had taken a strong public position in support of their demands.

Relations with Other Unions

For the most part, the few changes in relationships during the period were not of great importance. Johnston was not elected to the AFL executive council, nor was he successful in pressing for a resolution of the outstanding IAM claims. The AFL executive council took a pro-IAM stand in regard to the dispute between the carpenters and millwrights, but it completely failed to implement its decision. It refused to take any position regarding the elevator constructors' dispute, except to reiterate an old pious hope that the two would merge.

The IAM was not able to negotiate reentry into the Building Trades Department, although it tried to do so on several occasions.[49] For a while the carpenters' union was out of the Building Trades Department, and Johnston tried in vain to manage IAM entry in its absence. In general, the IAM concluded that the carpenters "ran the AFL executive council." But here agreement ceased; Johnston vowed to smash the system, if possible, and the old O'Connell partisans, particularly Charles Fry (business agent of Local 126 of Chicago), felt that readmission was not worth the fight. As long as Johnston was international president, there would be friction. The AFL group distrusted him, and he loathed them.

The IAM had been adjudged the offender in its dispute with the flint glass workers — the issue, described in Chapter IX, involved the IAM's attempt to establish a jurisdictional claim. During the previous period, 1912–1920, the IAM, although admitting its responsibility for the trouble, offered its compliance to the AFL order regarding the flint glass workers in exchange for the carpenters' compliance regarding the IAM.[50] The AFL executive council condemned the IAM. The IAM steadfastly refused to comply, even after the over-all position was thoroughly examined at the 1920 IAM Convention.

Agreements were consummated which arranged for the exchange of certain members between the IAM and several unions, with protection of the new members' previous status. These include protocols with the railway carmen in 1919, with the British Amalgamated Society of Engineers in 1920, and with the sheet metal workers in 1921.[51]

In 1924 a dispute flared with the street railwaymen over the question of who should repair buses. The problem grew out of the technological change associated with the replacement of electric trolley cars by buses. The work had formerly been that of the street railwaymen, but the IAM challenged the other union's right to the work once gasoline vehicles had been introduced. No settlement was reached during Johnston's time.

A remaining item of interest involved a jurisdictional agreement between the United Association of Plumbers *et al.* and the IAM.[52] It was negotiated by Fechner, Fry, Conlon, and President Coefield, Walsh, and Durkin of the United Association. It involved work division on flange pipes, air conditioning, and other materials. It is significant for two reasons; first because it was a stable understanding, and second, because it involved certain personal arrangements among the negotiators. Later, when all three IAM representatives were dead, the United Association claimed that the agreement was being breached, while the IAM asserted that the verbal codicils were unknown to any living officials. However, during the twenties the agreement worked well.

By 1925 there was virtually no possibility that Johnston could develop an entente with the AFL executive council. Gompers' death and Green's succession gave an even stronger position to the building tradesmen, to whom Johnston was ideologically objectionable. Even within the Metal Trades Department, hope for amalgamation of all craft unions into an industrial federation was virtually abandoned. If anything, the unions had become more craft-conscious.

The situation in the Railway Employees' Department was not materially different. The failure of the 1922 strike precluded any significant developments in this area.

Internal Affairs

It is in this field that the years from 1919 to 1920 were so fateful. Five major developments occurred. They were (1) the institution of a comprehensive, if unsound, life insurance scheme, (2) the establishment of a rigid anti-Communism policy as a basic IAM doctrine, (3) a reconsideration of the union's finances, (4) the development of a broadened interest in the labor movement, and last, but by far the most important, (5) a civil war leading to the practical abandonment of the two-party system in the IAM.

The development of the insurance department. In 1919 and 1920 the general executive board quite naturally turned to the problem of holding onto its enlarged membership. Traditionally, unions had borrowed a practice from the friendly societies, establishing death and disability benefits, which were contingent upon the retention of continuous membership. Thus it was reasonable for the IAM to consider modernizing its benefits program.

The effect of the army's First World War National Life Insurance program seems obvious. In 1920 the members voted 22,657 to 7420 (with almost 300,000 eligible to vote) to establish such a program. Three plans were considered: (a) a compulsory assessment plan covering all members to be carried by the union, (b) a compulsory group insurance scheme underwritten by an established insurance carrier, and (c) an optional insurance scheme underwritten by an established carrier. With its abhorrence for assessments, the IAM did not choose (a). It would have been better if (b) had been selected, since it would have minimized the risk, but the most that the leadership could sell to the rank and file was plan (c). In the 1921 referendum, the plan carried 33,802 to 4162 (with approximately 225,000 eligible to vote). Over 28,000 of those voting applied for coverage on their ballots.

The cost of this voluntary insurance scheme was 50 cents per month on the first $500 benefit. By paying an additional 25 cents per month, the base coverage would increase at the rate of $250 per year, until in the seventh year a maximum of $2000 would be reached. The local financial secretaries were given gratis term life insurance policies of $2500 (if they paid for the first $500) for the period they were in office — doubtless meant as an inducement for candidates for the office. A contract covering these policies was signed by the grand lodge with the United Life and Accident Company.

During the long shop craftsmen's strike, the grand lodge agreed to pay the insurance premiums of the strikers so long as the striking men held on to their membership. This program, announced in July, 1922, terminated on September 1, 1923.

The IAM did not abandon the death and disability program which existed prior to the adoption of the insurance scheme. In fact, the plan was adapted to the postwar inflation by readjusting the benefits in 1920: after one year of membership, $50.00; two years, $75.00; three years, $100.00; four years, $125.00; five years, $150.00; six years, $175.00; seven years, $200.00; eight years, $225.00; nine years, $250.00; ten years, $300.00. This was a compulsory scheme. Like the insurance plan, it proved to be actuarially unsound, but unlike the insurance scheme, it was not easily dropped. The problem with the insurance plan was that only the poor risks enrolled. Consequently the coverage was too narrow to support the size of benefits offered. The complaint with the death benefits plan was that it had not been figured on an adequate actuarial concept. In effect, it gave the family of almost every member of the IAM no less than $50.00 at the time of his death. The costs of this program are analyzed in Chapter VIII.

By 1924 the general executive board apparently wanted to eliminate the death benefits program.[53] However, the members felt that they had vested rights. Hence, the general executive board proposed that there would be no death benefits provision for any new members, that 15 per cent of the per capita tax revenue should be earmarked for paying off claims, and that a $1000 life insurance policy be made compulsory for every member. This plan would have eliminated the unsound death benefits program and would, through the compulsory feature, make the insurance scheme actuarially sound. The only alternative the general executive board thought practicable was complete abandonment of both the death benefits and insurance programs.

The 1924 convention refused to choose either alternative suggested by the general executive board. It specifically refused (1) to abolish the death benefits schedule, (2) to discontinue benefits to new members, (3) to make the insurance policy compulsory, (4) to discontinue the voluntary insurance program as it existed, and (5) to establish an autonomous insurance fund which, if made insolvent by reason of the demands put on it, would leave the regular IAM treasury untouched. Johnston and the general executive board had gone to great trouble to have the plans thoroughly examined and analyzed to no avail, because the delegates were unwilling to face the economic realities of the situation.

As in the previous period, Johnston tried to exercise greater grand lodge control over local lodge policies, but he was not always successful. In 1921, for instance, he ruled that the subordinate lodges, in this case District Lodge 9 of St. Louis, had to charge uniform dues for both journeymen and specialists.[54] The district lodge appealed, and on the first appeal Johnston was supported by the general executive board. On the second appeal, the general executive board reversed itself and let District Lodge 9 do as it pleased. It also permitted District Lodge 9 to establish a minimum dues rate for all its constituent locals. District Lodge 9 was antiadministration.

The Communism issue. Without any doubt the *cause célèbre* during this period was Johnston's campaign against some of his erstwhile supporters, the extreme radicals. In 1919 in Philadelphia, and 1920 in Detroit, he brought charges of dual unionism against some IWW partisans. In these cases the punishment was one year's suspension. In New York City, District Lodge 15 tried to crack down on a radical enclave, the "Machinists' Progressive Council." There Johnston held that the disbandment of the unit was sufficient and that there should be no individual prosecutions. The leaders of District Lodge 15 were antiadministration, and any foes of theirs were not foes of his. Johnston's antiradicalism was not simply a negative response. Far from it, he just wanted to see that local lodges did not involve themselves in what he considered dualistic activities. He favored reform movements and workers' education. In fact, the IAM endorsed the Brookwood Labor College during his administration, and set up scholarships for IAM members.

Seven members of Toledo Local Lodge 105 were charged with dualistic activities and tried in 1924.[55] It was claimed that they were "pledged to industrial unionism, that is, the substitution of the one big union idea for craft organizations." In point of historic fact, what the men had done was to affiliate with William Z. Foster's Trade Union Educational League. Vic Gauthier, a former general executive board member, was active in the prosecution. The men were all convicted, sentenced $50.00 and deprived of their so-called political rights within the IAM for a year, although steps were taken to protect their beneficiary interests. The men appealed to Johnston to reverse the conviction. But he was unwilling to support them — as much as he favored endorsing industrial unionism. Upon further appeal, the general executive board let the convictions stand, but set aside the punishments on the condition that the appellants would immediately and completely dissociate themselves from the Trade Union Educational League and the Workers' Party (later the Communist Party). There was a further appeal to the full convention in 1924. The delegates supported the general executive board's compromise — endorsing Johnston's anti-Communist ruling — but suspended punishment of the "Toledo Seven."

In effect, the IAM held that membership in the Communist Party was an act of dual unionism. This was explicitly stated in Circular 183, dated August 15, 1925, which explained "That regardless of the published aims and purposes of the Workers' or Communist Party and the Trade Union Educational League, their respective practices as disclosed by evidence in this case clearly indicates that their net purpose is the destruction of the Trade Union Movement of America."

It is easy to note that Johnston's antiradical stand developed in a period of great stress, and that radical influences could not be permitted if the IAM were to survive. But to note this in 1924, and to refuse to note it in the decade, 1901–1911, is inconsistent. O'Connell's interest would have been served if he could have outlawed all radicalism in the earlier period. As it was, he succeeded only in outlawing IWWism. This was done by the formal method of constitutional amendment. In 1925 Johnston outlawed Communism by ukase; that is, Johnston reinterpreted the constitution. That is the extent to which the powers of the international president had grown during the Socialist regime.

Finances and business operations. This was a period of great financial stress. Several steps were taken to increase revenue, including an increase in per capita tax for specialists to a par with that paid by journeymen (1920). Beginning in January 1921, the whole monthly per capita tax structure was raised: journeymen and specialists paid $1.00; helpers, 65 cents; apprentices, 50 cents; and the unemployment stamp was 20 cents. Except for one change, lowering the cost of an unemployment stamp to 10 cents after April 1925, the tax structure remained constant until the end of the Second World War.

In 1920 the membership voted to eliminate the differential in strike benefits between married and unmarried members. The various classes of members continued to be paid at different rates, however. The 1924 convention voted that the amount of the strike benefits would no longer be specified in the constitution, but would be determined by the grand lodge officers. The change was, of course, the direct result of the disastrous shop craftsmen's strike, when the grand lodge had borrowed $200,000 to meet its obligations. It was realized that paying fixed strike benefits could quickly bankrupt the organization during big strikes. Since then the grand lodge has always given donations to authorized strike efforts. The new system was decidedly more flexible.

The membership's "tight per capita tax policy," and the heavy drain upon resources of the postwar and 1922 strikes led Johnston and his colleagues to reduce their costs. They engaged in some experiments, most of which were richer in experience than in savings. After the war they built a union headquarters in Washington and rented out the first few floors. As a business venture, it appears to have been economically sound.

In 1920 the general executive board voted to buy a Norfolk, Virginia machine works for $15,000—believing it to be worth $27,000. Their direct motivations were to give some striking machinists a place to work, to reduce strike rolls, and to help fight the Iron Masters' Association "over the entire Atlantic Seaboard."[56] Similar ventures quickly followed. By 1921 the general executive board had become deeply involved in trying to run a ship repair yard in Hampton Roads, Virginia. This failed and by 1924 was abandoned.[57] The losses incurred were charged against the strike fund.

In Washington plans were on a larger scale. In 1920 the grand lodge bought a printing plant, with the hope that both savings and better service would result.[58] Neither did, and the plant was sold.

The major experiment in private enterprise was the Mt. Vernon Savings Bank, which opened in May 1920, with grand lodge officers doubling as officers.[59] The bank paid rent for its space on the first floor of the headquarters building. It also brought a good return to the IAM, which had purchased some of the original stock. It foundered in 1933—but for most of the thirteen years of its existence, it was a source of great pride to the grand lodge officers, particularly those who had earlier been loudest in their criticisms of O'Connell's supposed acceptance of the principle of profit maximization.

But none of these business attempts was particularly useful in meeting the union's pressing financial problems. The combination of low per capita taxes and expensive services was possible only through the resulting low salaries. The Socialist tradition that the union leader should get no more than he could earn in the shop was one maxim firmly observed.

But the tight funds policy served several purposes. As long as the grand lodge had little money to dispense, its power was checked. In a few cases, district and local lodges, with their own handsome stakes, were able to finance organizing and benefits programs, which the grand lodge was both unable and/or unwilling to support. Later it will be argued that this tight funds policy kept a balance of power between the grand lodge and the subordinate lodges. This balance has been an important element in maintaining genuine representative democracy.

Broadened horizons of the labor movement. Three developments during the period, 1920–1926, stand out as examples of Johnston's earlier desire to make the union perform wider functions. One was the program, supported but not initiated by him, of having the union go into business in order to save money for itself and the membership. Johnston also supported a program of cooperative buying—in which the union would purchase consumer commodities in carload lots, passing the savings on to members to whom the items were sold.[60] These consumer cooperatives had worked well in Europe — in the United States geographic distances plus great variations in consumer choices made the experiment unsuccessful. But Johnston tried the device in order to strengthen membership awareness of the advantages of unionism.

The second development was the result of governmental changes in Mexico.[61] In 1921 the Obregon administration sought the endorsement of the United States labor movement as part of its policy of coming to terms with the United States. The AFL, under Gompers, grasped the hand of friendship, and none on the United States side was more friendly than the IAM. Within a few months the Mexican government and the IAM had agreed that the IAM would handle, in part, the placing of Mexican orders for American machinery within the United States. In this way, the Mexican government would have an ally on the American scene, who could advise it regarding prices. On the other hand, the IAM would derive some bargaining power with American industry because it could use the Mexican orders as a tool in its own negotiations. The affiliation of the twenty-five thousand-member Mexican Machinists' Union with the IAM was also suggested. The agreement was implemented at first, but there is no record of much having been accomplished. Johnston and General Secretary-Treasurer Davison also contemplated a similar program for Soviet Russian purchases in the United States, but nothing came of that matter.[62]

The biggest opportunity to extend the social activities of the union came in 1924 when both the Republicans and the Democrats nominated presidential candidates who were obviously unacceptable to labor unions. The AFL, in spite of its earlier objection to direct affiliation with any set of political candidates had no alternative. It thus chose to endorse a third party, namely the Progressive Party. In 1920 the AFL had established a National Non-Partisan Political Campaign to elect prolabor candidates to congress. To this the IAM contributed 1 cent per member. But the 1924 effort was on a grander scale.[63]

At the 1924 convention the usual resolutions asking for a true labor party in the United States were sidetracked for a new reason.[64] No longer was it said that such plans were simply illusory (although Johnston, himself, felt them to be so), but now they were pointless because the LaFollette–Wheeler presidential ticket "seem[ed] to have the unanimous support of all the labor organizations and also the progressive element of all other classes." Johnston put the IAM into the fight wholeheartedly. LaFollette got almost three million votes and carried one state (his own). His defeat, however, indicated the futility of Johnston's earlier dream of uniting all liberal elements.

In all, Johnston's three attempts to reorganize and extend the union's influence came to naught. But it is evidence of his determination to make the IAM into something broader than the organization he found. His failure suggests that neither the organization nor the times were ready for these admirable aims.

Civil war in the IAM. The collapse of the Johnston administration was the result of developments within and without the union. He was never able to consolidate his control of the organization, nor to eliminate the hostility in several of the major local and district lodges. He was able, however, to stand off attacks and, in a few instances, to punish the attackers, but he could not turn opposition into support, which in a political organization where the division is nearly equal, is a serious failure. Secondly, his administration was not able to handle the financial problems which had brought O'Connell to defeat. In addition, he lacked some of the allies in the AFL which O'Connell had had.

Added to all this was considerable personal resentment toward Johnston. There is little record that he ever tightened control over his own faction — had he done so the result probably would have been the same, but the record would have been better.

Externally, Johnston had to come to grips with a much shrewder anti-union business community than the one with which O'Connell had dealt. The American Plan was harder to fight than the simple open-shop campaign. If anything, the Harding and Coolidge administrations were more openly unsympathetic toward organized labor than any administration since 1896, including Taft's.

The 1920 convention decided to increase the number of elective officials.[65] The decision was designed to meet the organizational needs of the enlarged membership due to wartime acquisitions. Hence the convention voted to increase the number of elected vice-presidents from two to ten, with each to be given an assigned area or industry. These men were not to serve on the general executive board or policy-making body, because it would make the latter unwieldy. Moreover, it seemed to have been generally understood that the ten vice-presidents would have to be subordinate to the international president, whereas the rationale of the general executive board was its semi-independence. At the same time all salaries were raised, the international president going from $4200 to $7500, the general secretary-treasurer to $6500 from $3600 and the vice-presidents to $5000 from $3600. Other salaries were also raised proportionately. A special election was held in 1921 to select the additional eight vice-presidents.

In 1922 there was a general election. The general executive board became anti-Johnston by a bare majority. Fechner, one of Johnston's personal friends, was elected with 25,740 votes, defeating Vic Gauthier (a Johnston critic, but also a Socialist) who received 25,541 votes. The closeness of the vote stirred up a suspicion that all was not well with the balloting. But no action was taken by either the administration or the antiadministration forces.

The 1924 convention was bitter. The administration moved quickly to reorganize the whole election slate. It abolished the semi-independent general executive board and reduced the number of vice-presidents to seven. The anti-Johnston group agreed that the reduced size of the membership made a cut-back in the number of vice-presidents mandatory, but it did not want to eliminate the independent character of the general executive board. C. W. Fry, spokesman for one antiadministration group, suggested three vice-presidents (with one coming from Canada), plus the old five-man general executive board. Other anti-Johnston spokesmen voiced fears that a change in form would result neither in savings nor a more representative officialdom. Several of the vice-presidents ridiculed both Johnston's policies and his abilities. Nonetheless, the convention accepted the administration's proposal, and elections were duly called for the new slate. Here the civil war began. The votes were as noted (names of the pro-Johnston men are italicized):

	Elected		*Defeated*	
International president	*Johnston*	18,021	J. F. Anderson	17,076
General secretary-treasurer	*Davison*	20,028	Stilgenbauer	14,648
General vice-president	*Conlon*	20,121	Taylor	16,948
"	*Thorp*		McMahon	
"	*Nickerson*		Nicholson	
"	*Brown*		Laudeman	
"	*Fechner*		McNamara	
"	Hannon		Knudson	
"	*Somerville*			
Editor	*Hewitt*	18,943	Williams	17,813

Even before the vote, the antiadministration candidates, dubbed the "Catholics" by their enemies (even though Anderson, their *de jure* leader was a Mormon), had their suspicions about fair play. As early as February they were finding it difficult to obtain membership lists. The administration men, called the "Masons" by the "Catholics," refused to order special precautions to ensure a fair count, claiming that strict adherence to the constitutional rules was sufficient.

Parenthetically, it is useful to note that the party designations "Mason" and "Catholic," although not descriptively accurate, were chosen by the partisans. Who were the "Masons"? They were the old-time grass roots Populist–Socialists, the southerners, and in most instances railroad machinists. General Vice-President Peter Conlon was one of them — he had come from the Union Pacific Railroad, and had been an ardent Socialist–Populist during the O'Connell regime. But his religion happened to be Catholic.

The term "Catholic" generally described the urbanized members, employed in job shops and in erection work, rather than railroad machinists. The writer knows one who is an active mason.

The administration also took the opportunity to issue an anti-Communist circular at the height of the campaign, believing the effect of it to be "anti-Catholic." [66] This paradox is explained by the fact that the "Catholics" were supported by many big city lodges, which also included Marxian radicals. Moreover, one of the antiadministration "Catholics," Martin McMahon, had been the author of an attack on Johnston appearing in the *Daily Worker*.[67] In attacking the Communists and the "Catholics," the administration thought it was killing two evil birds with one stone.

The voting was too close to be accepted, and within a few days the defeated candidate for international president, J. F. Anderson, charged fraud, in a pamphlet called *The Story of the Big Steal*.[68] His charge was leveled at Davison, but his claim affected Johnston. Moreover, he charged that in 1922 the ballot box had been stuffed in favor of Fechner and at the expense of Gauthier.

Johnston's reaction to the charge was to suspend Anderson (who had been a vice-president for almost ten years) until he would retract his story.[69]

Anderson appealed Johnston's suspension order to the executive council. He argued that the international president had no right to suspend him — saying that although he acknowledged the Persons rule, it had been modified by 1920 convention action ordering trials for situations like his. His appeal was heard by a subcommittee of three — Brown, Fechner and Somerville — who unanimously recommended continued suspension to the full council implying that Anderson had not been expelled, which was the basis for trial procedure. The council, with only Hannon dissenting, then adopted the report.

At this point one of the local lodges supporting Anderson sponsored a demand for his recall, to give him a chance for a vote of confidence. This was refused, and Anderson demanded a referendum vote on his suspension. In November the executive council issued a circular restating its position. It noted that Anderson had sent out "false and malicious" statements, for which reason he had been suspended, and that the suspension would continue until he had formally apologized. It noted, moreover, that even if the statements had contained some truth, there was no excuse for issuing the pamphlet, because better means existed for redress.

To add to the turmoil, six members of Local Lodge 132 of the New York city district (District Lodge 15) filed complaints against another of Johnston's critics, J. F. Dalton, their business agent. They charged that he had said:[70] (1) that Johnston had an antiunion arrangement with Westinghouse; (2) that the grand lodge officers had squandered the death benefits and other funds; (3) personally slanderous things about Johnston; (4) that he would see that no one supporting Johnston would be helped to find a new erection job; (5) that anyone involved in bringing charges against him would get no help in finding work; (6) that the charges levied against him were part of a general conspiracy, worked out at grand lodge headquarters; (7) that Johnston and Davison had tried to charge a 5 per cent commission on Mexican government purchases, which had disgusted the Mexicans and caused them to withdraw from the agreement.

Johnston summoned Dalton to Washington and ordered him to stand trial by the executive council. Dalton successfully pointed out that he did not have to stand trial by the executive council, because the latter could only hear appeals. And there had been no conviction. The executive council then took the responsibility for suspending him and ordered his local lodge to try him. This action was taken after Fechner had made an investigation on behalf of the council. After a trial wherein Dalton was declared innocent, the decision was appealed to Johnston, who debarred him from office for one year. At that point District Lodge 15 said that because it paid half his salary, it wanted a voice in the matter of his fitness to hold office in the IAM.

To review the situation, charges of malfeasance had been brought against both the international president and the general secretary-treasurer by two important officials, each with considerable backing. The charges implied that the executive council and the two major executive officials were at least guilty of conspiracy, and, at most, probably guilty of falsifying records. Both Johnston and the executive council, parties to the complaint, elected not only to sit in appeal, but they prevented the use of any other forms of redress through the duly constituted recall. On the other hand, in District Lodge 15 similar highhanded tactics were adopted against Johnston's partisans.

An impasse having been reached, Anderson was allowed to appeal to the membership via referendum. But the ballots were to be handled in the customary manner — implying that if chicanery occurred once, it could occur again.

It was clear that unless some firm steps were taken quickly, the union would divide. All the parties must have been under considerable personal strain, but Johnston was the first to break; he suffered a stroke in late September, 1925.[71] In November he was operated on for another ailment,[72] also a result of the nervous tension under which he had been living.

With Johnston out of the picture, the impasse began to be resolved, not because he had been the troublemaker, but because it was evident that he could not serve as international president, and that his partisans, the "Masons," had little chance of electing a successor. Anderson, on the other hand, seems to have been of the opinion that if he were selected as international president, the union would be destroyed.

Thus, in February 1926, the two factions met in Washington.[73] Davison, the general secretary-treasurer, was spokesman for the Johnstonites or "Masons," while Charles Fry, business agent of Chicago District Lodge 8, spoke for Anderson or the "Catholics."

Fry objected to the way in which the executive council had phrased the referendum on Anderson's appeal. Davison replied that the executive council was not responsible for wording, which had been devised by the autonomous Law Committee. Fry further alleged election irregularities for which, he charged, the executive council was responsible. The council voted down his allegations (Hannon dissenting). The council then passed a resolution attesting to its own innocence, which noted that the things said by both sides did the IAM no good.

Fry saw in this resolution the break he sought. He said that he and his colleagues agreed that there had been calumny on both sides, and that he, for one, was willing to acknowledge that Anderson's alleged victory was by such a small margin, that there may not have been fraud. He admitted the legality of Anderson's suspension and urged that the referendum ballots not be counted. In return, the executive council voted to reinstate Anderson and appointed a three-man committee to work out all existing grievances. The committee included General Vice-President Thorp (an administration man), General Vice-President Hannon (an Anderson supporter), and General Vice-President Conlon (who was proadministration, but also an ardent Roman Catholic).

This committee then went to New York where they worked out a formula for the settlement of the Dalton affair.[74] Dalton was reinstated, and the fines remitted. All the anti-Dalton members of Local Lodge 132 were to be given rotation rights on erection work, and Dalton apologized for the things he said.

In May, 1926, Johnston appeared before the executive council and tendered his resignation on the grounds of ill health. His successor was Arthur O. Wharton, president of the Railway Employees' Department, one-time architect of the Federation of Federations, and former public member of the

Railway Labor Board. In June Wharton appointed Johnston as a grand lodge representative — he was a poor man and needed the income.[75] Later in the year Johnston resigned (there had been considerable criticism of the appointment) and went to work for the Mt. Vernon Savings Bank, which was later to fail. He was given a small pension by the IAM, but died destitute in 1937.

Johnston's dream was of the same stuff as Wilson's New Freedom — Populism and self-determination in place of "cynical special plutocratic interests." The same thing happened to both dreams. They vanished in an era of wide-awake disillusionment.

Johnston's program of industrial unionism could not withstand the American Plan campaign and the disastrous shop craftsmen's strike. O'Connell was right — it was not good for the IAM to grow large too fast.

In addition, Johnston was not a shrewd leader. He did not see that what the IAM required was constructive integration. He paid far too little attention to developing a sense of community among the members.

Finally, Johnston faltered because the IAM was not stable enough to contain a genuine two-party system. Its continued existence was far too much in jeopardy to permit biennial or even quadrennial struggles for power.

What was needed in 1926 was a "cure" for Johnstonism, therapy for excessive disillusionment and enervating overstimulation. This was Arthur Wharton's mission. He had to rededicate the IAM to unifying job conciousness. To do this he decided to abandon industrial unionism. He remade the political structure into what elsewhere has been called "democratic centralism." And he encouraged no program which he believed would cost loss of loyalty. If Wharton's administration was not completely successful, it at least proved to be stable.

CHAPTER IV

Stability: The Wharton Administration

Unlike Johnston, Wharton entered the presidency with the best wishes of all factions. Thus his avowed purpose of conciliation met no initial obstacles. He held office for twelve years, throughout which time he consistently advocated a policy of conservative, job-conscious unionism, despite the drastic changes which occurred in the union environment.

This chapter covers the period from 1926 to 1938.[1] From 1926 until 1934, Wharton's conservatism reflected a judicious assessment of the IAM's possibilities in an essentially hostile world. In the light of later developments, the same conservatism after 1934 appeared unnecessarily restrictive.

The Wharton administration serves as a laboratory example of an administrative balance between effective, concentrated one-party authority, and the expression of factional views within the party. This is democratic centralism, which is supposed to combine administrative efficiency with vigorous and full discussion. By and large, Johnston had tried to rule as the leader of the majority party in a two-party system. Wharton, in contrast, did not seem to align himself with any faction or party. It is erroneous to assume that Wharton achieved harmony by avoiding the issues which had bitterly divided the union under Johnston. To the contrary, he was inclined to decisive action. As a result of the dissolution of what was actually an informal two-party system in the union, the consequent feeling that he acted not as a factional leader but as leader of the whole union, his interventions did not generally become political issues.

Wharton's earlier experiences prepared him in several ways for the task of trying to reunite the organization. He was a railroad machinist, having served an apprenticeship on the Santa Fe Railroad in the eighties. He became general chairman of the Missouri Pacific interunion organization in 1903 and was active in interunion affairs in the whole southwest from 1903 through 1910 when he led the Missouri Pacific strike. He played a leading role in the formation of the ill-fated Federation of Federations during the Harriman lines and Illinois Central strike. He also had had much governmental experience serving on a 1917 commission to standardize labor agreements on southeastern railways; as a labor adviser to the Lane Commission; and as a member of the Railway Labor Board after 1920. Thus his background as a trade unionist was, in terms of the IAM, somewhat more conventional than Johnston's had been, even though Wharton, too, had been slightly interested in the Socialism–Populism reform movement during the latter years of the O'Connell administration. In fact, he was elected to replace AFL delegate, J. J. Keegan, who was associated with the National Civic Federation interests of O'Connell in the IAM's first recall action (1912).

Withal, Wharton would have had a more difficult time had Johnston not prepared the scene for him in several senses. Johnston had replaced the semi-independent general executive board with an executive council, which was, in the fullest sense, an instrument completely dominated by the international president in 1925. If this change had helped to prolong Johnston's regime, it also served to maintain harmony during Wharton's incumbency. Even beyond this important administrative change, the organizational fratricide, which Johnston's experience seemed to encourage, had made the cost of intraunion civil war clear to all factions. Virtually all parties wanted to avoid strife, so that when an open conflict began to develop (as at the 1936 convention), there was a general willingness to avoid a showdown.

If the Wharton administration looks "better" (that is, smoother, more efficient, or less turbulent) than Johnston's, part of the explanation lies in the price paid by his predecessors. Part also, incidentally, lies in the price paid by his successor. Wharton did make some serious errors of judgment, and he was neither a better nor a more honorable man than Johnston. In point of fact, Wharton's most critical mistakes were not immediately noticed. His mishandling of a local autonomy situation in San Francisco was only corrected long after he died. His part in the CIO defection has only recently been "expunged" by the 1955 merger. Wharton had an easier time than any of his predecessors, and the burden of his errors rested on his successor.

From 1926 until 1934, the social and economic environment was not favorable to unionism.[2] Membership fell, reaching its nadir in 1933. It was an era when wise leaders acted conservatively. From 1933 onwards, the reverse was more probably the case. Wharton's program was better suited to the first, rather than to the second period, as we shall observe.

Constructive Consolidation: 1926–1933

Wharton's selection by a Johnston-dominated executive council signifies their support of him. Wharton's decision to be installed formally as international president in an anti-Johnston district lodge (District Lodge 8 in Chicago) symbolizes his wish to heal all wounds. His initial remarks to the membership indicate what he considered to be the outstanding problems. Of these, the need for harmony was the most pressing:

> It will be our policy . . . to restore harmony within our ranks, to organize our craft, to confine our principal activities to the business of our Association, to avoid craft jurisdictional disputes . . . to insist that the members of our Association shall perform the work of our craft, whether it be in the manufacture erection, installation or maintenance thereof, to refrain from meddling in the legitimate activities of all other bona fide trade unions . . . to reduce strikes to a minimum, to establish cooperative relations with every employer who is willing to recognize our Association and establish mutually satisfactory contractual relations.[3]

During the remainder of Johnston's unexpired term, Wharton moved particularly cautiously. He took the lead in "letting bygones be bygones" in regard to the lost 1922 shop strike.[4] *Circular 185* had offered reinstatement to those who had defected. When other members of the Railway Employees' Department criticized this permissive attitude, the IAM refused to budge or even to argue.[5] Wharton, in trying to consolidate groups within his union, announced that he wanted the men back — four years was long enough to mourn a lost cause. He supported the Baltimore and Ohio Plan, even though it was unpopular with other unions in the Railway Employees' Department.[6]

On the other hand, Wharton did not wish to break up the department and prevented District Lodge 29 (on the Baltimore and Ohio Railroad) from withdrawing from System Federation 30, when the latter cracked down on it.[7] Wharton counseled patience and tolerance, reminding the IAM local that more was gained by amity than by conflict. By ignoring Railway Employees' Department jurisdictional awards, he and the IAM ultimately forced the department to abandon that function. For one who had previously been president of the Railway Employees' Department, it represents a shift to a particularistic, if not parochial, point of view.

Wharton continued the policy of expelling Communists.[8] More than that, he had the IAM lend the ILGWU $15,000 to help it recover from the exhaustion of its conflict with Communists.[9] His attitude toward the Brookwood labor college outside New York City, for instance, changed abruptly when he learned that there was suspicion of a Communist taint not only among the student body, but also on the faculty. He withdrew all IAM support (as well as students). The quickness of Wharton's move, not even giving the Brookwood group an opportunity to discuss its side of the matter, is additional evidence of the unyielding antiradical side of his beliefs.

Wharton's attitude toward Johnston's banking experiment was mixed; he approved of it, while recognizing its limits:

Banking by labor unions has its proper place in the labor movement, but under no circumstances should it ever be interpreted or construed as a solution to Labor's problems. It can be, and it has been to a very great extent an important and influential factor in giving Labor Organizations prestige and standing. It has been the means of securing for the labor movement greater consideration from Employers, business men, financiers, statesmen, and the general public.

In 1927 he was elected international president without opposition. All the general vice-presidents were also reelected. However, Wharton decided to get rid of Hannon, his remaining opponent on the council. He assigned him to a distant territory, and Hannon took the only alternative open to him (which was just what Wharton intended him to do) and resigned. The council selected Harry Carr to fill out the term.

Wharton's relations within the labor movement were much better than Johnston's. He even became a vice-president of the AFL in 1928. Although he was not able to arrange a reentry of the IAM into the Building Trades Department, in virtually all other sectors his efforts at rapprochements were successful. He negotiated a 1928 agreement with the street and electric railwaymen, which gave the IAM jurisdiction over all jobs that were machinist in character.[10] It included an arbitration clause giving the president of the AFL authority in the event of an unresolved dispute between the two parties. The negotiation of the agreement is significant of a change in IAM attitude; but the giving of an arbitral power to the AFL president is probably the greatest indication of the new policy, because it represents a new-found confidence in the president of the AFL.

Though he was generally successful in pursuing this policy, he did run into difficulties in negotiations with the boilermakers over jurisdictional matters.[11] Both unions were members of the Railway Employees' Department, and negotiations were carried on under department auspices. He was convinced, after having made what he thought were major concessions, that the boilermakers were bargaining in poor faith and were, in effect, trying to take over the machinists' job territory. Wharton then directed "the IAM to decline to enter into any conferences . . . [or to continue any in progress] with any representative of the [boilermakers] . . . on any question of jurisdiction of work."

The boilermakers were not without good friends and controlled the department by voting regularly with the sheetmetal workers and the blacksmiths. Voting, it should be added, was on a unit basis, making it possible for several smaller unions to control the department. Invariably the boilermakers were given preferred treatment in matters affecting them and the IAM. When it became apparent to everyone that Wharton was going to make no further conciliatory moves, and that there was real danger that the IAM would try to smash the department, the department reluctantly agreed to suspend its usual voting rules, which had had the effect of discounting the IAM's larger membership on handling jurisdictional differences. The effect was to palliate, but not to eliminate, the machinists' anger.

The 1928 convention was held in Atlanta as part of the fortieth anniversary celebration of the association's founding. Discussion of national policies was eschewed — it was the year of the Hoover–Smith campaign and tempers as well as prejudices ran high. Interest in political developments remained keen, however, and the convention voted to make subscriptions to *Labor,* the political-action-oriented newspaper edited by Keating and published by the Railway Labor Executives' Association, compulsory for all IAM members.[12]

Wharton dominated the convention. The term of office was extended to four years, quadrennial conventions were ordered, and the anti-National Civic Federation plank (a thorn in the side of O'Connell's one-time supporters) was eliminated.[13] Nonetheless, when Wharton's ally and friend, Charles Fry (probably with Wharton's tacit support), tried to eliminate elections by referendum, the attempt was unsuccessful.[14]

The convention also approved some extensions of power for the international president and the grand lodge, including the granting of authority to the international president and executive council to expel Communists.[15] It approved an earlier ruling by Wharton, that a local lodge did not have full voice over the disposition of its funds.[16] The background of this decision is interesting. In 1921 Local Lodge 257 (Jacksonville, Florida) raised its dues in order to support a business agent. After 1924 when the business agency was discontinued, dues were not reduced. The result was an accumulation of funds. In 1928 the local decided to split the treasury surplus by giving each member a check equal to ten months' dues. Wharton held that this decision was *ultra vires:* "all monies accumulating in the treasury of [any] local lodge become the joint property of the Association, for which all bonded officers of the local lodge are responsible."

One development indicating the development of local, rather than central (grand lodge), authority was a decision to give district lodges a voice in the issuing of charters to new local lodges in a territory served by the district lodge.

The convention also voted to reduce death benefits because the old plan proved to be actuarially unsound.[17] The new plan of 1928 began paying a

$50.00 death benefit after three years of continuous membership instead of one. It caught up with the 1921 plan after seven years of continuous membership, with the payment of $150.00 but increased thereafter at a yearly rate of $25.00, reaching a peak of $300.00 after thirteen years. The 1921 plan, on the other hand, stayed at the $150.00 level reached after five years' continuous membership. The new plan did not prove to be much better and was modified in 1936.

Disability benefits were tightened. After one year's membership, payments up to $100 were awarded. An additional $100 for each extra year was also authorized, with the maximum payment amounting to $400.

Wharton, as we have noted, was reluctant to authorize strikes. But he was greatly interested in organizing the auto industry and did authorize one major strike there to gain a foothold.[18] In 1928 after a year of futile talks, the IAM struck the America LaFrance Company, an Elmira, New York manufacturer of fire-fighting machinery. The IAM did not get full cooperation from other unions in the plant, notably the carpenters' and the painters'. Nonetheless, after five months the company settled on the union's terms. Why? The IAM was able to organize support of its effort among local labor councils and federations. Fire equipment is primarily purchased by municipal governments, which are responsive to local labor sentiment. Thus the victory, although not to be minimized, did not indicate a "wave of the future." No one in the IAM, least of all Wharton, saw in this a precedent for future negotiations with the antiunion automobile industry. Earlier AFL efforts to organize the auto industry had foundered on the twin shoals of employer opposition and the refusal of several craft unions (notably the pattern makers, painters, and electricians) to waive their jurisdictional claims.

At the 1928 convention Wharton reported the almost insufferable difficulties which the union faced in attracting new members.[19] Some of the problems were basically economic; some were the result of inept administration; a few were the result of cultural conflicts; but most stemmed from the general fear of unemployment. In other words, Wharton was alert to the problems — yet, he was convinced that their solution in many instances was not within the grasp of union leaders. One consequent view was that it did the IAM harm to swell its ranks with newcomers who were not conservative, dedicated men. He wanted no repetition of the First World War experience. His judgment was, in fact, much like O'Connell's — accept men economically-tied to the trade, but avoid economic transients. The union was to be the tie between the member and his work opportunity. Wharton even advocated the state's licensing of auto mechanics in order to stabilized that labor market.

The membership voted in the postconvention referendum to accept all recommended changes; 1929 was a peaceful year with few new problems. An organizing department was established to secure the five-day, thirty-hour week, with a general minimum wage of $1.00 per hour and a model daily wage of $12.00–$14.00. Some believed that the America LaFrance victory should be the signal for a general push in the auto industry. Even the embryonic airplane industry came in for a share of attention.

For old-time members an exemption card system was devised.[20] The plan excluded all officers with experience on the national and local level. The plan, providing for a permanent release from dues payments, applied to members of over twenty years' continuous good standing, currently physically unable to work, and currently receiving no more than $50.00 per month as a pension right. Later it was extended to those who had been permanently victimized.

The indiscriminate use of unemployment stamps in lieu of full dues payment was stopped.[21] Membership could be retained with these reduced-price stamps only if no more than six were used in any twelve-month period. Administration of the death and disability benefits programs was also tightened, making the local lodge financially responsible for collection. In brief, Wharton used the period to consolidate the adminstrative policies of the grand lodge with regard to the members.

Immediately after the convention, the membership having voted for compulsory subscriptions to *Labor* (Keating's newspaper), the monthly per capita tax was raised 5 cents by the executive council, which interpreted the vote as authorization. This provoked a strong reaction among those who were not interested in American political matters (particularly the Canadians) as well as those who had no specific interest in Keating's views and reports.[22] By incorporating the 5-cent cost into the per capita tax, Wharton transferred responsibility for collection to the local lodges, with the penalty of loss of local lodge voting rights if there were delinquency. A move to repeal this referendum vote was initiated. It failed to pass in 1930 (13,371 to 6035), although it finally did in 1937.

The most far-reaching decisions in this post-1928 convention relate to the further growth of the power of the international president. Wharton's abrupt change of attitude toward the Brookwood Labor School has been noted. However, General Vice-President Fechner and Editor Fred Hewitt believed that Brookwood and its director, A. J. Muste, were entitled to present their defense against the charges raised by Matthew Woll and Spencer Miller in the AFL.[23] They signed a brochure, "The Injunction Against Brookwood," which compared the AFL executive council proceedings to the infamous Stuart Star–Chamber proceedings. It must be remembered that Fechner and Hewitt had been strong anti-Communist supporters of Johnston, and their reaction should not be attributed to a sentimental softness. They objected to the procedures employed.

Wharton's reaction was swift. He wrote each a personal letter saying:

> I was simply astounded to receive [the brochure] to which your names are attached as Ex-Directors and members of the IAM.
>
> I am even more astounded that you, as officers of the IAM with full knowledge of the action of the International [1928] Convention and the Executive Council should take the action you have without the courtesy of discussing this matter with me.
>
> I personally consider your action indefensible while you occupy an official position in the IAM . . . [The executive council had decided unanimously to suspend the affiliation with Brookwood].
>
> You and no other officer can hope to justify the use of your name as an individual and [ex-director] when by so doing you are taking an action that can only be construed as opposing your action as an officer.
>
> I will await with much interest your answer to this letter.

The council adopted two resolutions. The first forbade any IAM officer during the course of the "Brookwood defense" from participating in the activities of Brookwood. The second prohibited any IAM officer or member from using the IAM name directly or indirectly in any context contrary to the policies adopted by the executive council, except that an individual member of the council, who dissented from a majority decision, could have his vote formally recorded in the open minutes of the council. Otherwise he was required to support the majority. The only valid conclusion is that Wharton had successfully cracked down on the semipersonal activities of two officials. He tolerated nothing divisive on his council. In another move to extend his central authority, the executive council directed that all members of the delegation to AFL conventions vote as a bloc, in accordance with IAM policy made by the international president.

Wharton's attitude toward Brookwood was an expression of a pervasive if somewhat recent, antiradical attitude, itself a reaction to the dual unionism programs of the Communists. To a lesser, but by no means negligible, extent it was Wharton's device to consolidate power as the leader of a one-party system and as undisputed leader of the IAM. An incident particularly worth noting because it ties the two ends together involved one William Simons, a member of a Chicago lodge (Local Lodge 199).[24] Simons was found guilty by his lodge of being a Communist, and therefore a dual unionist. However, his prosecutors could not muster the two-thirds vote necessary to expel him. Wharton then intervened as international president and expelled the man, arguing that expulsion was mandatory under Article 23 of the constitution as well as Circular 183. After hearing Simons' appeal, the executive council supported Wharton. The importance of the incident lies in the evident expansion of the judicial powers of the international president, but it is also a clear example of Wharton's personal antiradicalism.

The Communist issue never died. The next year the executive council decided that too many radicals who were nonmembers spoke at IAM local lodge meetings.[25] Consequently it ordered that the floor be denied to all nonmembers except representatives of other AFL unions, the twenty-one standard railway labor organizations, or a local civic body seeking cooperation on local matters. At the same time, it forbade the use of the IAM name for local or national promotional schemes, year books, and the like. Again the existence of a radicalism threat was used to augment the grand lodge's power.

After the 1928 convention Wharton continued the policy of IAM rapprochement with other AFL unions. In 1929 there was an agreement with the International Alliance of Theatrical Stage Employees regarding the building, operation, and the repair of motion picture projectors.[26] The operation of the projectors and temporary repairs were given to the alliance. Jurisdiction over building, rebuilding, and major repair jobs went to the IAM. Agreements were also signed during this period with the teamsters, the operating engineers, and the printing pressmen. These were in addition to those signed earlier with the plumbers, steamfitters, and the street and electric railway employees. In 1931 after some preliminary skirmishes, Wharton managed to come to a tentative agreement with President Hutcheson of the carpenters.[27] The two unions agreed that they would assist each other "in bettering and maintaining hours, wages, and working conditions on [erection] work," and "that if a dispute arises [which] cannot be settled locally, no stoppage of work shall take place, but that the matter in dispute [shall] be immediately submitted to [the two presidents] for adjustment." Because of the opposition of the Building Trades Department, based on its view that the AFL "ratification" of the past constituted a major reallocation of responsibilities as well as jurisdictions, this agreement did not last many years. However, it illustrates that Wharton, in O'Connell's tradition, sought and reached some degree of understanding as leader of the IAM with the leaders of other big AFL unions.

The Great Depression hit hard. No sooner had the union paid off its bank debt (an aftermath of the strikes early in the twenties) than it had to reduce its income by suspending the rule limiting the use of "unemployed" stamps to six per twelve-month period.[28] Of course, this dried up a source of considerable revenue, and the rule was not again enforced until 1939. By late 1931 things were really bleak. In December the grand lodge representatives and auditors were given a month's leave of absence to save the cost of their salaries.[29] Eight months later the officers voluntarily cut their salaries 10 per cent, and all *per diem* allowances were reduced. The grand lodge contributions to local business agents' salaries were lowered to a maximum of $100. The bases for affiliation fees to the AFL and its various departments were made smaller. The journal staff was cut 25 per cent. Later, some were dismissed, and the rest were given frequent unpaid holidays. Even the 1932 convention was indefinitely postponed (after a referendum vote of 11,737 to 987) "until industrial conditions improve." These economy measures purportedly saved almost $125,000. Still it was not enough.

In February, 1933, the bank handling the IAM active business account closed, freezing all the IAM current accounts and checking funds.[30] The IAM's own savings institution investment, the Mt. Vernon Bank, failed on March 3, 1933, which further aggravated the IAM's financial condition, and it became immediately necessary to furlough all the field staff. Thus from mid-1930 until March, 1933, economic stress hindered the union's activities in an ever-increasing flood. The lowest point was reached in March, 1933.

During this first period Wharton's program bore a marked resemblance to O'Connell's, both because he worked efficiently within the general framework of the AFL, and because he held an antiradical, job-conscious philosophy of unionism. Unlike O'Connell he did much to strengthen the powers of the international president within the IAM. In essence, he tightened the IAM internally and exercised considerable skill in handling its external relationships with other unions. It was the latter factor which differentiates the avowed goal of his administration from his predecessor's. Considering the nature of the environment, caution was wise in either time. This part of Wharton's presidency can be fairly titled "constructive consolidation."

Wharton's Policies During the New Deal

The busy one hundred days following Franklin Roosevelt's going into the White House produced, as it well recorded elsewhere, a spate of administrative orders as well as legislative enactments. Most banks, after a brief "holiday" were opened — one exception being the Mt. Vernon Bank, which was ordered liquidated.[31] And business, protected by the NRA, was encouraged to establish codes in order to further economic activity. Unionism was given its own fillip in the form of Section 7a, and several unions, not including the IAM, borrowed heavily in order to finance organizing campaigns in new, or once-abandoned, territories.

The rationale of Wharton's decisions in the first five years of the New Deal was determined by the lessons he had learned during the Johnston administration. He had a fundamental distrust of "easy" gains in membership — maintaining that swollen ranks were likely to encourage irresponsible leadership. Instead, he favored locally planned organizing programs growing out of local demands, rather than situations in which the union engineered membership demand from the top. Wharton, in reminiscing on the pro-union policies of the first Wilson administration, also remembered the distorting effect the resultant increase in membership had had on stable, job-oriented union policies. He could feel nothing but mistrust for the enthusiasm of the industrial unionists of his period. He preferred to continue the policies developed prior to the depression years; consolidating grand lodge supervision over district and local lodge affairs, and working within the AFL executive council and the various AFL departments. Wharton's conclusions, based on the erroneous assumption that the Wagner Act would be no more successfully implemented than the Clayton Act, were obviously too limited for the New Deal period. He also faced other serious problems. The series of events which brought him to the presidency had already begun to be forgotten by the 1934–1935 period. On the district and local level new leadership was appearing, which first requested, and then demanded, serious consideration. Thus in analyzing the changes occurring during the second phase of Wharton's administration, we must first consider those stemming from the deteriorating equilibria in sectors where Wharton previously scored success. Then we will turn to the effects of new external developments, which not only required specific solutions, but also called for reappraisal of the place of the labor movement in general society, the IAM in the American labor movement, and the grand lodge in the IAM.

Grand Lodge and Local Lodge Relationships

It should be recalled that the IAM district and local lodges had a long history of relative autonomy because many critical aspects of union work had traditionally been carried on at the local level. Since 1895, however, there had been a chipping away at the autonomous rights of locals. This process had not been constant, but it reached high points several times during the Johnston and Wharton administrations. The passage and implementation of the Wagner Act accentuated the need to speed up the grand lodge's consolidation-of-authority process because it raised what previously had been local political and legal matters to the national level. That is, the ability of a union to get recognition from a local employer became a matter of federal governmental concern. Quite obviously a welter of uncoordinated local union requests for aid was not as effective as a determined, policy-oriented request handled through the IAM's grand lodge. Also, the IAM was competing for certification with the CIO unions, which were centrally directed; therefore irrespective of what might have been a balanced choice between a desirable efficiency level and a tradition of local autonomy, the grand lodge was forced to play a stronger role if the IAM were to win elections against the CIO.

The IAM locals should have realized that it was in their interest in the long run to work through their national organization, but in point of historical fact, they often tried to gain temporary local advantage even if it sabotaged the national organization. The result, therefore, was a lengthy struggle between the grand lodge and various strong locals intent upon maintaining their autonomy. On occasion, strong locals tried to use the Wagner Act to further their own ends.

Probably no local lodge had been more independent than Local Lodge 68 (San Francisco). Chronologically, it was older than the IAM. Geographically, it was far removed from grand lodge headquarters. And psychologically, it had always embraced a self-defined Populism, characteristic of communities isolated from the pressure of "eastern traditionalism." For example, at the end of the First World War in 1919, when jobs were becoming scarce, it had insisted, over the adamant and wise opposition of Johnston, upon strike action in support of wage advances.[32]

In 1932 when strike action would have seemed the quintessence of folly, Local Lodge 68 voted to strike the Matson (Navigation Company) shops in order to forestall a wage cut.[33] The vote did not carry by the required 75 per cent of those directly affected. The local lodge officers, however, decided that it did carry by 75 per cent of those indirectly affected — all the local's members coming under a general wage scale effective in San Francisco — and the strike was called. Their position, based on an interpretation of a clause debated at the 1903 convention, was rejected by Wharton, who ordered the strike to be terminated, offering, however, to consider men who had refused work offered at less than officially determined minimum rates, as victimized. Local Lodge 68 reluctantly bowed before Wharton's order, and the strike was called off. Considerable bitterness remained.

A few months later, Local Lodge 284 (Oakland) with whom Local Lodge 68 had strong ties, asked the executive council for the right to reinstate members who had been dropped for nonpayment of dues, without the special reinstatement payment, to allow the reinstated member to pay up his dues debts when he had a job. It also requested a waiver on subscriptions to *Labor*. This request, no doubt prompted by a desire to bring one-time, unemployed members back into the union, was denied both by Wharton and the council. Friction was again the result.

In 1935 Local Lodge 68 tried to improve the rates of its members so that every one of them would be working above the "official minimum," set jointly by all the locals in the area.[34] Business agent Hook wrote the grand lodge asking for permission to strike. Wharton's reply was that Local Lodge 68 must not strike until it had worked out a rate structure satisfactory to the other IAM locals in the area; when, and if, that was done, Wharton offered to recommend to the council that it sanction strike action.

Hook and the members ignored Wharton's order and struck without grand lodge sanction. Presented with a *fait accompli,* Wharton backed down, and the executive council agreed to sanction the strike and to pay strike benefits to those who had been working previously at the struck plants. At this stage, a further complication appeared. The executive council learned that Local Lodge 68 was putting on the strike roster — as well as permitting them to vote on the strike issue — not only the workers on strike, but also the unemployed who would have liked to work at the affected plants. Wharton's hand was thus forced by Hook and Local Lodge 68, and he had to concur in maintaining the strike action. These events occurred in late 1935 and in early 1936.

In July, 1937, Local Lodge 284 attempted to do the same thing.[35] It took a strike vote affecting thirty-seven firms and permitted all its members to vote — not only those directly affected. After the vote it declared strikes against the thirty-seven firms. This time, however, Wharton reacted differently. He countermanded the strike call and ordered negotiations. When his order was flouted, he sent a grand lodge representative to Oakland to audit Local Lodge 284's funds, prior to an order suspending the local. Such an order soon followed. In brief, Wharton seemed determined to break the growing spirit of "irresponsible" independence.

Business agent E. W. Dillon of Local Lodge 68 was asked by Local Lodge 284 to present its case to Wharton. Dillon got nowhere; Wharton was intent on preserving due process and on asserting his control. In the meantime Local Lodge 68 had fallen into debt to the grand lodge for nonpayment of the subscription price of *Labor,* and Dillon's own status as a delegate became questionable. At the Milwaukee convention held late in the summer of 1936 Wharton ordered, backed by the executive council, that Local Lodge 68 be disenfranchised until its *Labor* indebtedness was erased. Local Lodge 68 did so only because Dillon wanted to thrash out the whole matter of Local Lodge 284's suspension and to stir up an anti-Wharton, anti-grand lodge movement. Dillon very nearly succeeded, because his argument had a certain appeal. Local Lodge 284 was allegedly striking for the principle of higher wages. Wharton was deaf to these "legitimate" demands and was urging a policy which could be made to sound identical to the one advocated by the enemy, namely, the employers' association.

The debate over the suspension of the charter of Local Lodge 284 took the better part of two days. Dillon was doing very well until he ended his rebuttal on an emotional note: "I say that you [the delegates] are probably confronted with a situation and you are going to have to vote for the manufacturers there in Oakland or you are going to vote for the machinists. I implore you that you vote for the machinists of Oakland and not for the bosses." He sat down to prolonged applause.

Wharton then produced his extraordinary parliamentary skill. He immediately forced Dillon, buoyed by the emotional fervor of his own well-received words, to answer a direct question — "Will you personally support the decision of this convention?" Dillon's reply was, "It is according to what the decision is." This brought on "Laughter and Boos [*sic*] from the delegates and much confusion." Without any further delay Wharton adjourned the session for lunch to let the delegates appreciate the full impact of Dillon's threat of rebellion. They did. After lunch Wharton reviewed the whole story, emphasizing the danger of anarchy to the IAM and to the labor movement. When the vote came, the convention supported him and the grand lodge. Wharton had won the battle, but Dillon had not been vanquished; that is, the war was not yet over. The grand lodge was to pay well for Wharton's handling of the issue. Had he been consistent in the beginning and suspended Local Lodge 68, considerable trouble might have been avoided. The practical question, however, is why there was different treatment in the handling of the two locals. The answer lies in the timing, and in the ties which Local Lodge 68 had with other locals, and in those which Local Lodge 284 did not have. In any event, the former members of Local Lodge 284 joined the CIO and affiliated with the Steel Workers' Organizing Committee as Local Union 1304.

Dillon returned to San Francisco, unwilling to abide by the convention vote. In December his lodge, Local Lodge 68, levied an assessment on its own members to support the illegal strike in Oakland.[36] Wharton declared this levy illegal, whereupon Local Lodge 68 refused to accept the dues of anyone unwilling to pay. Wharton again compromised and merely authorized those refusing to meet Local Lodge 68's illegal levy to pay their dues directly to the grand lodge. This situation continued for several months.

In March, 1937, when Local Lodge 68 decided to press for new contractual terms, it took care to follow regular procedures.[37] At the same time it continued to levy its illegal assessment. And later, in June, 1937, Local Lodge

68 asked Wharton to pay part of the cost of a second business agent. It proposed Dillon — who, being *persona non grata* to the executive council, was turned down. Wharton informed the local that the grand lodge would accept almost anyone else, but it would not pay half of Dillon's salary. He was hired, nonetheless.

Wharton evidently could not bring himself to get tough with Local Lodge 68 and made at least one further concession. When Local Lodge 68 demanded payment of back dues from those who had paid directly to the grand lodge, Wharton authorized the general secretary–treasurer to refund the amounts to the men, so that they could pay the sums to Local Lodge 68.

In October, 1938, Hook tried to mend the differences between Wharton and suspended Local Lodge 284. The IAM had, in the meantime, chartered a new local, and Hook proposed that the "old" and the "new" merge, without prejudice to either, that the expellees be given their old standing unimpaired, and that the IAM accept without initiation fee all men signed up by the outcast local in the interim. The executive council agreed, qualifying that no expellee could hold a bonded office, and that the offer would expire on December 31, 1938. These restrictions were enough to prevent reassociation, and the split continued, having the effect of weakening the IAM's position in the Oakland area and the grand lodge's power in San Francisco as well.

In the meantime, old ties and alliances underwent strains elsewhere, and the grand lodge failed to assert its strength. In Chicago a young business agent (D. W. Burrows), representing an automotive local, challenged the control of Charles Fry, whose position had been virtually supreme in the area.[38] The conflict involved the right of Local Lodge 701 to organize the auto repairmen employed by the city, instead of the locals normally representing city-employed machinists. Burrows appealed to the convention for authority to claim the jurisdiction. Fry was shocked to find the convention ready to grant the young man's request. The only face-saver he could think of was delay, and Burrows' request was subsequently turned over to the executive council, where it was speedily granted. At the convention everyone took the opportunity to praise Burrows. Fry returned to Chicago disheartened. He died a year later. The net effect of these changes was to turn a personally pro-Wharton area into one that was, at best, neutral toward grand lodge proposals.

In other districts and areas the ties that made local units subservient to the grand lodge were reexamined, often with results not compatible with grand lodge traditions. Previously, in the depths of the depression, as a temporary relief measure, Wharton had allowed a local lodge to set up prohibitive transfer fees to prevent unemployed members of other locals from flocking into an area where a few openings had developed. But in 1938, despite a period of improved business conditions, he permitted a strong local unit (District Lodge 9 in St. Louis) to establish a special quarterly working card, which was required of all those seeking work in the contract and verbal agreement shops, in addition to the transfer fee.[39] In effect, he was agreeing to the proposition that the dues book was not a sufficient passport for the job rights of itinerant machinists. Locals would be allowed to charge a visa fee. It is relevant to add that District Lodge 9 was one of the strongest and best administered in the organization.

W. P. Thomas, a popular figure from Madison, Wisconsin, employed at headquarters, sought permission to buy "unemployed" stamps while ill.[40] He was a member of the huge government local (Local Lodge 174) in Washington. Local Lodge 174 changed its bylaws to keep him from his purpose. He appealed. Wharton refused to intervene, answering that local autonomy was desirable if it did not conflict with grand lodge policy. Again, a local lodge was too powerful to trifle with.

In other instances as well, the pattern of the local lodges' seeking a renaissance of their authority coming up against the grand lodge's desire for control can be found. In Cleveland the grand lodge played a vital role in suspending a business agent for incompetence.[41] His successor, selected by the members, had been anti-administration at the Milwaukee convention, and the executive council refused to contribute to his salary. This decision was later reversed when a newly appointed member of the council assured the others that the man "had changed his attitude." But here the point is obscured because of the man's flexibility. The local itself then reversed course and re-elected the original business agent. The executive council reluctantly agreed to support him. Here again the grand lodge first asserted itself and then backed down.

But the existence of active radicalism in one other case resulted in swift and decisive grand lodge action. It was charged that in Minneapolis, known Communists, one of whom Wharton had earlier suspended, had gained effective control of several lodges.[42] Thirty-seven officers, delegates, and members were tried on the spot by the executive council, which convicted all but three. In this case Wharton acted with dispatch, but it was the exception rather than the rule.

In brief, although Wharton tried to enforce his policies as he had done in the pre-New Deal period, he consistently failed after 1933. As suggested at the beginning of this section, the changed environment was partially responsible. The favorable climate engendered by the New Deal encouraged localism where it had once existed (at the expense of national unionism), even though localism was in the long run debilitating for the union movement. But it is worth adding that Wharton's uneven response to the challenge was also a significant factor. This will become more evident in the next two sections.

Changing Interunion Relations

The biggest development in the labor movement during Roosevelt's years in the White House was unquestionably the schism which resulted in a bifurcated labor movement in secondary industry. Walter Galenson and others have admirably traced the events leading to that split.[43] One aspect, however, which deserves special attention in this study of the IAM, was the stress and strain among the unions which stayed with the AFL. A good case can be made for the theory that it was the impasses between the various enclaves within the AFL which precipitated the crises.

The secession–expulsion of several old AFL unions, namely, the UMW, the ILGWU, the pressmen, and even that latecomer to the official AFL family, the Amalgamated, is only part of the story. What was occuring among unions like the machinists, the carpenters, and the teamsters is also relevant to the developments.

All unions believed that they were responsive to the potentialities of organization following 1933. Some, like the IAM, wanted to organize carefully, preserving wherever possible their claims to jurisdiction, while incorporating new members at a rate consistent with tradition.

The IAM had, at great cost to itself, worked out what seemed to be a basic *modus vivendi* with their most serious rivals, the carpenters. Nothing which was being done, according to this line of reasoning, should have jeopardized the 1931 agreement. Thus when the aircraft workers, over whom the IAM had earlier exercised a claim, appeared ready to join, and when the carpenters put forth a rival claim, Wharton proceeded with caution.[44] After negotiations within the AFL executive council, the IAM was given the jurisdictional green light. Only then was Wharton ready to take them in.

The auto industry was even harder to handle. Wharton undoubtedly recognized the desirability of securing the auto jurisdiction, but he was also well aware of both the cost of organizing the industry, and the bitternesses which would result with other unions if the IAM handled the job on its own. He knew, too, how the IAM would react if another union were to be given rights over the machinists, tool makers, die sinkers, and mechanics working on tools and dies, as well as on experimental models.

In short, Wharton well remembered the IAM's difficulties with the AFL during Johnston's time. He was not prepared to run the risk of repeating the experience. Because he was alert to the need of organizing the mass production industries, he obviously felt a responsibility for supporting alternatives which would allow one union to exercise hegemony over a major secondary industry. He offered two; the first was that the AFL issue charters to federal unions for the workers in these industries, and that the old-time craft unions could work out jurisdictional details as time went on. The second drew upon his earlier experience with the Federation of Federations. He suggested that the organizing drives be carried on by the AFL departments — there, effective action would be possible, but not at the expense of any particular constituent union. Division of the newly organized members into separate competent unions would occur, but in facing the employer, all the crafts would bargain together. For a while the second plan looked possible — in fact, its chances appeared to be so favorable that the IAM executive council thought it wise to increase its level of participation in the Metal Trades Department in order to increase its voice when the ultimate division occurred.

In the light of these factors, it is not surprising that the IAM bitterly opposed William Green's granting of a charter to the International Union of Auto Workers.[45] Although Green had tried to assuage IAM fears by explicit exclusions in the charter of jobs "involving tools, dies and machinery as well as job [contract] shops," the new International Union of Auto Workers lost no time in asserting its claim to them.

The IAM executive council was informed that two stumbling blocks in the way to successful IAM organizing drives were its initiation fee and high monthly dues, in comparison with those of federal labor unions. Consequently, it sought, and received, referendum authorization to eliminate (when thought necessary) the former, and to issue helpers' dues books (with a lower rate of payments) to auto industry machinists. An organizing drive was undertaken almost immediately, but the move was too slow and too late. The CIO drive had begun, and the initiative had been wrested from the hands of the AFL.

The actual secession of the CIO unions provided the IAM with some immediate problems. IAM members who accepted CIO offices were expelled. Some IAM leaders, notably Michael Quill and James Matles (neither of whom had been in the IAM very long) took their local organizations with them when they defected. Almost 8000 members were involved and the grand lodge estimated a loss of approximately $13,000.[46]

Besides the question of defection, there was also the issue of what relationship IAM locals were to have with the new CIO unions. Local Lodge 203 (Akron, Ohio), for example, wanted to know whether victimization benefits were to be paid when machinists in local rubber plants were unable to work as a result of the rubber workers union's sit-down strikes.[47] In other words, would the payments traditionally intended for workers locked out by employers be paid to workers locked out by a CIO union? Wharton ruled in the negative, saying that victimization benefits were paid only when the employer wilfully tried to harm the IAM. In the event of a plant's being closed because of inclement weather, no benefits normally accrued. And none would accrue now. Nor would there be any strike benefits paid to IAM members refusing to cross picket lines.

Another direct effect of the CIO drive was the renewed IAM effort to gain members. As the new members came, they, too, presented problems. Some newly-picked-up unskilled workers were earning high rates of pay, and it seemed illogical both to charge them low tax dues and to pay them lower benefits rates. Eric Peterson, then grand lodge representative in Cleveland, produced a solution with profound consequences.[48] It was that any worker earning more than 60 cents per hour should pay $1.75 per month as dues; all others, $1.25.

Obviously, its first significance is that in translating the divisions of membership from skill to income, it provided the rationale for the development of modern industrial unionism and paved the way for absorbing a greater variety of members. The evolution of tests for machinists — (1) is he a good man? (2) is he generally competent at all operations? (3) can he handle one of the standard machine operations? — became (4) does he earn as much as those theretofore acknowledged as competent for first class membership? In retrospect, this shift constituted a major redefinition of job orientation. Much earlier when the fact of specialists was accepted, the old touchstone of "a machinist is an all-round man" had been modified to "a machinist is what a machinist does." Now during the New Deal wave of organizing, the union had made a further move — "a machinist is a man working in the metal industries who gets paid about the market rate."

In a most important sense, this was a shift away from the type of craft unionism associated both with O'Connell and Wharton. But the shift was made necessary not only because the CIO was organizing the mass-production industries, but also because the NLRB assumed the responsibility and right to determine bargaining units. It was not so much the enthusiasm of CIO organizers, with their songs, their publicity, and their money that rang the death knell of old-style unionism, as it was the active sponsorship of the right to organize (if necessary, by the intervention of the federal government, with the entry of the NLRB into the jurisdiction-granting business). The fact of the NLRB (particularly sections 9 and 10 of the Wagner Act) caused the change within the IAM — far more than the "fact" of the UAW, the SWOC, or the rubber workers. That an industrial orientation was in the offing, was clearly evident as early as the 1936 convention, when the "woman worker" category was changed to "production worker." But the critical stage of the evolution occurred when the amount of pay became the criterion for the type of membership. The final step in this direction was taken in 1953, when all name categories of membership were abolished. But that was many years later.

At the time Wharton was having his greatest success in smoothing relationships within the AFL executive council, he ran into further difficulties with the boilermakers. There were two reasons; relationships had never been good, and such successes as had occurred had been handled by Grand Vice President Conlon (who died in April 1931).

President Franklin of the boilermakers claimed a verbal jurisdictional agreement with Conlon.[49] Wharton disclaimed Conlon's alleged concessions and, in order to make the IAM position absolutely clear, announced that the "supposed agreement is cancelled and declared null and void." At about this same time he was mending his fences with the other AFL unions.

The 1931 basic agreement with the carpenters was augmented by some protocols (1932–1933). These provided that the IAM would accept qualified millwrights as members and would give them credit for continuous membership in both organizations, in computing death benefits eligibility. This concordance did not work out because of the opposition of the Building Trades Department, which in time led the carpenters to annul the Wharton–Hutcheson accord.[50] Little trouble actually occurred until 1937, although the carpenters' preference for the Building Trades Department's views kept alive a relative undercurrent of hostility. In 1937, however, what remained of the *entente "not very" cordiale* was definitely ruptured when the carpenters disregarded IAM jurisdictional claims at the Firestone Plant in Detroit, and in the millwrights' field in Bellingham, Washington, and Newark, New Jersey.[51] The IAM executive council resolved "that the IAM observe [only] the jurisdiction of all trades that respect the jurisdiction of the IAM." The executive council decided to appeal for relief to the AFL executive council. Wharton's attempt failed and he then tried personally to work out a *modus operandi*. He was too ill to succeed. Moreover, it is doubtful that success was possible because both unions felt keen senses of rivalry.

There can be no doubt that the proverbial powder keg was full. So long as Wharton was on the scene, however, the IAM was not going to light it.

Wharton was a sick man. Bronchial asthma made his retirement almost mandatory. In May 1938, however, a situation developed in the Railway Employees' Department, which, President Jewell, in the midst of a personal crisis of his own, was not able to handle. The conflict with the boilermakers was only one of many in which the IAM was trying to define its area of jurisdictional authority. The system of representation within the system federations as well as the Railway Employees' Department, itself, made the IAM position very weak. Voting, as was mentioned earlier, was on a unit rather than a proportionate size basis. Because it would have been extremely difficult to find an acceptable successor to Jewell, there was no thought of removing him. Yet, he was not able to handle the job. Wharton pressured him into seeking medical leave and returning to his post later. Wharton, in turn, postponed his own full retirement in order to handle the critical 1938 negotiations with the railroads. When these were completed, and Jewell was active once more, Wharton retired not only as international president, but also as a member of the AFL executive council. His successor as international president was Harvey W. Brown rather than Robert Fechner, who had technical seniority over Brown and who was also a more able administrator. Fechner had gone on leave in 1933 to become Director of the Federal Civilian Conservation Corps (Emergency Conservation Works), and was thus passed over. The IAM was left without a representative voice on the AFL executive council.

Changing Relationships with Private Employers

In retrospect, the latter part of Wharton's administration represents the period when the IAM's relationship with the diehard segment of American antiunion employers changed. We have already indicated that the change was associated with the enlarged role played by the government, particularly by the National Labor Relations Board. But it is erroneous to assume that the unionization of American industry was no more than the result of the waving of the governmental wand.

No experience better characterizes the slowness of the shift in attitudes and policies than that of the Remington Rand Corporation, an upstate New York firm.[52] Traditionally, this employer had resisted the unionization of its plants, a policy which was easy to practice because most of the plants were in small, one-industry towns, where the workers had no alternative opportunity for employment. Moreover, upstate New Yorkers appear to be an insular group, unlikely to respond to the leadership of those from metropolitan centers.

But this does not mean that the machinists employed by Remington Rand were unaware of the advantages of unionism, they simply doubted its efficacy. In 1931, for instance, of the eighty machinists employed by the Remington Rand Corporation in Ilion, New York, seventy-four were members of the IAM and had been in the union long enough to become beneficiary members (entitled to strike benefits). The men asked for sanction to strike, which was granted. The company immediately laid off almost two score machinists without any deference to seniority, and any probability of successful strike action quickly disappeared. In short, the men faced a monopsonistic market situation, and unionism appeared to have a very limited effectiveness in such a case.

In 1933 and 1934 the IAM, acting in accord with Section 7a of the National Industrial Recovery Program, sent organizers into the area, who made some headway. By 1934 the IAM had signed contracts with the company, covering plants in Ilion, Tonawanda and Syracuse, New York, as well as Middletown, Connecticut, Norwood, Ohio, and Cambridge, Massachusetts. In the fall of 1935 these locals, as well as several from other unions with whom the company had signed, formed a joint protective board under the general protection of the AFL Metal Trades Department.

The joint protective board sought first to get a wage increase, and when that move failed, it conducted a strike vote. That vote authorized strike action, which the IAM executive council confirmed. The men then struck, taking possession first of the Syracuse, New York, plant and then walking out in a more conventional fashion from the company's other plants in late May. From the union's viewpoint the strike was costly. The grand lodge's donations were in excess of $35,000 each month, until September when the strike donation rolls were cut an arbitary 25 per cent. Eleven months after the strike began, the IAM executive council voted to declare defeat. In all, the effort cost the grand lodge approximately $300,000

The more interesting side of the story, however, deals with the efforts made by the company to defeat the union. It developed a program, which it called the "Mohawk Valley Formula," similar to the program of the NMTA some thirty-five years before. The company simply told each community in which it operated that it would close its plant unless the community took steps to keep the union out. In Ilion, New York the threat succeeded, and the plant reopened as a company union affair. Similar developments occurred at the other plants. The only difference between these events and the 1901 NMTA affair was the response of the government. The NLRB held hearings and published a full transcript of the range of schemes to which the company had resorted. The short-run effects were the same, but the unfavorable publicity ultimately caused the company to reconsider its open-shop policy.

As a result, the plant did make a limited effort to come to terms with its discharged union employees. It agreed to reinstate the strikers and to pay token severance or unemployment pay to those for whom jobs no longer existed. The burden of the fight was taken over by the NLRB which, in the words of one author, "pursued the company through the courts in an endeavor to force disestablishment of [the] company unions and abstention from interference with the employees in the exercise of their bargaining right." The company eventually abandoned its position during the Second World War. A contract was signed in 1943 recognizing the IAM.

In one area, at least, the IAM was able to overcome the remaining opposition in an industry. By 1936 the association had contracts with all the "Big Five" manufacturers of printing presses.[53] Three of these firms had had a long history of cooperation; but the other two had been noteworthy as open-shop advocates — the Duplex Company,[54] which had successfully taken its fight against the IAM to the U. S. Supreme Court, and the R. Hoe Company, which had dissolved its formal relationship with the IAM in 1923.

But aside from these special areas of success, the IAM's victories were not spectacular. Yet many new members were signed up. Between October 1, 1935 and June 30, 1940, the IAM resorted to National Labor Relations Board procedures in 976 cases; of these, 669 were unfair labor practice cases, and the remaining 307 involved representation questions. Of the 976, 729 were settled prior to a formal finding.[55] Thus, the great majority of cases were settled by direct negotiation with the employer.

Between the same two dates the IAM participated in 140 NLRB elections; in 81 cases it was victorious and in 59 it lost. Of the 81, 54 were without organized union opposition and 18 were victories over CIO unions. Of the 59, 22 were without organized opposition (the workers preferring "no union"), and 26 were won by CIO unions. Compared to the accomplishments of some of the CIO unions, this was not an overwhelming achievement. But in these 140 elections a total of 45,000 workers was involved. And when one recalls that the IAM in 1935 numbered only 88,000 members, the relative increase is impressive, particularly because a large portion — possibly half the members — had been in the railroad shops, an area isolated from NLRB activity. In any event, the NLRB was a boon to the IAM. It proved to be even more so later on, when, to avoid the possibility of having to negotiate with the UAW–CIO, some employers in the aircraft industry modified their traditional anti-union policies and withheld the full force of their hatred from affecting IAM organizing efforts. This change would not have occurred if the Wagner Act had not been the law.

Wharton's administration is of particular interest because of his conscious attempt to end internal friction. Earlier we termed this a move toward "democratic centralism." "Democratic centralism" was his answer to the problems posed by the legacy of the two-party system.

We have seen that "democratic centralism" was needed, because no union could survive, much less grow, when all energies went into never-ending internal conflict. Wharton sought to establish concerted, stable leadership, and by 1933, despite outside events, his program appeared to be successful.

But there are problems in a policy of "democratic centralism." The greatest is the maintenance of a dynamic quality in the leadership. Attempts to muffle unnecessary rivalry within the organization must not kill debate or discussion. In other words, care must be taken to prevent the development of rubber-stamp character among the leaders.

Few can dispute the existence of Wharton's abilities. His responsiveness to changes prior to 1933 (when there weren't many) shows up well, but after 1933 (when there were more) it was less impressive. He dominated his council during both periods. And lacking an effective internal opposition, the policies implemented after 1933 tended to reflect his own assessments. Thus, the IAM, particularly during the last years of Wharton's rule, suffered the obverse side of the democratic centralism policy. It leaned too heavily on Wharton; and he was not up to the burden. On the other hand, because he kept the lesson of the civil war during Johnston's incumbency always in mind, he was loath to permit the crystallization of any opposition to his views.

This was the problem facing Harvey Brown when he became international president. Added to the memory of the debilitating conflict of the Johnston regime was a realization of a stultifying democratic centralism of Wharton's last years. No wonder then that the Brown administration was stormy. Action was needed, but the debate necessary for deciding the direction of that action was forcibly restrained. The result, therefore, was a series of explosive actions, each the result of informal politicking within the organization. The lack was an orderly appraisal of alternatives, because it seemed that such an appraisal would lead to a revival of the polarization of views found in the early twenties.

CHAPTER V

Midpassage: The Brown Administration

Harvey Brown served as international president for ten of the most turbulent years in the association's history. Born in Schuylkill County, Pennsylvania, he joined the IAM near the end of his apprenticeship in 1905. Within ten years he became business agent for the anthracite region, and later served in the same capacity in Syracuse, New York, and Newark, New Jersey. He became a vice-president in 1921, and a general vice-president in 1925. He was brought by Wharton to IAM headquarters in 1934, where he acted as Wharton's substitute from 1938 to 1940. He was subsequently elected to two full four-year terms of his own. An objective assessment of Brown's efforts and achievements, in response to the challenges he faced during that decade, yields a mixed judgment. The results of his efforts may be underestimated because there is an understandable tendency to confuse his personality with the problems of his administration, and he was a stubborn, pugnacious man.

Aside from personality, his problems stemmed from two sources. The first was the legacy of bad guesses and improvised arrangements from the latter phase of Wharton's administration. The other was the rapidity of environmental change during the years of his own administration. Between the two — this difficult inheritance plus a complicated set of problems — he more than had his hands full. This chapter is intended primarily to explain how he went about reshaping the grand lodge's policies, and his treatment of new issues as they arose.

In the previous chapter the characteristic strengths and failings of the Wharton approach were analyzed under the heading of "democratic centralism." This approach did not successfully meet the challenges of the National Labor Relations Act or the rise of new local lodge and district lodge power blocs. Because the NLRB exercised an effective voice, as did the CIO unions, in working out jurisdictional disputes, the old AFL executive council's ritual of jurisdiction-making had been radically changed, and grabs for job territory, even within the AFL itself, became less affected by the historical niceties of charter grants. Thus, Wharton's reliance on his friendly contacts with other union leaders in the AFL executive council proved excessive.

This change in the atmosphere of the AFL executive council is too frequently overlooked. At least, in Gompers' time, there had been a belief that the right to a jurisdiction was something more than an open show of force; rather, it was a complex ethical system of definitions of craft hegemonies, phrased in terms of tools, materials, and work processes. But with the rise of the CIO and the contemporaneous emergence of the teamsters and carpenters as dominant AFL unions, the old system, which even then had lost its vitality, became hardly more than a façade.

One factor which had changed only in degree was the attitude of certain employers. In the pre-Wagner Act days, an employer was legally able to choose the union he wanted. This was no longer true after 1935, although the law was occasionally violated in spirit, if not in fact. Within the AFL, which was no longer sovereign in the business of carving jurisdictions, the result was that jurisdictional questions more frequently seemed to be decided along unsophisticated power lines, with unions taking what they could hold.

Perhaps no union was more adversely affected by this change than the IAM. Certainly few unions became more regularly involved in interunion conflicts. This development was inevitable, perhaps, because the IAM had never had more than passably good relations with the Building Trades Department, dominated as it was by the carpenters. Nor was the IAM solidly enough entrenched in the Metal Trades or Railway Employees' departments, to use what strength existed there for its own bargaining advantage with other enclaves in the AFL. So long as Wharton remained active, he did manage to keep the other unions' antagonisms somewhat in check. But once he was off the scene, far more than average tact and guile would have been required to prevent explosions. Brown was not endowed with either of these qualities; moreover, he had a large sense of personal righteousness. Thus, his relationship with the dominant figures of the AFL executive council deteriorated steadily.

The period covered in this chapter involves years when the country was first preparing for, and later fighting, a major war. The most direct effect of this was industrial prosperity of a degree never before known in the United States. It must be remembered, therefore, that at no time was Brown given an opportunity to consolidate his gains, to postpone further actions until he had had time to consider their consequences thoroughly, or to reflect leisurely upon the decisions previously made. Recessions and depressions, unfortunate and disastrous as they are, do offer trade-union leaders a much needed respite, which Brown did not have. He was pitched into one titanic struggle after another. Moreover, very little preparation for the types of conflicts he faced was ever given him.

This chapter chronicles five developments, each related to the others. It seems wisest to tell the most bitter story first, and then to fit the others around it; the others being no less complicated, although less explosive. First we shall consider the history of the IAM's long fight with the AFL. Then we shall discuss the impact of technological and social changes on the union, and the union's rebirth as an industrial organization. Third, we shall turn to the reassertion of grand lodge dominance over the more rebellious and autonomous local lodges — thereby "correcting" Wharton's historical error in handling Local Lodge 68. Fourth, we shall examine developments in the relationships with employers. And finally, we shall turn to the most difficult subject for analysis, the changed nature of the relationship of the IAM to the community at large.

Conflict with the AFL

There had never really been more than an uneasy truce between the carpenters and the IAM after the 1914 expulsion of the IAM from the Building Trades Department. This holds true even in the face of the 1931–1932 agreement between Wharton and Hutcheson, which was annulled at the Cincinnati convention of the AFL in 1932. Thus, the eruption of full-scale warfare was always a possibility, not only because the parties were unwilling to come to full agreement, but because other unions banked on and, indeed, encouraged the incipient IAM–carpenters antagonism, to further their own ends. Harvey Brown seemed to believe that the IAM's will could be made to prevail by the force of his own irrefutable logic. Hence, for several years he tried to demonstrate the carpenters' aggressive intent to the AFL. On the other hand, President Hutcheson of the carpenters did not depend upon logical arguments in jurisdictional matters, knowing that in matters of this sort, votes were what counted. Moreover, he seems to have understood that ethics are frequently operational rather than revelational, and that the ethical implications of his case, so long as his parliamentary motions would carry both in the AFL executive council and in the full AFL convention, would transcend those of the IAM's case.

The open rivalry between the two unions resulted not only from their own differences, but were also a consequence of IAM disagreements with the operating engineers and the street railway men. Open conflict started in February, 1938, when Wharton put through the AFL executive council a short summary of the machinists' jurisdiction, which was to be sent by telegram to any employer trying to determine whether he was to deal with the machinists or some other union contending for the exclusive right to a job.[1]

Wharton's plan went awry the following month, when Hutcheson of the carpenters bluntly told the AFL executive council that his organization would stop paying its per capita tax to the AFL unless President Green ceased using the telegram system. The AFL executive council, responding to the carpenters' threat, ordered Green never to send out the message again without its specific sanction.[2] Naturally the IAM became angry, and all attempts at smoothing out the differences failed.

In December, 1940, Brown by then international president, sent an ultimatum to the AFL executive council — that the council order the carpenters to comply with the old 1914 AFL convention resolution summarizing the IAM jurisdiction (much of which was summarized in the disputed telegram message), or else the IAM would cease to pay its per capita tax to the AFL.[3] The actual issue which tipped the scales was the famous Anheuser–Busch Case (sometimes called the Hutcheson Case). Much to Brown's surprise, the AFL executive council did not quail and capitulate. Consequently the IAM ceased paying its per capita tax.

At this point Brown's strategy was to present the whole issue to the AFL convention in such a way as to emphasize his contention that the carpenters were again threatening a major segment of the IAM jurisdiction. "The position I want to be placed in, if this matter is to be argued before the AFL convention," he wrote to Grand Vice-President Laudeman, "is to be able to tell the convention that the controversy is caused by the carpenters wanting us to give up a part of our trade, and which we are unwilling to do."[4] Laudeman carried on extensive negotiations with the carpenters' leadership, but reached an impasse when it became evident that the basic difference involved a claim to installation work customarily done by millwrights. The machinists wanted that jurisdiction for its own men — the IAM claimed that millwrights frequently handled jobs for which only machinists were trained. Thus, the issue was joined; millwrights were usurping machinists' rights.

After a few months, and on sobering second thought, the IAM resumed payment of its per capita tax in order to qualify for attendance at the AFL 1941 convention. There it sought to convince the delegates that justice demanded that the AFL executive council be ordered to issue the telegram message confirming the IAM jurisdiction. Moreover, the IAM wanted the convention to direct the Building Trades Department to stop interfering in jurisdictional questions involving nonmembers of that department (that is, the IAM). And finally, it wanted to have its jurisdiction regarding the operating engineers and the street car employees' unions, reconfirmed. (The latter unions appear to have joined forces with the carpenters in order to harass the IAM.) Brown was completely unsuccessful in his demands. Evidently believing that the influence and latent power of the carpenters (which he thought he could counter with reason) were the only causes of his troubles, he neglected to note first that Hutcheson actually had the "law" on his side. Hutcheson could therefore point to the AFL constitution, which forbade the convention from acting on any matter that it had referred to the AFL executive council until the executive council had reported back. A whole fabric of jurisdictional relationships had been woven since the time of the 1914 convention's endorsement of the IAM's jurisdiction, and so Brown and the IAM were stymied.[5]

In February, 1943, Brown again asked the AFL executive council to confirm the IAM jurisdiction.[6] The executive council had just fulfilled a similar request for the teamsters, structural iron workers, and the operating engineers. But it refused. His reaction was to call for a referendum vote authorizing the IAM's withdrawal from the AFL.

Although Brown carried the referendum 78,811 to 20,179, the figures are misleading. For the importance of the issue, the vote was believed small; only 20 per cent having cast ballots.[7] More important, however, Brown lacked support in critical quarters; General Vice-President Lyons (Canada), for one, was opposed to withdrawing from the AFL and argued that it would force the IAM to fight a two-front campaign against both the CIO and the AFL. Indeed, General Secretary–Treasurer Davison, no small adversary, was full of doubts about the legality of the whole proceedings. Nonetheless, Brown refused to turn back and took the necessary steps to withdraw the IAM from the AFL on May 31, 1943.

Troubles developed almost immediately; the existence of which was clearly known to the AFL executive council.[8] The big Chicago district lodge intimated quite openly that it might bolt the IAM and affiliate with some AFL union if the separation continued, and the important government workers' district (District Lodge 44), when asked for a vote of confidence by Brown and the grand lodge, refused. Accordingly, Brown concluded that the better part of valor was retreat. In Boston, in the spring of 1943, the IAM quietly withdrew its formal disaffiliation notice and sent in the overdue per capita taxes, presumably having secured a commitment from William Green to do what he could to help the IAM work out its difficulties with the carpenters and the other offending unions. All Green did, however, was to arrange some meetings for the IAM with the leaders of the other unions, and to issue a general letter pointing out that the Building Trades Department had no control over nonmember unions.[9]

Even greater disharmony resulted from these meetings. Hutcheson and the carpenters blatantly insisted that their jurisdiction included the right to work on all goods and processes which involved wood or wood products, as well as the right to install all that they manufactured. On the other hand the operating engineers decided that they were entitled to repair all machinery which they normally operated. In brief, the IAM claimed that it was being "jurisdictionally" squeezed out of existence. Again Green and the AFL executive council tried to reach a reasonable compromise, but no one was ready to abandon any claims.

Brown then decided to hold a convention in order to marshal his forces, and to ascertain the degree to which he could muster membership support. Here again he was thwarted by external events. The Office of Defense Mobilization had ordered the convention put off until the end of the European and Pacific wars.[10] It was not held until late 1945, at which time there was a thorough reappraisal of Brown's policies. In several hours of executive session the whole situation was aired, with both sides given ample opportunity to express themselves. Even William Green was allowed to come, so that he might try to prevent secession.[11]

Brown summarized, in great historical detail, the IAM's difficulties with the carpenters, the Building Trades Department, and the operating engineers. He alleged that the AFL executive council was not amenable to rational argument because it was clearly controlled by four unions (the carpenters, operating engineers, teamsters, and the railway clerks). The possibility of working out a satisfactory solution seemed to him to be hopeless, and he urged the delegates to support his proposal to end the tie with the AFL. As he put it, paying $100,000 annually to an organization intent on ignoring one's rights and humiliating one's representatives was illogical.

Several of the senior general vice-presidents disagreed with Brown. General Vice-President Carr argued that the IAM should remain within the AFL because some hope for redress might develop in time; to be out, would only serve to make negotiations more difficult. To leave the AFL, he implied, was to declare war on everyone, and to be fair game for anyone.

General Vice-President Nickerson, probably more than a little influenced by the pro-teamster views of the Chicago district lodge, felt that it was membership in the AFL which gave the IAM the legitimacy necessary for day-to-day local relationships.[12] Secession would result in big struggles fought on state and local levels. Struggles, he suggested, that the IAM would probably not win.

General Vice-President Lyons, expecting a postwar recession with consequent unemployment, opposed any move toward internecine strife in the labor movement. He felt that the IAM should concentrate its energies on fighting the employers' expected efforts at wage deflation. Moreover, leaving the "security" of the AFL would open the question of subsequent affiliation with the CIO — a step which, he feared, would lead to bitter factionalism within the IAM itself.

Others said much the same thing. General Vice-President Melton voiced fears that the IAM would not be able to handle its isolation from the other segments of the labor movement. Don Burrows, the leader of the Chicago auto mechanics' lodge, suggested that the IAM should do nothing to affect the AFL adversely, irrespective of provocation, while Anthony Ballerini, leader of the San Francisco production workers' local, cited the danger of fighting simultaneously on more than one front. N. P. Alifas, leader of the government workers' District Lodge 44, also was opposed to leaving the AFL and urged that the IAM accept the AFL's terms, remain in the federation, but carry on its fight later when the issues and the times were more propitious.

On the other hand, the younger leadership of the IAM tended to support Brown. General Secretary–Treasurer Peterson did not think it worth paying $100,000 to be humiliated. General Vice-President Newman suggested that it was morally wrong to ally the IAM "with people who stole our virtue." General Vice-Presidents Walker, Brown, and Hayes all felt that withdrawal was the only answer, and that it was conceivable that some sort of victory could be secured. When the vote was taken, the convention recommended ending AFL affiliation. Its action was later endorsed in the post-convention referendum, and the bond was broken.[13]

Shortly thereafter the IAM was expelled from the Metal Trades Department as well as many state and local labor federations. John Frey, president of the Metal Trades Department, even urged IAM members to resign from the now "isolated" union and to join federal locals, directly chartered by the AFL.[14] Of course, more cautious views did prevail. Frey, himself, was quicker to speak than to act. Although the IAM was driven from state and local labor federations, this was more in name than in fact. The IAM was permitted to "remain in the house of labor" until the expiration of the existent contracts, jointly signed by it and other unions with employers.

Brown was thus placed in a most difficult position. He had advocated leaving the AFL. In fact, he chose to bear the major part of the responsibility for the final action.[15] Yet, it was obvious that some attempt should be made to compose differences before the IAM would really become an outcast. Part of the answer was to set up an IAM bargaining committee which would earn the confidence of the various factions.[16] The committee included Carr and Nickerson (both having opposed the withdrawal), and Peterson and Hayes (who had supported Brown). Another part of the answer was to try to convince the AFL leadership that the IAM did not "need" the AFL as much as the AFL needed it. This was done by attempting to secure a resounding majority in a 1947 referendum disaffiliation vote; however, only 21 per cent of the membership voted. In the meantime the AFL, although maintaining a slight pressure to isolate the IAM, took conscious care not to carve up its traditional jurisdiction. A third part of the answer was to formulate the bedrock terms which the IAM would insist upon in future negotiations. These terms consisted of having the AFL executive council admit the IAM's right to construction work and to the repair of automotive vehicles, and of having the council rescind the letter sent by Green on the council's authorization, giving the operating engineers the right to man the machinery on ships during their trial runs.

Here the matter rested. Brown was not able to effect re-entry, although he and all his supporters on the IAM executive council recognized the difficulty of trying to maintain their position. Later in 1950, after Brown had retired as international president, and when the carpenters' influence in the AFL had begun to wane, Hayes, Brown's successor, led the IAM back into the AFL. Hayes's action was supported by a referendum vote of 87,852 to 23,579. This development will be discussed in the next chapter.

In retrospect it is hard to see just what Brown could have done to avoid friction. The salient facts are that the carpenters and operating engineers were aggressive, as were the machinists. Brown might have realized that his opponents' unassailability would be taken care of by time. Just as Wharton's retirement weakened the IAM's influence, so the passing of the older Hutcheson would do the same for the carpenters. But it is a rare man who can keep historical perspective about his own times. Yet time was on the side of the IAM, and within a few years these changes came to pass. Thus, it seems clear that Brown's insistence on a formal resolution of the problem was unwise. On the other hand, all this must not becloud the clear fact that the IAM was poorly treated by the AFL executive council. Even if the excuse were political circumstances, one could not expect a growing organization with a proud tradition to accept it meekly.

The New IAM

The change of the IAM to industrial unionism was the most significant development during the years of Brown's presidency. Factors affecting developments in this direction had already occurred prior to his accession, but they were accentuated considerably during his incumbency. In the previous chapter we indicated that one of the basic causes for the shift was the passage of the Wagner Act, giving a governmental body an effective voice in the determination of jurisdiction, and thereby taking from the labor movement and employers their plenary authority. Another factor undoubtedly was the existence of aggressive CIO organizing teams, for without them much of the motivation for changing the character of craft unions would not have existed. One writer aptly refers to this as competitive unionism.[17] To extend his analogy, we suggest that the NLRB provided the "market" in which competitive unionism flourished, and that the effect of competition was originally to homogenize the product. In turn, it leveled the producers (that is, the unions "selling" representation service).

During Brown's years in office, however, other factors accelerated the speed of the shift. The Second World War caused a rapid change to full employment in the metal trades industries, and the building of plants both in formerly small industries (that is, aircraft, shipbuilding, and munitions), and in formerly nonindustrialized communities. Thus the union was confronted with a vastly increased opportunity for bargaining. But it also faced the difficult problem of trying to handle a labor force with little or no general experience in the ways of unionism, and particularly, in the IAM. The obvious result was a compromise — the IAM had to accelerate its rate of change to industrial unionism by de-emphasizing its old shibboleth of craft solidarity, and the new membership had to acquire a willingness to tolerate, if not actually follow, the craftsmen's leadership. These adaptations required patience, forbearance, and even luck, and it is not surprising that the IAM was unable to organize under its hegemony all to whom it had an AFL-authorized claim.

To clarify this point further the new industries were developed under full-employment conditions, with considerable upgrading of personnel. The result was that the line between the "journeyman" and the "helper" or "production worker" all but disappeared. Consequently, it was impossible to draw the type of classification line between the skilled and the unskilled, which the IAM had traditionally used to distinguish itself from purely industrial unions. In other words, "dilution of the trade" (to use the British expression) served to minimize the effects of craft consciousness largely because many of the new craftsmen had not enjoyed the status long enough to demand the privilege "normally pertaining thereunto." The integration of diverse social types into the union also contributed to the speedy change in attitudes. The rapid expansion of war-time industries involved the incorporation of not only unskilled white, urban males, but also the incorporation of Negroes, females, and rural workers. Educating them in the ways of unionism had the result of affecting the teacher (the IAM administration) as well.

The IAM had to make a choice of retaining its craft character, or expanding in the direction of industrial unionism. It resolved to expand. The choice was originally presented at the 1934 San Francisco convention when Hutcheson of the carpenters agreed to give the IAM nominal hegemony over the aircraft manufacturing industry. His willingness to do so probably attests to his estimate of the difficulty of organizing that industry, more than to any innate generosity, but whatever the cause, the outcome of the IAM's decision to organize the aircraft industry was a further step toward industrialization.

This is not meant to imply that there were no counterforces. The old-time craftsmen in the organization had great fear of losing control. To protect their relative position, they resisted attempts to force them to take unskilled and semiskilled members into their locals, preferring that the grand lodge organize separate lodges for the new members. A concomitant development was the renewed assertion of local autonomy, retaining for the established craft-oriented units their accustomed control over their own policies. The attitude of these old locals was not irrationally selfish. Many, remembering the First World War aftermath, were duly hesitant about a too rapid increase in membership, when the newcomers would not be experienced unionists.

The result was a curious type of adjustment. Many of the railroad locals (where there was little opportunity for expansion) clung to the old ways, while many of the automotive and contract shop locals, already accustomed to heterogeneity in membership types, took the initiative in incorporating the new membership. These automotive and contract shop groups provided the leadership for organizing drives, and, taking a leaf from the CIO's book of experience, relied to a much greater extent upon NLRB elections than AFL tradition was wont to encourage. In addition, whenever possible, IAM leaders tried to secure a basic agreement with many managements, taking advantage of management's distaste for the CIO.

Within a very few years the IAM clearly ceased to be primarily a craft-oriented organization. True, the dominant type of leader was one who had come up through the railroad shops, but despite this, the typical leader was now no longer overwhelmingly committed to craft principles. It is worth adding that the experience under the Railway Labor Act made the use of the NLRB organizing process somewhat easier, for these leaders having had experience with the Railway Labor Acts of 1926 and 1934 were not averse to using governmental agencies whenever it seemed simpler to do so.

The change from craft to industrial orientation happened in four ways.

The first was in the increased number of unskilled and semiskilled members. As had been the experience in 1918, the change in the relative number of journeymen did not immediately make a difference in policies. The journeymen, by continuing to play their old active role in the organization, for some time exercised a voice disproportionately large for their number. But as the number of nonjourneymen increased, it became more and more difficult for the old group to retain its effectiveness, although as long as it could, it held on to critical positions in the grand lodge. At the same time many old type locals fought to retain local autonomy to reduce the policy changes wrought by the grand lodge.

A second change was in the area of union–employer negotiations. Here, the tendency was toward bargaining centralization — that is, plant-wide and industry-wide contracts. Once more the same paradox appears. The grand lodge, run by craft-trained individuals with a new orientation, was opposed by the craft-oriented lodges because the latter feared the future. The grand lodge overcame much of the resistance, and set standards for new contracts, even if it did not negotiate them.

The third change involved the government. If the IAM were to use the NLRB, it had to try to exercise influence behind the scenes. This could best be done by lobbying within Congress. The immediate necessity became one of political action. Here, however, the change was not thwarted by the old railroad lodges, for they, too, had much earlier seen a similar need in their own negotiations. As a result there was no resistance to the marked shift toward political lobbying and political education.

The final change resulting from the new orientation dealt with the union's public relations program. Such cherished traditions as the "whites only" clause in the ritual became an expensive luxury. No state which had passed fair employment practice acts could be sympathetic to any semiprivate organization which defeated this legislation. Although the old membership was reluctant to let this particular tradition go, many of the newer locals were taking in Negro members. It was debated in convention after convention, but invariably the resolution was negative; the majority of the delegates remained adamant. Eventually the grand lodge, actually the executive council, using a self-authorized power, struck out the offending clause despite convention refusal to do so.[18] Thus, the handling of the fourth change was resolved by an extension of the same grand lodge authority involved in the second.

The Airplane Industry

The history of the IAM's efforts in organizing the aircraft manufacturing industry contains several strange elements.[19] From the beginning, the industry had used its romantic aura to attract and hold part of its labor force; although, to be sure, since the Second World War much of that aura has been lost. In the early thirties, however, the romance was still there. In fact, there seems to be good reason to believe that the first steps in organizing that industry came about only when the romantic tradition in the aircraft industry came into contact with a similar one in the cinema industry. It was in 1933 when a few aircraft workers were helping in Howard Hughes' film, *Hell's Angels.* When they saw what the technicians and workers had managed to accomplish in the movie industry as a result of union activity, they became interested in developing a union of their own.

Unfortunately their efforts became mired in the conflict over jurisdiction among various AFL international, as well as federal, unions, and many of the men became disheartened. At the Douglas plant an independent union was established, which later affiliated with the UAW–CIO. The men at Northrop, as at Douglas in California, also went to the UAW–CIO. But when Homer Martin, the UAW leader, left the CIO for the AFL, they went with him.[20]

In the meantime the IAM had succeeded in establishing what seemed initially to be a fairly stable organization in Seattle at the Boeing plant, Local Lodge 751. Because of the apparent stability of the Boeing relationship, the Lockheed Company reconsidered its earlier anti-IAM attitude and refrained from fighting the IAM's organization of some of its plants.

By 1940 the IAM had contracts with Boeing in Seattle, as well as with Lockheed and Consolidated in southern California. It was trying to get recognition at North American and Douglas. All was not well in the industry, however.

In mid-1940 the Boeing local sought new concessions from the management. The management countered with a suggestion that jobs be reclassified and rates of some grades be cut. The local asked the grand lodge for sanction to strike. The grand lodge was hesitant because interruption of military defense production would result. The Boeing management had in its employ many German-trained engineers, products of Anthony Fokker's First World War, and post-First World War, plants. Quite a few of these men were avowedly pro-Nazi. On the other hand, the union local was dominated by several pro-Communists. Neither group was very eager to see rapid strides being made in the production of military aircraft. The grand lodge was powerless to handle the pro-Nazi problem, but it could, and did, try to clean up the Communist nest. Acting upon the authorization of the executive council, International President Brown sent a grand lodge representative to Seattle to organize a clean-up. A trial committee was appointed, and it soon became evident that the degree of Communist penetration was too great to permit the situation to be handled in the normal manner. The executive council then intervened, suspended the local's charter, and took over the running of the trial proceedings.[21] Almost fifty members were found guilty of subversion (that is, being advocates of Communism, an affiliation outlawed at the 1928 convention); each was fined $1000 and expelled. Nine more were fined $25.00 but not expelled; charges against thirteen others were dismissed.

The extent of the Communist infiltration into one of its relatively new locals naturally worried the grand lodge. The executive council decided on a course of action designed to prevent similar episodes from occurring at Boeing or elsewhere in the aircraft industry. It provided that when the charter was returned to local control, the local would be effectively divided into several political subsections. Each subsection was to carry the old number 751, and, in addition a letter suffix (751A, etc.). Together all would make up a district lodge (District Lodge 751). In this way it would be easier for the grand lodge to keep an eye on developments. Each unit would of course be smaller than the old local had been, and there would be far greater opportunity for individual recognition and participation. This idea seemed to work effectively, and the locals of the two other aircraft firms organized by the IAM were similarly divided (District Lodge 727 at Lockheed, and District Lodge 1125 at Consolidated).

Unionization of the aircraft industry did not proceed easily. Many of the workers were inexperienced in unionism and were easy targets for demagogues. Their living conditions were often bad, and they had virtually no pride in craft. Even worse, assignments relating to shifts, shops, and even plants were frequently changed for production-control reasons. And in many instances, no sooner had a man become well enough known to be elected shop delegate, than his seniority made him eligible to be reassigned to another location, or shift, at an increased rate of pay. Consequently, it was difficult for the union to develop stable internal local leadership. In many senses this development paralleled the First World War defense plant experience, but in this instance the grand lodge exercised great care to keep control over the development of local autonomy. Whenever an insurgent group, led either by Communists or by pro-radical elements, appeared to be gaining control, the grand lodge suspended the charter and handled all matters through one of its own representatives. The result was that while the mushrooming industry did contain many elements of instability, the situation was not impossible on the whole.

One development out of the experience of organizing the aircraft industry was the appearance of a new type of IAM staff individual. For the most part he did not come out of the railroad shops, but from old contract locals. His sense of craft orientation differed from the one traditionally associated with railroad machinists. He was more flexible (less precedent-conscious) in his choice of means. In some ways he seemed to be indistinguishable from his counterpart in the UAW–CIO, but because the two organizations had vastly different organizational histories, it is easy to see that the role of the IAM's staff representative was not really identical with the other. In the aircraft industry, where the IAM was equally new, the organizing and administrative patterns were more nearly alike than in any other sector. During the war the IAM also tried to organize some of the aircraft plants for which the UAW–CIO had sought recognition as well as some that had resisted both unions' attempts. For several months in 1942 the IAM spent over $1800 monthly on organizing at the Douglas Long Beach (California) plant, as well as almost $20,000 at the Glenn Martin plant in Baltimore, and a somewhat smaller amount at Bell in Buffalo and Atlanta.[22] It did score some success in the Douglas campaign. There was suspicion regarding the NLRB's tabulation of ballots; the IAM believed that it had won several elections, where the NLRB certified the UAW–CIO. In any event, by 1943 the IAM had been recognized only at the Douglas El Segundo plant.

By the end of 1943 the UAW–CIO tried to end its bitter organizing competition with the IAM.[23] It is to be recalled that this was the time when the IAM was moving out of the AFL. Although there were rumors that talks were held regarding a merger of the two organizations, all that evolved was an agreement to refrain from raiding each other's NLRB-certified territories for the duration of the war. The agreement was not immediately extended at the war's end because Brown suspected that the UAW–CIO intended to conduct large-scale organizing operations in the automobile service and repair business. By that time (1945), the IAM was back in the AFL (for the moment), and the grand lodge referred to the auto workers as "the dual labor movement."[24] During the rest of Brown's administration no new accord was reached, although it is obvious that toward the end, attempts were made by the CIO. Brown's successor, A. J. Hayes, signed an enlarged no-raiding agreement, going well beyond the wartime arrangement in 1949 and then again in 1954.[25] Later in 1948 and 1949 the teamsters conducted a major raid on the Boeing Seattle plant.[26] Shortly beforehand, the Boeing district lodge had insisted on striking in the wake of declining production and had lost the strike, with the men forced to return to work on the company's terms. The company, motivated by what seems to have been a desire to have Dave Beck's union (the teamsters) represent their employees, petitioned the NLRB to decertify the IAM. Pending the subsequent NLRB election the company pursued a hiring policy calculated to increase teamster representation in the Seattle plant. The IAM responded by putting forth a Herculean effort. The IAM saved its certification, and District Lodge 751 remained active. Beck, it should be added, got at least a limited endorsement from the AFL executive council — but this was at a time when AFL President Green was trying to pressure the IAM to negotiate with the AFL.

As the decade passed, the relative importance of the membership in the aircraft industry increased; by 1950 it was the largest single element in the IAM. Because it was industrially organized, its needs and its practices became one of the prime factors shaping union policy. It is interesting to compare this development with what had occurred during the Johnston administration, when there was a concerted policy to "industrialize" the union. Earlier it had not worked because the employers, not being compelled to deal with the union, broke off negotiations as soon as governmental contract work was completed and they were able to revert entirely to their own decisions. After 1937 it succeeded largely because of the NLRB certification process, forcing the employers to deal with the union chosen by their employees.

The Assertion of Grand Lodge Dominance

In the previous chapter we discussed the handling of the 1934–1935 "revolt" by Local Lodge 284 in Oakland, California, and how its cause was espoused by Local Lodge 68 of San Francisco. The narrative ended with the 1936 convention, where Edward Dillon, the delegate from Local Lodge 68, was defeated by Wharton — but only on the Local Lodge 284 matter. Our conclusion was that Wharton had erred, and that in failing to come to grips with Local Lodge 68, he had seriously weakened the grand lodge's control of the union.

By 1939 the continuing friction between Local Lodge 68 and Washington headquarters was clearly apparent when the executive council refused to approve Dillon's appointment as business agent. An allegation, attributed to Wharton, was that Dillon was "high up in the councils of the Communist Party." [27] Nonetheless Dillon did become a business agent, although without grand lodge funds.

In March, 1941, Local Lodge 68 sought sanction to strike the shipyards in the Bay area. Limited sanction was given, to take effect only if, and when, a particular shipbuilder refused to sign the area master agreement, which had to be worked out without a general work stoppage. Nonetheless the local called a strike.[28] President Roosevelt then intervened and asked Brown and the grand lodge to call off the strike in order to restore production. The grand lodge was far from convinced at this point that the strike was simply the local's fault, but it withdrew all sanction. Bowing to the combination of pressures, Local Lodge 68 sent its members back to work. Brown decided to travel to the Bay area and survey the situation personally.

He found that Local Lodge 68 was acting as a law to itself. It still insisted that those who had refused to pay the Local Lodge 284 illegal strike assessment could not be readmitted to membership. Moreover, Messrs. Hook and Dillon (the latter being paid entirely from Local 68 funds) were working closely with the suspended Local Lodge 284 group (then chartered as Local 1304 SWOC–CIO). In fact, so great was this cooperation that it was correctly said that the two unions were collaborating to the detriment of all other IAM locals in the area. Brown formally asked Local Lodge 68 to refrain from "further assisting or cooperating with Local 1304 SWOC–CIO and in future cooperate in every way with [the new IAM] Local Lodge 284 and other IAM lodges in the Oakland area." There is no indication that his request was honored.

In 1944 Local Lodge 68, seeking to apply pressure to the War Labor Board in regard to some wage issues before it, refused to permit any of its members to work overtime until the War Labor Board had processed its claim.[29] The War Labor Board refused to knuckle under and ordered Local Lodge 68 to rescind its ban. Again Brown and the grand lodge were in the position of having to crack down on Local Lodge 68 at the request of governmental authorities. And again Brown's intervention went largely ignored. All Brown could do was write to Undersecretary (of War) Patterson, Admiral Land, and Donald Nelson complaining that the War Labor Board had not handled the matter diplomatically, that the grand lodge had asked Local Lodge 68 to comply, but that there was an old IAM tradition of local autonomy, making the grand lodge powerless to take stronger steps.

After the surrender of Japan in August, 1945, the conflict between the grand lodge and the local officers reached a climax when Dillon asked the executive council for strike sanction. Brown replied the next month by asking Dillon whether Local Lodge 68 was planning its negotiation approach to the California Metal Trades Association in cooperation with the old 284 (now Local 1304 SWOC–CIO). Dillon replied to Brown's letter, but not to the question. Keeping in mind Dillon's record of capriciousness, Brown and the executive council agreed to consider Dillon's application for strike sanction only if Local Lodge 68 took the prescribed type of strike vote, ceased collaborating with Local 1304 SWOC–CIO, refrained from violating the Pacific Coast Master Agreement, and complied with the War Labor Disputes Act. Local Lodge 68, realizing how unpopular Dillon was with the grand lodge, sent Hook and one of his associates to persuade the executive council to abandon this stringent position. It refused to do so, and when Local Lodge 68 went on strike, grand lodge authorization was denied. Brown and the executive council went to San Francisco early in 1946.

In the meantime District Lodge 115, also of San Francisco, had agreed to a contract with the California Metal Trades Association involving a 15 per cent wage increase, six paid holidays, and two weeks paid vacation. But in January, 1946, Local Lodge 68 rejected these terms and asked for elimination of all wartime special production clauses, a 23 per cent wage increase, a starting rate for apprentices of 52 per cent of the journeymen's rate, a liberal vacation schedule depending upon length of service, and a wage reopener for September, 1946. Brown thought that the District Lodge 115 terms were quite liberal and asked Dillon to have his men discuss them as a basis for their contract. Dillon ignored the suggestion, and so the grand lodge on its own called a meeting of the members of Local Lodge 68 for February 26, 1946, to discuss the terms. Dillon and his associates forbade the members to attend. The executive council then took the action Wharton should have taken years before and suspended Local Lodge 68 as well as many of the key figures within it. The executive council noted that the strike had never been authorized, that it had not been called off when strike sanction had been categorically refused, that Local Lodge 68 had aided and abetted Local 1304 SWOC–CIO in defiance of orders to the contrary, and that the officers and leaders of Local Lodge 68 had thwarted the grand lodge's meeting of February 26.

Local Lodge 68 did not respond as the executive council would have wanted. The local refused to appear at the trial, retitling itself instead the (independent) Machinists' Lodge 68. The grand lodge, however, acted swiftly and blocked all the bank accounts of suspended Local Lodge 68 and declared the illegal strike off. At the trial subsequently conducted by the executive council, Local Lodge 68 was found guilty and its charter was indefinitely suspended. Machinists' Lodge 68 had previously tried to turn the charter in voluntarily, but the grand lodge refused to jeopardize its position and allowed no face-saver. Hook and Dillon were fined $1000 and expelled. Thus ended the autonomy of the most autonomous local in the IAM. Two years later the members of Local Lodge 68 (now under trusteeship) asked for the return of their charter. At that time the request was turned down, but later during Hayes's administration the charter was given back.[30]

It is important to realize the significance of the action taken against Local Lodge 68. In Wharton's time the executive council had been wilfully blind to that local's activities, and by refusing to see, it had condoned a wilful and flagrant violation of the IAM's governmental process. Local Lodge 68 had repeatedly struck at the several most fundamental principles of American trade unionism; that is, disregarding the rules for declaring strikes, cooperating with a dual union, and punishing those members who refused to comply with the conspiratorial directives. All these "mortal" sins had gone virtually unpunished during Wharton's administration, and were not really dealt with in a serious fashion until the end of the Second World War. Several hypotheses have been suggested to explain why strong action was not taken earlier. From 1934 through 1936, there is reason to believe that the executive council, influenced in good measure by General Secretary–Treasurer Davison, believed that the trouble was caused by personal antagonism between Wharton and the San Francisco leaders. Thus the executive council was unwilling to sanction strong action against the local, believing that time would straighten out the difficulties. If this were the hypothesis, time showed it to be erroneous.

A second explanation refers to the events of 1941. It alleges that the San Francisco group was dominated by Communists, and that a showdown would have occurred in 1941 had not Hitler turned on Stalin just when the shipyard crises began to mount. The implication was clearly that Soviet Russia's needs, rather than America's, were determining factors. But this explanation does not really cover the militancy at the end of the war (1944–1945), when the Communist line was peaceful labor relations with the union at any price, quite the opposite of what Local Lodge 68 advocated.

The most satisfying explanation is the one which suggests that little more than a tradition of fierce autonomy was involved. San Francisco, geographically separated from the east, prefers to live in isolation from national movements. Local Lodge 68 is representative of the California attitude. Its members were loyal to it even though their work carried them from San Francisco to the Middle East (Saudi Arabia) or to far Pacific islands. Seen in this light, what were the issues? The grand lodge wanted to dictate local policy with very little knowledge of local situations. The European war was not as immediate a question in 1941 in the west as it was in Washington. And finally, who knew better how to negotiate with the California Metal Trades Association than those who had been doing it for decades? Thus, a reasonable excuse could be constructed for the actions of Dillon, Hook, and company. But this rationale depended upon the assumption that Local Lodge 68 was in fact isolated, and that its activities would not materially affect other less powerful locals or the organization's national structure. By 1945 it was clear that California was economically more integrated with the east than it had been before the Second World War. In addition, federal rather than state labor policy prevailed throughout the country, having the immediate effect of limiting the tradition of local autonomy. In other words, it was clear that the conditions which had earlier made for local autonomy were no longer present. Thus Brown and the executive council could not possibly have winked at what was going on in the Bay area, even if Wharton had done so. So one can see that the passage of the Wagner Act and the establishment of the War Labor Board had done more than inaugurate a new epoch of industrial unionism, it had made American unions integrate the policies pursued by their locals. Barnett, Slichter, Dunlop, and Ulman have all noted the economic factors causing the development of the national union.[31] The Wagner Act, particularly its certification procedures, was a political factor aimed at the same result, but speeding up the process considerably.

Wharton should have cracked down on Local Lodge 68 in the mid-thirties. His not doing so was an error in judgment, but it did not seem at the time to be a step toward disaster. Had Brown refrained from cracking down, it is probable that the consequences to the whole IAM would have been considerable. It is important to reiterate the major conclusion. The Local Lodge 68 episode was the normal outgrowth of craft unionism which permitted considerable autonomy. The disposition of the 1944–1946 incident was virtually mandatory because of the major changes resulting from the passage of the Wagner Act and the implementation of a federal labor policy under the aegis of the War Labor Board. The significance of the suspension of Local Lodge 68 lies not so much in the fact that a rebellious faction was severely punished, as it does in the lesson it taught all other locals with aspirations for autonomous isolation.

It is entirely possible that the whole Local Lodge 68 mess would never have developed had Wharton acted differently from 1934 through 1936. But if we realize that the importance of Brown's actions is not in the "correcting" of Wharton's mistake alone, but is an illustration of the type of change in American unionism engendered by a "positive" federal labor policy, then the full meaning of what occurred becomes apparent. From a historic viewpoint, the disciplining of that San Francisco local marks a major step toward the end of the fine tradition of local self-determination. Our point is not that Hook and Dillon ran a popular, democratic organization, but that decisions were made locally. Brown and his executive council realized that the IAM could not suffer this cost if the burden fell on other locals. Consequently, they had to act.

The IAM and Public Labor Policy

We have been considering the effect of the development of federal labor policy on traditional local autonomy, and have concentrated on the irresistible force of a national labor policy on an allegedly immovable object like economically-oriented, autonomous, local unionism. This development of a federal labor policy under the Roosevelt administration was not the only shift to "the method of legal enactment" occurring during the period. The various states developed their own policies. These are well described in Charles Killingsworth's *State Labor Relations Acts* and several other sources.[32] Of course, the switch to the method of legal enactment involved a considerable reorientation of time-honored techniques. One obvious change was the whole IAM experience vis-à-vis leaving the AFL, since with the protection afforded by the Wagner Act, a union could exist outside of an established labor federation.

Another obvious change was the increased attention directed toward influencing Congress and the various state legislatures. In the last section of this chapter we shall discuss the significance of increasing the union's political consciousness on the national level. Here we are concerned with what transpired on the state level.

Brown and his executive council had great doubts about the desirability of developing state-wide IAM lobbying bodies. Nonetheless these bodies did develop in response to the need for directing legislative developments. As early as 1939 the Oregon "Machinists' Council" sent the grand lodge a set of bylaws for approval; it was not forthcoming because the executive council claimed that there was no constitutional authority for such an organization.[33] By the war's end, however, quite a few of these "councils" were operating. They were duly authorized at the 1945 convention, but even then the executive council remained doubtful and did what it could to discourage their development because the councils were rallying points within the IAM governmental structure for anti-grand lodge factions. The most that the grand lodge could do, however, to minimize their influence was to limit their activities to strictly political programs. In other words, these councils were forbidden to handle economic questions or topics involving jurisdictional matters.

Perhaps no state council gave the grand lodge more trouble than New York. It should be remembered that District Lodge 15 in New York City had both radical and pro-O'Connell elements — in fact that was the combination making up the so-called "Catholic" party in the early twenties. The dominant figure in the New York state council was one Robert Schrank, who at the beginning of our story was considered to be "friendly" by Brown.[34] Schrank, however, had many enemies within some of the New York City locals, who used their influence at grand lodge headquarters to put District 15 under trusteeship in 1945. At that time the grand lodge deposed Peabody, a regularly elected business representative, who refused to accept his displacement "gracefully." Brown had set aside a District Lodge 15 vote of acquittal on charges of malfeasance. Thereafter Peabody sought and was granted injunctive relief from Brown's order.

Throughout this time Schrank, who had opposed Peabody, was enjoying solid grand lodge support, particularly from General Vice-President Newman, who ran the New York territory. Schrank finally arranged a testimonial dinner for Newman, not only to honor Newman but to create an opportunity for asserting his own leadership in the area. The relationship between Schrank and the grand lodge deteriorated when Brown became aware that Schrank opposed the move to leave the AFL, and when FBI reports indicated that Schrank was a Communist. Brown went to a meeting of the New York state council to question Schrank, whose answers were evasive. After the passage of the Taft–Hartley Act, Schrank wrote a pamphlet not only criticizing that legislation, but also condemning Brown for signing the non-Communist affidavit. This made the break complete, and a new bitter fight was on. In April 1948 Brown wrote a formal letter to Schrank in which he said that Schrank was a liar — since he had denied ever having been a Communist, when it was a known fact that he had been one. The letter noted that at a later date Schrank had even privately admitted to Brown that he had lied, but, the letter added, the admission was publicly presented in such fashion as to cast suspicion on Brown's veracity. And Schrank's pamphlet, which was issued only after it had been partly rewritten, still "contain[ed] a veiled criticism directed against the International Association of Machinists." These were the reasons given by Brown for suspending Schrank as president of Local Lodge 402 and as president of the New York state council of machinists.

Local Lodge 402 not only stood behind its erstwhile president, but went to court to question Brown's right to suspend anyone prior to a hearing. The local lodge implied that Brown's order was a result of Schrank's victory over Brown's program in the New York area, and that Brown, having failed to silence Schrank the "legitimate" way (through elections), was now using an improper method. The grand lodge's case was not well prepared, and in at least two instances, the courts directed the grand lodge to withdraw its submissions for reasons of legal error.

Eventually the whole issue was passed on to the Grand Rapids convention, which debated it thoroughly. Brown was deeply involved in the matter, and lost no time in putting forth his side. In due course both Schrank and Local Lodge 402 were given the opportunity to answer all charges, and for reasons that seem to confirm that Brown was substantively right, refused to do so. The matter was put to a vote, and Local Lodge 402 was found guilty of impugning the motives and character of Harvey Brown. The convention also voted to instruct the executive council to take over the administration of the lodge. Finally the convention found Schrank guilty of similar offenses and voted to expel him.

Thus, although the matter ended as a nominal victory for Brown, he paid a heavy price for his participation. It was the last convention before his retirement and he had chosen (more precisely, had been forced) to make the convention choose between him or his assailants. From a procedural viewpoint, his actions were without shrewdness, much less skill. It would have been far better had Newman or some other member of the executive council brought the charges, so that Brown could have played the role of spectator. As it was, Brown was in every sense a committed litigant, and as such, his position was being continually challenged. In this sense, his pugnacious personality did not serve his personal interest. It also tended to obfuscate the most important issue in the case.

Putting aside consideration of both Brown's personal role and the general question of technical procedure, what can be said of the episode? The facet most neglected in the discussion was the prominence of the New York state council. What Brown was originally trying to do was to keep the "conciliar movement" from developing into an important administrative unit within the organization. The councils, if allowed to prosper, could both afford nonadministration voices an opportunity to present their views before a great number of lodges, and could shift union concentration from economic to political matters. In 1947 the executive council declared that the state councils could not institute referenda, although they could pass resolutions regarding federal legislation.[35] Moreover, when the New England states' conference (and "interstate council") took upon itself the responsibility of debating the desirability of a pension plan for rank-and-file members, the grand lodge told it to mind its own business. Later when that same body discussed the grand lodge's handling of the Schrank affair (he had good friends), the grand lodge, through General Vice-President Newman ordered it to be indefinitely recessed for *ultra vires* action. Brown and the executive council, having ratified Newman's order, for what appears to be simple political advantage, then withdrew it. The convention was approaching, and a gag over the mouth of any debating body would call down the wrath of the convention delegates. The convention voted to establish lines of reference for procedure in councils, and conferences for handling charges against them.[36] Brown wanted to keep the organization, job- or economy-oriented. And although he had to recognize the increasingly important role of legal enactment, he was wary of letting the politics-first movement develop to the detriment of the economic. The point here is perhaps complex: Brown was opposed to the development of councils or politically oriented conferences because he saw in them the basis for an undesirable concentration on political matters. Nonetheless, the passage of much state and federal industrial relations legislation required increased attention to legislative matters. The solution, therefore, seemed to be to create lobbying bodies, but to restrict them to legislative enactment. So long as they could not consider any other matter, it was relatively easy to retain for the conventional subbodies (the local, district, and grand lodges), the determining voices in basic policies. Where the local lodge was too small to cover a market (considering a railroad as a product market unit), the district lodge had been encouraged to fill the breach. And when, as a result of both economic and political changes, the nation commenced to turn into one single product and factor market unit, the grand lodge naturally tended to assume an increasingly important role. Thus, Brown believed that there was danger in letting state or interstate political units grow any stronger. Schrank threatened to promote another source of power (as Easton had done years before). Whether the Schrank dispute was caused by radicalism, charges of prevarication, or something else, the fight served the grand lodge's purpose of asserting its suzerainty.

In retrospect, the grand lodge during Brown's administration clearly exhibited its jealousy toward other levels in the organization. The Local Lodge 68 episode was the culmination of a long dispute about local autonomy. In this sense Brown finished a major chapter in the organization's development. In cutting off the challenges offered by the New York state council and the New England states' conference, he prevented episodes of serious proportion from dveloping.

Relationships with Employers

Brown was international president at a time when relationships with employers were in an easy phase. During the Second World War a sense of wartime urgency overcame the usual concern for cost reduction. And during the postwar period there was such a high level of economic activity, that employers worried far more about holding their labor forces than they did about wage rates and wage costs.

There were, however, additional developments during this period, which are worth noting. First, the grand lodge expanded its own role in the shaping of labor contracts with employers; it intervened more frequently and to a greater degree, particularly through its representation on wartime labor agencies. Second, after 1940 the IAM took an increasingly positive attitude toward the establishment of additional apprenticeship-training programs, not only because it felt a need to express a significant interest in the economic future of the industries within which it was operating, but also because it needed an expanding supply of journeymen to preserve its own union traditions.[37] Historically, it should be recalled that the IAM like other unions had feared the proliferation of apprentices. Employers were loath to invest in the training of a young man, who, upon completion of this training, would so often leave to work for another employer. The union was hesitant in urging the training of apprentices, but by 1940, there was a pressing fear that there would be so few journeymen in the industry who had matured through the apprentice system, that the union, itself, would suffer.

Consequently in 1941 the union took steps to coordinate its policy with that of the Federal Commission on Apprenticeship, in order to increase the number of apprentices. The eventual policy provided for joint employer–IAM committees, expansion of age limits for trainees to include those between sixteen and thirty-five years of age, length of the apprenticeship period to be 8000 hours with a probationary period of 1000 hours, and pay to be increased so that by the end of the 8000 hours the apprentices would secure the full rates given to journeymen — with graduated wage steps based on 1000 hours of training being incorporated in each plan. For every 1000 hours on the job there were to be 144 class room hours. The IAM offered to waive its own rule limiting the number of apprentices for every ten journeymen for the duration of the war, if this plan were accepted by employers. The grand lodge's importance was spelled out in other ways too.

After the war in 1947, the IAM partly revised the approach.[38] It defined twelve areas of the machinists' trade: (1) general machinist, (2) tool and die maker, (3) maintenance and erecting machinists, (4) auto mechanics, (5) automotive machineshop men, (6) automotive body and fender shop men, (7) auto body builders, (8) road and construction machinery men, (9) aircraft service mechanics, (10) cash register repairmen, (11) business machine repairmen, and (12) farm equipment service mechanics. But for these twelve different areas, four types of apprenticeship training would suffice — (1) general machinist, (2) tool and die maker, (3) auto mechanic, and (4) aircraft mechanic.

In acknowledging the division of the craft into four parts, the IAM was, in effect, further emancipating itself from the ties that bound it to its old railroad machinist tradition; it had become a cosmopolitan organization. But this change marked more than a mere disintegration of the former craft exclusiveness, because by initiating plans for a broad-gauged comprehensive apprenticeship program covering many industries, the union was widening its range of interests.

In the early war years the grand lodge decided that it would have to handle most of the cases arising out of grievances in defense plants, in order to circumvent a policy decision taken at the 1940 convention; where it was decided to permit everyone in a local lodge to vote on specific strike actions, once uniform standards had been written into the local lodge constitutions. This Populist maneuver, undoubtedly a reaction to the grand lodge and Local Lodge 68 fracas, had the economic rationale of recognizing the need to standardize conditions in the factor market. Nonetheless, it was administratively unworkable, and the grand lodge, itself, processed what would have been strike-causing issues. In 1941 the executive council spelled out the procedures to be used by local organizations on "sincerely cooperative employers," but that step proved insufficient.[39] For a brief time the council directed that arbitration be used to forestall strikes, but that order was rescinded.

Early in 1942 the executive council enunciated the IAM's policy on overtime:

> Where no stagger system is in effect, time in excess of 8 hours and work performed on Saturday shall be paid for at the rate of time and one-half, double time for work performed on Sundays and holidays. Where a stagger system is in effect, there shall be a guarantee of six days' work. Work performed after eight hours and on the sixth day shall be paid for at the rate of time and one-half. Work performed on the seventh day and on holidays shall be paid for at the cost of double time.

The significance of this action by the grand lodge should not be missed. True it was a wartime situation, but even more relevant is the fact that the grand lodge recognized that the factor and product markets had become national in scope, and it was necessary for the union to undertake the task of determining policy at the national level. This particular policy statement was later reinforced by President Roosevelt's authorizing the substitution of the forty-eight- for the forty-hour week.

One of the most significant reversals of IAM policy by grand lodge fiat came about at the end of the war in 1945, when the executive council decided that it could no longer close its eyes to the practice of incorporating job evaluation plans into labor contracts. It therefore directed all local or district lodges negotiating such contracts to contact the grand lodge for instructions and information before concluding any agreements which incorporated any of the phases of job-evaluation systems or so-called "objective standards."

To handle the burden of work, which all these activities put upon the grand lodge, a sizable technical staff became necessary. There had been a research staff for almost fifteen years, headed not by a machinist but by a university-trained expert, David Kaplan. His reputation soon brought him offers from other unions and he left.[40] The executive council decided that in the future it would be better to give the job to one who could be expected to stay. Thus it came about that the economic research staff, performing a technical function, also became machinist in character. Similar reasoning was involved in a decision to train grand lodge representatives to replace the lawyers who had previously handled much of the IAM's NLRB work. A training program (run by Lee Thomas, who later briefly became editor of the journal) for IAM grand lodge representatives was established for the purpose.[41]

Other policy changes emphasizing the growth of grand lodge influence include the grand lodge's specification in 1946 for wording to eliminate wartime escape clauses in postwar contracts.[42] First in 1947 in a tentative way, and then in 1948 in a directive, the grand lodge sent out "pattern agreements" for use in local bargaining sessions. It included a recommendation in favor of grievance arbitration, but it strongly urged against commercial arbitration services. It favored incorporating clauses which would award dismissal pay. It also specified that no standard wage policy was to be adopted until the IAM grand lodge Research Department had analyzed national wage and cost-of-living indices. The executive council directed that, except in the railroad industry, no IAM unit should sign joint contracts with other unions.[43]

This new emphasis on direction from grand lodge headquarters rendered obsolete and misleading the journal's traditional policy of discussing each new major contract. Instead the grand lodge sent out a professional type of field service bulletin to local negotiators each month. The implications were clear. Negotiation of contracts in the postwar world was too technical a job to be entrusted to "amateurs," not only because contracts had become more complex, but because the result of market integration made the negotiation of one contract affect the negotiation of many others. In a major sense, this change in policy coming as a result of basic economic changes in the nation marks the passing of the Populist–Socialist phase in the union's development, and the tradition that "every private carried a marshal's baton in his pack"—instead, a professional officer class had been created with specialized training in the new technical arts of making war.

The grand lodge asserted the supremacy of its views in two other issues developing from 1947 through 1948. Because of the unfortunate effects of the Supreme Court's decision in the Mount Clemens Pottery Case, a great many employers became liable to suits for back pay for time spent in getting to work benches after entering an employer's property. At first, the executive council was reluctant to take a stand. On the one hand, the council did not think that it was wise to use a legal loophole to collect additional pay—presumably the contract specified a "just" amount; but on the other hand, the membership was not going to be put off by such ethical niceties. The council's dictum was this:

As a general policy, our Organization is opposed to the use of courts in any matters related to or growing out of collective bargaining unless court action is absolutely necessary as a last resort in order to protect and promote the best interests of the membership, but this case involves more than collective bargaining. Therefore, try to gain the amount through direct negotiation with the employer.

This implied settling for less if necessary.[44] Only in the case of absolute failure were the local and district lodges to revert to legal action, and even then, no local or district lodge was permitted to hire lawyers on a contingency fee basis. Fortunately the Congress and later the Supreme Court (with its *de minimis* rule) took most of the pressure off the issue.

The other ruling grew out of the overtime dispute, which also came up through the courts.[45] On this matter the grand lodge was firm: the IAM asks for overtime only after eight hours in any one working day, after forty hours in any seven-day period, for the sixth or seventh day worked in any seven, or when explicitly noted in the contract.

Internally there were significant changes too. Probably nothing reflects this so well as the discussion of the apprenticeship program. One or two episodes illustrate the tenor of the IAM–employer relationships during this period. They are perhaps exceptions to the usual practice, but they stand out as examples of the frontiers of thinking.

At the beginning of the defense emergency, one Bill Jacks, a former business agent in Cleveland, went into the machine shop business, operating an antiunion open shop.[46] In 1940 the IAM struck his firm, the Jacks–Heintz Company, but made very little headway, getting a contract only much later. Jacks operated under a profits-sharing scheme, which appeared on the surface to be very lucrative to the workers, although closer examination showed that the workers, in order to justify their higher pay, were actually working under a spectacular speed-up. Jacks' methods were well publicized by the *Reader's Digest,* and the IAM's struggles with him attracted a good deal of attention. In 1945 the IAM executive council took the unusual step of suspending the charter of Local Lodge 439 (with which Jacks had a contract) because it had become obvious that he was actually dictating lodge policies. In other words, one IAM local had become company-dominated. The experience is worth noting because it came at a time when there was considerable feeling that unions and employers had to work together. The IAM executive council took care to see that cooperation meant bilateral, rather than unilateral, decision-making. Later in 1946 the executive council gave approval to a new labor contract negotiated with Jacks, but only after perusing it carefully. There seems to be little doubt that Jacks had his employees with him all the time, but the IAM executive council was not willing to let them become employer-dominated, even if they wanted to be.

In the postwar period the executive council also took steps to establish systems conferences on the airlines, using the similar arrangements on the railroad as models. Strenuous attempts were made to organize several airlines; success was hampered by opposition from such rival unions as the transport workers', the UAW, and the teamsters'.[47]

The IAM and Community Problems

Several community problems developed during the Brown administration, which are well worth discussing. But we shall leave the consideration of racism and the growth of antidiscrimination legislation until the final chapter. Here it suffices to note that community and, above all, governmental pressure forced the executive council to eliminate the "whites only" clause from the ritual.

Our point in this chapter relates not so much to specific actions taken by the IAM in response to public pressure, but to the growing awareness within the union leadership of the importance of that pressure.[48] Historically, the IAM had not shown much interest in the public's response to its activities. To the IAM, the ones who counted were the members, the employers when confronted with demands, and the judges when presented with cases. By the end of the thirties, however, with the growing importance of public agencies, notably the NLRB, the IAM became more aware of the advantages of "a good press." A good press made for congressional friends, and congressional friends could put pressure on the NLRB. Consequently more and more attention was paid to public relations matters. The disaffiliation from the AFL also accentuated this tendency because it stripped the IAM of the support of other AFL unions that had remained after the carpenter pressure.

By the end of the Second World War it also became apparent that the journal no longer served its traditional function. The IAM had become far too large to permit the journal to be a clearing house for personal notices and information pertaining to technological matters. Moreover, the new member was most frequently not a skilled machinist, nor a sophisticated reader and had little, if any, interest in either the technical or the basic political questions which previously made up such a large part of the old journal's message. In order to reach the new member, some other medium was needed; for if the new member could be effectively reached he could be used to put pressure on the members of Congress, who in turn would come to the "aid" of the IAM before the NLRB and other governmental agencies. A weekly tabloid newspaper of the read-and-throw-away variety was deemed the answer and came into existence in 1947.[49] By 1957 it had completely supplanted the old journal. Its editor was the public relations director of the union, and its columns were meant to be read by anyone having an interest in IAM policies, whether he were a member or not.

The union was also asked to contribute to worthy charitable and political causes. It became increasingly willing to do so, not only because the postwar period was prosperous and the money available, but also because it was a nationally prominent organization, whose social activities were watched by the public at large, and particularly by the newspapers. Some of the charitable causes included Guiding Eyes, Inc., an organization led by a former machinist to provide trained dogs for the blind; the American Veterans' Committee, a reform-minded organization of exservicemen; cancer research committees; and Red Cross relief funds.[50] On the political side, it aided the Americans for Democratic Action (until it was forbidden to make political donations by the Taft–Hartley Act). It also favorably publicized the Marshall Plan and its successor, the Point Four Program, as well as the United Nations and the latter's appeal for aid to undernourished children. In 1947 the executive council joined in the nomination of Mrs. Eleanor Roosevelt for the Nobel prize.[51]

One area of public activity which was not new to the IAM, but which it extended greatly during the Brown administration was its program for participation in international trade-union affairs. Shortly before the First World War the IAM had affiliated with the International Metal Workers' Federation (IMWF) because it provided organizational publicity for the IAM among immigrating European machinists.[52] During that war the IMWF went into serious decline, but somewhat later, when it became active

Thomas W. Talbot,
Grand Master Machinist, 1889–1890

James J. Creamer,
Grand Master Machinist, 1890–1892

John O'Day,
Grand Master Machinist, 1892–1893

William L. Dawley,
Grand Secretary, 1889–1895 (Title changed to Grand Secretary-Treasurer in 1893)

PLATE I

1. Atlanta
2. Florence
3. Augusta
4. Mobile
5. Wilmington
6. Galveston
7. Birmingham
8. Macon
9. Marshall
10. Richmond
11. Norfolk
12. Houston
13. Pueblo
14. Memphis
15. Louisville
16. Harrisburg
17. Springfield
18. Vicksburg
19. Nickerson
20. Emporia
21. Ottawa
22. Argenta
23. Savannah
24. Topeka
25. Denison
26. Palatka
27. Kansas City
28. Trenton
29. Horton
30. Wellington
31. Omaha
32. Columbus
33. Charleston
34. Pensacola
35. Arkansas City
36. San Antonio
37. New Orleans
38. Palestine
39. Garrett
40. Tallahassee
41. St. Louis
42. S. Kaukauna
43. Laredo
44. Columbia
45. Tyler
46. Battle Creek
47. Denver
48. New Decatur
49. Selma
50. The Dalles
51. Pine Bluff
52. Pittsburgh
53. Pocatello
54. Logansport
55. Columbus
56. Ridgedale
57. Moberly
58. Knoxville
59. Temple
60. McKeesport
61. Water Valley
62. Sacramento
63. Albino
64. Indianapolis
65. Laramie
66. Milwaukee
67. Denver
68. San Francisco
69. Delphos
70. Fort Wayne
71. Sedalia
72. Jackson
73. Huntington
74. Waycross
75. Fort Worth
76. Plattsmouth
77. Evansville
78. Tacoma
79. Seattle
80. Newark
81. Bloomington
82. Detroit
83. Cleveland
84. Mt. Vernon
85. St. Louis
86. Fort Madison
87. La Grande
88. S. Butte
89. Cheyenne
90. Marion
91. Anaconda
92. Kansas City
93. Wadsworth
94. New Albany
95. Jackson
96. Mattoon
97. Raton
98. Bay City
99. New Brighton
100. Chicago
101. Erie
102. Manchester
103. Stratford
104. Waukesha

PLATE II

James O'Connell,
Grand Master Machinist, 1893–1912 (Title changed to International President in 1899)

George Preston,
Grand Secretary-Treasurer, 1895–1917 (Title changed to General Secretary-Treasurer in 1899)

Douglas D. Wilson,
Editor, 1895–1915

PLATE III

William H. Johnston,
International President, 1912–1926

Emmet C. Davison,
General Secretary-Treasurer, 1917–1943

Peter J. Conlon,
Vice-President, 1907–1916, 1921–1931 (Title changed to General Vice-President in 1925)

Fred Hewitt,
Editor, 1915–1945

PLATE IV

Arthur O. Wharton,
International President, 1926–1939

James F. Anderson,
Vice-President, 1913–1925

Charles W. Fry,
Business Agent of Chicago District Lodge 8
during Johnston's administration

Lee O. Thomas,
Editor, 1945–1952

PLATE V

Harvey W. Brown,
International President, 1940–1949

Albert J. Hayes,
International President, 1949–

Eric Peterson,
General Secretary-Treasurer, 1944–1959

Elmer E. Walker,
General Secretary-Treasurer, 1959–

PLATE VI

Headquarters on Mt. Vernon Place

Headquarters on Connecticut Avenue

The 1956 Convention, San Francisco

PLATE VIII

once more, its affiliation with the IAM was renewed. During the Great Depression the IAM suspended payments as an economy measure.[53]

During the Second World War the IAM became seriously interested in world labor-union politics, and established anti-Communist (as well as anti-Fascist) policies.[54] It endorsed the Free Trade Union Committee, and it sent donations to starving civilians, to exiled free trade-union leaders, and after the liberation, to French, and later, German unions. It supported an active organizer–reporter in Europe, Irving Brown (who had come to the IAM from the staff of the UAW–AFL). In 1948 the IAM (at a time when it was disaffiliated from the AFL) played host in Washington to a meeting of the central committee of the IMWF.

During the Versailles Peace Conference, Editor Hewitt went to Paris as a delegate to the founding session of the International Labor Organization. After 1945, key IAM leaders, notably Hayes, Peterson, and Walker, served as delegates to that and to other international gatherings.

Thus, the level of IAM involvement in international affairs grew, and as it developed, became more complicated. The IAM chose to separate its program from the AFL's Free Trade Union Committee and to concentrate its support on Irving Brown's projects. This decision was taken only after much discussion, and the executive council also decided to detail one grand lodge representative as its full-time advisor on matters of foreign labor policy.

Another aspect of the union's concern with public relations was the development of an educational department to acquaint the rank-and-file members with the IAM's specific mission and general place in the community.

In most respects the turbulence of the Brown administration was the result of external pressures, although, as we noted at the very beginning, President Brown's intransigence of manner often turned mere disagreements into major crises. Personal frictions between him and General Vice-President Laudemann led to the latter's early retirement in 1946.[55] Brown also forced the retirement of General Vice-President Nickerson and General Vice-President Carr.[56] Thus by the end of his last term of office, he had removed most of the Old Guard. In the long run this was an aid to his successor.

So much has been said of Brown's difficulties, it is only fair to list some of his accomplishments. Under his leadership the union underwent a major metamorphosis, turning it into a large industrial organization. He asserted grand lodge suzerainty — a necessary step after Congress had decided upon the establishment of a national labor policy. He left the union bigger, stronger, and with less internal conflict than he had found it. The only question is — was personal unpopularity necessary to accomplish these things?

After being retired on an IAM pension, Harvey Brown accepted a U.S. government job in Germany. For accepting both pension and government salary, he was severely criticized by many local leaders; but the executive council ruled that he was within his rights.[57] He later asked for an opportunity to explain his position at the 1952 convention, but his successor thought that it would merely open old wounds and refused to recognize Brown when he tried to speak. Brown then fought with the executive council over the size of his pension. The matter in dispute was a trifling $40.00 per year. He appealed the executive council's ruling to the 1956 convention, but he died on the eve of the convention, and the appeal was never ruled upon.

Brown's administration was certainly shaped by the rapid events on the national level. The development of a national (federal) labor policy required greater concentration of control within the IAM. The Second World War furthered the integration of many factor and product markets, which previously had been local or regional in scope. The rise of new industries, like airframe and air transport, presented the union with new challenges.

The speed with which Brown responded to these challenges is commendable. That frictions developed was inevitable, for such is the nature of periods of midpassage.

CHAPTER VI

The Period of Reconciliation: The Start of the Hayes Administration

This chapter attempts principally to cover a few of the episodes in the first years of Albert J. Hayes's administration as international president. In the previous chapters we have attempted to consider each administration as a whole, noting changes in policy or in the effectiveness of policies. In this chapter we discuss only those events in the Hayes administration which reveal how the IAM returned to the AFL, and how it broadened its relationship with other unions in order to make stable its claim to jurisdiction.

The IAM and the AFL

By the end of Brown's administration it was quite obvious to the IAM that little purpose had really been served by its withdrawal from the AFL. True, the IAM had saved the amount normally spent in per capita taxes, but there had also been some real losses incurred by the disaffiliation. Except in some areas where unionism was "new" (as in southern California), and where there was little or no dependence upon the union movement as a whole, considerable burden had fallen on locals with long histories of co-operation with other metal trades, as well as the teamsters' unions. There was, therefore, great local pressure to get back to the old relationship with other unions.

On the other hand, the AFL was also embarrassed by the rupture of relationships. Not only did it have difficulty in getting local labor bodies to comply with the order excommunicating the IAM, but the Canadian Trades and Labor Congress had flatly refused to expel the IAM.[1] Moreover, the IAM, excluded from the deliberative bodies which normally processed disputes between AFL affiliates, was turning, with what the AFL believed to be distressing frequency, to the courts and the National Labor Relations Board, for resolution of its problems.

Added to these factors was the retirement of Harvey Brown, whose pugnacity had irritated many of the key figures on the AFL council, and the succession of Albert J. Hayes, whose reasonableness appealed markedly to Brown's "enemies" on the council. Thus, although President Green had taken steps to repair the breach almost immediately after the formal disaffiliation, it was not until February, 1949, after Brown had retired, when serious talks about a formula to resolve the impasse began.[2] By that time the fight with the operating engineers had become less important as a result of the postwar reduction in the shipbuilding program, and even the bitter dispute with the carpenters seemed less vital in view of the relatively small number of men in question (many of whom were actually carrying membership in both unions). Also, the passage of the Taft–Hartley Act (and its retention even in the face of the "Truman mandate of 1948") made responsible labor leaders aware of the perils in any kind of division in the labor movement.

Thus it was that after a year of talks, William Green could write formally to the IAM executive council in March 1950 suggesting a formula under which the IAM could reaffiliate with ease.[3] It would be given its old jurisdiction and be treated like all other AFL unions. Moreover, Green would withdraw his letter to the operating engineers regarding trial ship runs, would notify the Building Trades Department that it could not assign jurisdictions affecting nonmembers of the Building Trades Department, and would, if the Building Trades Department or one of its members did go so far as to render an unauthorized opinion, personally nullify that opinion.

The IAM executive council agreed to set up some committees to negotiate with Green as well as with two of the dominant AFL unions, namely, the teamsters and the carpenters. The council's willingness to reconsider the IAM's position did not completely contradict its realization that the IAM had to proceed very carefully lest it find itself once again outmaneuvered by some of its "enemies" on the AFL executive council.

By this time the IAM acknowledged that the AFL executive council was, in the truest sense, a legislative body responding to the private interests of particular factions. Beyond this, it also recognized that President Green was an old man who was unable to stand fast when pushed. Thus in the midst of the negotiations, the IAM executive council decided that it had to call a spade a spade. It turned down a Green proposal which appeared to give ground from a position that he had taken earlier.[4] The IAM executive council drafted a letter outlining its position and had it presented to Green by its negotiating committee. The letter's tone was important not so much because it categorically informed Green of the IAM's distrust of him, but because it made quite clear under what conditions reaffiliation was possible. The negotiating committee reported to the other members of the IAM executive council the tenor of their interview:

Several days later we delivered our letter to President Green. He read it and stated that he was in complete accord with everything in it and that he personally could confirm the five points of understanding set forth in the letter as the agreement reached in Miami Beach. At this point we pointed out . . . that we were certain some of the members of the AFL Executive Council, in a subtle way, were trying to keep our Organization from reaffiliation.[5] Because of this we told Green we were convinced that if he again submitted his letter to his Council that everything which had been accomplished up to date would just be a lot of wasted effort because some members of his Council would find some reason to object to the letter. We further stated that unless he felt that he had the authority to confirm in writing what he had confirmed verbally, that we might just as well forget about the whole thing. We told him some other things too. For example, we told him that we did not believe he had to fear any of the AFL Council Members any longer and he should draw upon some of the courage he displayed in past years and make a decision which we believe to be in line with his authority as President of the AFL.[6]

The IAM got its desired letter on June 23, 1950. It came not so much because President Green had suddenly had a change of heart, but because many of the dominant old anti-IAM figures had left the scene. Tobin of the teamsters was no longer strong; nor was Hutcheson of the carpenters any longer fully active. Moreover, Hayes and Peterson of the IAM both had a good deal of moral stature. In addition, both were known to have extremely good judgment. Consequently, any of the arguments previously trotted out against the IAM (mostly anti-Brown views) were no longer usable.

The IAM executive council voted to hold a referendum on reaffiliation. It passed 87,852 to 23,579.[7] By then, the Korean War was in progress, and the IAM had been accorded a special voice in the government agencies because it could not nominally be represented by the usual AFL delegates. The AFL then initiated some moves which precipitated new expressions of IAM distrust. The AFL asked the IAM not to use the NLRB against any other AFL union in an interunion dispute.[8] President Hayes replied that he would make no promises and that he would abide strictly by the terms he had outlined in his earlier letter accepting Green's amended proposals. Hayes believed that there was some envy on the AFL executive council of the IAM's role in the war agencies, and that that envy might be used to block the reaffiliation move. He told his colleagues that he would call off the whole settlement if any bad faith were shown. He was aiming at reasonable indifference—if the AFL wanted the IAM back, the IAM would return, but only if the AFL stood by the letter of its commitments. The IAM did not want any eagerness for AFL affiliation to blind it to past experience with AFL perfidy. In mid-1951 the IAM did reaffiliate.

Shortly after President Green's death in 1953, AFL President Meany tried to persuade Hayes to become a member of the AFL executive council. Hayes, in keeping with his previously determined policy of asking no favors from the AFL, was noncommittal. Meany offered to name him as an AFL delegate to the ICFTU Stockholm conference, but Hayes refused, suggesting Peterson as his substitute.[9] Meany first wanted a union president, and Peterson was not appointed. Eventually General Vice-President Walker replaced teamster President Beck, and thus a machinist was an AFL delegate.

Late in 1953 Hutcheson in a moment of pique led his carpenters out of the AFL. Much to his surprise, George Meany accepted the carpenters' withdrawal and suggested that Hayes replace Hutcheson as first vice-president of the AFL. Meany's intention and Hayes's response remain obscure. Beck took the vacant space, and Hayes's reaction was to decide that he did not want the IAM to do any lobbying on his behalf for the next vacancy.

In 1953 Hayes and Maurice Hutcheson both became members of the AFL executive council.[10] By the 1955–1956 period, Hayes had developed one of the more important voices on the council. This was according to his plan, for unlike Johnston he made no move to be included; but when he was included, his disinterestedness became useful. In many senses Hayes became the leader of a third force in the AFL executive council, but that is a chapter beyond the purview of this study.

The IAM and Other Unions

Hayes's policy with regard to the rest of the labor movement also resulted in a plethora of agreements after 1953. In February, 1953, a jurisdictional division was agreed upon by the teamsters, who, it may be recalled, had earlier tried to raid the IAM's territory in the Seattle Boeing plant. They had also tried to get a foothold in the air transport industry, particularly in the New York City–Newark, New Jersey terminal areas. But the IAM had, on the whole, resisted these efforts successfully and by 1950 Dave Beck, the teamster president, wanted to make peace and to show his good faith.[11] Preliminary negotiations between representative committees were held, and toward the end of 1952, Mr. David Kaplan, the IAM's former director of research (by this time filling the same function for the teamsters), was able to arrange a meeting of the leaders of the two unions. The outgrowth was the agreement of February 4, 1953, which not only specified respective jurisdictional territories, but also provided for jointly financed organizing campaigns in the auto sales, servicing, and repair industries.

A new agreement was also entered into with the UAW–CIO in 1953, building on a no-raiding pact between the two organizations negotiated

September 9, 1949.[12] It provided for a regular institutionalized grievance system to handle disputes between the two parties, as well as a system of interunion consultation to apply to industries where "both unions have organized a substantial number of workers." One interesting additional feature was the provision that if either union had 50 per cent or more of the production and maintenance employees in a multiple plant corporation, and if the other union had no history of a contract, the latter would make no attempt to organize the workers for itself, but when both unions had had contracts, they would do their individual best to win the NLRB election, abiding by the results. Much of the 1953 agreement was extended to Canada in 1954.

New agreements were entered into with the rubber workers on July 24, 1953, which generally followed the outlines of the 1953 UAW–CIO accord;[13] and with the pressmen on January 4, 1954, which stated that practice should be considered along with logical precedent in the resolution of any disputes between the two organizations.[14] The old 1925 agreement with the United Association (the plumbers), the terms of which had often been observed in the breach, was also renovated and modified on April 29, 1954. The new contents, following the pattern of specifying particular craft skills, functions, and types of materials to be worked upon, included a provision explicitly disavowing "all decisions rendered (previously) by the American Federation of Labor, or the Building and Construction Trades Department."

But the biggest *coup* of the new agreement-making epoch was the signing of a workable accord with the carpenters on September 18, 1954.[15] Talks with Hutcheson's union had actually been in process since 1950, but had repeatedly bogged down. Early in 1954 Presidents Hayes and Hutcheson resolved that some sort of arrangement had to be worked out. After much bitter wrangling, the two unions, aided by Father Leo Kelly and Professor John T. Dunlop of Harvard University, actually did reach an agreement, ending more than forty years of sporadic conflict. It allocated to the IAM all the work of manufacturing and handling, installing, and repairing all printing presses and auxiliary machinery, most brewery equipment, and all machine shop work in connection with construction, on the site or in the shop. The carpenters were to have conveyors, machinery, and motors in new construction work, and also in plants where the carpenters' union had had a long-term contract. Work on the installation of turbines was to be divided equally between the two unions. And a grievance system was devised to work out any disputes arising under the terms of this new accord. Thus ended one of the longest and most debilitating conflicts between two American unions.

Why did this agreement come about? It completely ignored the 1932 Cincinnati convention *dictum,* and it appears to have been fashioned out of an experience which was not greatly influenced by the 1914–1916 Building Trades Department attitudes. Thus we can conclude that the major reasons for this agreement were that there were new people who negotiated it, that is, individuals who were not emotionally committed to reliving earlier episodes. Secondly, the IAM probably realized that its claim to turbine-installation work was becoming ludicrous in the light of its relative inability to drive the carpenters out of the actual jobs. In fact, if machinists worked those assignments individually, they generally carried membership cards in both organizations. Third, there is reason to believe that the carpenters, more than a little annoyed at the machinists' constant reliance upon the courts and the NLRB, felt that the only way to resolve that time-and-energy-consuming litigation was to conclude a proper agreement once and for all. Fourth, the mediators may have had influence in leading the parties, particularly the carpenters, along a conciliatory path. In any event, whatever the reasons, this accord has managed to survive at least six and one half years.

In the following years other agreements were established; between the IAM and the ironworkers in 1955 (providing for a no-raid clause as well as joint organizing endeavors), the boilermakers in 1956 (following in general the type of pattern suggested in the 1954 plumbers treaty), and with the Air Lines Pilots' Association in 1957.

These two efforts, the one bringing the IAM back into the AFL, and the other involving a reorganization of the IAM's relationships with other unions, represent the answer of the Hayes administration to the questions it initially faced. As such they raise an interesting question of history and unionism. It is to this that we now turn.

The IAM in Perspective

Our discussion of the history of the IAM has focused on the challenges to, and the responses of, the various administrations. Two major generalizations emerge: one pertains to the mechanism of response to a challenge, and the other to the "historical group personality" of the IAM.

Administrative Challenges and Responses

Each president of the IAM concentrated his greatest efforts on the greatest problems of the time of his first election. Wharton became president at a time when it was necessary to secure internal administrative stability. Brown was elected when it seemed most necessary to develop an aggressive organizing campaign among industrial workers, and Hayes was chosen to restore friendly relations with several unions that had become bitter rivals. But it is often the case that problems, other than the ones to which the international president was dedicated, do develop. Invariably new conditions or crises appear, which are not the incumbent's "meat." For example, once O'Connell ran into the bitter organized opposition of the NMTA, his success required changes in the IAM approach far beyond his capacity. Similarly, Johnston, elected on the wave of the pre-World War I Socialist movement, was not particularly fitted to adjust the IAM program to post-World War I "normalcy." Wharton, by way of contrast, was well adapted to function in the post-World War I period of normalcy, but was a relative disappointment during the heyday of the New Deal. Brown, aggressive and imaginative, but also pugnacious, eventually caused tremendous problems in dealing with the AFL. Thus, if one is to generalize, one can only suggest that the criteria for selecting a president at a particular time may be so specialized as to become erroneous later on. There is a parallel between these figures and the epic characters of the Old Testament, each of whom had a "fault" which time was sure to expose.

However, it is not true that every incumbent must be proved ineffective by time. Such would be quite contrary to our point, since we merely emphasize the shifting nature of the problems to be faced by union administrators. O'Connell functioned quite well in most areas, even after the 1901 NMTA fight. Johnston was able to adapt his policies to some of the post-World War I developments; in fact, what is remarkable is the degree to which he successfully modified his earlier views to conform with changed conditions. It can also be said that Wharton and Brown also showed limited flexibility. Our conclusion is not Hegelian. It is not the response which breeds the new problem; it is time and external developments which makes an administration's response to the problems it faces anachronistic.

The "Group Personality" of the IAM

Several aspects of the IAM's "group personality" are worth mentioning. These include its attitude toward the social order, its attitude toward its own internal check-and-balance system (that is, the role of factions), and its attitude toward the rest of the labor-union movement.

In its general social orientation, the IAM can be characterized as a bargaining, rather than as a doctrinaire reform, institution. If it has had any consistent approach, it has been one of concentration on job benefits (rather than general social benefits). This policy has been called by one writer "job-conscious" unionism.[16] "Job-conscious" unionism, however, has changed its form during the lifetime of the IAM. Originally it emphasized craft solidarity, but the effect of national integration of the factor and product markets, plus the development of a federal labor policy, now has rendered such particularism out of date. Industrial unionism as practiced by the IAM today is not the same thing advocated by the Socialists in 1911, when it was the expression of working-class consciousness. Today, industrial unionism is the former craft union's response to the specific economic challenges implicit in the integration of markets and the development of federal labor policy. To put this in another way, it is not the union which has abandoned job-consciousness in favor of working-class solidarity, but a change in industrial organization which has expanded the expression of job-consciousness from a craft to an industrial level. Members of the IAM are undoubtedly less Socialistically inclined today than they were previously; in its general social orientation the IAM has, if anything, moved slightly to the right.

In matters of its internal orientation, the IAM has also undergone several important administrative changes. The self-government process, originally centered on the local level, has been "nationalized" in order to cope with new conditions. The development of a federal labor policy, particularly the Taft–Hartley Act, requires the union to streamline its administrative process. These changes, coupled with those induced by the national integration of markets, have resulted in a vast increase in the powers of the international president. Effective use of these powers has presented the union with some of its major crises. Democratic centralism, one answer, has not proved to be completely satisfactory because the international presidents have on occasion been excessively sensitive to criticism from within their own administration and have silenced it by driving their opponents out of office or into retirement, and then replacing them with less independent-minded men. On the whole, it should be added, the record of the several international presidents has been remarkably good, and our point is not that these men have been inferior to the international presidents of other unions, but that the system requires superhuman judgment.

Local autonomy remains important in the IAM. Contracts are still generally negotiated on the local level; and although at present there is more interregional competition than formerly, the prevalent pattern remains highly local. So long as local autonomy in the negotiation of contracts remains widespread, it is highly unlikely that the IAM will become administratively controlled from the center like the United Auto Workers, United Steel Workers, or even any of the railroad brotherhoods. Our conclusion, therefore, is that the problems of internal administration remain somewhat unresolved. Two opposing tendencies are at work: one, centripetal in nature, stems from the integration of markets and the development of a federal labor policy. The other, centrifugal in nature, stems from the historic traditions of localism. It is worth adding at this point that the district lodge has generally replaced the old local lodge as the critical autonomous unit. Just as once it could be argued that provincialism was a unifying factor in overcoming parochial sentiment, later to become an obstacle to nationalism, so too it can be seen that the district lodge has now become an obstacle to national integration of policy.

The third general administrative trend relates to the union's orientation as part of the labor movement. Here, one is entitled to ask — for what does the American labor movement stand? [17] Is it simply a response to the conditions engendered by industrialism? Or, is it a least-cost method of increasing workers' real pay and improving their working conditions? Or, alternatively, is it best understood as the extension of representative government to industry? In the early years membership in the IAM was probably not the least-cost method of improving wages and working conditions. Quite the contrary, those who joined the union paid a steep price for their membership and joined because they believed that, in the future, the union might stand as the guarantee of their job right. Without the union the early members knew that they were at the mercy of their employers, and even with the union, it was conceivable that they could not defend themselves. However, labor solidarity in the shop, gained by simple association or under the aegis of the NLRB, rendered the need for union protection somewhat less obvious to many workers. Many who joined unions did so simply because unions were there, and not because they saw in them job protection. One can almost say that the membership in unions came to be like membership in the American Red Cross. To refuse to join is difficult; to join involves little cost and virtually no effort.

Taking the American labor movement as it appears, one can see that the IAM seems to have completed a great circle in its relationship to other unions. So long as O'Connell was president, the IAM cooperated closely with the top leadership of the AFL (Gompers). Under Johnston, the IAM leadership and AFL leadership were poles apart. Concord of some type was reestablished under Wharton; although, under Brown, once again there was great divergence between the two camps. Hayes has led the union back to the policies of O'Connell. Hayes, Wharton, and O'Connell on the one hand, in contrast to Johnston and Brown on the other, were politically "in." They had helped formulate major AFL policy because of their prestige on the AFL executive council. (Possibly Wharton was not as important in the AFL deliberations because he did not pack the weight that the leaders of such unions as the teamsters and carpenters did.) Influence is a relative matter, and to enjoy a strong position one must not only have a clear voice, but the others must want to listen. The size of the IAM under Hayes plus its excellent reputation for honest and efficient administration, particularly in these times when so many unions are charged with maladministration, have given Hayes and the IAM an authoritative position which they had not enjoyed since O'Connell's time.

The development of complacency, associated with the member who believes that joining involves little cost and ultimately no effort, presents unions with problems familiar to all social movements. Success breeds a *blasé* quality, and the enthusiastic cadre who could be depended upon to furnish local leadership is no longer readily available. Our point is this, the development of indifference in the whole labor movement undoubtedly has touched the IAM as well, but this change is characteristic of all social movements and is not irreversible.

One can, of course, ask where the American labor movement is going. "More, more, and yet more" seems to be a policy with a limited objective. It is not easy to argue that this type of reasoning is not in the end self-limiting. The impressive side of the IAM's history is the adaptability of its policies and its administration. "More, more, and yet more" is simply descriptive of a quantitative appetite. It does not necessarily imply that this appetite will be confined to wages, shorter hours, or even "fringe benefits." It merely suggests that in a bargaining society the American labor movement (of which the IAM is simply a major part) will seek to bargain on a wider range and with increasing success. The conclusion in this sense is simply that the administrative flexibility of the IAM is its major resource. The sixty-five or seventy-year history of the organization which we have described presents an excellent summary of the exploitation of that resource. Indifference affects the movement not so much because old demands are dropped (more, more, and yet more is no longer needed), but because doubt is expressed of the need for the institution. It is that kind of indifference which kills social movements.

PART TWO

The Government and Its Growth

CHAPTER VII

The Government of the Grand Lodge

The grand lodge is the national organization of the IAM. It consists of the international officers, the staff appointed to assist them, and the convention of representative delegates from the local lodges.

This chapter presents a formal analysis of the governmental process in the grand lodge.[1] Its purpose is to give a view of the evolution of various institutions and practices, as well as to put into perspective the different agencies making up the grand lodge. It consists of several major sections. The first discusses the IAM constitution and ritual. The second is an analysis of the legislative function. The third considers the component parts of the executive branch. And the fourth explores the judicial process. This chapter is intended primarily to portray the formal development of the IAM government, and only secondarily to describe present practices.

The Constitution

The constitution, now consisting of over eighty small, closely printed pages, comprises several sections. From time to time their contents have changed, and to facilitate the discussion we consider the parts not in the order that they appear, but in light of the function that they are meant to perform. We take up one after another (1) the platform, which is basically an idealized version of what the future ought to offer, (2) a statement of jurisdiction or claim to sovereignty over a particular job territory, (3) a discussion of grand lodge and subordinate lodge relationships, (4) an examination of the grand lodge's relations to its members, and (5) the ritual.

Here it is timely to note that the constitution was first adopted at the 1889 convention. Until 1895 it could be modified only by the direct vote of the delegates. Between 1895 and 1916, modification was also possible by referendum vote. After 1916 all basic policy changes, even those adopted by the delegates to the convention, had to be referred to the full membership for ratification. Thus, since 1916 modification of the constitution has come only after a referendum vote.

How are modifications to the constitution effected? Prior to conventions, the subordinate lodges as well as the executive council are authorized to propose amendments. These proposals are subsequently processed by the Committee on Law, a lay committee now elected by the whole membership at normal four-year intervals according to the usual procedures. The next step is to hold committee hearings at a convention and then refer the matter to the floor with a committee recommendation. If the convention favors the change, the matter is then referred to the membership. If the matter passes the referendum, the Committee on Law is then charged with the responsibility of preparing the precise language of the new clause.

The constitution is interpreted by the international president. In practice, this means that a specific constitutional authorization is what he rules it to be. However, since 1911, an aggrieved lodge, with sufficient backing from other lodges, can appeal to a convention or to the membership by referendum vote to reverse a president's ruling. In spite of the fact that this has rarely been done, the international president exercises great restraint in making his rulings. His is a political office, and he realizes that an abuse of this all-important power is the one thing which can unite the critics of his administration. Historical experience reveals that the international president has been most careful to consult with the executive council, recognized lay members (unpaid individuals active on the local level), particularly those on the law committee, and the convention, itself, when he has doubts about any matter.

The Platform

In Chapter I we indicated that the union had been under the "Southern" or quality influence in its earliest years, but that this had lessened, finally to disappear at a fairly early date. This influence was most readily seen in the examination of the first platform — where a five-point program was embraced. It included (1) building up the educational and social qualities of machinists, (2) adoption of a job-finding program for unemployed brothers, (3) provision for a sick benefits fund, (4) endorsement of the apprenticeship system, and (5) a plank opposing strikes and "any attempt to antagonize the interests of capital and labor." Of these, the first and the last were the most obvious by-products of the Southern influence. And they were the ones most quickly dropped.

By 1891 the platform had begun to have more of a "pure and simple" trade-union flavor. It called for the admission of every competent machinist who had worked four years at the trade, it urged the adoption of the eight-hour day; as if to retain some of the earlier Southern flavor, it justified this demand by noting the necessity of giving members opportunities for self-improvement and social enjoyment. It abandoned all reference to sick benefits, but retained the requests for retention of the apprenticeship system and a program for finding jobs for unemployed members.

Tracing the platform after 1891 is analogous to tracing the development of American industry or to tracing the rise and fall of the Socialist–Populist influence in the union. Until 1920 the union asked for the eight-hour day–presumably meaning the forty-eight-hour week. In 1920 this plank was changed to ask for a forty-four-hour week, implying a half holiday on Saturdays. In 1929 the demand was changed to a forty-hour week, and then, after the depth of the depression it was further amended to the thirty-hour week. In 1941 a plank advocating paid vacations was incorporated. Looking backward, it is clear that the incorporation of a plank sometimes lagged behind the fact as found in contracts. In a few instances there is reason to believe that demands were granted by some employers, before they became generally voiced. In this sense, the plank was something other than a pious hope—it may at times have been a practical request for standardized costs. As far as the hours–vacation issues were concerned, the demands were obtained soon after they were first generally proposed.

The demand for a job-finding program underwent only two changes. In 1911 a clause was appended asking that employers give up their blacklists and other record-keeping systems on ex-employees. Moreover, physical examinations were also opposed. It is hard to believe that the employees' physical health suddenly became a matter of concern to employers. Certainly, the enactment of workmen's compensation acts came later, and they cannot be blamed. More probably, it was simply the consequence of the growth of the scientific-management movement, which constantly raised physical standards in order to encourage new production levels. Taylor had specified that one of the four steps necessary to true scientific management was "picking the right man for the job," and this involved some examination of the individual's health and physical abilities, in order to eliminate the weaker (and older) workers. Also there is good reason to believe that the standards for passing the physical examinations varied directly with the examinee's enthusiasm for unions. The other change in the demand for developing a job-finding program was introduced in 1920. It was a plea for a social policy of full employment. As such, it was well in advance of its time but has proved to be not an unreasonable request.

The Jurisdictional Claim

Observation of this aspect of the IAM's history is most like studying the pulse of the organization. The claim to jurisdiction typifies the growth of the organization because it categorizes who is and who is not eligible for "citizenship" in the "job republic." Major changes occurred so many times that it is useful to refer to the various administrations to keep them in perspective.

In 1888 the basic requirement for membership was simply that the applicant be a white, male citizen of some civilized country as well as a practical machinist, capable of commanding the average rate of wages given in some well-regulated machine shop in his district. Moreover, he had to be practicing his craft.

By 1891 the emphasis on citizenship quality began to change and included economic as well as social criteria. The new quest was for competent, sober, industrious white machinists who had either served a four-year apprenticeship or who had worked at the trade for four years and could command the average rate of wages paid in their locality. The qualifications went on to specify that a practical machinist was one who could do "general work on the floor and vice [*sic*], and who "[could] use a majority of tools used in the average machine shop."[2] Quite clearly the social quality or Southern theme was still present, although, to be sure, it was now sharing attention with some technical details. Apprentices, incidentally, were eligible for membership after three and a half years of their indenture.

The following list gives the year that different elements of the platform were adopted, illustrating the evolution of the union's nominal philosophy. The first three clauses, emphasizing the Southern tradition, were eliminated very early, in 1891. In 1953, after half a century of inclusion, two other clauses, advocating public ownership and the election of trade union members to public office, were also dropped.

The emphasis on social and educational qualifications	1889
Sick benefits fund	1889
The anti-strike plank	1889
Helping members find employment	1889
Further apprentice system	1889
Favoring arbitration	1889
Admission clause relating to eligibility	1891
Shorter hours	1891
Stimulating political education and activity of members	1899
Electing trade unionists to office	1899
Favoring public ownership	1903
Advocating Populist program — i.e., direct election, popular control of courts	1909
Cooperation with shop craft unions	1911
Against firing older workers	1925

Supremacy of Congress over Supreme Court	1925
Anti-injunction in labor disputes	1925
Bargaining over arbitration	1953

The O'Connell Administration. Further changes came about in 1895 when the four-year time requirement (involving either apprenticeship or experience as a practicing craftsman) was abandoned. The criteria were restated and expanded; (1) ability to command the average local rate, and (2) ability to perform one or more of the following functions: (a) general machine work, (b) general floor work, (c) lathe work, (d) vise work, (e) planer work, (f) milling machine work, (g) slotting machine work, (h) die-sinking, tool making, or boring mill work, (i) linotype repair work. Each member was to have the appropriate category noted on his card. In effect, these changes indicate the entry of specialists into the union, although the issue was not recognized as such until later.

By 1897 the pressures for recruiting and admitting less than fully trained men had mounted. In his report to the convention O'Connell said:

> Every day our trade is becoming more and more specialized, and if we hope to successfully protect our craft it is necessary that our qualifications for membership be radically changed. The multifarious industries in which our membership are employed warrants this convention in taking steps that will bring into the association thousands of new men, who, under our former laws, would not come up to the qualifications required. *Women are being rapidly introduced into the trade, and we should change our laws so that we can take them in when they are qualified.* [Italics supplied.] [3]

Nonetheless, not enough of the delegates concurred, and in place of opening membership to specialists, the old four-year rule was restored. The convention specified that anyone falsely claiming general competence would be subject to a small fine. Apprentices had their path to membership eased—they could join after two and one half years of indenture.

O'Connell continued his advocacy of recasting membership requirements, and in 1899 the convention agreed to substitute the minimum rate in place of the average rate paid in a locality. Moreover, it directed subordinate lodges (over the objections of the convention committee) to specify the minimum rate applicable in the community, and it forbade anyone to work for less. A proposal to take in semiskilled men and apprentices (after nine months) was defeated; its opponents claimed that their entry would "prostitute" the union. Its proponents argued that other unions had had to agree to "dilution of the trades" (upgrading the semiskilled).

By the 1901 convention, pressure for modifying requirements of skill began to bear results. Although the disadvantages of abandoning emphasis on skill or competence were recognized, the delegates realized that it had become absolutely necessary to control every man in machine shops. Thus the new eligibility clause claimed "[every] workman *performing the work of a machinist.*"[4] providing, of course, that he earned the minimum rate of wages paid in his locality. Besides, apprentices could join after nine months, although they were segregated in auxiliary lodges until they had completed their second year of indenture.

The validity of O'Connell's position could not be denied, particularly since it was based on an accurate assessment of the growth of industrial technology. More and more, unions had to face the reality that they had to control all who were competitors for jobs, irrespective of whether they were fully qualified in the traditional sense. In 1903 O'Connell pointed to the miners, printers, molders (core makers), brewery workers, and the steelworkers, whose unions had had to try to gain control of their industries' labor force. O'Connell was not an industrial unionist and was unwilling to take into the IAM all types of skilled workers employed in machine shops, but did urge that the IAM enter into mutual agreements with every other craft organization which had members in these shops. This position was debated for many years, leaving two questions to be answered: should the IAM give specialists full recognition? And, should the IAM admit unskilled helpers?

One possible answer was "yes" to both queries, and it was argued that admission was economically essential, morally important, and historically in line with Socialistic principles. In addition, there was the point that groups which once had looked to the IAM were beginning to lose interest and to affiliate elsewhere. These included the millwrights (who went to the carpenters), the elevator constructors (who formed their own association), the steamfitters, the toolmakers, and the general mechanics.

A second possible response was "no" to both questions. Here it was held that the IAM stood for certain levels of skill and, in the words of one delegate, "[if] we take these men in we will have to change our name. . . . I want to belong to an association of machinists and none other."[5] Besides, it was observed that the purpose of including handymen was to gain control of job territory, then to turn it over to regular machinists, and, in that way, kill the original job classification. It was questionable whether so devious a move could really be executed. Probably the biggest single factor was a fear that inclusion of men, not fully qualified, meant the end of machinist control of the union.

The third possible response was to temporize. "I am in favor of this movement to take [others] in," said one delegate, "but not with equal rights or privileges. Take them in as a separate organization, as an auxiliary for two years, and then, probably, we can take them in without conditions."

The geographic side of things should not be overlooked. The westerners coming from small railroad towns wanted to maintain the *status quo;* the easterners, more aware of the pressures of local competition in the labor market, urged inclusion.

A decision to bifurcate the membership emerged. One group was termed *journeymen machinists;* the other, *specialists*. Wherever possible each group was to have separate lodges, except where numbers were too few, then they could be in a single lodge. The jurisdictional claim was amended to include "any person *working in a machine shop and engaged in any manner with the making and repairing of machinery* . . . providing that he is working at the trade (and gets the local minimum wages of his class)." [6] Unskilled helpers, as such, were not included. However, merger with the bicycle mechanics' union, for instance, was now possible. Thus, the two questions were answered differently; to the first, the answer was a qualified "yes"; to the second, the answer remained "no." O'Connell was not fully satisfied with the outcome; he was not certain that the specialists actually belonged in the IAM. He continued to urge putting them in their own auxiliaries, which the IAM would naturally control.

At the 1905 convention, the language of the constitution was made explicit about the mode of organization: "In localities where there are [enough] . . . machinists, die-sinkers, die or tool makers, or specialists, separate lodges *may* be organized." In 1907 the constitution directed that all machinists or specialists working in railroad shops had to join the local railroad lodge, if one existed. The effect, of course, was to expand the railroad lodges, which were efficiently run by the regular journeyman group.

Additional changes were made during the period of O'Connell's leadership including some modifications in language in 1909, when the definition of jurisdiction was sufficiently modified to imply the existence of a significant qualification difference between a "journeyman machinist" and the lesser categories. This was a return to the old apprenticeship or four-years' experience rule. Thus, what had occurred between 1900 and 1909 was both the expansion of eligibility and the creation of classes of citizenship.

Although O'Connell was a lame-duck officer at the 1911 convention, his views on jurisdiction were accorded respect. Two changes which he advocated were adopted. It is worth adding that these changes were not in line with his previous thinking. One involved taking women into the IAM. The other was the taking in of helpers.

O'Connell was not personally sympathetic to the idea of women in industry. In her *From Pinafores to Politics,* Mrs. J. Borden Harriman commented that she found O'Connell in the 1913–1915 period most hostile to working women.[7] Nonetheless, he argued at the 1911 convention that it was necessary to face the fact that women were in industry and would have to be organized. Actually women had been in the IAM since 1904 when a Miss Nellie T. Burke joined the Wilkes-Barre local. Parenthetically, it should be added that Miss Burke was granted all the privileges of membership.[8] She was not in the "Ladies' Auxiliary" category which had also first appeared in Wilkes-Barre in 1899, and which had by 1909, thirty-six chapters as well as its own grand lodge organization (established in 1907).[9] Hence in 1911 the constitution, which previously referred to "anyone,' was changed to specify the organization of women.

The situation of helpers remained little changed, except that they were being organized by the AFL in federal unions. O'Connell pointed out the dangers to the IAM of having the machine shop helpers independently organized, and now urged that they be admitted into their own separate lodges, whenever there were enough of them. Otherwise they were to go into specialists' lodges. In addition, their cards and dues books were to be stamped *machinist helper*. They were to receive two-thirds of the benefits payments accorded to journeymen. Their lodges were not allowed to call strikes unless that action was also sanctiond by the local journeymen's lodge.

It is clear that the admission of helpers was a bitter pill swallowed only out of necessity. The IAM's organizing them was only slightly better than leaving them to be organized by others. In other words, they were the third estate — made up of the unskilled, even though they were adequately paid. If the journeymen had found the admission of specialists hard to tolerate, the acceptance of helpers was harder. Of course, there were some dedicated Socialists or levellers who wanted equal treatment for these untouchables, but theirs was not an important voice. In brief, it was economic necessity, not democratic sentiment, that brought them in.

O'Connell's administration saw the IAM grow from a quality-conscious organization into a "pure and simple" type. It changed from a small railroad-craft-dominated community to an industrial "house of many mansions." By and large he encouraged this change, even though at times he found it difficult to accept. But his eye was always on the facts of industrial development. Consequently, he steered a consistent, and realistic, course. He charted the IAM's development toward industrial control, while seeking to retain hegemony for the craftsmen. This point is too frequently overlooked. He did not oppose incorporation of the unskilled — but sought to keep the prerogatives of citizenship primarily for the "educated." His notion of social organization was republican — but patrician or noble, rather than plebian or egalitarian.

The Johnston Administration. After the 1911 changes, little remained to be done. Thus Johnston's Socialism did not result in spectacular developments. In 1913 the specialist category was redefined de-emphasizing the absence of general knowledge of all machine processes, and replacing it with a stress on the absence of personal skill on the part of the member. In other words, a journeyman was held to be skilled; a specialist, semiskilled, and a helper, unskilled. Each category paid its own per capita tax; there were four, (including apprentices) and four monthly rates — 60 cents, 45 cents, 35 cents and 20 cents respectively.

In 1915 the qualifications of "working at the trade" and "being paid the minimum local rate of his class" were dropped because they were meaningless in the face of unemployment and the need to organize. And in 1916 the journeymen category was once again tightened and changed to require "apprenticeship or four years' experience and (in place of or) is competent to command the minimum local rate."

The biggest changes during Johnston's time occurred at the 1920 convention, where it was decided to admit helpers into the regular lodges. This change meant the end of segregation of the "unworthy" — and the old penalty clause for misrepresentation of skill was changed from "falsely representing self as a *general workman* to *"competent workman."*[10] Moreover, steps were taken to erase the line of distinction between the general machinists and the specialists. Although their dues books were stamped differently, they now paid the same per capita tax, irrespective of any differences in general levels of pay, and got the same benefits. Women, who in 1918 had been offered a special category, now paid lower dues (and received lower strike and death benefits). The classes of citizenship became (1) journeyman machinists and specialists; (2) machinists' helpers; (3) apprentices and women workers. Apprentices were ordered admitted after their sixth month (instead of after their 24th, as previously).

The Wharton administration. During Wharton's time, two significant changes were made. In 1929 increased emphasis was put on organizing automobile and aircraft mechanics, which, in time, was to become most important. And in 1937 the category of production worker (with the obligations and benefits of the machinists' helper) was established. The production worker was defined as "one employed in the mass production industry, and engaged in repetitive machine, assembly, or bench work, requiring less training, experience and skill than that necessary to qualify one as a machinist."

The Brown Administration. The adaptations made during this period reflected continued jurisdictional adjustment to technological change. For instance, the air conditioning manufacturing industry and the plastics industry were added to those in which the IAM exercised a claim. In addition, the trend towards full industrial unionism continued — in 1943, for instance, a local made up of firemen and guards was chartered.

In 1942 a member was fined $100 by Local Lodge 1 (Atlanta) for falsely claiming to be skilled, when he was merely a helper,[11] but the rarity of this is perhaps the best evidence of the changes which had occurred.

In 1946 the definitions of categories were once again revised. The production worker category, which was earlier described as having less skill than a machinist, now specified less skill than a specialist. And the fact that the specialist had less skill than a journeyman, was once again made explicit.

The Hayes administration. The next step in the democratization or levelling of membership responsibilities and rights, occurred in 1953 when the per capita tax was made uniform for all members and when it was accordingly decided to abandon the practice of stamping the member's category on his dues book. Thus the process entered its last stage. Although the categories of skill were nominally retained, the meaningful distinctions between them had been eliminated. Moreover, clerical employees, "working in conjunction with the trade,"[12] were admitted.

Clearly, by 1953 the IAM had become an industrial union, and virtually every formal vestige of its craft origin had either been erased or remained only in an informal sense, because the union's customs had their own staying power. This change was caused in great part by the technological development of American industry, including not only the growth of the mass production factory, but also the decline of the steam locomotive and the railroad roundhouse — which had been the original *raison d'être* of the organization.

But the change was accomplished gradually — in two ways. The first was the formal one outlined in these pages. The second, even more profound although far less noticeable, was the decision to organize the excluded categories. By this we mean simply O'Connell's obvious decision to bring the specialists into the fold. They were admitted even prior to the authorization.

A similar development occurred in the late 1930's when Wharton and Brown sent organizers into the mass production industries. Thus, one can see that the exercise of the jurisdictional claim was not simply the will of the convention, molded as it was by technological changes, but, in good part, the wisdom of the international president as seen in his instructions to the IAM organizers.

Grand Lodge and Local Lodge Relationships

The nature of grand lodge and subordinate lodge relationships reflects several strong influences. Foremost of these is the historic fact that the subordinate lodge has generally been the principal negotiating agent for the members. This means simply that the union's power and influence vis-à-vis employers is not funnelled through the grand lodge. Consequently, it has been not only desirable, but also absolutely necessary to preserve some degree of independence and importance of the local units. In the IAM there has been a constant "functional" force serving to restrain the grand lodge from what in several other large "industrial" unions is the natural development. That is, the grand lodge has not swamped local autonomy.

A second influence which has buttressed local lodge autonomy has been the existence of large, powerful districts. These have served to balance the influence of the grand lodge officers. In fact, the historical strength of District Lodge 8 (Chicago), District Lodge 9 (St. Louis), and District Lodge 15 (New York) serves both as a reminder of the actual existence of non-grand lodge power groups in the IAM and as the protector of other would-be autonomous factions.

Third, it is worth noting that the grand lodge has rarely had very much money to spend on strike benefits so that it has been chary of extravagance toward those on strike or those in need of any form of unauthorized aid. The power of the subordinate lodge has also been significantly protected by the policy of authorizing only a small per capita tax to be paid to the grand lodge (See Table 2). In other words, the subordinate lodge, through its "power of the purse," has maintained a leverage on grand lodge policy and development.

It should be added that there have been many dynamic forces making for developments in the other direction. That is, there have also been strong factors tending to make the grand lodge dominant. Principal among these are the development of national factor and product markets, the emergence of a positive federal labor policy, rivalries between factions in the IAM leading first to national conflicts and then to national "victories," and technological change outmoding craft solidarity.

The development of a national product market in the machinists' sector has been in process for over a hundred years. Once mass production had been adopted as a general technique, the need for custom-made repairs diminished. Moreover, mass-produced units are selected on a price basis; the result is that areas compete for orders, and the national union emerges to police the wage effects of that competition. What is most remarkable is the delayed nature of this change. However, so long as the IAM was a steam-locomotive-oriented

Table 2. *Authorized per capita tax, 1889–1953.* (unless otherwise noted, amount due monthly) (in dollars)

Effective year	Journeyman	Apprentice	Specialist	Helper	Woman	Unemployed member	Production worker
1889	up to 0.25/qrtr	—	—	—	—	—	—
1891	.25/qrtr	—	—	—	—	—	—
1897	.20 plus .25/qrtr	—	—	—	—	—	—
1901	.40	0.20	—	—	—	—	—
1906	.55	.25	—	—	—	0.20	—
1914	.60	.25	0.45 [a]	0.35	0.45 [a]	.20	—
1918	.60	.30	.45 [a]	.35	.30 [a]	.20	—
1920	.60	.30	.60	.35	.30 [a]	.20	—
1921	1.00	.50	1.00	.65	.50	.20	—
1925	1.00	.50	1.00	.65	.50	.10	—
1937	1.00	.50	1.00	.65	—	.10	0.65
1946	1.05	.55	1.05	.70	—	.10	.70
1949	1.30	.80	1.30	.95	—	.10	.95
1953	1.30	1.30	1.30	1.30	—	.10	1.30

a If earning .25 an hour or less.

railroad union, the impact of the national product market drift was limited, simply because steam engine repairs could not be mass-produced.

The emergence of a positive federal labor policy was largely the result of the wave of railroad strikes prior to World War I. The Adamson Act (1916) was only the first of several important laws which put the government squarely into the railroad industrial relations process. The IAM, like all unions having a large railroad membership, was required to conduct a large share of its negotiations through the good offices of its friends in Congress, because nothing influences any governmental operation so much as an indication of congressional interest. Marshalling support from congressmen required the building of a national organization. And this, in effect, meant the emergence of the grand lodge as a critically important unit. It is worth noting here that even prior to the emergence of railroad legislation, the IAM had recognized the need of using friends in Congress. Industrial relations in the naval yards and arsenals had long been affected by the same procedural necessities. District Lodge 44, the government workers' lodge, had needed the grand lodge for this purpose even in the mid-nineties. But because District Lodge 44 did not represent a dominant group, such as the railroad workers were until the mid-thirties, it was not able to get the grand lodge to devote itself fully to lobbying, until the railroad workers realized the similarity of their own needs. It follows that the passage of the National Industrial Recovery Act (1933), and the Wagner Act (1935) even further increased the importance of there being a national organization for political purposes. Besides, the Wagner Act provided for a continuing process — involving hearings — and in that area, the grand lodge was the best prepared unit to render consistently good service.

We have cited at length the conflicts within the O'Connell and Johnston administrations. In so doing we have indicated that the parties carried political and later "religious" labels, but that they were in effect basically "big city" versus "small railroad town" factions. (It is only fair to add that as in most political squabbles the lines were not clearly drawn.) The conflicts became national in scope — emerging from time to time as efforts to elect Johnston rather than O'Connell, to recall Keegan, Keppler, Preston, and Anderson, and also as efforts to defeat Gompers and to outlaw the National Civic Federation. In each of these, the fight was bitter, and the triumph of the winning side was quickly followed by an attempt to regroup for the next round. Because Johnston and the "Socialists" won in 1911, and in spite of their previous endorsement of "democratic localism," they looked forward to using their new instrument, the grand lodge, for their own purposes. What resulted was their endorsement of national union dominance.

Technological change, as much as any of the other factors mentioned, caused the growth of the grand lodge. Technological changes created a great demand for machinists. The demand was initially largely satisfied with the appearance of the semitrained specialist, whose relatively low common denominator of skill made him more replaceable (thereby lessening the bargaining advantage formerly enjoyed by the old craftsmen) and more of an industrial transient — i.e. willing to enter or leave the trade without a thought to what economic effects his decision would have on other machinists. In short, there was need both to increase bargaining effectiveness and to police the transients. In most instances these required national coordination. Briefly, this too led to the growth of the national organization.

Let us now turn to the record and examine how the relationship between the grand lodge and the subordinate lodges changed.

The basis of grand lodge authority is the constitution. In 1891 the constitution categorized the grand lodge's powers as executive, legislative, and judicial. The executive authority was the implementation of the convention's resolutions. It also stated that the grand lodge was the ultimate tribunal; however, the grand lodge was made to share this authority in 1895. The grand lodge initiated all legislative changes. It determined the customs and usages relative to the practice of the craft. Legislation could also be initiated by the subordinate lodges resorting to referendum. In fact, by 1911, the grand lodge conventions were no longer authorized to repeal anything that had been passed by referendum; and in 1916 the decision to require the submission to referendum vote of all amendments to the constitution was taken.

The generalization here is that the independence of the grand lodge, meaning the national officers and convention delegates, was technically greater at the beginning than it was after 1916. In fact, the powers of the grand lodge declined from 1895 (when the referendum was first instituted), through 1905 (when election of officers was no longer left to the convention, but was decided by referendum vote), through 1911 (when it was held that salaries and per capita taxes could only be changed by referendum action), until 1920 when the grand lodge was at the nadir of its formal authority. Since then no additional steps have been taken to limit grand lodge authority; and, in practice, the development of an administration machine has informally succeeded in undoing most of this formal stripping of power. The means, of course, have been to control the referendum instrument, and this is accomplished by "bringing out the vote" and devising policies which will "split the opposition."

From the first (1889), the grand lodge has been authorized to charter subordinate lodges. And from 1891 it has had the power to accept or reject the constitutions and bylaws proposed by the local lodges. From 1891 until 1895, however, provision was made for the existence of railroad or geographic district lodges, which came into existence upon the petition of five to twenty local lodges, and with the consent of the grand master machinist and the general executive board. Where district lodges did not exist, the grand lodge exercised the right to intervene and to suspend, call in, or revoke charters, if the local officers were incompetent or negligent. But where district lodges were created, the district lodge was given plenary power (under the general limits of the grand lodge constitution) to superintend local matters. For instance, the district lodge could levy assessments, adopt laws and regulations for the government of trade and local affairs, and settle grievances (negotiate with employers). The right of appeal from the district lodge officials to the grand lodge was stated, however. In 1893 local lodge participation in district lodges (where the latter existed) was made obligatory. Moreover, the minimum number of local lodges required to form a district was reduced to three.

It may be recalled that O'Connell and the general executive board became alarmed about the development of power blocs in the IAM and in 1895 successfully cancelled the constitutional provisions giving the district lodges their autonomous powers. What remained was a simple statement that local lodges on a railroad or in a geographic locality could, when they deemed it advisable, form a district lodge "for their mutual protection," providing that its existence and policies did not conflict with the grand lodge constitution. Presumably the grand master machinist (O'Connell) decided all questionable points.

In 1895 the grand lodge also strengthened its supervisory relationships over local lodges — it could revoke an individual's membership, if he hurt the organization by sins of commission or omission.

In 1897 the subordinate lodge officers were made directly responsible to the grand lodge for the property and monies of their lodges; in effect, this gave the national officers full authorization to probe local affairs.

From 1903 to 1905, the rights of district lodges were re-enumerated, although it was abundantly clear that their exercise was subject to the international president's approval. In 1907 the district lodges were given the right to levy assessments, but only if two-thirds of those present so voted. The assessment-levying authority was amended in 1915 to provide for at least seven days' notice of the meeting. It continues much in the same form up to the present.

In 1907 an attempt was made to set up five consolidated district lodges on the railroads, each comprising a large geographic territory. This attempt was abandoned in 1911, although, to be sure, an interest in industry-wide bargaining on the railroads persisted. As a matter of historical record, this action was taken at the time of the calling of the Harriman lines and Illinois Central strikes. Populism caught up briefly with the railroad district lodges from 1937 to 1946, when election of officers by referendum vote was required.

Going back to 1907, the powers of the international officers relative to the revocation of charters were revised; the charters were revocable only after a subordinate lodge was proven guilty of violating the IAM constitution. (In 1920, violation of the provisions of its own bylaws was also made grounds for revocation of the charter.) And in 1941, no doubt as a result of several experiences during the Wharton regime — above all, the Local Lodge 284 episode — the rule was amended to provide for the trial *before* the revocation. Moreover, the trial was to be held on the local scene. The procedure was finally established completely in 1949, when the constitution provided a trial procedure and determined that the international president, with executive council approval, could take over the supervision (suspend the charter), pending the filing and disposition of charges against a lodge. Thus, what has transpired since the earliest days has been the establishment of a definite procedure for the grand lodge's disciplining of subordinate lodges. In one sense, the powers of the international officers have been cut back, because the enumeration of certain rights implies the nonexistence of others. Yet, in practice, this same spelling-out of procedures makes the implementation of the grand lodge's rights possible. A fair summation might be: in spite of the appearance of limitations of grand lodge authorizations through the incorporation of tighter verbiage into the constitution, this same tightening of terms suggests that there has been a greater exercise of supervision by the grand lodge.

What of the position of the local lodges in relation to the grand lodge? From 1889 until 1920 they were enjoined to furnish statistical data on wages, employment, extent of union organization among machinists, and cost of living (retail prices) to the national organization. Starting in 1892 they were given an explicit role in amending the grand lodge constitution; and, as we have already noted, by 1895 this role was co-equal with that of the grand lodge convention. By 1916 it had grown greater than the convention's.

In the mid-nineties the institution of the "walking delegate" (the business agent) spread to the IAM. This meant that local lodges had their own full-time business agents. They were thus developing a professional bureaucracy of their own. In 1899 the grand lodge participated in this development by offering to pay one-half the salaries of these business agents up to a fixed amount, providing that the particular business agent was *persona grata* with the grand lodge; or in the words of Article IX of that constitution, "The grand lodge shall assist lodges maintaining business agencies . . . [approved of by the international president and general executive board] . . . if after due investigation, it is found that [it] . . . warrants the expense. Where it is found that the business agent [*sic*] is a failure, the grand lodge shall . . . withdraw this assistance." Moreover, in 1901, all business agents were made subject to instructions given by the international president; and in 1909 the agents were required to send him monthly statements of their activities. In practice, the grand lodge was not able to "capture" all the business agents. Many did take their lead from the grand lodge (which paid part of their salary), but a few showed no sense of subordination. In fact, they have been the effective opposition on the local level to the aggrandizement of grand lodge functions. They are the ones who have most strongly resisted increasing grand lodge funds and powers. In practice, these "independent" business agents are few in number; but the size of their group is not an accurate reflection of their power. They are frequently the bureaucratic heads of large city organizations (district lodges); they negotiate many contracts involving large numbers of members, and they have behind them sizable treasuries.

The grand lodge, it is worth repeating, has not "tamed" them yet; until it does, local autonomy is still a force to be reckoned with.

Two or three additional small points remain. In 1925 the grand lodge was authorized to subsidize slightly the Ladies' Auxiliary, an organization which started in Scranton, Pennsylvania, near the turn of the century, and which has grown considerably. By giving the grand lodge this authorization, it was hoped that the international officers could have influence over the ladies. They should have known better. Even as skilled a diplomat or politician as General Secretary-Treasurer E. C. Davison reported in 1926 that he could not get them to reform their financial program because they resented any interference.[13]

In 1946, at a time when the IAM was leaving the AFL, it nonetheless required all local lodges to affiliate with the local and state AFL organizations or give an adequate excuse why such affiliation was not feasible. This was obviously an attempt to influence AFL policies locally through the one avenue then remaining open. As such, it was not successful.

And in 1946 the grand lodge authorized what in fact already existed; namely, state councils or conferences. Their purpose was to promote cooperation in the fields of education and legislation. They were enjoined from infringing on the rights of any other IAM organizations—i.e. the grand lodge or any subordinate lodges. The 1949 constitution required that each of these councils or conferences have bylaws, subject to the approval of the grand lodge. Again the motivation for this effort at control was an outgrowth of the Schrank affair.

The local lodges have close ties with the membership. Putting it another way, the members are the local lodges. The power to admit, suspend, try, expel, and reinstate individuals belongs essentially to the local lodges, although some regulations regarding fees have been promulgated by the grand lodge. Certainly from 1889 until 1909, all nonpecuniary regulations clearly were exercised by the local lodges. Then in 1909 the grand lodge laid down some explicit rules regarding reinstatement and directed that it would have a voice in the matter—those who were expelled could not be reinstated without grand lodge permission. At the same time the grand lodge took action which would require its approval in the levying of fines in excess of fifty dollars.

The local lodge keeps the membership records; that is, it issues dues books and sells the grand lodge per capita tax stamps to the members. It levies dues and collects initiation fees; however, the grand lodge has specified the minimum for each in the constitution since 1891 and 1893, respectively. (See

Table 3. *Minimum monthly dues to be charged by local lodges, 1891–1949.*[a]
(in dollars)

Year	Journeyman	Specialist	Apprentice	Helper	Woman or production worker
1891	0.50	—	0.25 [b]	—	—
1897	.50	—	.25 [c]	—	—
1901	.75	—	.375 [d]	—	—
1905	1.00	1.00	.50 [d]	—	—
1911	1.00	1.00	.50 [d]	0.65	—
1913	1.00	.75 [e]	.50 [d]	.65	—
1918	1.00	.75 [e]	.50 [d]	.65	0.50
1921	1.50	1.50	.75 [f]	1.00	.75
1929	1.75	1.75	.875	1.17	.875
1949	2.00 [g]	2.00 [g]	1.00 [g]	1.33 [g]	1.00 [g]

[a] Woman worker category existed from 1918–1937; production worker category, after 1937.
[b] After 3½ years of apprenticeship.
[c] After 2½ years of apprenticeship.
[d] After 2 years of apprenticeship.
[e] When earning 25 cents per hour or less; otherwise, journeyman's rate.
[f] After 6 months of apprenticeship.
[g] Reduced rate applicable to those having to carry membership in another AFL union to qualify for job.

Tables 3 and 4.) Its powers to expand its treasury are somewhat limited; since 1891 it has been forbidden to levy compulsory assessments to aid other unions (the Local Lodge 68 episode notwithstanding).

The local lodge also has issued traveling cards to members. (The traveling card was standard between 1889 and 1899, when it was replaced by the dues book.) It issues withdrawal cards to those leaving the trade and the union, insofar as they have been authorized. They were used from 1891 to 1899, when they were retermed "honorary retirement cards." From 1946 until 1949, they were issued only to those leaving for the armed forces. All others who left were just "dropped." But after 1949, traveling cards were once more in general use.

From 1889 until the present, the local lodges were authorized to pay sick and disability benefits, but it was mainly a function of their own choice. In 1925 the grand lodge tried to assume this burden, one which it later was only too willing to lay down.

Besides these services, the local lodge has served as a job clearing house. Those who are unemployed or dissatisfied with their jobs look to the local lodge for aid in finding the work they desire.

Local lodges not only conduct most negotiations with employers, but from

Table 4. *Minimum initiation fees to be charged by local lodges, 1893–1953.*[a]
(in dollars)

Year	Journeyman	Specialist	Apprentice	Helper	Woman or production worker
1893	2.00	—	1.00 [b]	—	—
1897	2.00	—	1.00 [c]	—	—
1899	3.00	—	1.50 [d]	—	—
1911	3.00	—	1.50 [d]	2.00	—
1913	3.00	2.00 [e]	1.50 [d]	2.00	—
1918	3.00	2.00 [e]	1.50 [d]	2.00	1.50
1921	5.00	5.00	2.50 [f]	3.00	2.50
1929	5.00	5.00	2.50	3.00	2.50
1949	5.00	5.00	2.50	3.00	3.00
1953	5.00	5.00	5.00	5.00	5.00

[a] Woman worker category existed from 1918–1937; production worker category, after 1937.
[b] After 3½ years of apprenticeship.
[c] After 2½ years of apprenticeship.
[d] After 2 years of apprenticeship.
[e] When earning 25 cents per hour or less; otherwise, journeyman's rate.
[f] After 6 months of apprenticeship.

1899 until 1937, they were directed to set the local minimum wages—i.e., the amount below which no machinist should work. Since 1937 this provision has become voluntary—they may or may not set local minimum for machine erectors (involving to some degree those traveling in from outside). Local lodges conduct strike votes and, subject to grand lodge approval, strikes. For this purpose they may pay strike benefits and levy assessments to meet their cost. Since 1920 each local lodge has had to have a relief committee to deal with hardship cases among the members.

From 1903 until 1909, the local lodges were to pay superannuation benefits, for which amounts they were to be reimbursed by the grand lodge. The scheme never worked and was abandoned.

The number of local lodges has grown. The minimum number of members in each lodge was 7 until 1916, when it was increased to 15. In 1916 there were 865 local lodges, the number going as high as 1286 in 1921. There was a steady yearly decline after this period, to a low of 642 in 1933. Then another steady surge from 1934 up to a high of 1883 in 1952.

Grand Lodge Relationship to Members

The earliest grand lodge constitution (1889) defined the eligibility for membership, in the broad sense. It set up the minimum "dues" and the initiation fee. Thus, the requirements for "citizenship" comes from the grand lodge, even though the application of these requirements has been the responsibility of the subordinate lodges.

The IAM's relationship to its members was further specified in 1890 when the grand lodge arrogated to itself the determination of the rights of reinstatement. In 1891 the grand lodge constitution was amended to stipulate the grounds for expulsion of individuals. Hence, by 1891 the grand lodge had extended its authority over the "citizenship right," to include stipulation of the requirements for taking it away as well as those for giving it back.

In 1891 the grand lodge further exercised its authority by defining the apprenticeship system and the rules by which it operated. And although there were several other minor changes, no other substantial claim to grand lodge suzerainty was exercised until 1895, when the record-keeping function was assumed by the general secretary-treasurer.

Table 5. *Death benefits, 1910–1937.*
(amounts paid to journeymen unless otherwise specified) [a]
(in dollars)

Length of service	1910	1911 [b]	1921	1929	1937
1 year	50	40	50	—	—
2 years	75	50	75	—	—
3 "	100	65	100	50	50
4 "	—	—	125	75	—
5 "	150	100	150	100	75
6 "	—	—	175	125	—
7 "	200	135	200	150	100
8 "	—	—	225	175	—
9 "	—	—	250	200	125
10 "	—	—	300	225	—
11 "	—	—	—	250	150
12 "	—	—	—	275	—
13 "	—	—	—	300	175
14 "	—	—	—	—	—
15 "	—	—	—	—	200
16 "	—	—	—	—	—
17 "	—	—	—	—	225
18 "	—	—	—	—	250
19 "	—	—	—	—	275
20 "	—	—	—	—	300

[a] Benefits paid to other classifications, unless specified, were proportionate to the per capita taxes paid.

[b] The amounts given are for helpers; the amounts paid to journeymen were the same as in 1910. From January 1, 1917 until April 1, 1953 no one initiated at age fifty or over was eligible for benefits.

Chapter VIII treats in some detail the cost of benefits developed by the IAM. Here, however, we are concerned with the authorization of benefits.

The method of mutual insurance, the beneficial side of unionism, serves a dual function. It aids those who need help; and it offers the others a reason for continued membership, when the size of benefits relates to the length of continuous association. The benefits can be grouped under three headings: strike, disability, and death. That the grand lodge took a positive role in furnishing any of these, is indicative of two factors. The first is actuarial in nature—only the national organization could handle the nature of the risk. The other is the more important for our purposes; by controlling benefits, the grand lodge built up the members' sense of loyalty to the national organization itself. Table 5 illustrates the changes in authorized death benefits rates paid from 1910 to 1937. Table 6 shows the changes in authorized weekly strike benefits from 1891 to 1925. In 1925 a decision was reached to pay varying amounts depending upon the availability of funds.

Table 6. *Weekly strike benefits, 1891–1925.*
(amounts paid to journeymen, unless specified)[a]
(in dollars)

Status	1891	1895	1903	1907	1925
Single	5.00	4.00	5.00	6.00	[b]
Married or single with one dependent	8.00	6.00	7.00	8.00	[b]

[a] After 1905, apprentices were given one half the journeyman's benefit; after 1913, specialists paying lower rates, received three-quarters the journeyman's rate; after 1918, women workers received one half the journeyman's rate.

[b] Explicit payments replaced by special donations, voted by the international president and the executive council, and distributed in proportion to the members' per capita taxes.

In subsequent sections of this chapter, the tendencies toward central control (grand lodge dominance) over autonomy (subordinate lodge hegemony) are discussed with regard to the legislative, executive, and judicial functions. A complex set of conclusions emerges. Here it suffices to suggest that the grand lodge exercises its control over the members directly (as in the cases we have suggested), and laterally through its determination of subordinate lodge general policies, on the one hand, and its practical assertion of the international president's power as the organization's judicial authority, on the other.

The Ritual

In one major sense, the significance of the ritual lies in the uses to which it was put. It is interesting to note that at no time was the purpose of the ritual simply racism. This point is generally ignored by those who do not appreciate the social movement aspects of unionism.

The avowed purpose of the ritual was to endow the union with a sense of dedication. Briefly, its purpose was to establish within the new members' minds the principle that the IAM represented both a general purpose and a consecrated membership. For these reasons the ritual was surrounded with a solemn air, and its performance was restricted to the most serious part of the lodge's meeting.

In its nature, the ritual appears to have many Masonic characteristics. The explanation of this similarity is simple. Most nineteenth century fraternal and friendly societies had rituals based on Masonic tradition, because many members were Masons and because the Masonic order is the oldest of the present fraternal organizations. New fraternal organizations, bent on becoming traditions in their own right, adopted the established pattern. The Knights of Labor, for instance, drew heavily upon the Masons. And the founders of the IAM drew heavily upon the Knights. Barnett in his study of the printers' union notes that the printers also patterned their constitution and ritual upon similar documents of the Right Worthy Grand Lodge of the Independent Order of Odd Fellows of the United States of America.[14] Be that as it may, the basic pattern was the semireligious one associated with the Masons.

Bitterness over the race issue forced all discussion of the ritual to be done in executive or closed sessions at the conventions. Voting was generally by voice, and it is hard to sense the degree of feeling that existed. (The minutes of executive and closed sessions are not printed; consequently, few who were not at the conventions can appreciate the position in which officers found themselves. They were damned if they moved to strike the offending clause; and they were even more damned if they did not.) It is worth adding that both O'Connell and Johnston wanted to see the clause deleted. Wharton was probably indifferent, although by strict interpretation, he was not eligible for membership, since he was not a "pure white" (he was partly Indian). Brown's feelings are not clear; on *a priori* grounds, it should be assumed that he was neither *pro* nor *con;* and the record only indicates that he held in 1943 that the ritual could only be amended by the convention (meeting in executive session), and not by referendum. Yet he was international president when the executive council finally did take the step.

It is hard to judge whether anything significant remains of the ritual now.

Technically, it still exists, and according to the IAM law it is to be observed. Discussion with a small sample of local lodge members led to the conclusion that the divesting of its contentious character has not revived its original purpose. Moreover, the executive council has had to change its form so that members take the obligation when they sign their membership applications. This change was precipitated by a case before the National Labor Relations Board. Good or bad, the sense of dedication no longer seems to be apparent when members join.

The Legislative Function

The legislative function involves the choice of policies. Normally it is performed by the convention with the subsequent consent of the membership, but it can be performed directly by the membership through referendum vote. In practice, the international president as well as the executive council (including its predecessor, the general executive board) also choose policies by being generous or niggardly in their implementation.

In formal terms, the legislative function is performed by the convention (with subsequent ratification by the membership) or by direct referendum action, alone. The prerogative, defined by Locke to be the exercise of the legislative right between the meetings of the regular legislative body, is vested, in theory, in the referendum instrument.

The Convention

The regularity of conventions and the methods of calling them have changed from time to time. In general, provision has been made for conventions at either one- two- or four-year intervals, with the sole modification that from 1912 until 1916 there was no provision for calls at a specified time.

In general, conventions have been called in three ways. The most direct manner was to have the constitution specify that conventions were to be called at set intervals. The conventions of 1897 (Kansas City), 1899 (Buffalo), 1901 (Toronto), 1905 (Boston), 1936 (Milwaukee), 1940 (Cleveland), 1948 (Grand Rapids), and 1952 (Kansas City) were held under this type of provision. A slightly different manner was also used. In this case, the constitution provided that conventions were to be held at specified intervals, but only after the membership had been polled as to whether the time was appropriate. They always agreed, and conventions were held under this rule in Chicago (1892), Indianapolis (1893), Cincinnati (1895), Milwaukee (1903), St. Louis (1907), Davenport (1911), Rochester (1920), Detroit (1924), and Atlanta (1928). From 1889 through 1892, and from 1912 until 1916, there was no provision in the constitution for calling conventions, except one which permitted referendum votes on any issue. The Atlanta, Louisville, and Pittsburgh conventions (1889, 1890, 1891, respectively) as well as the Baltimore convention (1916) were called according to this means. Referendum votes were used to cancel conventions in 1932 and 1944, because of economic difficulties engendered by the Great Depression and transportation regulations in effect during the Second World War. The New York convention (1945) was called by special referendum as soon as the war was over.

As the organization has become larger, the frequency of conventions has diminished. Since 1916 the practice has been to plan conventions on a quadrennial basis. A second observation relates to the method of calling conventions. The Socialist–Populist influence, strong in the years prior to the First World War, emphasized the use of a referendum vote to authorize holding of conventions because the Socialist leaders had a general fear of O'Connell's organizational machine being turned against them. Therefore, they wanted conventions to be held only when they were confident that they were in control of the situation.

It is worth noting, for instance, that O'Connell, who was adept at controlling his administrative machine, and who was a strong advocate of convention (rather than referendum) control, sought to have conventions held at regular intervals. When he was strong (in 1895, 1897, 1899 and 1905), use of the referendum was reduced. When he was relatively weak (in 1901 at the time of the NMTA strike), the other procedure was preferred. In 1911 when he was defeated, the Socialists–Populists took full control and substituted use of the referendum in place of the convention.

By 1916 it was clear that a convention was sorely needed, and as we have noted, one was called. Johnston never abandoned his preference for requiring a referendum to call a convention. Wharton preferred O'Connell's to Johnston's way. Quadrennial conventions, without referenda vote, were authorized at Atlanta in 1928, which was Wharton's first real opportunity to reconstruct the constitution. The 1932 convention was to have been held in St. John, New Brunswick, but for reasons already given, was not held.

The 1891 convention provided that all delegates coming to conventions were entitled to travel pay of 3 cents per mile. This allowance proved to be too heavy a strain on the grand lodge treasury, and provision for paying these grants was withdrawn. In 1916, however, a limited return was made to the practice, when it was decided to have the grand lodge pay the traveling expenses of one delegate per lodge. This practice has continued to the present time.

In general, voting at the convention has always been associated with the size of the local. This is to say, each lodge has generally been entitled to twice as many votes as it has delegates. Thus, even for the very smallest lodges (which are entitled to bare representation and a vote), every delegate casts at least one vote. If, however, a lodge sends fewer delegates than it is entitled to send, each delegate may cast more than his double vote. Delegations usually vote as a bloc, but delegates have the right to vote as individuals, if they so desire.

The 1903 convention decided to require that each delegate be a member of his local lodge at least three months prior to his selection. At the 1909 convention it was further required that the delegate had to have been working at the trade for at least six months prior to his nomination. Later in 1911 a further exception had to be made in favor of unemployed members who were unable to find work because of their union membership: that is, in favor of those "discriminated against." By 1920 this exception had proved insufficient, and was further modified to include those unable to obtain employment as a result of a strike, lockout, discrimination, or temporary physical disability. What is evident is that there were to be no chronic deadbeats or unemployables as delegates. This policy has continued to the present time. It is worth adding that since 1920, grand lodge employees and officers as well as those employed by some agency of the AFL can be delegates but must go off the grand lodge payroll for the duration of the convention.

Representation of local lodges at conventions has been changed only three times. From the beginning (when a regular procedure was established in the constitution), 1891 until 1897, the basic pattern was one delegate for every 50 paid-up members. Actually this meant that every lodge was entitled to at least 1 delegate, and that those lodges having more than 50 members, could send an additional delegate if they had at least 76 members, or they could send three delegates if they had 126 members.

At the 1897 convention, action to change the ratios was taken, making it 1 delegate for every 25 members or major fraction thereof, with all lodges entitled to at least one delegate.

Starting with the 1903 convention the ratios were again changed. The basic unit was raised to 100 members. But at that convention the number was raised to 200, where it has since remained. Thus beginning with the 1905 convention, the basis of representation has been 1 delegate for every 200 members.

The convention sessions are usually open to any interested party. However, on occasion, each convention has gone into closed session, when all nonmembers are excluded. The ritual, purportedly a secret known only to members (and ex-members), is then discussed. On a few occasions the convention goes into "executive session" where only delegates and officers are permitted.

The duration of the conventions vary, but seven to ten days is the average length. The first few days are frequently taken up with addresses given by outside dignitaries. In the meantime various committees are named, and they hold hearings on resolutions. The resolutions are initially presented by local lodges or, on occasion, by the convention or the executive council.

The Committee on Law, the one responsible for amending the constitution, has been elected by the membership since 1911. About the same time the power of selecting the other convention committees was explicitly given to the convention; previously it can be assumed that the international president made the appointments. In 1913 this rule was modified to give the international president the right to choose the Rules Committee, and in 1920 the constitution was changed to give to the international president the right to select the Resolutions Committee 15 days prior to the convention. In 1929 he and the executive council were given the right to nominate all committees (except the Law, Rules, and Resolutions Committees), with the convention itself charged only with ratifying the nominations. In 1936 the convention thoroughly reconsidered the question of who was to select the other committees, and after Wharton pointed out that having the convention elect the committees (as had been proposed by the Rules Committee) would result in added expense in time and money, the convention struck the Rules Committee proposal, leaving things as they were.

The conventions are run according to Robert's Rules. Roll call votes are fairly infrequent, although in every convention there has always been at least one. The tradition has been to give the international president considerable latitude in describing his position and recommendations, but this tradition is watched carefully by his opposition. O'Connell had a sense of convention-timing, which Johnston did not share. Wharton's abilities in this area were between the two — his masterly handling of the Local Lodge 284 appeal at the 1936 Milwaukee convention is a positive example. Harvey Brown's technique was not good.

Certain generalizations regarding the use of the convention as a governmental instrument stand out. It is primarily an educational experience because, except for matters of ritual, its vote on legislative matters is not final. It is an opportunity for the delegates to meet and hear the national officers, to convey to them grass roots sentiment. It is also a proving ground for talent. Leadership shows itself in the committee hearings and on the convention floor. But the convention is not an active instrument of democracy, because it is subordinate to the referendum and because the IAM is too large and complex an organization to be able to respond to a "town meeting" type of government.

The Prerogative

We have already noted that the prerogative is in theory vested in the referendum instrument. By this we mean simply that the legislative function between conventions is purportedly exercised only through the referendum.

The decision to use the referendum instrument was taken in 1895: "Article I, section 5. All legislative powers hitherto vested in this body [the grand lodge, convention assembled], shall be vested in the subordinate lodges, to be carried out under the referendum system. This clause to go into effect on the first day of October, 1895." In order to amend the constitution, any local or district lodge had to get the endorsement of 5 per cent of the total number of lodges prior to requesting a vote. Having fulfilled this requirement, however, the local lodge had the right to insist upon a speedy vote, for the change also provided that the "grand secretary" could be fined $25.00 to $50.00 if he failed to carry out the provisions enacted. To amend the constitution, the referendum had not only to get a majority of votes cast, but at least 50 per cent of the eligible membership had to participate in the voting process.

In 1897 use of the referendum was made easier. Instead of requiring endorsement of 5 per cent of all the local lodges and the voting of a majority of the members, endorsement of only five lodges and a simple majority of those voting were all that was required. Thus the effect of the 1897 changes was to liberalize the use of the referendum. Two years later, a move was made to prevent regional enthusiasms from precipitating referenda votes; it was required that no two of the five endorsements could be from lodges in the same state.

Further steps were taken in 1905 and 1907 to reduce the ease of getting a referendum vote. In the former year the number of required endorsements was raised to twenty-five (with a maximum of three coming from any single state, province or territory); and in the latter, the number was increased to one hundred (with no more than five from any single state).

After the 1907 convention, as O'Connell's influence waned, reliance upon the referendum instrument grew more pronounced. In 1909 the number of regional endorsements was reduced to forty (with not more than five from any single political unit — as formerly). But it was in 1911, the year of O'Connell's defeat, that the referendum really "came into its own." The constitution was changed to require that all questions of grand lodge officers' salaries and per capita taxes could only be changed by referendum, instead of at conventions, and that any action once voted in referendum could only be changed by similar (referendum) action.

In 1911, as was noted earlier, a decision was reached to refer all matters to referendum vote even after they had been passed by convention action.

Consequently, conventions seemed unnecessary, and no future provision was made for calling them. The Law Committee, elected by referendum vote, met each odd numbered year to consider any amendments which had been submitted (properly endorsed) by various local lodges. After due consideration, the Law Committee was to make its recommendations and the various proposals would then be submitted to the rank and file. Upon passage they would then be incorporated into the constitution.

The next change was in 1913, when it became evident that administrative efficiency dictated that amendments be voted on no more frequently than every other year. It was as though the earlier experience with conventions was being repeated. Frequent conventions were both expensive and conducive to instability; the same results were similarly evident with semiannual referenda votes on constitutional amendments.

When, in 1916, it was decided that conventions were necessary after all, use of the referendum was not sacrificed. Instead, it was resolved that the rank and file would have to ratify all amendments voted by the delegates. However, it was decided that in the years when a convention was held, the delegates would vote first on all submitted amendments, and only if they took affirmative action, would the rank and file be given an opportunity to voice their views.

Use of the referendum was once more reduced in 1920, when the number of required endorsements was expanded to 10 per cent of the number of local lodges (with no more than ten coming from any single state).

On the whole, however, we can conclude that the use of the referendum as an instrument for exercising the prerogative has been neither efficient nor particularly equitable. Membership apathy, minority group enthusiasms and collusion, as well as the absence of thorough discussion before voting, have made this method less than desirable. Similarly, when the referendum has been employed as a means of ratifying convention decisions, it has caused the conventions to become less solemn and responsible bodies. On several occasions the conventions have, after full debate, voted to raise per capita taxes, minimum dues, officers' salaries, and pensions for employees, only to have the matters defeated in the subsequent referenda. This situation could be construed to be the will of the membership if a reasonably large number of the rank and file voted. But generally, such has not been the case. Often, needed changes have been unreasonably delayed because a minority group, after having been outvoted at a convention, chose to stage a last-ditch fight on the "grass roots level."

The question of the value of the referendum as an instrument for exercising the prerogative, goes back to one's faith in representative government. The referendum was introduced because faith was lacking in the good, disinterested judgment of the convention delegates. It is hard to see, however, how venality or stupidity among them can be prevented by referring all questions to the electorate who selected them. Table 7 shows the largest number of members voting in a referendum on any issue, including election of officers, for each year from 1904 through 1952. The percentage of total membership

Table 7. *Number participating in referenda votes, 1904–1952.* (in thousands, using maximum vote for each year) [a]

Year	Membership	Maxima referenda vote	Per cent	Year	Membership	Maxima referenda vote	Per cent
1904	55.7	10.4	19	1929	71.6	21.0	29
1905	48.5	9.5	20	1930	69.4	19.2	28
1906	50.0	N.A.[b]	—	1931	63.6	20.6	32 [c]
1907	69.4	11.2	22	1932	58.9	12.7	22
1908	57.1	11.2	20	1933	61.1	13.1	21
1909	48.2	14.3	30 [d]	1934	88.3	16.9	19
1910	61.0	13.4	22	1935	88.9	18.1	20
1911	67.4	28.9	43 [e]	1936	105.1	25.8	25
1912	63.0	13.9	22	1937	152.1	36.7	24
1913	74.0	22.9	31 [e]	1938	155.3	27.8	18
1914	74.2	11.2	15	1939	161.8	34.6	22
1915	75.0	16.9	23	1940	187.7	45.5	24
1916	107.4	29.1	27	1941	284.5	34.4	12
1917	127.5	35.2	28	1942	444.9	54.7	12
1918	229.5	58.7	23	1943	616.7	99.0	16
1919	331.4	56.1	17	1944	661.8	51.3	8
1920	282.5	35.6	13	1945	609.2	46.6	8
1921	206.9	38.0	18	1946	519.2	58.3	11
1922	148.3	55.9	38 [f]	1947	545.6	115.0	21
1923	105.0	N.A.	—	1948	541.9	N.A.	—
1924	79.6	15.3	19	1949	518.5	84.1	16
1925	72.0	34.8	48 [f]	1950	509.9	51.8	10
1926	71.6	19.1	27	1951	621.1	111.4	18
1927	71.0	21.4	30 [g]	1952	734.1	99.6	14
1928	69.0	11.9	17				

[a] *Machinists' Monthly Journal.*
[b] Not available or none held.
[c] Against raising salary of international president.
[d] Constitutional amendment.
[e] Election of Johnston.
[f] Election of editor (Hewitt).
[g] Election of general secretary–treasurer. (Davison).

voting has never reached 50 per cent and generally has been below 25 per cent. Since the end of the Second World War, in particular, the proportion of those choosing to exercise their voting rights, has been even smaller.

Nonetheless, the history of the use of the referendum exemplifies resistance to the process of centralization. In fact, the legislative process has become centralized, insofar as the international officers are the initiators of most of the important programs, and they, through their endorsement of personnel for the Committee on Law, in effect screen subordinate lodge proposals. But so long as all changes must go to the rank-and-file membership, it is necessary to conclude that the movement toward centralization of authority has been, in good part, circumscribed.

The Executive Function

This function involves the implementing of basic policies. It is presumed that wherever the policies were spawned, they were officially determined at the conventions and/or in the referenda. In the grand lodge of the IAM, the executive function has always been exercised by the international president and a consultative body. To aid the president, staff members have been appointed, who in time have come to assume much of the burden (but none of the responsibilities) of his office. In addition, he has been assisted by vice-presidents. There has also been an office of the general secretary–treasurer, which of recent years has had its own "professional" staff.

For reasons of lucid exposition, we shall discuss in sequence the evolution of the various offices. First come the general questions of the selection of officers, and what happened to them as individuals. Then we shall discuss the duties of the office of the international president (called the grand master machinist prior to 1899). After that, we turn to the office of general secretary–treasurer (prior to 1893 the two functions were separate). Then, the vice-presidents and those designated to assist the president. And finally, the consultative body. Throughout, however, it should be borne in mind that the president has virtually always been the dominant member of the executive. Occasionally the general secretary–treasurers have developed influence and power, but that was because of their long tenure in office and their personalities. Even when the president has been opposed by a critical consultative body (i.e. the general executive board during part of Johnston's administration and the executive council during Brown's), his has invariably been the strongest influence.

The Election and Retirement of Officers

In the beginning (1888) there was no formal provision for the election of officers, although, in fact, they were elected by the grand lodge "in convention, assembled." In 1891 provision was made for having the convention carry on the elections by ballot and an absolute majority was required for victory.

In 1892 the constitution was changed in order to permit any seven delegates, who wished, to demand a roll call vote. The following year, when O'Connell became grand master machinist, the roll call was established as a mandatory part of the election process.

The next change was made in 1905 and was major in its implications. Instead of having the convention select the officers, they were to be nominated by the local lodges and voted upon by the entire membership. In short, the referendum supplanted the convention as the instrument for selecting the officers. In 1905 a further change required that a candidate have a simple voting majority to gain victory. In 1907, however, this vestigial remnant of the convention procedure was dropped, and only two candidates (those receiving the greatest number of endorsements) ran. A plurality was all that was required for victory — thus, blank or partly voided ballots did not count against the winner. The system of elections has remained unchanged until the present, in spite of a 1907 attempt to limit a man to two consecutive terms. This proposal went to referendum and was defeated 8175 to 3073.

In 1911, however, a system of recall was adopted. Part of the Socialist–Populist program, it became a two-edged threat. It permitted any subordinate lodge in good standing, which had garnered the endorsements of eighty other lodges (not more than ten of which were in any single state, province or territory), to demand the recall of any officers. Upon notice of the demand for his recall, the affected officer was allowed to write a two-hundred-word statement, which was then circulated officially (at the expense of the grand lodge).

If he sought reelection, he was paired against the eligible candidate receiving the greatest number of endorsements. If not, the two eligible candidates receiving the greatest number of endorsements ran against each other. The victor served only the unexpired term.

From 1912 until 1920 the threat of the recall instrument was fairly frequent; no changes were made except in 1915 when the recalled man was allowed to make a five-hundred- rather than a two-hundred-word statement. During this period J. J. Keegan was recalled as delegate to the AFL and subsequently defeated by A. O. Wharton. Keegan, one of O'Connell's friends, was charged with entertaining pro-employer (i.e. National Civic Federation) sympathies.[15] In 1915 an attempt was made by Local Lodge 126 (Chicago), to recall Vice-President J. J. Keppler. Keppler was reelected 8369 to 6403. In

1916, as an aftermath of the Preston incident, he was recalled, and Emitt Davison was elected in his place. And in 1919 Local Lodge 582 (Chicago) sought the recall of International Vice-President Anderson, on the grounds that he had not prosecuted the IAM demands before the United States Railroad Administration with adequate vigor. Balloting was held in early 1920, and Anderson was returned to his post 20,292 to 11,702.

At the 1920 convention, steps were taken to make the recall instrument less easy to wield. Instead of the endorsement of eighty lodges, endorsement of no less than 15 per cent of the total number was required (with not more than fifteen coming from any single state, province, or territory). Moreover, unless someone else got at least twenty-five lodge endorsements, no one could run against him.

In the 1925–1926 period Anderson was not recalled, but suspended instead. He sought vindication by appealing to a membership referendum. These were the ballots which were never counted.

There have been no recalls of officers since 1920.

One problem involving elections, which the IAM has sought to solve, is the prevention of slander, or what Wendell Willkie once euphemistically termed "campaign talk." In 1905 the convention voted to authorize the fining and/or expulsion after trial, by the man's local or district lodge, of anyone convicted of circulating "malicious or untrue statements" about the character or standing, "private or public," of any officer or member, or of impugning his motives. The right of appeal was granted — appeal to be heard by the general executive board.

By 1909, as a result of IWW inroads, this clause was broadened to provide for punishment of those whose actions encouraged secession or disruption of the IAM organization. Furthermore, if the local or district lodge failed to take action, the international president and the general executive board were authorized to try the individual, and impose punishment. The actual disciplining of secessionists has been limited to Marxian "radicals," later to CIO enthusiasts, and much later to actively antiunion members, who were involuntarily recruited by means of union-shop contracts, and who sought to reduce union power through disruptive tactics. Here it suffices to note that by 1909 the grand lodge had the right to initiate trial proceedings. By 1916, it may be recalled, Johnston had exercised that right in the Carl Persons case.

As a result of the bitterness of the Johnston–Anderson feud in 1925, there was some discussion of restoring the election process to the convention, but it was neither adopted then nor later in 1928, when it was again proposed. Instead, in 1926 the membership adopted by a bare 188 vote majority out of over 19,000 cast, a provision that provided for an identification number for each ballot — thus, a check could be made later on the validity of the count.

Of recent years there has been a trend toward uncontested national elections for the two top positions. This change is indicated in Appendix I.

It can be seen that the number of unsuccessful candidates for offices where contested elections remain the rule has also fallen. In 1952 no election was contested.

Appendix I traces the election careers of the national officers. All victories and defeats are not homogeneous; for example, O'Connell ran ten times between 1907 and the end of his life and lost only twice. Both defeats were particularly bitter because they terminated what seemed to be time-honored recognition. By way of contrast, Johnston ran eight times in the same period and lost twice—but these defeats were prior to his great victory of 1911; consequently it is fair to say that his election history was qualitatively better than O'Connell's. Wharton ran nine times and lost twice (early in his career). Davison ran ten times and lost twice (early in his career). Conlon lost once in mid-career—running a total of ten times; like him, Fechner lost only once, running nine times. The great loser was Anderson, being defeated three of the seven times he ran (and at the end of his career, as well).

Election opportunities, involving the number of offices, length of term, remuneration, power to participate as part of the policy-making body, as well as designating the electorate of the officers (which has already been discussed), have frequently been changed. In general, the major trends have emphasized longer terms of office, fewer officers relative to the size of membership, and until fairly recently, an inflexibility in the upward revision of salaries, as seen in Table 8. Only the relevant qualifications for office holders were included—other points such as the Caucasian clause (violated in letter if not in spirit in the case of Arthur O. Wharton), the non-Communist clause, the National Civic Federation membership prohibition, plus a citizenship clause are not included. They were, however, mentioned in the historical chapters.

The remaining topic is the retirement of officers. Some retired simply because they failed to be reelected. Others retired because of ill health. A few retired for other reasons, or resigned. But the majority died in office. Table 8, giving the salaries authorized at different times, indicates that until recently no one could have left office with any great savings from his union remuneration.

In the early years when an officer died "prematurely," the organization made some sort of *ad hoc* arrangements for his widow and family. These arrangements were rarely satisfactory, and by 1920 there was some sentiment for providing a regular pension or survivor's benefit. In spite of some interest shown at the 1936 convention, nothing happened until 1937, when the officers were brought into the Railroad Retirement Administration scheme.

Table 8. *Elected officials: Changes in salary, 1899–1953.*[a]
(prior condition prevails unless otherwise noted)
(in dollars)

Salaries	1899	1901	1903	1905	1907	1909	1911	1915	1916
International president	1500	1500	1800	—	2400	—	—	—	—
Vice-president & editor [b]	1000	—	—	—	—	—	—	—	—
Vice-president [c]	—	1000	1200	—	1500	—	—	—	—
General vice-president [d]	—	—	—	—	—	—	—	—	—
General secretary-treasurer	1200	—	1500	—	2000	—	—	—	—
Editor [e]	—	1200	1500	—	1500	1800	—	—	—
General exec. bd. mbrs.[f]	4.00 per diem	—	—	—	4.00 per diem, plus 25 per qtr.	5.00 per diem plus 25 per qtr.	—	—	1500

Salaries	1918	1921	1925	1929	1941	1946	1953
International president	4200	7500	—	—	—	12,000	18,000
Vice-president & editor [b]	—	—	—	—	—	—	—
Vice-president [c]	3600	5000	—	—	—	—	—
General vice-president [d]	—	—	4500	—	—	8,000 [g]	12,000 [g]
General secretary-treasurer	3600	6500	—	—	—	10,000	15,000
Editor [e]	3000	4500	—	—	—	8,000	12,000
General exec. bd. mbrs.[f]	3000	5000	—	—	—	—	—

[a] Salary does not include expense allowance.
[b] Two offices separated in 1901.
[c] Office abolished, effective 1925.
[d] Office created, effective 1925.
[e] Office created in 1901.
[f] Office abolished, effective 1925. Incumbents called "lay trustees" from 1899 to 1901. During the period 1899 to 1901 two members of the "board of trustees" were hired as full-time assistant organizers.
[g] Plus additional $1000 for general vice-president stationed at headquarters.

Then it was decided that at its own option, the executive council could pay the difference between one-half the officer's (or grand lodge employee's) railroad pension and his regular salary when he reached sixty years of age. Retirement was made mandatory (with or without the IAM "pension contribution") at seventy, however.

After the 1940 convention this plan was adopted by the membership, except that the pension became a right and was calculated on the basis of the man's average salary for the last twelve months of his service.

Retirement at age sixty-five became obligatory in 1945. In addition, limits were developed allowing everyone no less than $200 per month (including his benefit from the railroad retirement or old age survivors plan), and forbidding the grand lodge to pay amounts which would make the total more than $320 a month. Those previously retired also benefited by the new plan.

General Vice-President Carr, elected close to his sixty-fifth birthday, tried to complete his term, but was forced by Harvey Brown to retire. He appealed to the executive council but lost five to four. The issue went to the 1948 convention. The resolution of the dispute did not benefit Carr, personally, but the convention ratified the proposal that any officer who on his sixty-fifth birthday had less than a year to complete his term of office, could do so.

The limits on the grand lodge contributions to individual pensions were again liberalized in 1952. Here it suffices to note that the IAM, unlike most other American unions, does not permit the superannuated to remain in office, nor does it turn them out without decent regard for their economic needs.

The International President

Because the central structure of Part I was largely a discussion of the evolution of the executive powers of the international president, only a few special topics will be handled in this section; the organizing program, the research program, the legal staff, and the educational program. The development of a newspaper and public relations program come later in this chapter.

The Organizing Function. Except for the beginning years, the international president has always had the title of "chief organizer." This, of course, means that he has been responsible for administering the organizing campaigns. His selection of assistants has, at times, been a matter for constitutional determination — as in 1897, when he was directed to select his staff from lists prepared by local lodges.

After 1901, vice-presidents were elected by referendum, and one of their principal functions was to act as organizers. In fact, one of the criticisms of O'Connell's administration was the degree of his reliance upon the seven vice-presidents and the consequent limitation of organizing campaigns. Thus in 1911, at the time of the change in administrations, provision was made for the appointment of special organizers, to be selected by the international president. Johnston's response was to appoint as many as he thought the budget could afford. The bulk of the organizing burden fell on the special organizers, not only because the number of vice-presidents was reduced in 1915, but also because the officers had to devote an increasingly large part of their time to negotiating with employers on war work. In 1915 an organizing department was formally created with one vice-president given nominal responsibility. By 1917, however, it was agreed that not all appointments had been wise, and steps were taken to cut the number from forty-three to twenty-five. This decision provoked a major dispute between Johnston and the general executive board — each side insisting that it had the sole right to determine who was to be retained. The dispute was quite bitter but came to an unexpected resolution, when it was discovered that both sides were in general agreement regarding the action to be taken — in the case of individual men. Later in 1917 a constitutional provision was enacted making two years' continuous good membership and lack of dues delinquency the qualifications for appointment. The position of grand lodge representative was established — to be, in effect, a "commissioned officer" on the international president's staff.

Here it is interesting to note the case of Mrs. Ella Reeves ("Mother") Bloor who was given a membership card and hired in 1918 to organize women workers, although she had never worked at the trade. "Mother" Bloor, well known in her role as "labor agitator" in the mine fields, remained with the IAM until 1922, when the general executive board directed that she be dismissed on the grounds that she was not a machinist in the necessary meaning of the term.[16]

In the early twenties the organizing question became particularly acute. And in 1924 President Johnston and the general executive board introduced a "bounty" system for new members. This meant that each member who brought someone into the union was given $1.00 as a reward. This system was continued until May 1927. It was estimated that well over twenty-thousand members were thus recruited — in any case as of January 1, 1927 "commissions" totalling $22,788 had been paid.[17]

In restrospect Johnston's use of the "profit motive" as an organizing technique seems incongruous. For a Socialist, dedicated to unionism as a working-class movement, his reliance upon this most "capitalist-oriented" gimmick is hard to explain. Nonetheless, when it was abandoned during Wharton's time, several local lodges complained claiming that the system "worked." The executive council simply told them that if that were so they could pay the commission out of their own treasury. The technique is mentioned here because it was a temporary step away from the professionalization of union administrative activities. By the thirties, organizing was as professionalized as it had ever been with, of course, some differences.

The big CIO organizing drives were eventually matched by IAM efforts. The generalizations to be noted, however, were that the function of organizing became at a very early period a grand lodge responsibility, and that a class of professionals — grand lodge representatives — was developed to perform this function. This is not to imply that local business agents do not also serve as organizers. To the contrary, since 1939 the executive council has authorized the grand lodge to pay business agents for their time and expenses while undertaking organizing efforts. Nor are the grand lodge representatives exclusively concerned with organizing. But, historically speaking, organizing has long been one of their principal assignments.

The position of grand lodge representative has become increasingly important. They are actually "commissioned" representatives of the international president, or when so designated, of a general vice-president. Since 1925, they have had to have five years of previous membership experience (free of delinquencies), before they are appointed. In this way, it is assured that they are a group of IAM career men, and not, as might otherwise be the case, intellectuals or do-gooders, doing a stint with the IAM before moving on to some other union job.

The salaries paid to grand lodge representatives have been reasonably good, considering the IAM belief that union employees should not receive more than men in the shop are paid. From 1920 until 1945, they got $300 per month plus expenses. In 1946 their pay was raised to $5000 a year for the first six months; $5500 a year for the second six months, and $6000 a year, thereafter. In 1952, these amounts were again raised to $7000, $7500 and $8000 respectively.

The Research Function. The need for accurate wage and employment data has always been felt by those in the American labor movement whose duty it has been to bargain with employers. In the earliest years of the IAM, provision was made for local lodges to have a "statistician" who would record wage, employment and cost-of-living data. These, in turn, would be put to use by the local lodge during negotiation sessions.

It is not possible, except by inference, to tell how successful this system of local reporting was. From time to time the journal published reports of wage rates, unemployment, and even local cost-of-living estimates. But little check was made for accuracy; and certainly no check was made for comprehensiveness.

One effect of World War I, however, was the establishment of a national market for machined materials. Consequently, to prevent inter-area competition from driving down wage rates, it became mandatory for the grand lodge to play a role in the collection, preparation, and application of statistical data. There were at least two difficulties. The first was a natural defensiveness by local lodges for their own autonomy. (It stands to reason that the grand lodge collection of statistical data was viewed by those who favored local autonomy as the first step in eventual grand lodge control of the bargaining process.) The other problem grew out of the acute shortage of technically trained labor economists within the ranks of the IAM or even the American labor movement as a whole.

At the 1920 convention, Resolution 40 was adopted which tried, in part, to meet local criticism. It tied the collection of data to the need for furnishing information to local lodges so they could carry on bargaining. Nothing came of this attempt, first because the following period was one of general retrenchment and reduction of grand lodge costs; second, because the national market for machined goods, inspired largely by wartime demands, diminished in size and importance.

It was not until 1930 that we find the grand lodge systematically organizing a research and development program. At the end of 1933, Wharton appointed David Kaplan, of whom we have spoken earlier. Kaplan, in turn, hired other assistants, including two Wisconsin graduate students, Philip Taft (later Professor of Economics at Brown University) and Hans Lehmann (previously a judge in the Weimar Republic's labor courts and later a staff member of the Labor Bureau of the Midwest). In 1937 other regular staff members were appointed, including Paul Hutchings, who succeeded Kaplan when he accepted a similar position in the teamsters' union. Hutchings left in 1945, and shortly thereafter, Carl Hundorff, a business agent from Texas, was made research director. This list of names is included because it typifies the problem facing the grand lodge. Kaplan and Hutchings left the organization primarily because they were given bigger opportunities elsewhere. They were not "consecrated machinists" (which, of course, does not imply that they were any less dedicated). Beginning with Hundorff's appointment the decision to train a machinist as research director, rather than the reverse, was made.

The responsibilities of the research department grew during and after World War II. This department has become responsible for the analysis of contracts in order to determine trends and patterns of settlement. It analyzes changes in membership composition as well as the effects of change in grand lodge expenditures. It has also prepared a model or standard contract, and during the Second World War, a manual for handling piecework. And when, as in the aircraft industry, there has been a growth of standard bargaining, the research department serves the international president in a staff capacity, prior to his recommendations regarding standard rates and conditions.

In short, the increased intervention of the international president into the collective bargaining process was the natural result of the growth of American industry, greater government activity, and the role of wartime labor boards. In turn, the development of a research department was the result of the added pressure put on the international president. In order to give the department stability, it was decided to give it a career man as director. He could then hire such technicians and professionals as were necessary.

The Legal Program. Almost from its inception the grand lodge has been involved in litigation. And litigation has created a need for legal advice and aid. However, it was not until 1907 that pressure to authorize the regular employment of a single law firm to give aid and counsel began to mount in the conventions. It was pointed out that the National Metal Trades Association had a regular legal staff, and that the IAM needed one no less. But the proposal did not obtain sufficient delegate support.

The question of having regular counsel was brought up at successive conventions, and in 1911, when it was made abundantly clear that it cost more not to have consistent legal advice, the convention authorized a sum for legal retainers. The attorney selected was Frank Mulholland of Toledo, Ohio — not related to the William Mulholland of the same city who had been the leader of the bicycle workers. Mulholland had handled IAM litigation for several years previous to this appointment. And he and his firm remained IAM counsel until the end of Brown's term (1948).

From time to time other firms were also used. In 1938 Joseph Padway, the AFL's general counsel, was given a retainer to advise on matters going before the National Labor Relations Board. This arrangement had to be modified during World War II, when the amount of litigation before the board became too great for any one firm to handle. In 1946 an order went out giving the grand lodge authority over the arguments used by the attorneys of IAM locals. This move came after finding that, in one case, the IAM had been proposing the very argument which it had been resisting in another. The consequence, quite naturally, was the establishment of a "coordinator of arguments" in the international president's office. The obvious choice for this task was a full-time legally trained assistant.

In 1947 several moves were made which further illustrated the need for coordination. A general counsel was appointed to coordinate the NLRB work as mentioned above. Each general vice-president also hired a counsel to help process NLRB cases. And the resident officers (the international president, the general secretary–treasurer, and the general vice-president stationed at headquarters) collectively arranged to get advice from one of the leading law firms in Washington. These arrangements proved costly, and in 1948 all the arrangements were reconsidered. The regional counsels for NLRB cases were discontinued, and a full-time attorney was hired to take charge of the whole operation. His office is in the grand lodge headquarters. This change does not mean that he handles all litigation — rather, he is a staff officer who advises the international president and the executive council regarding policy. The actual litigation is usually farmed out.

Membership Education Program. For many years, the education of the worker was considered either to be the normal by-product of the journal, or beyond that, the responsibility of local lodges. As a matter of fact, it is still considered to be the by-product of the newspaper and attendance at local lodge meetings. Since 1899 the constitution for local lodges was provided that, "Each lodge, under the 'good and welfare' may discuss the subject of Political Economy for twenty minutes," and since 1905, "providing such discussion does not include partisan politics or religious creeds."

But this reliance upon self-direction has proved to be insufficient for its purpose. Partly as a result of the development of employers' education programs, partly from the collapse of the American Socialist movement with the consequent realization that education was vitally needed prior to attempting large-scale reforms, and partly as an outgrowth of the extension of popular free education, the grand lodge has assumed some degree of responsibility for providing direction for the IAM workers' education program.

In 1925 the Workers' Education Bureau received ½ cent per member, per annum, for the services it provided. When, two years later, the Workers' Education Bureau doubled its rate (to one cent per annum, per member), the IAM dropped the service. And in spite of repeated requests from the bureau for IAM reaffiliation, it was not until the relatively lush year of 1940 that the executive council voted to restore the service.

In 1947 the executive council hired a full-time director of education, Tom Tippett, and since that time, has had a grand lodge educational program. This program has been generally focused on developing organizing aids and on awakening membership interest in union problems. It has been conducting training institutes for local leaders and grand lodge representatives, and has prepared many training aids.

Perhaps the most significant aspects of this development has been its relatively late start, and the care which has been exercised to respect local autonomy. From time to time, as in 1914 and later, the grand lodge has summoned its representatives as well as the business agents which it helps to support, to inform them of decisions regarding policy or to discuss with them issues which have to be resolved. But the grand lodge has moved cautiously in attempting to mold rank-and-file membership opinion.

The General Secretary–Treasurer

In the seventy-five years since the founding of the association, there have been only four individuals serving as secretary. This smallness of number is perhaps misleading, because the office has always been regarded as a political plum, and the incumbents have generally had to play the political game actively to hold onto it. Of the four, three have served for sixty-three of the first seventy-five years. And of these three, two were, without question, leaders in the factionalism which at times rent the union.

In the earliest years (1889–1891) the function of what is now called the general secretary–treasurer was performed first by W. L. Dawley of Atlanta. He bore the title "grand secretary, finance." In 1890, however, he turned over part of his duties involving the treasury, to J. R. Miles of Mansfield, Ohio. Miles was not reelected to the post at the 1891 convention, and being a poor loser, was reluctant to give up such monies as existed. J. J. Creamer, then grand master machinist, instructed the member of the general executive board, who was beneficiary of Miles' $1000 surety bond, to get the money or the sheriff. He got the money. But as a result of the experience, it was decided that, in the future, the treasurer was to bring the treasury with him to the conventions.[18]

Miles was succeeded by John O'Day who was "grand treasurer" for one year (1891–92). In 1892 he became grand master machinist, and John J. Lamb, who had been at one time assistant doorkeeper of the House of Representatives, became his successor. Lamb was described in the journal at the time of his election as having "sound judgment and conservative principles [which have] brought him to the front."[19] The description seems to have been more than generous since Lamb ran off with the funds when he was not reelected to the office in 1893. By the time the police apprehended him, the money (over $3000) was gone. He went to jail, and the association went back to having Dawley serve as treasurer, as well as secretary. Lamb's defalcation was particularly resounding because the bonding company, taking advantage of a legal technicality arising from an error in phrasing the surety policy, refused to meet its obligation.[20]

Dawley remained general secretary–treasurer for only two years and was defeated by George Preston in 1895. He gave up his office easily and even made a graceful retiring speech, in which he said that he could not rightfully resent the result of the election.[21] His successor, George Preston, took over the job close to the beginning of O'Connell's administration. Like O'Connell, he was dedicated to making the IAM into an efficient trade union, and he did much to straighten out the tangled finances.

Preston's job was to save money, and, as was indicated in Chapter III, he was loath to pay when he could think of a reason not to. As a result, he was forever fighting with local lodge financial secretaries and calling them to account for their handling of grand lodge moneys. To his credit, however, it should be added that he was generally right and appeared to be completely uncorruptible.

The details of his removal from office have already been covered in Chapter III. Here it suffices to summarize their implications. First, it is clear that the qualities which made him a careful secretary–treasurer were the same ones which made him politically vulnerable, if not actually ridiculous. Second, even when he was openly challenged by the international president and the general executive board, he was able to put up a strong fight. And it is this point which is worthy of further examination.

Many members distrusted the international president because they feared that he was committed to dissipating the organization's wealth. Moreover, they saw in the scope of his power considerable opportunity for its abuse. They therefore looked to the general secretary–treasurer as the sole independent, nationally-elected officer who could offset the power of the international president. In other words, they preferred to have the two men somewhat at loggerheads, believing that from that division there would result some form of balanced control.

It was from this belief that the general secretary–treasurer was allowed to create his own staff, independent of the international president. Starting in 1905 there has been a provision for the appointment of an assistant general secretary–treasurer, the sole national officer who is not elected by the membership. But later, as the international president built up a staff of grand lodge representatives, the general secretary–treasurer was allowed to build up his own organization of grand lodge auditors. The seeds of this development were not only planted but had actually begun to flower during Preston's incumbency. Our point, in brief, is that Preston tried to counterbalance Johnston, and nearly succeeded.

Davison, the one selected by the Johnston group to run against Preston in the 1917 recall election, came from Richmond, Virginia (Local Lodge 10). He had once been offered the assistant general secretary–treasurership, but had declined because personal problems made it difficult for him to move to Washington. In the recall election subsequent to the 1916 Baltimore convention, Davison defeated Preston 19,006 to 16,235. And for thirty-seven years thereafter, he occupied the office.

Davison seems to have been far more astute politically than Preston. He worked closely with Johnston, and was in fact the spokesman for the Johnston faction in the Anderson affair. Like Johnston, he eventually favored union investment in private enterprise, and he took a keen personal interest in the printing plant venture (which was his special responsibility), and in the Mount Vernon Savings Bank. He did not get along as well with Johnston's successor, Arthur O. Wharton, but the reason for that may well have been Wharton's own suspicion of an officeholder who predated him. In any event, it was during Wharton's term of office that the hiatus separating the two departments (the international president's and the general secretary-treasurer's) began to be most evident.

If Preston were, by nature, a stickler for precision, Davison was a lover of politicking. Davison developed some intense personal ties among the membership; in some cases, in areas where Wharton was not strong. For instance, there is much reason to believe that the leadership of Local Lodge 68 had Davison's confidence at a time when Wharton was trying to discipline the lodge.

Davison and Harvey W. Brown, Wharton's successor, got along even less well than Davison and Wharton had. Brown was clearly jealous of Davison's independence, and Davison quite obviously felt himself to be the equal of Brown on a good many matters. Davison did many things with which Brown had no patience. He ran for, and was elected, mayor of Alexandria, Virginia. He ran for Congress against Howard W. Smith. In short, Davison was, much to Brown's displeasure, a national figure. And Davison took care to maintain his personal independence.

When Davison became ill in 1944, he instructed his assistants not to inform Brown, or anyone in the international president's office, of the serious nature of his health. Eventually, however, the news did become known and shortly before Davison's death, the executive council appointed Eric Peterson as general secretary-treasurer *pro tem*. Peterson was reappointed when Davison died, and occupied the position until 1959. Peterson's background was in the international president's department, and he took care not to contribute to the distrust of that office which was part of the Davison legacy.

This illustrates the role played by the general secretary-treasurer's department. Its formal role is to keep records, collect per capita taxes, and to pay out benefits. The general secretary-treasurer is a bonded officer, entrusted not only with the collection and the investment of the association's moneys, but also with the keeping of its records, both of individuals and of the executive council.[22] He also has since 1911 supervised the bonding of local, financially responsible officers. This he has accomplished either by running his own bonding service or by selecting the surety company which the locals are to use. In practice, he has become the only national officer whose duties are not directly circumscribed by the international president, and as such, they are pretty much what he chooses to make of them, providing that he does not run explicitly counter to the international president's policies.

Moreover, because the general secretary–treasurer often has longer tenure in office than the other officers on the executive council, his views are accorded particular respect by the other members of the council. And in spite of the *Brookwood rule,* prohibiting debate after a vote, if it is known that the general secretary–treasurer's position is in opposition to those expressed by others, the implication is that his has the added virtue of being independently arrived at. In practice, the general secretary–treasurer has become the comptroller of the grand lodge and is the effective check within grand lodge headquarters on the international president and the executive council.

The Vice-Presidents

The senior elected assistant to the chief executive was originally called the foreman. He was so termed from 1891 until 1893, when his title became slightly more elevated to grand foreman. (Originally there had been an elected assistant foreman, as well.) Prior to 1895, the grand foreman worked as the grand master machinist's deputy in organizing and conducting grand lodge affairs throughout the country. But in 1895, he became the editor of the journal, and no provision was made for him to travel on grand lodge business except to the convention. There were probably two reasons for this change in duties. The first was unquestionably tied up with recognition of the need for full-time work on the journal—previously the grand master machinist had been devoting such time as he could to the journal. The second was probably the result of dissatisfaction with Harry Easton, and a resulting determination to give the second highest elected officer a function which need not make him a competitor with the grand master machinist. Thus it was the grand foreman, from 1895 until 1899, and the vice-president from 1899 through 1901, who were the editors of the journal.

At the 1901 convention five new vice-presidents were elected. None was concerned with the journal, and all were designated as assistant organizers, which meant that they were clearly subordinate to the international president. They helped organize and to handle any business that he assigned to them. They were designated in numerical order and were slated to succeed the international president in that order. They had "power" to "settle all disputes in [the] district [assigned to them by the international president], subject to appeal, but [could not] call a strike unless their action has been approved by the [general executive board]." [23]

After the 1903 convention the number of vice-presidents became seven, with no two permitted to come from the same state, province, or territory.

Over the next decade there were no changes in the number of vice-presidents nor in their nominal duties. The system appeared to be working quite harmoniously, except that the lay members of the general executive board often found it difficult to take time off to attend to union affairs. In 1915 it was proposed that the members of the general executive board be put on a full-time basis, to be used as organizers and trouble shooters when they were not directly employed on board business. The logical result was a diminished need for vice-presidents. Consequently, in 1915, the membership voted to have only two vice-presidents, one of whom was to be from Canada. Both worked out of the Washington grand lodge headquarters, although in practice the Canadian vice-president had to be in Canada most of the time.

After World War I, the failings of excessive centralism came to be generally realized. Hence the 1920 convention created ten vice-presidents (with two from Canada) who were to be assigned by the international president and the general executive board to particular areas, and who were to be responsible (subject to directions from the international president and the board) for the administration of those areas.

The overpowering need to economize became evident after the 1922 shopmen's strike fiasco, and the 1924 convention chose to combine the vice-presidencies and the membership of the general executive board, with the result that the latter was abolished and the number of vice-presidents reduced to seven. These seven, now termed general vice-presidents, together with the international president and the general secretary–treasurer, made up the present executive council. This development is analyzed more fully later in this chapter.

In 1927 International President Wharton forced General Vice-President Hannon to resign by assigning him to a territory in which he was not popular. The 1936 convention moved a constitutional amendment prohibiting the assignment of a vice-president to any territory where he has not received a majority vote in the latest election.

During the Second World War, because of the press of work, two additional "temporary" general vice-presidents were authorized by special referendum vote. The augmented number (nine) was further formalized in 1946 when the two "temporaries" were confirmed as regulars. At the same time provision was made for one general vice-president to be stationed at headquarters to assist the international president directly.[24] Termed the "resident general vice-president," he receives extra remuneration annually.

The only other change was after the 1952 convention, when it was voted to assign one general vice-president to look after the interests of the railroad membership. This change was the result of pressure by what then amounted to a minority, although earlier it had been the dominant voice in the IAM. This demand suggests a departure from its regular rule, one of the basic choices which the union has made — that is, to administer the union geographically rather than by industry or combination of industries. The rationale of this choice is primarily political — it permits autonomy on the local level. The sole deviation from the rule was the case of the "railroad" general vice-president, although at recent conventions there has also been agitation for a vice-president to look after other branches, notably marine, aircraft, and automobile repair. It seems clear that administration along geographical lines has merit. To administer the union "functionally" would require a more precise delineation of industrial categories than is possible. And failing the establishment of this precision, there would be conflict of authority between general vice-presidents or a resurgence of personal dependence upon the international president for the making of decisions.

As the situation exists, each general vice-president is relatively dominant in his assigned territory. The railroad general vice-president does not get "in the way," because the handling of railroad industrial relations has been treated as a special case by the government since 1916.

The resident general vice-president was in the case of Albert Hayes, heir-apparent. Moreover, Harvey Brown had handled a similar assignment without title or extra compensation toward the end of Wharton's regime. There are actually few logical reasons why the resident general vice-president should succeed to the international presidency. It is possible that because of his propinquity to the international president, he is more in touch with a wider range of issues. But by the same token, he can be more vulnerable to criticism if a change in administrations is accompanied by a change in policies.

The Executive Council

This council, as presently constituted, includes the international president, the general vice-presidents, and the general secretary–treasurer. All are professional union officers, employed full time in their IAM duties. This has been the pattern since 1925, when the council was established.

The previous development reflected not only the smaller size of the IAM, but also the English tradition of lay executives. Except for one year (1899), when the lay executive was called the board of trustees, the group was known as the general executive board. The board was first authorized in 1891, when the election of five practicing machinists, each to be paid $5.00 for every day spent on IAM duties, was authorized.

The size of the board has varied. At first it had five elected members (the grand master machinist or international president was always a nonvoting member). From 1892 until 1895 the number was increased to seven, only to be reduced again to five at the 1895 convention. It remained five until 1925, when the board was replaced by the executive council.

The details of election and remuneration are presented in Appendix I and Table 8. It can be added that starting in 1899 no two members could come from the same state, and that in that year the nonprofessional aspect of the board's composition began to disintegrate. In 1899 two trustees were employed on a more or less regular basis as assistant organizers. This change resulted in a nominal loss of their personal independence, since the international president, as chief organizer, was able to send them where he chose, as well as make their personal lives easier or harder in other ways. Actually, such loss of independence did not result from this cause alone, because there were other ways in which the international president could dominate the board. Not the least of these was to lend his personal support at election times and, if the member failed to be returned, to offer him full-time professional employment.

All the same, several members of the board refused to consider full-time work for the union, and others, hoping for greater careers than the ones offered by the international president, refused all blandishments proffered by him. In practice, the points of conflict were usually not serious, and there was generally little reason for subordination.

It should be added that the members of the board were frequently strong-minded individuals, who cared little for the type of honors that any international president could bestow. P. J. Conlon, for instance, was a devoted Socialist at the turn of the century and was ready to stand up for his principles or, if necessary, return to the shop to earn his livelihood. Others, like Stuart Reid, actually left the board because they could earn substantially more outside the industry. Reid resigned in 1900 to become a labor reporter for the Chicago *Daily News*.[25]

In 1910 O'Connell reported that all members of the board were currently working in shops. That he chose to make reference to the fact, is evidence of his awareness of criticism that he was "looking after" the job interests of some. At the previous convention, for instance, it was proposed, but not voted, that the board should consist of five business agents from the five cities with the largest membership. Evidently, some lodges believed that there was a need for the board members to be professionals, but men not stamped with the grand lodge point of view.

In 1915 the general secretary–treasurer became a nonvoting member of the board. At the time the board was badly split between Johnston and anti-

Johnston factions. As it turned out, Preston's relations with the board were far from good. Davison, his successor, got along better, but that was because he was the "board's man."

The board was eventually abolished because Johnston and his group saw an opportunity to consolidate their hold on the administration at the 1924 convention. Their plan was to consolidate the vice-presidencies (of which there were then ten) and the board (who were all paid for full-time work), so that a total of seven would result. Annual savings in salary alone would amount to over $43,000, which, in view of the union's then impoverished condition, was worth considering. Best of all was the fact that the general vice-presidents "when not in attendance in meetings of the Executive Council . . . shall act as General Organizers, performing such duties and in such localities as may be decided by the International President to be for the best interests of the Association." [26]

This change did not make Johnston's position immediately easier, because some of his antagonists did manage to get elected. Moreover, he was immediately precipitated into the Anderson affair, which precluded his giving much attention to many other matters.

Wharton, upon taking over the union, was not so hampered and within a year had forced the resignation of General Vice-President William Hannon, and, as we noted earlier, also used the Brookwood incident as a means of gaining control over dissident council members.

Wharton's grip on the executive council loosened toward the end of his administration. He designated Harvey Brown as his successor, and the council accepted him, although Robert Fechner, on leave from the council to serve as director for President's Roosevelt's Civilian Conservation Corps, did assert a superior claim. And Wharton's control was also limited by the growth of an enclave about General Secretary–Treasurer, E. C. Davison. Thus, it is inaccurate to assume that the 1924 reform alone made the council a rubber stamp for the international president.

In 1941 the council established several of its present procedural rules.[27] A quorum consists of a majority of the members. In regular sessions, the vote of a majority of those present is required to make decisions. When in session, there will be no telephone call interruptions. In 1945 some additional rules were made. The first order of business at the second day of each regular session was to be devoted to an open forum, with each member allowed to talk fully and freely on any topic. Starting in 1946 policy or planning meetings were held once each year, at which time the sessions would be devoted to general rather than specific questions.

Both the old general executive board and the present executive council act on issues by means of recorded vote. These are called propositions. They are taken when the body is in session or by telegram or mail when the body is not assembled. Until 1945 the vote on most propositions was announced, although commencing in the late 1930's more and more of the votes were withheld as confidential. They were thus classified because they dealt with topics which could be embarrassing to individuals, because they referred to matters of relationship between a single local lodge and the grand lodge, or, occasionally, because they might have tended to put the union or the council in an unfavorable light.

In 1945 the council ceased publishing the vote on its propositions, because the growth of the organization no longer made the practices which had been applicable earlier, appropriate. Where once the council voted on ten issues a year, it was voting on over a thousand a year in 1945. And publication of the results of a thousand separate votes a year was unwieldy and appeared to serve no pressing need.

The executive council reflects both the personality of the international president and the capabilities of its members. When the president is prudent, and when the members recognize the need for full discussion prior to decision and are willing to abide by council vote thereafter, the council operates most effectively. It breaks down when the international president becomes stubborn or when he becomes unwilling to tolerate full discussion. It also breaks down when the other members lack ability and look to friendship or some other form of alliance to indicate how to vote. Most of all it collapses as an effective instrument when the members lack the courage to stand for what they think right, or the maturity to know when to cease opposing the majority will.

Traditionally the council has been dominated by men trained as railroad shopmen. Recently this trend has been challenged. If the council were to operate under the true principle of American political representation, where each delegate represents the views of his constituents, it would lead either to organizational immobility on the grand lodge level or to ennervating factionalism. The alternative is for each council member to vote as he thinks best for the whole organization.

The "Journal" and Related Publications

The *Machinists' Monthly Journal* appeared during the first year of the Association's life. Subsequently it matured into one of the country's finest union publications, only to decline in recent years.[28] The purpose of the journal was to inform the membership of developments within the trade and the grand lodge. Originally edited by Thomas Talbot, and in the three years following his resignation, by the grand master machinist, it got its own regularly elected editor in 1895. He was D. D. Wilson, who established its form and continued to run it until his death in 1915. Wilson was succeeded by Fred Hewitt, who remained the editor until his retirement in 1945. The next editor was Lee Thomas who died in 1952. The last editor was William V. Dameron.

One problem which continually plagued the journal was the question of its use as a reflection of membership sentiment. Two polar positions were possible: one, as the voice of the grand lodge administration; the other, as the voice of the rank-and-file membership. In practice, the editor's real responsibility was to steer a midway course. That was no easy task. On the whole, he tended to make the journal reflect his views, which were occasionally, as in the case of D. D. Wilson, not in complete accord with those of the administration, at that time, James O'Connell. At other times, as was true when Johnston and Wharton were international presidents, Fred Hewitt pretty much saw eye to eye with the administration.

It was at the 1911 convention when the value of the journal was thoroughly analyzed for the first time.[29] It was then edited by Douglas D. Wilson, who had a loyal following among the rank and file. He had made the journal into something akin to a machinist's version of *Harper's* or *Scribner's* magazines. In it he published general discussions of political and economic philosophy, articles describing technical developments in the trade, and much material pertaining to union matters. The latter included regular reports from the vice-presidents, occasional reports from business agents, and a good many letters from ordinary members. In addition, he also devoted several pages of each issue to his own running comment on current issues. Politically, he seems to have had a moderate Socialist slant.

President O'Connell was appalled at the cost of the journal (in excess of $34,000 annually), and wanted to see it replaced by a small inexpensive newspaper of eight pages. He also wanted to place it on a subscription basis, rather than have it sent to all the membership. The convention established a committee to consider O'Connell's recommendations. The committee reported on its deliberations, which "carefully considered the relative value of our *Journal* from the following standpoints, viz: educational value, practical value from a technical standpoint, industrial value from a trade union and economic standpoint, social value from a cooperative and news-distributing standpoint, and the devoted attachment our membership in general bestow [*sic*] upon it." Their conclusion (which did not amplify each of the criteria) was simply that it "is the richest asset the International Association of Machinists possesses."

O'Connell was unimpressed and returned to the fact that it was excessively costly. The journal, however, remained unchanged. At the time, it was running around ninety-six pages per issue.

After World War I, the importance of the journal decreased because its role as an educational instrument was curtailed.[30] It should be recalled, for instance, that prior to 1911 the union was largely composed of self-educated men, who were not only politically conscious (as Socialists or anti-Socialists), but who had a tremendous personal stake in understanding the technical implications of mechanical innovations. Thus, to them, the journal was both a forum for discussing their class grievances against the social order, and a vehicle for informing them of all the aspects of craft development.

By the end of World War I, the political issue was no longer Socialism, and workmen had little "class awareness," insofar as "return to normalcy" was concerned. One major effect of the war had been to institutionalize mechanical training, with the obvious result that other media than the journal were used for that purpose. Besides these two points, the union had become larger and older, and the close personal ties which had earlier been the rule were swamped by the numbers of newcomers, as well as thinned by death and retirement. Thus, after 1920 the journal no longer performed a critical role.

But if a new role were required, what was it to be? It was not effective as a weapon for political action because it took too long to appear. Unlike a newspaper, where the mechanical problems of production are simple enough so that it can be sent out within minutes of copy submission, the journal required a full month, if not more, for publication. It became a sort of monthly diary of developments, a permanent record of changes, and a running essay on their implications. It continued to carry news of grand lodge activities, including reports of the vice-presidents and general executive board members. It continued to have articles on technological changes. But now the emphasis was on putting things into perspective, rather than informing the membership. Perhaps the best example of this was a series of articles on the history of the IAM, written by Vice-President P. J. Conlon from 1922 through 1923.[31] In it he tried to tell the members what the union had done and what it had become. Earlier in Editor Wilson's time, the emphasis had been what should be done and why. Briefly stated, the journal, which had once been an instrument for the education of machinists in the problems of the world about them, became after World War I an instrument for worker education in the advantages of unionism.

Partly because the journal had a devoted following, partly because Editor Hewitt had his own political ties, and partly because of inertia, little thought was given to abolishing the journal until after World War II. President Brown did not get along well with Hewitt, and when the latter retired, Brown sought successfully to make the editor subordinate to him.[32] Thus after World War II the first effort was to make the journal a part of the international president's program. It was assumed that in this way the journal could be made into a more effective organizing and workers' education device.

But such did not prove to be the case. The reason lay in the changed character of membership as well as the changed reading habits of the American worker. Here it should be noted that the old type machinist was a serious man; perhaps he read little, but what he took up, he thought through. The new member was not a reader. He was accustomed to picking up his information from the radio or from television. The most he could be expected to peruse were the headlines in a newspaper. The obvious conclusion was that the traditional need for the journal had disappeared, and it was discontinued. For the years it appeared, however, it furnished a splendid record of the union's activities. It was never a "canned" or trite publication. And if it did not attract as much reader attention as it might have, it was probably read by the devoted membership. As a vehicle for conveying sophisticated information to local lodge leadership and potential leadership, it has not been replaced.

"Labor." After World War I, quite unlike the situation prior to it, American labor did have a policy. Considering that the Socialist movement died during the war, this seems to have certain elements of a paradox. The explanation lies in the shift from long-range to short-run interests in the political area. The last stand of the prewar Socialists was the embracing of the Plumb Plan, a program devised by Glenn Plumb to retain public ownership of the railroads. The plan was not adopted, and its proponents turned to more limited objectives, objectives which could be achieved through one's friends in Congress.

It will be recalled that Johnston was an ardent supporter of the Plumb Plan, and he succeeded in getting the union to indorse it. Thus, like the other old-time Socialists, who had had to turn from remaking American society on a grand scale to doing what they could to assure American workers of protection of their job-rights, he became interested in using the journal for political education. As we noted above, the journal was not a very good medium for this purpose — one could not appeal to one's readers to write to their congressmen quickly enough to be effective.

The passage of the Railway Labor Act of 1926 was a triumph of grassroots pressure. It was in large part the salvation of the limited-objective type of American unionism, although it was operative not in the area of bipartite, but tripartite, collective bargaining. However, it required that an instrument be created to put pressure on the members of Congress. And former Representative Keating, who had been a prime mover of the Plumb Plan, became editor of *Labor,* a weekly newspaper put out by the unions which had considerable interest in the administration of the Railway Labor Act. Because it was a newspaper, it could be distributed quickly and cheaply. In short order it became a potent political force.

At the 1928 convention President Wharton, who had had favorable experience with Keating's newspaper in his previous job as president of the Railway Employees' Department, recommended that subscription to *Labor* be made a mandatory part of membership in the IAM.[33] Because the IAM at that time was dominated by the railroad machinists, and because it was generally believed that *Labor* was the key to moving the hearts of congressmen, and that Congress was in the long run the prime mover for the improvement of labor relations in the United States, the delegates accepted Wharton's recommendation. And the membership ratified the decision in the subsequent referendum vote.

The breadth of the decision is, upon reflection, more than a little startling. All members had to subscribe, irrespective of whether they read English or not. If they were unemployed, they had to maintain their subscriptions until after the seventh month of unemployment. And all IAM members had to subscribe through the IAM—which meant that they were to cancel any other subscriptions that they may previously have had. The subscriptions were not part of the per capita tax; in other words, membership fees were not increased to cover the additional 5 cents per month cost. And when a delinquency occurred, that is when any individual failed to remit his subscription fee, the amount was charged against the local lodge's account. It was only in March, 1932, when the depression was well recognized, that the general secretary-treasurer was permitted to use his own discretion in discontinuing the subscriptions of unemployed members.

By 1936 both the grand lodge and the local lodges realized that the mandatory subscriptions to *Labor* were proving to be a divisive influence. In 1930 an attempt had been made to repeal the mandatory provision, but it failed 13,731 to 6309. It passed in 1936, when the economy-consciousness of the depression was voiced; the vote was 15,264 to 10,176. Although there was considerable fussing about collecting old debts, the experiment was pretty much abandoned by the end of 1937. A few lodges were reluctant to pay up, but eventually they did. The 1936 referendum, the one repealing the mandatory subscription, also voted 11,513 to 14,161 against permitting a delinquency over the *Labor* subscription to be a basis for cancellation of membership.

Notwithstanding the reversal of policy over an eight-year period, the experience is worth noting for several reasons. It emphasizes that the union was railroad-administration-oriented. Moreover, it points up the belief that the journal was not a satisfactory vehicle for the communication of news and views prior to putting pressure on Congress. Last of all, the vehemence of the protest from several locals is good evidence of the preservation of a strong sense of local autonomy.

"The Machinist." Toward the end of World War II, the executive council authorized the establishment of a weekly newspaper, as proposed by President Brown. By then the IAM was no longer a railroad-oriented union; consequently, what was wanted was something significantly different from *Labor,* which was directed primarily at treating the problems of those coming under the jurisdiction of the Railway Labor Act.

The new publication was called *The Machinist.* In makeup, it was of tabloid size. It contained many pictures and has been of an "easy-to-read" nature. From the first, it has had the services of a full-time cartoonist. Since 1947 it has been edited by Gordon Cole, who is also the IAM's public relations director. Perhaps it is this doubling of roles which characterizes the quality of the newspaper best. In other words, unlike the journal in its earlier days, *The Machinist* is not geared to a more or less systematic discussion of the pros and cons of economic, political, or social issues. It is rather a well-prepared information sheet giving factual information, written in a lively journalistic vein by professional newspapermen, as well as presenting certain views authorized by the executive council.

In short, the journal as it originally appeared, and *The Machinist* as it now appears, were aimed at different types of people. The journal was more reflective; *The Machinist* more inspirational. Use of the journal was largely confined to theoretical, as well as practicing, leaders; use of *The Machinist* is much more widespread, and should be particularly appreciated by the rank and file.

The journal departed from its original function. It, too, became a "once-over-lightly" type of publication. As such it was less efficient, per unit cost, than *The Machinist.* But there has been no replacement for the old journal; nothing put out by the grand lodge has succeeded in giving the serious "organization-minded" members a comprehensive discussion (including pros and cons) of alternative policies.

The closest approximation is the *Research Bulletin* published by the research department. But it is sent only to business agents and to grand lodge representatives. Moreover, it, too, is principally a fact sheet, although in this instance, because of the greater technical competence of its readers, its facts are more complex, and its discussion of them more sophisticated.

What about the question of the centralization of power and authority? It is apparent that the executive function has on the whole become partly centralized. The international president clearly dominates both his own immediate office and the executive council. But he does not dominate the local business agencies — he leads them; he cannot push them. And he has obviously sought to increase his leadership power by providing research, educational, and legal services.

It is also true that the international president does not exercise suzerainty over the general secretary–treasurer's department. Thus it might appear that the forces tending toward local autonomy (decentralization of power) retain their earlier importance.

On the whole, that is not the case. The international president has become the dominant influence in the organization. To a great degree, he personally controls the international purse; he assigns the organizers; he pays strike benefits where he thinks they should be paid. Most of such planning for the future as exists is done under his direction. It is for these reasons that this conclusion seems valid: the grand lodge has become the province of the international president.

The Judicial Process

No aspect of labor-union custom has been more open to misinterpretation than the handling of internal disputes and disciplinary problems. Much of the confusion has originated in a lack of appreciation of the operational environment surrounding union activities. In addition, there has been a strong tendency on the part of trade unionists and their critics to shun technicalities in an unseemly haste to embrace what they consider to be basic ethical or moral realities. Consequently, many phases of the judicial process are not well handled and often not well understood. For purposes of clarification it is wise to turn to first principles.

The judicial process within unions (as within political society) has been developed to maintain a practical balance between individual independence and social need. In other words, the judicial process is fashioned to preserve the group and also to protect the individual. As a rule, the more secure the group, the more generous the judicial process has been in handling nonconformists. Conversely, the less secure the group, the less tolerant the process becomes in its treatment of "rebelliousness."

Here it is useful to refer to developments in areas other than the trade union. In the normal, peacetime situation, the usual civil judicial process is more likely to protect the individual's rights (his nonconformism or expression of personal dissidence), than it is in times of war. The same situation also holds true for the military judicial process — although in the latter case, a move toward wartime stringency has occasionally been modified because the character of the soldiery shifts from a professional to a civilian makeup. Our point, however, is that the effectiveness of the process as a protection for the individual is frequently a function of how threatened the society believes itself to be.

Besides this point, there are two others. First, the rights of the individual are better protected in the case of criminal charges than they are in the event of civil action. Thus, what society frequently considers to be basic safeguards, are simply no more than the protection afforded to those against whom the state has initiated juridical, particularly criminal, proceedings. In other words, a jury sitting in a criminal case must find for the defendant unless his culpability is demonstrated beyond a reasonable doubt; in civil cases, the jury finds for the side having no more than a slightly more plausible argument of the two presented to it, and it can award punitive damages. In civil cases, be they between individuals or between a person and the government, A alleges that B failed to act properly; B answers that A is mistaken. The jury decides which of the two sides has a more believable position and so votes. Possibly B then must pay his whole fortune to A. Nonetheless, even if there is only a slight advantage for A's argument, B is the complete loser.

Our third point is that the law, right or wrong, has come to consider procedural technique as important as the substantive question. It is frequently held that the technique of hearing the case is as important as the question of whether "right" is done. As a result, the judicial process becomes a highly technical one, and guilt or innocence, culpability or acquittal, or, as in civil cases, responsibility or nonresponsibility are as much a function of observing procedural details as a function of right or wrong. This development has been particularly noticeable when the bar has lost its sense of professional or social ethics.

In addition to these three points, which affect the usual civil or military judicial process, there is one other particularly worth mentioning. Perhaps it is the most important one of all. The judicial process deals with absolutes. Unlike the legislative process, it does not operate through compromise. And unlike the administrative process, it is not concerned with practical hazards. A man is ultimately guilty or he is not guilty; he is culpable or he should escape responsibility. For this reason those who participate in the civil judicial process are generally required to announce their position and can be expected to justify their decisions. This does not mean, of course, that uncertainty is not rampant here as elsewhere; but it has to be grappled with and eliminated. For better or worse, a clear choice has to be made; it cannot be postponed.

The judicial process in the IAM has logical elements; it also has had defects. The history of its operation has been an attempt to compensate for some of these defects. One point stands out. The IAM has generally existed in an unfriendly environment. Its insecurity as an organization has caused it to emphasize the importance of its own protection even while grappling with the problems of justice for its individual members.

Its process is most correctly compared to civil suits. In civil cases, A alleges that B has failed to perform as he should have. B responds that A's allegations are erroneous. The community, sometimes acting through a committee or para-jury system, decides which story it believes. The loser then appeals on the merits of his case. A higher court examines the record, and may sustain or reverse the first finding. So it is with the IAM, where M brings charges against N. A trial is arranged. M's charges are accepted or rejected; in either event, the loser appeals; and the issue is thoroughly considered by the international president. Our point here is important; the accused (respondent) may have been acquitted of the charges in the original trial; but the international president may reverse the decision and find him guilty. As in a civil suit, having been acquitted at one stage does not preclude the opposite result later. The important point to understand is that the judicial process in the IAM is conceived as comparable not to the criminal law, but to civil suits.

Procedural technique, our third point, has also developed into an art over the years. In the beginning, little attention was paid to the formal conduct of trials. As the years passed, more and more care was taken, and within the last decade a formal procedure gradually evolved. Now grand lodge representatives regularly appear as observers in order to witness the proceedings and to report to the international president. And within grand lodge headquarters there is a small cadre whose major assignment is to review appeals for the international president and to make such recommendations as they believe the facts and precedents warrant. In truth, a judicial bureaucracy is developing, assisted by an embryonic bar.

It is surrounding our fourth point that the greatest question lies. The practice in the IAM, when charges have been brought against a member, has been for the president of the local lodge to appoint a trial committee to hear the litigants and render a report to the whole local. The report is then voted upon by the whole membership of the local lodge. Thus the judicial process has a distinctively democratic flavor, in the true political sense. The dangers are that the local president may "load" the committee, and that the plaintiff or the respondent may "pack" the local lodge meetings. Consequently, the international president has emerged as the union's real judicial officer. Added to his stated power of interpreting the constitution, it is he, who because of his practical experience in the ways of unionism, is expected to guard the judicial process from political abuses. By this we mean simply that the political tendencies toward compromise or expediency, must be countered by him. Only rarely can local personnel under pressure be expected to show a restraint as well as an absolute impartiality, necessary for the successful functioning of the process, equal to his.

Here it is necessary to emphasize one point. The trial system actually works well in the great majority of cases, and our observations implying a logical breakdown in the design of the system, do not apply most of the time. We stress this failure simply because it explains the international president's growth as the judicial guardian of the organization, and it explains why a centralizing tendency has occurred in the area of the judicial process. We could also add that the international president often stands as the protector of the individual, and that in many instances he has found for the respondent, when local pressures have reached almost hysteria-like proportions. In these instances, irrespective of the local short-run consequences to him, he has acquired critical functional importance, as well as prestige. But the main point refers not to the prestige, but to the causes for the development of his peculiar function, namely, that the confusion of the legislative process (a popularity contest) with the judicial process, has led to the centralization of judicial authority with the key political figure, and that this change has been necessary in order to protect the Association as well as the rights of individual members.

The judicial process in the IAM proceeds through (1) an analysis of the trial procedure, (2) an analysis of the appeals procedure, and (3) a discussion of several leading cases which have significantly shaped subsequent developments. In short, we shall discuss procedure, and then precedent.

Trials

The basic features of trials were incorporated into the first constitution (1889). There, provision was made that all charges that an individual had violated the constitution were to be made in writing at the local lodge level. Then the local master machinist was to appoint a committee within one week, and the accused was to be notified and invited to appear before the committee. He could defend himself or ask some other member to defend him; and he or his "attorney" were to be allowed the right of cross-examination. In the event that the accused failed to appear, the proceedings were to continue as though he had been there. After hearing all the testimony and examining such evidence as was presented, the trial committee was to report its findings of guilt or innocence to the local lodge. It was also to make such recommendations as it found desirable. At that point, the local voted to accept, or to reject, the committee's findings. If the accused were held to be guilty, the local could then vote to expel, suspend, fine, or reprimand him. After 1890, it required a two-thirds vote of those present to vote expulsion. And since 1909 no fine in excess of $50.00 may be levied, without explicit approval of the international president and the general executive board (now, the executive council).

Thus, from the first, the judicial process in the IAM carried within itself strong overtones of the legislative process. The trial committee fulfilled only a recommendatory function. Guilt or innocence were determined by popular vote. And punishment, too, was similarly felt to be the will of the members present at the meeting of the local lodge.

There have been only a few changes in the trial procedure. From 1911 until 1915 the constitution did not require that the accused be served with a written copy of the charges, but in 1915 that requirement was restored. The most significant change was a result of the inability or unwillingness of local lodges to punish those accused of dual unionism or of defaming the leadership of the IAM. Thus, starting in 1909 the grand lodge (through the international president and the general executive board) could serve as a "court of original jurisdiction" (i.e. indict and try the accused) if the local lodge failed to take necessary action. In practice, this change meant that the administration of the judicial process was partly removed from local pressures and interests. More will be said of this change shortly. Here it suffices to add that it was only after 1941 that these grand lodge trials had to be held locally, if the defendant so desired.

Standard trial procedures were introduced in the 1946 constitution. Their enunciation was partly the result of the codification of experience. They were also partly the union's recognition that protection of the accused, as well as a more general need to protect itself, required greater attention to matters of procedure. The outcome was a spelling out of details:

(1) The trial committee is to come to order.[34]
(2) The dues books of those present are then to be examined. (This establishes the right of the trial to be held.) After 1949 all nonparticipants, except a grand lodge representative, were to be sent to anterooms. All present, except the reporter, must hold IAM membership.

(3) The defendant and the plaintiff are identified and segregated. Each is to remain in the trial chamber until the trial is over. The charge is read, and the defendant enters his plea.
(4) The plaintiff (or his "attorney") presents the case supporting the charge. Witnesses are to be called one at a time. They are subject to cross-examination.
(5) Defense witnesses are called. They, too, are subject to cross-examination.
(6) At the conclusion of the presentation, everyone but the trial committee is to withdraw.
(7) Later at the meeting of the local lodge, the trial committee makes its report, explanations, and recommendations.
(8) Finally the lodge votes without debate, and by secret ballot.

A postscript to the foregoing should be added. In 1953 the constitution was amended to permit the convention to serve as a court of original jurisdiction in the event that a body, such as a district or local lodge, as well as a council or conference, were brought up on charges. This change grew out of concern over what should be done with local and district lodges pursuing courses of action inimical to their own welfare or the good of the IAM as a whole. In practice, problem situations rarely have occurred, but when they have arisen, it has been necessary to provide some machinery to authorize grand lodge intervention. For example, in the event of financial irregularities, in cases where local leadership has become rampantly anti-grand lodge, and at times when employers have come to dominate local leadership, the international president and the executive council have suspended a local or district lodge's autonomy and have sent in a grand lodge representative to administer its business and political affairs. Recent testimony before the United States Senate's McClellan Committee indicated that the question of union receiverships has become vitally significant in some unions. Not so in the IAM; there, receiverships are very few in number, limited to fewer than ten per year, and in almost all cases they have been of less than one year's duration. The 1952 convention also authorized convention trials of individuals, in the event that the local had failed to do so; in these cases the international president was the one to decide whether the trial was to be conducted by the convention, or by the executive council.

To put the trial process in perspective, it is necessary to emphasize that in the IAM the great majority of issues are successfully handled on the local level. The interest of the grand lodge in original trials is limited to insistence upon using adequate procedures, as well as special issues like radicalism, dualism, or defamation of character of the IAM leadership. On the whole, IAM trial procedures contain about as many safeguards for defendants as the law provides for defendants in civil suits. It is true that the IAM procedure does not provide the type of protection for the defense that normal peacetime criminal law provides. But on this subject our points have been made earlier. In spite of the loose use of verbiage, the IAM has no ability to order capital punishment, the payment of fines on pain of imprisonment, or imprisonment itself as a punishment. True there are evils and problems attendant to the handling of justice within a semiprivate organization like the IAM; but these are not generally tied up with the unreasonableness of the law or the harshness of the punishment. Rather, they are the by-product of local pressures being reflected in trial procedures. And this, any fair-minded observer must admit, is an evil not unknown to the state's judicial process.

Appeals

Implicitly, there has always been a right to appeal on procedural grounds. By 1891 the constitution actually provided that when the convention was not in session, judicial authority rested in the hands of the international president and the general executive board.

But the handling of appeals has varied. In 1899 the law was changed to require the international president (or as a deputy, the vice-president) to visit the lodge personally, prior to considering the verdict on its substantive merits.

The manner of handling appeals from all local lodge "decisions," was put into explicit form in 1911. The loser (plaintiff or respondent) was authorized to appeal first to the international president. Either party could then appeal that decision to the general executive board, and a final appeal could then be made, if desired, to the grand lodge convention. During the period of the last appeal to the convention, the defendant's financial position within the IAM was not to be impaired—that is, his dues and assessments were to be collected as formerly, and he was entitled to all the normal benefits. In the event he was finally expelled, the loss would be borne by the grand lodge.

In 1915 the law was further modified to permit appeal to the membership through the referendum. Moreover, no party was to resort to the civil courts while a case was *sub judice* in the IAM judicial process or while any IAM avenue of redress remained.

In 1925 the law was changed to prohibit any member of the executive council from voting on any appeal in a case on which he has previously rendered a judgment. This, of course, precluded the international president from participating in the executive council's vote. It also prevented any general vice-president, who had acted as deputy for the international president, from doing the same thing.

The 1946 revisions also required that appeals be taken within thirty days of the judgment.

The Evolution of the IAM's Common Law

Until now we have examined the IAM's judicial process as though it were comparable to the type of litigation generally practiced in most American courts of civil law. Previously, however, we suggested that IAM was not a sovereign institution, and as a result, many of its practices were influenced by extrajudicial situations. Putting this another way, the penalties which the grand lodge can invoke are not strictly comparable to anything in the normal civil process. In fact, they can be likened only to the state's resort to siege law or the abandonment of the civil process.

In certain circumstances, the international president has resorted to the suspension (of IAM constitutional rights) of lodges and individuals. His reasons for such actions have always been the same; the necessity to preserve the organization. On occasions, the international president has not openly moved to accomplish his purpose. This is to be expected, since such a move is actually an open extension of his powers and, as such, politically dangerous. But on other occasions, the moves have been overt — and once the glove is thrown, the international president has had to rally political support.

The Warner episode, discussed in Chapter II, was one illustration of the extension of grand lodge quasi-judicial rights. Warner was *persona non grata* to the organization, but his own district lodge liked him. O'Connell forced the district lodge against its wishes, and in direct defiance of the results of the local "due process" clause, to expel the man. To do this, he had to resort to a referendum. But having done this, he was able to assert grand lodge hegemony vis-à-vis the good name of the Association and its officialdom. Much the same thing was done in 1909 in the case of Nathan Cole, whom O'Connell held to be ineligible for office — not having been a practicing machinist. It is hard to term O'Connell's action in these cases a "judgment" — but it resulted in what we can fairly call the "Warner rule" — namely, the supremacy of grand lodge decisions, levied according to due process.

The great steps in the rise of grand lodge hegemony, however, occurred not during O'Connell's administration, but during Johnston's, when the union was larger, and more bitterly divided. In 1913 one B. Tennebaum was fined $50.00 by Local Lodge 112 (St. Paul) for conduct unbecoming a member. On September 25, 1913, he sought to pay his fine and a $5.00 reinstatement fee (he had allowed his dues to lapse). The local refused to accept him, and he appealed to Johnston and the general executive board. They ordered the local to accept him, and when it did not, they had the grand lodge issue a dues book to him. The grand lodge thus gave notice that it would protect those against whom it felt local lodges had discriminated. This "Tennebaum rule" was invoked again in the 1930's against San Francisco Local 68.

In 1916 Johnston suspended Carl Persons for slandering and libeling him. In fact, Johnston did not prefer charges against Persons, but suspended him pending an apology and retraction. In this case Johnston assumed the mantle of a judge holding a citizen in contempt. Technically, no case was made against Persons — that is, no attempt was made to prove that what he said and what he wrote were untrue and presented with malice aforethought. What Johnston claimed was simply that the organization could not exist if Persons's allegations went unchecked, and that if Persons believed what he said, there was a proper constitutional remedy via due judicial process. Persons's refusal to employ this avenue made him liable for suspension, at the pleasure of the international president. That the international president also happened to be the object of Persons's animus purportedly had nothing to do with the decision. Johnston's decision would have been the same had Persons said the same thing about someone else. The Baltimore convention upheld Johnston, and what emerged could be called the Persons rule, that is, that the international president can hold a member in contempt until the member makes a formal retraction. To do this, no formal charges need be levied, and no trial need be held. Johnston invoked this rule in the 1925 Anderson case, and if his attempt to use it partially failed, it was because the matter was clearly political and not judicial.

In Chapter IV we referred to Wharton's extension of grand lodge powers — mentioning in particular, the "Brookwood rule," which limited post-vote debate in the executive council. Wharton made other quasi-judicial interpretations which became precedent-setting in nature. The "San Francisco 1936 rule" forbade any local lodge from levying assessments to aid a defecting member or local. An earlier 1927 "Peoria rule" held that no local lodge could require its members to buy stock in local labor temples, and a 1927 "Sleeman rule" held that no member could be fined or suspended without a trial, for working overtime. In 1932 Wharton enunciated a "no opposition, no elections rule," which implied that write-in names were illegal; in other words, if no one were nominated in opposition to any slate of officers, the election need not be held.

H. W. Brown also issued many regulations which affected trials and procedures. Most of these were the result of appeals to him by individuals having grievances. Some of them were:

(1) The "Alconada rule" — the accused has no vote on the verdict or the penalty when on trial.
(2) The "Warren rule" — no shop chairman can be removed by simple impeachment. He must stand trial.
(3) In case of a tie vote, all ballots not fully marked are invalid.
(4) No member can be legally elected to an office unless he is present when election is held or gives written notice of his willingness to accept the office.

The international president's department has of recent years codified both the important judgments rendered from time to time, and the administrative policy rulings carrying the force of law. These two compilations are not binding in the full sense of the common law and *stare decisis,* but they act both as a prediction of what may be expected in events or cases that occur, and as an insight into the thinking of the administration. On the whole, the *Decisions Book* reflects the practical drift to grand lodge control; it indicates a high degree of individual membership responsibility (rather than local lodge responsibility) for dues and similar grand lodge obligations; and it stresses the need for due process in the handling of most IAM business.

In the main, the development of the judicial process in the IAM has not been particularly advanced. "The life of the law," wrote Oliver Wendell Holmes (known best as a dissenter), "has not been logic; it has been experience." Such is the truth also in the case of the IAM. But where the Anglo-American societies have had no less than four centuries to perfect their judicial institutions, the IAM has worked at it for less than a fifth of the time. It is little wonder then that instances of political chicanery (not unknown, by the way, in justice as it is administered by the courts), creep in from time to time in the world of unionism.

Our final point on this subject, however, reflects a somewhat different concern. Unions are basically representative democracies. As such, both responsibility and authority have to be delegated to key officials. In a civilized society some checks must be maintained on these officials, lest in the name of efficiency (or some other value), they abuse their powers. To hamstring them is as wrong, however, as to give them unlimited judicial control. The one area which society, generally, and unions, no less, have had trouble handling is that of equitable yet reasonable redress of individual grievances. The IAM, like most American unions, has traditionally, resisted all external institutional controls on its handling of individuals. The development of trial and appeals procedures, as well as a codification of its law in a constitution, a *Policies Book,* and a *Decisions Book,* are indications of the evolutionary phases through which that institution (or any other democratic one) travels in the quest for a reasonable solution of the question of how to handle dissident individuals. Those who think the problem simple are generally as ignorant of the history of the legal process, as they are naive regarding the power conflicts within contemporary society.

CHAPTER VIII

The Quantitative View of the IAM's Development

This chapter considers the quantitative aspects of the growth of the IAM. It consists of three parts, which analyze in turn membership, grand lodge revenue, and grand lodge expenditure.

Quantitative analysis is a useful technique in discussing institutional growth and change, because it suggests easy comparisons. However, it presumes homogeneity of quality, a characteristic which can be elusive because things do not always go by the same name at different times; worse yet, different things may go by the same name in separate periods. One other shortcoming of quantitative analysis is a tendency to presuppose that the interpretation of numbers is simple. It is not, particularly because change is often brought about by the intensity of feeling of a small, even numerically-insignificant, group.

Membership

Membership figures for the IAM are presented in Table 9. Fluctuations in the union's size are the result of several variables, some of which are partly within the union's control. These include its decision to organize new members in previously unexplored territory, its decision to expand or modify its admissions policy and jurisdiction, its decision to expand its efforts to serve its membership, its decision to secure favorable changes in collectively-bargained contracts with employers, including such union security provisions as the union shop, or within broad limits, its decision to change the cost of union membership (dues above the constitutional minimum are set in local lodge by laws; the latter must be approved by the international president).[1] The factors beyond the union's direct control include the size of the labor force in the industries handled by the IAM, the exigencies of the business cycle, the government's labor policy, the extent of employers' willingness not only

Table 9. *Membership figures.*

Year	Membership [a]	Unemployed [b]	Year	Membership [a]	Unemployed [b]
1899	18,000	—	1926	71,647	—
1900	22,500	—	1927	71,042	—
1901	32,500	—	1928	69,011	5,499
1902	35,500	—	1929	71,609	3,580
1903	48,800	—	1930	69,397	8,178
1904	55,700	—	1931	63,625	15,062
1905	48,500	—	1932	58,932	21,151
1906	50,000	—	1933	61,079	20,955
1907	69,361	—	1934	88,337	18,495
1908	57,091	—	1935	88,887	14,575
1909	48,220	—	1936	105,063	9,672
1910	60,970	—	1937	152,022	11,447
1911	67,411	—	1938	155,267	28,137
1912	63,005	—	1939	161,828	17,089
1913	73,957	—	1940	187,738	11,219
1914	74,206	—	1941	284,514	7,433
1915	75,002	—	1942	444,892	8,607
1916	107,444	—	1943	616,662	10,531
1917	127,484	—	1944	661,843	13,849
1918	229,468	—	1945	609,178	21,509
1919	331,449	—	1946	519,213	26,339
1920	282,496	—	1947	545,593	23,910
1921	206,922	—	1948	541,861	26,829
1922	148,342	—	1949	518,456	40,980
1923	104,692	—	1950	509,877	31,041
1924	79,648	—	1951	621,074	19,005
1925	72,025	—	1952	734,068	24,758

[a] 1899–1911 figures come from 1916 convention *Proceedings,* p. 17; 1912–1952 figures come from official records, general secretary-treasurer's office.

[b] Included in membership figure.

to engage in collective bargaining, but more specifically, their acceptance of the IAM as a preferred union, as well as social and cultural factors which shape an individual's attitude toward union participation.

The accuracy of these membership figures is greatest since 1912, when, as noted in Table 9, we have the data collected for the use of the grand lodge officers. At times the executive council has seen a need for inflating these true figures for public relations purposes. At other times, the officers have chosen to save money by paying on less than their full membership to the AFL. And it should be recalled that Wolman, for one, based his estimates of union size on the AFL per capita tax figures.

The periods of greatest membership growth since 1912 have been 1915–1919, a war period; 1933–1934, a depression; 1935–1937, a period of great unemployment; 1939–1944 and 1950–1953; also war periods. As noted on the graph, the conditions during these five intervals are not homogeneous; nor were the conditions homogeneous in the three periods of membership decline: 1919–1925, except for a short depression, a period of prosperity; 1930–1932, intense depression; 1944–1946, period of postwar industrial reorganization. One point that stands out is that the exigencies of the general business cycle do not control the levels of IAM membership. That they affect union growth is not denied; but they make up only one of several critical factors. On the other hand, it is clear that government labor policy does play a major role, suggesting that the growth of the union's interest in the public reaction to union activities is based on some form of sound reasoning. The government's attitude is an important factor, but not conclusive. Later in this chapter the effectiveness of union expenditure on organizing campaigns is considered.

The map (Plate II) illustrates the IAM's early expansion along certain major railroad lines. By 1893 lodges had been established in every part of the continental United States except Maine, South Dakota, Nevada, and Oklahoma. In addition, Canadian and Mexican lodges had also been chartered.

Recent changes in the geographic location of membership have done much to shape the union's development. One need only recall the abandonment of the Southern tradition to note geography's role. Moreover the im-

Table 10. *Distribution of membership by region, 1947 and 1952,* (per cent distribution)

Area	1947	1952	Percentage growth [territory by territory]
Northeast – Middle Atlantic	19.4	21.7	52.6
South	9.3	9.3	45.7
Eastern Midwest	16.6	13.6	15.6
Western Midwest	23.4	24.7	46.2
Southwest	17.8	17.6	42.1
Pacific Northwest (including mountain states)	8.2	6.7	16.2
District of Columbia	1.0	0.6	−2.7
Canada	4.1	5.8	86.0
Membership totals	482,151	677,344	
Per cent growth of whole organization			40.5

Source: Executive council memorandum. Territories were designated by responsible general vice-president.

portant "Catholic–Mason" fight in the period, 1905–1925, was basically a conflict between rural towns and big city organizations. The cultural homogenization of the United States which started in the twenties, and which was intensified by the Second World War, erased the sores, if not the scars, of the experience.

Canadian membership has played a significant role, largely through its buttressing of the important tradition of local autonomy. Size of the Canadian membership can be seen in Table 10. (See p. 207.)

Table 10 illustrates some relatively recent changes in the location of the membership. Although the organization has the bulk of its numerical strength in the midwest, it is important to note that the strength in the southwest is more remarkable because it is of fairly recent vintage (the Second World War). In the period following the Second World War, the greatest relative growth was found in Canada, the northeast–middle Atlantic area, the western midwest area, the south, and the southwest. The relative growth of these four areas exceeded the growth of the whole organization. Short reflection will reveal the striking importance of the western midwestern territory because it started as the largest and managed to increase its relative importance. The two Pacific coastal territories increased their membership, but not enough to maintain their relative importance.

Table 11 shows the disposition of membership among the different industrial groupings, as indicated by lodge classification for the IAM as a whole, as well as within each of the regions. Our data are limited by the cut-off date of our analysis and naturally cannot indicate recent changes.

Lodges are classified according to the primary industrial orientation of their members. The airframe, air transport, auto repair, and railroad lodges consist of members employed in the indicated industry. The tool and die lodges contain members with a special skill, when not organized as part of another IAM local. The contract lodges are those having joint agreements with a variety of employers in diverse job shops and other unspecified types of plants in the metal-fabricating industry. Production worker lodges are composed principally of unskilled workers in mass production industries. Mixed lodges contain railroad workers as well as some other category of worker. Almost one member in four was connected with the airplane industry; only approximately one in ten was connected with railroads. Almost 50 per cent of the members were associated with the production of general metal goods (the contract and production worker categories). The craft elite, the railroad men and the tool and die men, hardly numbered one in eight. Each of the territories can be characterized by a model type (or model types) of membership. For example, the northeastern–middle Atlantic area

Table 11. *Members working in different industrial categories, according to geographic distribution, 1952.*
(per cent distribution)

Area	Air-frame	Air trans.	Auto repair	Contract [a]	Mixed	Production worker	Rail-road	Tool & die	Total
New England – Middle Atlantic	19.7	1.6	4.8	58.2	2.2	6.6	6.9	0	100
South	33.3	4.7	2.4	28.0	16.0	1.9	13.7	0	100
Eastern Midwest	0.3	0.4	7.8	56.7	6.8	9.4	16.4	2.1	100
Western Midwest	16.6	2.5	10.4	42.8	7.1	8.9	8.0	3.7	100
Southwest	41.0	2.9	13.6	12.8	17.3	6.9	4.6	0.8	100
Pacific northwest (including mountain states)	23.4	1.6	24.6	24.8	13.2	1.3	11.0	0.1	100
District of Columbia	0	20.1	7.2	58.3	2.7	7.9	3.8	0	100
Canada	28.7	6.3	4.2	28.6	3.0	4.9	24.3	0	100
Total	22.0	2.6	9.2	39.4	8.8	6.7	10.0	1.3	100

Source: Executive Council memoranda. Territories were designated by responsible general vice-president.

[a] Also welders and foremen.

concentrated on contract shops; the south on contract shops and airframe production; both midwest territories on contract shops; the southwest on airframe production; the Pacific northwestern territory is divided largely between auto repair shops, airframe production, and contract shops; and Canada on airframe production, contract shops, and railroad shops. In one sense, these are significant observations because each general vice-president has an equal vote in the executive council, irrespective of differences in geographic size or membership size in their respective territories. But in the aggregate, the division of membership is not the same as seen in the various territories (see Table 11, for a distribution of membership according to type of lodge). The larger part of the aggregate membership was in contract and airframe lodges. Only about 10 per cent of the membership was in railroad lodges (allowing 50 per cent of the mixed lodge membership to be associated with railroads, builds up the railroad sector to a bare 14 per cent, or less than one in six).

Table 12 indicates where the various industrial classifications were concentrated geographically. The contract lodges were most strongly represented in the New England–middle Atlantic, and midwestern areas. The airframe lodges had the bulk of their strength in the southwest, New England–middle Atlantic, and western midwest areas. Thus it was entirely logical that the general vice presidents of these areas were particularly responsive to the needs of these industrial classifications. The other categories (except for railroads, unique for reasons of leadership in the IAM's history), were not sufficiently large in the aggregate to deserve special voices. Nonetheless, in the name of historical sentiment, the railroad lodges were given special consideration, and a general vice-president was detailed to attend their interests.

In the historical chapters as well as in Chapter VII the tradition of the skilled craftsman has served as a frequent point of reference. By the end of the Second World War, emphasis on skill as a qualification for membership had been abandoned. Nonetheless it is interesting to examine what we can of the formal membership structure at that time, in order to determine how much of the earlier craftsman emphasis may in point of fact have remained. Table 13 is useful for this purpose; the major caveat being that there is no way one can be sure that the personal skill classifications reported reflect competence as measured by thorough training, or simply skill as measured by the ability to demand, and get, typical journeymen's rates.

Withal, it is useful to pause at this point to examine the implications of the data. So much has been said of the passing of the heyday of the journeyman that it is worth noting that in 1952 two out of every five members still claimed to be skilled; that is, claimed to be journeymen. Beyond this first

Table 12. *Geographical distribution of members within each industrial category, 1952.*
(per cent distribution)

Area	Air-frame	Air trans.	Auto repair	Contract [a]	Mixed	Production worker	Rail-road	Tool & die
New England – Middle Atlantic	19.2	13.1	11.2	31.5	5.4	21.1	14.6	0
South	14.8	17.6	2.6	6.9	17.8	2.7	13.3	0
Eastern Midwest	0.2	1.9	11.5	19.5	10.6	19.1	22.2	21.5
Western Midwest	19.0	24.4	28.5	27.1	20.3	33.1	20.1	68.3
Southwest	32.2	19.5	25.6	5.6	34.0	17.7	8.0	9.9
Pacific northwest	6.9	4.0	17.4	4.1	9.7	1.2	7.1	0.3
District of Columbia	0	5.1	0.5	1.0	0.2	0.8	0.2	0
Canada	7.7	14.4	2.7	4.3	2.0	4.3	14.4	0
Total	100.	100.	100.	100.	100.	100.	100.	100.

Source: Executive council memoranda. Territories were designated by responsible general vice-president.

[a] Also welders and foremen.

Table 13. *Distribution of types of members within each region, 1952.*
(per cent distribution)

Area	Journeyman	Apprentice	Specialist	Helper	Production worker	Unemp.	On strike	Others [a]	Total
Northeast and Middle Atlantic	29.4	0.8	10.1	7.1	40.4	3.2	0.2	0.2	100
South	40.2	2.6	10.9	9.6	32.6	3.6	0.2	0.2	100
Eastern Midwest	35.6	1.4	16.7	8.6	30.5	5.7	1.1	0.4	100
Western Midwest	37.0	1.8	10.1	7.1	40.4	3.2	0.2	0.2	100
Southwest	52.8	1.6	6.7	4.5	29.9	3.6	0.7	0.1	100
Pacific northwest and mountain states	61.7	2.8	5.4	6.9	17.2	4.6	0.1	1.2	100
District of Columbia	83.5	3.1	1.2	4.0	5.9	1.8	0.0	1.4	100
Canada	42.2	2.9	2.6	12.6	35.3	3.0	0.0	0.5	100
Total in IAM (1952)	40.5	1.7	11.2	7.2	34.6	4.0	0.4	0.7	100
Total in IAM (1947)	46.8	3.7	11.0	9.5	23.0	5.1	0.3	0.5	100

Source: Executive council memoranda.

[a] Includes the retired categories.

point, it is important to add that in the areas where airframe production was most important and where one might expect the quantitive importance of having the skilled classification to have diminished most, the quantitive importance of the craftsman classification was still very strong. For example, in the southwest, 41.0 per cent of the membership was in the airframe industry, yet 52.8 per cent of the members were journeymen.

On the other hand, almost one third of the members in all regions claimed to be no more than production (relatively unskilled) operatives. In other words, the size of the operative classification was becoming almost as large as that of journeyman; and the disparity was diminishing between 1947 and 1952. The numerical importance of the apprentice group was also falling; in fact, it was relatively about half as large in 1952 as it was in 1947, although its absolute size held up well.[3]

One important insight is that the union grew most in the midwest, and it is in this geographic area where the unskilled operative has made his most significant numerical impact on the union. This is a point to emphasize. It is not in the "frontier areas" (the south or the Pacific coast sections), but in the "settled areas" (the western midwest) where the levelling-down or industrialization process has had its maximum impact numerically. Qualitatively, we know that this same area has been one of the bastions of journeyman or tradition-oriented strength. The inference is therefore that where the traditional journeyman group is strong, there is the greatest resistance to swelling the journeymen's ranks through "payroll-authorized" dilutions of the trades.

Sheer numbers do not show directly but can reflect intensity of feeling. It is this intensity of feeling which must always be considered.

Revenue [4]

While it is true that there are other important political reasons for limiting the grand lodge's influence in all IAM matters, the biggest single factor working in the direction of local autonomy is without any question the difficulty of raising large revenues. Large sums of money have to be raised with not only the acquiescence but also the cooperation of the membership. That is, the difficulty of actually collecting authorized amounts is far less than the difficulty of increasing those amounts. On several occasions even after it has been possible to convince the convention delegates of the need for putting larger sums at the disposal of the grand lodge, the rank and file have rejected the proposal. Thus the compulsory referendum on raising per capita taxes has had the effect of restricting grand lodge activities, in the first instance, and grand lodge influence thereafter.

From a technical viewpoint, there are six sources of IAM grand lodge funds: dues stamp sales, assessments, merchandise sales, income on investments, voluntary contributions, and special grand lodge fees. Stamp sales are, by all odds, the most important. This is illustrated both by Table 14 and the graph below.

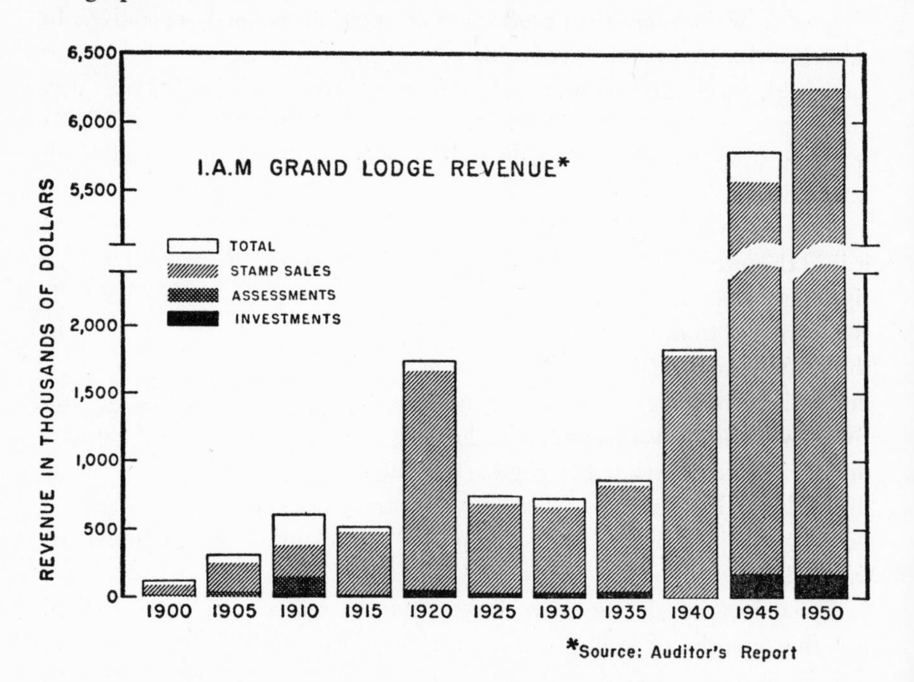

The monthly revenue from stamp sales is a function of three variables: the price per stamp, the size of the membership, and the number of delayed payments. Some delinquency in dues payment has always been tolerated; generally delinquency of three months has been permitted. The price per stamp has changed several times (see Table 2, Chapter VII), and for many years different classes of members paid different monthly per capita taxes, and unemployed members were permitted to substitute low-cost unemployed stamps for six months out of any twelve-month period.

Stamp sales are not a perfect indication of membership in short time intervals. Not only does individual delinquency occur, involving delay in purchasing the stamps, but local lodges occasionally stock up on stamps.

Assessment, the second source of grand lodge revenue, was regularly used during the O'Connell administration. As a program, assessment was hard to

Table 14. *Sources of grand lodge revenues, 1899–1952* (in thousands of dollars)

Year	Total	Stamp sales	Assessments	Investments
1899	56	51	0	—
1900	111	89	18	—
1901	186	126	63	—
1902	196	170	22	—
1903	317	266	48	—
1904	298	270	19	—
1905	286	250	29	—
1906	350	292	59	—
1907	289	273	61	3
1908	481	354	109	3
1909	459	334	118	2
1910	603	388	155	5
1911	583	396	164	4
1912	520	364	73	4
1913	527	441	11	5
1914	478	459	1	5
1915	504	487	0	5
1916	717	698	0	5
1917	880	842	0	4
1918	1618	1554	0	13
1919	1990	1919	0	39
1920	1728	1654	0	49
1921	1512	1507	—	1
1922	1172	1068	6	56 [a]
1923	904	778	0	65
1924	771	705	0	55
1925	739	690	—	27 [b]
1926	770	707	—	51
1927	790	710	—	70
1928	775	706	—	63
1929	875	750	—	54
1930	728	689	—	29
1931	617	557	—	56
1932	478	432	—	42
1933	490	445	—	34
1934	870	746	—	25
1935	859	822	—	29
1936	1112	1032	—	72
1937	1514	1485	—	14
1938	1325	1312	—	5
1939	1519	1501	—	6
1940	1813	1799	—	2
1941	2793	2762	—	5
1942	4126	4078	—	29
1943	5441	5369	—	44
1944	5977	5824	—	114
1945	5773	5573	—	164
1946	4854	4594	—	220
1947	5423	5165	—	221
1948	5482	5195	—	263
1949	5795	5611	—	149
1950	6456	6250	—	158
1951	8123	7879	—	789 [c]
1952	9555	9360	—	227

Source: Auditors' reports.

[a] Includes rental in IAM Building.

[b] Excludes interest on first half of year.

[c] Includes sale of bonds.

administer. Johnston abandoned this as a regular method after he took office, although he called for voluntary contributions during the shopcraftmen's strike in 1922.

Merchandise sales have been a source of a relatively small income. They refer to such supplies as dues books, stationery supplies, and jewelry insignia, which are sold at a moderate markup.

Investment income, on the other hand, has at times achieved significant proportions. On the whole, the IAM has done well in its real estate transactions. Its ventures into business, whether shipyard, printing shop, or banking, have not resulted in comparable success. Changes in accounting procedures confused the investment income pictures, particularly prior to 1925; but it has been increasingly important as a source of revenue.

Voluntary contributions were significant only prior to Wharton's administration. They represented an answer to rank-and-file opposition to the paying of increased per capita taxes as well as assessments. As such, they represented an ineffectual alternative.

The last source of revenue was grand lodge income from members unaffiliated with local lodges, as well as income from initiation and reinstatement fees.

One can see that the grand lodge has not been a wealthy organization. It has had to rely on a grudging membership for most of its authorized revenue; that is, for per capita taxes. Large annual income from investments, the only significant alternative to high per capita taxation, requires either speculation, or a big financial base from which to start. The former is so hazardous politically, that it has not been used extensively; and the latter has clearly been all but impossible, except in wartime (which is invariably followed by periods of intense strike activity).

Expenditures

How much the grand lodge spends, and on what, is determined by external factors such as the phase of the business cycle, the nature and extent of outstanding lawsuits, and the costs of affiliation with other labor organizations. It also reflects the lines of policy favored by the international president and the executive council, the extent of the benefits program currently in force, to say nothing of the size of membership and the level of funds on hand. In this section we consider first the allocation of expenditures among the several needs or uses. Then we turn to the consideration of the pattern within each of these categories.

Table. 15. *Proportion of expenditures for principal grand lodge activities, 1920–1952* (in per cent)

Year	Direct benefits	Grand lodge service function	"Overhead" cost	Affiliation costs	Other costs	Total
	a	b	c	d	e	
1920	13.1	29.1	13.8	3.8	40.2	100.0
1921	48.4	25.7	14.2	2.4	9.3	100.0
1922	44.1	23.2	17.1	3.4	12.2	100.0
1923	20.0	31.4	29.4	3.6	15.6	100.0
1924	18.7	30.0	28.4	3.9	19.0	100.0
1925	17.7	32.6	28.8	3.2	17.7	100.0
1926	16.5	31.9	21.4	4.1	26.1	100.0
1927	16.4	38.5	23.7	4.5	16.9	100.0
1928	22.9	33.1	21.4	3.7	18.9	100.0
1929	20.3	37.6	23.8	4.5	13.8	100.0
1930	16.1	33.2	22.8	3.1	24.8	100.0
1931	17.4	32.3	22.3	2.5	25.5	100.0
1932	19.3	27.8	22.2	3.2	27.5	100.0
1933	18.2	22.2	22.1	3.1	34.4	100.0
1934	16.7	33.4	19.7	2.8	27.4	100.0
1935	17.4	36.4	18.7	2.7	24.8	100.0
1936	29.9	30.9	15.5	2.6	21.1	100.0
1937	20.0	40.5	18.4	3.2	17.9	100.0
1938	15.4	46.8	17.2	4.7	15.9	100.0
1939	13.9	47.3	18.6	4.7	15.5	100.0
1940	15.5	46.2	17.2	4.5	16.6	100.0
1941	10.0	45.7	15.1	4.3	24.9	100.0
1942	8.1	61.9	17.1	2.4	10.5	100.0
1943	6.9	62.9	14.0	4.8	11.4	100.0
1944	6.3	62.8	13.6	7.2	10.1	100.0
1945	8.6	62.2	12.0	4.6	12.6	100.0
1946	18.7	61.7	8.7	3.1	7.7	100.0
1947	18.0	63.1	9.7	1.8	7.4	100.0
1948	26.4	55.0	8.8	0.7	9.1	100.0
1949	14.9	62.8	12.5	0.9	8.9	100.0
1950	14.2	62.1	12.8	1.0	9.9	100.0
1951	9.9	64.2	13.0	3.5	9.4	100.0
1952	11.2	60.0	10.0	4.0	14.8	100.0

Source: Auditors' reports.

[a] Death benefits, strike benefits and strike appropriations.

[b] Grand lodge's business agent program, organizing program, publications (journal and weekly), research cost.

[c] Executive expenditure (salaries). General headquarters cost.

[d] Payments to AFL, its various departments, its Canadian counterpart.

[e] Conventions and referenda.

Relative Amounts

Table 15 shows the pattern of expenditures on principal activities since 1920. For purposes of quick examination we have listed most of the major items under four separate headings: (1) direct benefits to individual members, (2) the grand lodge cost of performing its service function, (3) grand lodge "overhead" or administrative cost, and (4) the cost of affiliations. Several years present some accounting anomalies because considerable funds were used to replenish reserve funds, and although accounted as expended for that purpose, they were in a larger sense merely shifted from the surplus account to some other account. The accounts have been audited regularly, and designation of expenditures has occasionally changed, thus the opportunity for comparing expenditures has therefore been greatly complicated or even lost. Here it is pertinent to note that the union's books have been audited on a six-month basis since the beginning, but that this half-yearly period has been made to coincide with the usual January-through-June, July-through-December intervals, only since 1919. It is for this reason that we have elected to confine our analysis to the period after the First World War.

Generally the IAM seems to spend between 15 and 20 per cent of its annual budget on so-called direct membership benefits, i.e. death benefits and strike payment allocations. This was the pattern in fifteen of the thirty-three years between 1920 and 1952; in only four years was more than 25 per cent spent in this area, and three were years of great postwar strikes (1921, 1922, and 1948). More will be said regarding this point later. During the four years of the Second World War, less than 10 per cent of the budget went to what we have termed the "direct benefits program"—this situation prevailed because virtually no strikes were authorized during the months of active military hostilities. And again during the Korean conflict a similar policy prevailed. Thus if we exclude from our calculations the war as well as the abnormal postwar years, we conclude that the "range" of direct benefits expenditures was between 15 and 20 per cent, but on some occasions close to 10 per cent, and on others rose as high as 25 per cent. The years of "relative parsimony" were 1920 (when much money went for other things, including a new building) and 1939. The years of relatively generous appropriation were 1928 and 1929 (periods of prosperity following the replenishment of funds in the similarly lush preceding two years), and 1936 and 1937 (a time of big organizing strikes—particularly in the plants of the Remington-Rand Corporation).

The role played by the grand lodge in servicing membership needs (as distinct from giving them straight or direct benefits) has grown since 1920. These include organizing programs, business agencies, research, and legal expenses. Admittedly, expenditure in this area has been variable and reflects grand lodge prosperity as much as it does the growth of grand lodge responsibilities. Excluding the gravest year of the depression, when it tumbled to less than one quarter of the expenditure, the level of expenditure on servicing membership needs has risen from about 30 per cent to a share roughly twice as large.

By way of contrast, the relative share of grand lodge "overhead" costs, which includes general headquarters expenses and the salaries and expenses of the elected and appointed officials, has been reduced. The advantage of large-scale operation, that is of a larger and larger membership, is nowhere so well revealed as in the cost of maintaining headquarters. For example, the number of officials and their salaries have been kept relatively inflexible; consequently their cost has become relatively smaller as total expenditures have risen. In addition, economies of scale, plus improvements in operating efficiency introduced by the officers, have brought the overhead cost of the Washington staff down to about 10 per cent of total expenditures or about one-half the prewar level. Of course, this reduction is not in itself necessarily impressive — too radical reductions in such expenditures may result in losses elsewhere. On the other hand, it might also have been possible to pare even more, and 10 per cent could thus be a high residual share rather than a low one. But, it is a low enough figure to dispel any notions that headquarters has grown fat during the years of plenty following the Second World War.

This leaves only the relative pecuniary cost of being part of the "house of labor." This generally amounted to about 3 to 4 per cent of the IAM's annual budget. It rose to its maximum during the latter thirties, and in 1944. It was at its minimum during the period when the IAM had withdrawn from the AFL. Actually the amounts allocated for this purpose were direct functions of the percentage of membership used for reportorial purposes and the per capita cost of affiliation. Indirectly, they were functions of the willingness of the IAM to participate in AFL activities, its departments, and other labor organizations (railroad, as well as the Canadian counterpart of the AFL); and the affluence of the treasury.

Since the Second World War, the "other," or residual, expenditures — those not accounted for by the four principal categories — have dropped to a figure usually less than 10 per cent of the IAM's budget. During the twenties the proportion was roughly twice as great, and during the depression the proportion was even larger.

Now let us turn to a discussion of specific expenditure patterns. For this purpose a per capita analysis is probably the most useful, although consideration of the absolute amounts as well as the precise relative share of the budget is helpful.

Death Benefits and Strike Allocations

In Table 16 the direct benefits are separated into death benefits and strike allocations. The death benefits program has been so popular with the rank-and-file membership that all moves to eliminate it or to put it on an actuarially sound basis failed until 1960. The most that has been possible has

Table 16. *Grand lodge expenditures in direct benefits: Death benefits and strike allocations, 1921–1952*

Year	Death benefits			Strike allocations		
	Absolute amount (thousands)	Per capita expenditure	Per cent of annual expenditure	Absolute amount (thousands)	Per capita	Per cent of annual expenditure
1921	122	$0.59	5.8	897	$4.33	42.6
1922	136	.92	7.9	621	4.19	36.2
1923	128	1.22	12.1	84 [a]	.80	7.9 [a]
1924	107	1.34	13.0	47 (special)	.59	5.7
1925	105	1.46	13.9	27	.37	3.6
1926	122	1.70	14.3	19	.27	2.2
1927	107	1.51	14.5	14	.19	1.9
1928	123	1.78	15.5	59	.86	7.4
1929	127	1.77	16.3	31	.44	4.0
1930	122	1.76	15.0	9	.13	1.1
1931	123	1.94	16.0	11	.18	1.4
1932	127	2.16	18.4	6	.11	.9
1933	129	2.12	18.1	1	.02	.1
1934	142	1.61	14.7	19	.21	2.0
1935	152	1.71	15.2	22	.25	2.2
1936	148	1.40	11.6	233	2.21	18.3
1937	171	1.12	12.3	107	.71	7.7
1938	158	1.02	10.5	74	.47	4.9
1939	148	.91	10.5	48	.30	3.4
1940	180	.96	11.4	65	.35	4.1
1941	164	.57	7.3	60	.21	2.7
1942	191	.43	7.9	4	.01	.2
1943	222	.36	6.9	0	0	0
1944	215	.33	6.3	0	0	0
1945	228	.37	5.7	116	.19	2.9
1946	255	.49	4.3	856	1.65	14.4
1947	267	.49	4.0	927	1.70	14.0
1948	304	.56	3.9	1,744	3.22	22.5
1949	314	.61	5.3	571	1.10	9.6
1950	324	.64	5.4	502	.99	8.6
1951	350	.56	5.5	283	.46	4.4
1952	386	.53	4.6	549	.94	6.6

Source: Derived from auditors' reports.

[a] The shop craftsmen's strike accounted for $49,000 (46% of annual expenditure).

been to lengthen the membership requirements necessary to qualify, a point discussed previously. In the light of this situation, these benefits have had to be financed to a large degree out of current income or general reserve funds. Moreover, during the years of lessened membership, it appears that it was often the "old-timer," who kept his membership active. Because these benefits were a matter of right, nothing could be done by the administration to reduce the cost. On the other hand, when the membership had expanded, this burden on the budget decreased. Examination of Table 16 quickly points up the situation. In absolute amounts, the death benefits program has had a marked secular rise. As a share of the budgeted expenses, however, it hit its apogee in 1932 and its nadir after World War II. During the worst depression years it cost the IAM over $2.00 per member, at a time when the average grand lodge per capita tax, even after allowance for unemployed stamps is made, was about $10.00. Considering the lack of direct usefulness of these benefits in the bargaining or representation function of unionism, the benefits program at that time weighed heavily. On the other hand, by 1951 its cost was approximately 55 cents, at a time when the per capita tax to the grand lodge was bringing in over $15.00 per member.

The strike benefits program had to be suspended during the railroad shopcraft strike of 1922–1923 because of the drain on the union's treasury. As shown on Table 16, it represented approximately 40 per cent of total expenditures. Subsequently, as we have noted, strike payments became a matter of privilege rather than right, giving the grand lodge a degree of discretionary power regarding the use of its funds. Previously, of course, the grand lodge could refuse to authorize strikes, but its grounds for so doing had to be made explicit. Insolvency, or the threat of it, was not the kind of information which enhanced the IAM's chances in any situation. As a result of the change in grand lodge policy, it became easy for the IAM to hide its pecuniary difficulties and, what is more to the point, to choose which strike situation it wanted to press to victory, and which it could afford to neglect.

Strike expenditures are associated with periods when employers are attempting to resist union pressures for hourly rate increases or union attempts to organize previously unorganized areas. By and large, they occur during periods of rising prices or during periods of recession when the likelihood of union victory is small. During war periods strike expenditures shrink completely.

The years of heaviest absolute expenditure were immediately after the two world wars and during the years following the enactment of the National Labor Relations Act (1935). The strikes of 1921–1923 were associated with the union's efforts to maintain its First World War gains. These efforts certainly were not successful, although it is impossible to adjudge the expenditures either unwise or unsuccessful, since what would have occurred had the effort not been made can never be known. On the other hand, the great expenditures following the Second World War, despite the union's gains in membership, as well as contract advantages, may have been unnecessary, but again one cannot judge. Suffice it here to observe that there are many intangibles which affect the formation of bargaining — and strike — policies. One tangible factor is the state of the union's financial reserves.

Occasionally, as in the cases of the shopcrafts strike or the Remington Rand strike (which cost the grand lodge almost $300,000, about 89 per cent of the strike expenditures from 1936 to 1937), stalwart employers may press the issue and all but force the union to spend on strikes. Even so, union leadership has to watch expenditures carefully lest the struggle develop into a war of attrition — a situation in which the odds favor the employer.

Analysis of Table 16 indicates that the years of heaviest per capita expenditure on strikes were during the postwar periods, during the Remington Rand conflict, and during 1928. Explanation for the first and the last, although largely speculative, involves an appreciation of what might be termed the psychic costs of recuperative or postponed bargaining policies. During war periods work is plentiful, pay is high, and hours are long. When peace comes, workers are ready to "take a vacation" and are apt to bargain closely, knowing that strikes may well result. In brief, union policies become pugnacious because of the enforced period of cooperation. The 1928 figure can be explained in like manner. For five years, 1923–1927, the union could not afford to strike because its reserves had been wiped out, and the little it was accumulating was tied up with interfactional fighting in its own ranks. By 1928 a semblance of normalcy had returned, and it was then able to assert not only its own accustomed degree of aggressiveness, but to try to compensate for the lean years.

We now turn to a detailed analysis of three of the grand lodge's service functions. They are the organizing program, the business agent program, and its research activities. Table 17 presents total outlay, the per capita cost, and the per cent of annual expenditure for each of these items.

The Organizing Program

The grand lodge's effort to organize new members has been one of the major items of expenditure. If one omits the blackest years, after the disastrous shopcrafts strike and the Great Depression (when all variable expenditures were pared to a minimum), the grand lodge, according to its own

Table 17. *Grand lodge expenditures on selected service programs, 1921–1952*

Year	Organizing			Business agent program			Research		
	Amount (thousands)	Per capita	Per cent of annual expenditure	Amount (thousands)	Per capita	Per cent of annual expenditure	Amount (thousands)	Per capita	Per cent of annual expenditure
1921	$260	$1.26	12.4	$141	$0.68	6.7	—	—	—
1922	169	1.14	9.8	122	.82	7.1	—	—	—
1923	129	1.22	12.1	137	1.31	12.9	—	—	—
1924	83	1.04	10.1	100	1.25	12.2	$ 3	$.04	0.4
1925	105	1.46	13.9	93	1.29	12.3	4	.05	0.5
1926	111	1.55	13.0	97	1.35	11.3	3	.03	0.4
1927	115	1.62	15.6	98	1.38	13.3	2	.03	0.3
1928	96	1.39	12.1	97	1.41	12.2	2	.02	0.3
1929	128	1.79	16.4	94	1.31	12.1	3	.04	0.4
1930	110	1.58	13.5	94	1.35	11.5	2	.03	0.2
1931	92	1.45	12.0	91	1.42	11.8	2	.04	0.3
1932	62	1.05	9.0	77	1.30	11.1	2	.03	0.3
1933	46	.76	6.5	62	1.01	8.7	2	.03	0.3
1934	173	1.96	17.9	70	.79	7.3	2	.02	0.2
1935	196	2.20	19.6	83	.94	8.3	2	.03	0.2
1936	200	1.91	15.7	90	.86	7.1	4	.04	0.3
1937	308	2.03	22.1	113	.74	8.1	8	.05	0.6
1938	385	2.48	25.5	145	.94	9.6	12	.08	0.8
1939	357	2.20	25.3	149	.92	10.5	14	.09	1.0
1940	375	2.00	23.7	170	.90	10.7	16	.09	1.0
1941	539	1.90	24.1	240	.84	10.7	13	.05	0.6
1942	858	1.93	34.9	324	.73	13.2	22	.05	0.9
1943	1251	2.03	38.6	426	.69	13.2	28	.05	0.9
1944	1302	1.97	37.9	513	.78	14.9	26	.04	0.8
1945	1561	2.56	39.2	563	.92	14.1	27	.04	0.7
1946	2042	3.93	34.4	653	1.26	11.0	53	.10	0.9
1947	2223	4.08	33.5	770	1.41	11.6	75	.14	1.1
1948	2215	4.09	28.6	823	1.52	10.6	80	.15	1.0
1949	1826	3.52	30.6	851	1.64	14.3	83	.16	1.4
1950	1745	3.44	30.2	870	1.71	15.0	87	.17	1.5
1951	2184	3.52	34.1	943	1.52	14.7	87	.14	1.4
1952	2684	3.66	32.3	1078	1.47	13.0	93	.13	1.1

Source: Derived from auditors' reports.

accounting system, has spent between one-fifth and two-fifths of its budget in order to expand its ranks. This pattern of effort is confirmed by examination of the per capita expenditure.

Why is this such an important activity? In other words, does it benefit the existing membership or just the newcomers? Obviously, the most direct beneficiaries of this massive effort are the new members; for this reason alone the IAM can well be said to have some of the earmarks of a social movement with a mission. This point is all too frequently overlooked by those who can see in unionism nothing more than a cynical bargaining institution.

The truth is that the organizing effort benefits old members as well. By standardizing the union's wage rates throughout product and factor markets, the union reduces the economic pressure on employers to take back the concessions secured in previous contracts. Similarly, it makes it easier for the union to secure additional advantages in future contracts. Sums spent on organizing are to some degree substitutes for sums spent on strikes. If money were not used to bring the unorganized into the IAM's ranks, additional money would have to be spent on strike funds to protect the IAM's gains, which are jeopardized by cheaper products manufactured by cheaper labor. Optimum balance between the two types of expenditure is hard to determine precisely, but, in general, it is far better for the individual member to see his per capita "returned to him" in the form of new members than as a strike payment.

The Business Agent Program

In addition to the strike payments, and the organizing program, the grand lodge spends sizeable amounts on helping to finance business agencies, the units responsible for the negotiation of contracts as well as their policing. This aspect of unionism is in the case of some CIO unions largely the responsibility of the national organization; such is historically not the case in the IAM, where the tradition of local autonomy remains strong. Here it will be recalled from Chapter VII that the grand lodge pays only half the cost of these agencies up to a fixed sum, and in return, the grand lodge is able to exercise some degree of control over local contracts.

In practice, the extension of grand lodge control does not seem to be reflected by the expenditure picture indicated in Table 17 (columns 5 to 7).

No sharp increase either in the percentage of the annual budget or the per capita expenditure can be seen, although of course the absolute amounts have expanded significantly, along with growth in union size (as well as price inflation). Why, it can be asked, accepting the fact of a general price inflation as well as the assertion that grand lodge authority has expanded, does no clear pattern of relative expenditure increase exist in this area? The answer reflects two forces, one political and one economic. The political force is the reluctance of the rank and file to authorize large increases in officials' remuneration (see Table 8, Chapter VII); thus, there is little upward movement associated with price inflation. The other, or economic, factor reflects economies of scale in union representation. By and large, one union business representative can handle either a small or large number of contracts; to be more precise, fifteen local contracts require the same number of business agents (one), as do fifty. Moreover, it makes relatively little difference whether each contract covers ten or one-thousand employees. Consequently, as the union has grown in size, and the number of contracts it has negotiated has expanded, it has not been necessary for the size of its business agency staffs to increase in comparable proportions. It has been necessary, however, for the grand lodge to increase its technical service to the business agents.

The Research Program

Traditionally, contracts were negotiated by trial and error—the union asking for more than it expected, the employer offering less than he could afford. The point of resolution, brought about by pure bargaining, ultimately reflected the employer's estimate of the maximum he could afford (involving also the possibility of substituting machinery or cheaper labor for machinists), and the union's ability to hold its membership united. More recently, as product and factor markets have become better integrated, the union has seen the need to base its bargaining position on some form of economic analysis pertaining to wage patterns of alternative labor sources, as well as the price of machinery which could be substituted for its members. There is no reason why local business agencies could not hire their own research staffs to perform this function, except that it is much more economical for the grand lodge to provide the service for the agencies. This is just what has occurred and although the absolute cost is small (it did triple after the Second World War, but was still less than one-tenth the cost of the grand lodge's business agent program), it is extremely important. The research program is not only economics-oriented, but it also provides some basic legal references for the wording of clauses.

The size of figures indicated in Table 17 (columns 9–10) does not reflect their usefulness. Whether additional expenditure in this area would be helpful, however, is not clear. Presumably the expenditure pattern on each item should be such that the usefulness of additional money should be greater on no one than on any other. That is, the organization's budget is optimally arranged if there is no net advantage to shifting a dollar from one account (such as strike allocations, business agencies, research, or savings) to another.

PART THREE

The Policies

CHAPTER IX

The Meaning of Jurisdiction

The concept of jurisdictional claims and boundaries has probably been the biggest single obstacle to the understanding of the American trade-union movement. In this chapter we consider the meaning of jurisdiction, first in a general and abstract sense, and then we turn to the history of the IAM for applications of the concept. Together the two treatments yield an analysis which clarifies what might otherwise appear to be an inconsistent, if not contradictory, policy. This discussion is confined, however, to the areas of contested jurisdiction. In other words, the problems of colonizing in open, undisputed areas, while truly an exercise of the jurisdictional claim, are not part of our consideration.

JURISDICTION ANALYZED

Although we have already considered the evolution of the IAM's policy of admissions through sixty years of history, we have not consciously put down a definition of jurisdiction, nor described the set of factors which determine jurisdiction.

By jurisdiction we mean two exclusive claims: one over the job area, and the second over the workers, who at one time or another fill these jobs. Jurisdiction starts with the claim for exclusive control over a craft or an industrial function but frequently stretches to incorporate a similar demand for controlling all the individuals who presently perform the function. Put together, the two claims constitute the definition of union jurisdiction. This, however, does not explain the pattern of changes in the jurisdictional claim. The historical fact is that unions not only redefine their jurisdictions, asserting new claims and exchanging old ones, but frequently the claims are "created" or "modified" by what are actually employer preferences. For this reason we shall consider the type of conflict occurring between two or more unions, when the employer's role is thoroughly passive. Afterward, we shall examine the roles that employers can play, and superimpose the latter situations on the former.

Unions expand their claims, make deals or exchanges, or redefine their legitimate job area in several ways. It often happens that first there are *de facto* conquests. That is, a union gets a foothold in a new shop or industry, at the workers' request. But our interest is in the desire for *de jure* recognition, which is the union's desire to "legitimize" its claim. Characteristically, the *de jure* claim appears earliest in the union constitutions or circulars, and only after such due notice has been afforded to other parties, will the union press its advantage in confronting employees; and this to be done within the councils of the federation (AFL or AFL–CIO) and its sub-bodies, like the Building Trades Department, or before the government agency authorized to consider the matter. On the surface the claim in some way usually reflects the product made by the workers, the materials used, the tools employed, or the skills required in the process.[1] Quite naturally, the less rapidly technology and/or the product changes, the less likely this rationale can be used for broadening the claim. One example of a relatively static industrial process might be the making of molds for iron castings. There the claim could well be phrased in such broad terms as the simple right to make molds for iron castings, the right to jobs using molders' sand, or even the right to those jobs using molders' sand to make iron castings. In this example, the factors listed earlier are fairly constant or stable, and few jurisdictional disputes, for the reasons cited above, should develop. On the other hand, where industrial technology and/or the product are not constant, there will be many jurisdictional claims, because unions must adapt if they are not to shrink and disappear. In these latter instances the changes tend to follow lines suggested by the use of tools or materials. For instance, the carpenters' union at times has argued that their jurisdictional claim is properly exercised over all products made of wood and all products which at one time (if not currently) have been made of wood. Here it is obvious that the claim is tied to the product; but it is important to add that the carpenters have not limited their claim to a simple touchstone.

Some unions have associated their claims with the skills employed on tools or machines. The IAM, for example, believes that the operation of metal lathes, boring mills, as well as several other machines, is inherently its territory. The teamsters have similarly claimed the use of the wheeled vehicle as their area. And the broad claims made by two unions may conflict because each has tried to create a general justification for asserting its rights.

Unfortunately for the cause of industrial peace, the rate of change of the industrial arts has been great, and unions have tried to retain control over jobs and the workers who at one time performed them, by broadening their claims of control. The net result has been, as every student of American labor history well appreciates, a marked proliferation of interunion conflicts. The first conclusion one can draw is that jurisdictional problems are often created by changes in the industrial arts because jurisdiction is generally conceived along lines which are affected by changes in the industrial arts.

It is inadequate to suggest that jurisdictional problems are created only by technological change. They can also be a product of a hunger for work, that is both actual employment and all the rights that pertain to controlling a job territory. Two unions may compete in their attempts to organize an unorganized industry, or one union may eye a group of jobs being filled by members of another union. With this, comes a desire for assimilation of either the jobs or the jobs and workers. In the former instance, the first union will baldly assert its right to the jobs and the rights of its present members to the employment opportunity (that is, to the detriment of those presently holding the jobs); in the second instance, it will assert its right to control the workers already on the jobs involved and its right to their fees and dues. There are several reasons why this hunger develops. At times the appetite, as the French put it, comes with eating; in other words, rank union imperialism. But there can be a reason; that is, the economic motivation coming from the knowledge that a union must control certain subsidiary jobs if it is to strengthen its position in its traditional job territory. A union may discover that the only way to organize the factory or manufacturing side of an industry is to control a relatively small number of installation jobs on the job site. For this reason a union may be forced to expand its jurisdiction to cover workers whom it did not originally want as members (or workers who do not particularly want to join that or any other union), simply to protect the interests of its regular members.

Another cause of jurisdictional conflict is the exercise of the political strength and abilities of unions and their leaders. The proclivities for making, or for not making, personal alliances and agreements, have frequently accentuated the importance and the frequency of jurisdictional disputes. O'Connell's influence within AFL circles, to cite one example, was such that he could "get away with" claims which Johnston could not. Often this personal factor, stressing the ties or influence of union leaders (and reflecting their financial power as well as their personal good-fellow reputations), has reached a level of significance in the development of jurisdictional patterns. Coupled with the importance of the key national figure, is the similar possibility of intraunion differences between national and local officials. It can and does happen that the national representative may agree to one pattern of resolving conflicting claims but is powerless to carry out his promises effectively at the scene of the dispute. Thus, the political abilities and proclivities of national union leaders may run up against local attitudes, and true intraunion fighting can be the product.

But it is also possible for employers, willingly or unknowingly, to precipitate interunion discord. In a situation where there is relatively little need for a particular craft's participation, or where confusion reigns, and it is believed that there is no need for the representatives of a particular craft to be employed on the job, an employer may direct another worker "to help out"; that is, a carpenter may be told to take over some other craft's regularly assigned function. Not only will the aggrieved union resist this discriminatory treatment, but other unions may well ask, "If it is not to be the regular craft, why the carpenters in preference to us?" Conflict frequently follows, because one union is said (sometimes with reason) to have the "inside track" with an employer.

Because all crafts are not paid the same, employers have an understandably great temptation to divert work from one union toward a lower-paid one. Traditionally, production workers employed in factories earn less per hour than construction workers employed on job sites, and employers, intent on minimizing costs, may try to shift work to the lower-paid group (assuming that productivity as well as simple hourly rates are considered). This almost inevitably leads to conflict between the two unions involved—a fight between those working on the "inside" (in the factory) and those on the "outside" (at the site of the new construction).

Favoritism on the part of the employers is another factor. Some employers try to play up union rivalries, or favor one union over another. The consequence in both instances is more or less interunion conflict in the form of rival jurisdictional claims. It is also true that the effects of employer policy may intensify intraunion difficulties either between the national and local levels or within the local, where politically ambitious individuals may use the results of an employer's policies to foment discord. This aspect of the problem ties into the question of the political strength and abilities of union leaders.

There is also the problem of employer willingness or unwillingness to countenance graft. This pertains to the moral imperfection of man generally, and of a union leader or official specifically. It involves a local union leader making an unjustified threat in the hope of "being paid off"; that is, of receiving a remittance not "to make trouble for the employer." Failing to get his "cut," a business agent may raise the question of appropriateness of jurisdiction, as a subterfuge. Situations of this type unfortunately do occur. Employers know it and by accepting it, they encourage its spread.

In addition to the "union causes" and the "employer causes" of jurisdictional disputes, there is a third force generating difficulty. The government has come to play a large role in the definition of appropriate bargaining units as well as protecting the rights of dissident workers. The National Labor Relations Board, by defining appropriate areas for bargaining purposes under the direction given it from time to time by Congress, can and does precipitate disputes, in much the same way it resolves them.

Unions are involved in jurisdictional disputes because of changes in technology, job hunger and the need to protect previously organized job territory, and because of the political conditions inherent in any self-administered social movement. To these factors may be added certain employers, who are ignorant of past practices of work division, or who, for reasons of economy or politics, feel they gain an advantage in reassigning work. Graft and the promise of pay-offs involving employers, should also be listed. Finally the government, as its policy is administered by the NLRB, plays a vital role. The phenomenon of jurisdictional conflict, however, is an inherent, probably necessary, part of a dynamic, pluralistic society and can be eliminated only by an autocratic assignment of new or disputed job territories. The latter, for other institutional reasons, notably its completely authoritarian nature, is undesirable.

A Brief History of Jurisdictional Disputes

The classic example of tight jurisdictional control is the International Typographical Union, which gained the closed shop early in the nineties at the time of the introduction of the Mergenthaler linotype. Because the IAM's members normally fabricated and repaired all types of printing machinery, it is not surprising that the earliest violent fight involving the IAM's claim to jurisdiction, was with the ITU over the right to repair linotypes. The dispute continued for several years, in spite of attempts at a solution by the AFL, ending only when the IAM recognized that the ITU's control over the job floor was so great that the ITU could not be successfully challenged.[2]

Originally (in 1895) the ITU had agreed to give IAM members the right to repair linotypes. Within a few months after the agreement, however, the ITU permitted some expelled New York City members of the IAM to form a linotype machinists' local within its own organization. O'Connell quite naturally took the matter to the AFL executive council, where he obtained a resolution directing the ITU to rescind the local's charter and directing the men to return to the IAM fold. The ITU not only ignored the resolution, but amended its own constitution in 1897, to provide that ITU members should properly make all linotype repairs. Considering the strength of the ITU in printing shops, this decision meant the virtual expulsion of the IAM from the linotype shops. However, President Donnelly, of the ITU, then (1898) worked out what he hoped would be a satisfactory compromise; the IAM could have the large plants (in the cities where they had numerical strength); the ITU, the small shops. But this effort came to nothing, for by 1899 the ITU, guided by the preferences of some of its local organizations, defied the IAM and the AFL executive council and ordered all linotype repairmen to join the ITU. The ITU locals took this step just at the time Donnelly was trying to conciliate both the IAM and the AFL leadership.

Motivated, in part, by local sentiments, Donnelly's union had taken action, ignoring his own protests. (Whether he actively fought the imperialism being exercised by the ITU is unknown, but he certainly must have opposed its timing.) He could not have argued that the ITU had any historical right to the job territory. Nor could he argue that ITU membership was "better" for the men, because it was believed that the IAM hourly rates were higher than the ITU rates. Moreover, the ITU did not require control over the repair work in order to assure its own security in the industry; the closed shop was more than enough for that. Yet, from a political standpoint, what could Donnelly do? He could either try to modify the ITU's stand or the one taken by the AFL executive council. Eventually he chose the latter course and with the aid of Peter McGuire (the AFL secretary–treasurer), he had the motion condemning the ITU watered down to the point where it merely urged the two unions to compromise their differences, and in the event of a failure to do so, directed the establishment of a nine-man arbitration panel.

In the meantime open antagonism between the two organizations increased. In Buffalo an IAM member sued the ITU and was awarded $600 damages as compensation for having been frozen out of his job. The ITU, in turn, protested the signing of an agreement between some Pittsburgh employers and the IAM, in scathing terms.

The ITU refused either to conciliate its differences with the IAM or to arbitrate them. And the fight ended with an ITU victory. The IAM had to admit that it was powerless to change the situation, although it did assert that it would never forego its right to linotype repair work.

This refers us back to our analytical framework. The conflict was caused by technological development, by job hunger, and by the politicking of employer and union leadership. What kicked off the dispute was the substitution of a mechanical process for a hand process. Insofar as the linotype was a machine, its repair traditionally should have been reserved for machinists, but the ITU wanted the job territory because it believed it desirable to have exclusive control over all printing shop jobs. There was, therefore, a conflict between two of the traditional touchstones of jurisdiction, namely, the tools and the product. The ITU won, in part, because Donnelly prevented ITU expulsion from the AFL, but more because of the ITU's solid grip on the industry. The employers presumably did not want to court chaos by fighting. In other words, the IAM lost mostly because it lacked effective political power in the shop.

Technological change was at the root of the trouble with the ITU, but the outward manifestation took the form of the ITU's claiming, as its "tool" (machine), the type of thing which the IAM had previously considered to be exclusively its own. In other words, where machinists had formerly repaired machines (including linotypes), the ITU now successfully asserted that it repaired certain printing machines — an incident illustrating the dominance of the adjective over the noun. The important point is that both unions formed the rationale of their positions in the same way — each claiming that the criterion was simply a decision regarding "craft ownership" of a particular machine.

It is worth adding that the pressmen, a breakaway from the ITU, did not have the strength in the shop or with the employers that the ITU did.[8] Consequently when the IAM raised the question of defining jurisdictions, the pressmen agreed to negotiate a pattern for settlements. This agreement, occurring in 1916 and later expanded in 1953, set up a two-man "International Board of Relationship" to handle those disputes which could not be resolved on the local level. In general, the pressmen's union was to have as members those operating "all printing and lithographing machinery," while the IAM was to have those who manufactured all presses and accessories. Nothing was specifically said about the repair of the equipment. The method of dividing the work, that is, listing of equipment, was not dissimilar to the ITU case; the only difference was probably the level of union influence with employers. In the ITU case, the employers were relatively beholden to that union; the employers were much more independent regarding the pressmen. The ITU could, and would, refuse to work equipment that its members hadn't repaired, and what is more, could get away with their threat. The pressman were not that well organized. In other words, jurisdictional lines have their own rationale, but whatever it is, it cannot get very far from the pattern set by "the real power structure."

In the building trades, however, "craft ownership" of a tool or machine has not been used as the criterion for assertion of jurisdiction, because the use of this criterion presupposes a type of job continuity not generally existent in the building trades. There, it has traditionally been difficult to use tools or materials as jurisdictional touchstones because of the discontinuous nature of construction work. Each particular job contract tends to have a large number of individual characteristics, involving brief use of one or another tool or process, so that building crews must exercise a "jack-of-all-trades" ingenuity. Part of this situation can also be explained by noting that the carry-over of skill among building craftsmen is, as a result, probably greater than is generally the rule elsewhere. Because of the ephemeral nature of jobs in this industry and of the carry-over of skills, jurisdictional disputes, when they arise, seem to cause immediate work stoppages in the building trades; whereas, in the railroad shops or the other metal trades, the settlement of a dispute, even if it should require little time, carries with it so much precedent-forming impact, that the unions are willing to continue work prior to the formal decision, and are prepared to trust to a sort of *stare decisis* to preserve their subsequent interests. In the building trades, however, a large number of small, perhaps even trifling, disputes encourages "horse-trading"—that is, Union A gives several decisions to Union B, providing Union B does the same for Union A. Jurisdictional dispute settlement in the building trades appears to the historian to be somewhat more "bargain-prone" than in the metal trades (the railroad shops), for example, where it is relatively "precedent-oriented." In the building trades, unions get along by overtly recognizing the economic power of their rivals and by bidding as high as their own strength permits; in the metal trades (and particularly in the railroad shops, the most static of the metal trades' universe) unions strive to maximize their ends by watching the establishment of precedents with a most careful eye. The result is obvious—the metal trades unions view jurisdictional dispute settlement in the building trades as overt power-bargaining; the building trades unions return the compliment by considering similar dispute settlements in the metal trades as typical of the operations of Philadelphia lawyers.

The best example of this diversity of approach was the long struggle between the IAM and the group of unions which clustered about the carpenters. The struggle lasted almost five decades and was caused by the IAM's insistence that the pattern for settling the dispute follow the one found in the metal trades. The carpenters, by way of contrast, really cared little for precedents based on the definition of craft ownership of tools and machines. In the ensuing struggle the IAM fared poorly because the carpenters' approach was not only far better adapted to hit-and-run political tactics, which paid off with victory, but was also more realistic considering the rapidity of technological change. In the council halls the IAM did well at first because it prepared a logical case. But repeated losses on the job made successes in the council halls empty victories, and in time those who ran the council hall (the

AFL executive council and conventions) preferred to have the IAM grievance overlooked because its continued reiteration publicized the impotence of the council hall. For this reason the IAM became increasingly frustrated until it eventually withdraw from the AFL.

Resolution of the conflict with the carpenters occurred when the IAM and the building trades unions realized the true nature of the conflict and agreed to bargain over jurisdiction in a fashion consonant with economic reality, as well as the tradition of the building trades unions. In a 1954 agreement, described in Chapter VI, the IAM agreed to recognize the "right" of the carpenters to 50 per cent of the jobs in erecting turbines, and the carpenters (who, in point of fact, actually were doing the work) agreed to give 50 per cent of the work to the IAM.

The earlier history of the conflict deserves some attention. The trouble appears to have begun with an IAM decision, some time around 1908, not to accept millwrights as members, on the grounds that they were insufficiently skilled for anything but the rigging of power belts.[4] Behind this decision were several factors, including a belief that the IAM could have squeezed the millwrights' craft into oblivion and have inherited for itself the latter's job opportunity. The millwrights, however, turned to the carpenters and, instead of disappearing, emerged as active rivals to the IAM for the erection of machinery in shops and factories.

In the meantime the elevator erectors' union also was having its difficulties with the machinists; the latter wanted amalgamation not only because it would increase the job area somewhat, but also, we have noted, because control of elevator erection was essential to the IAM's job sovereignty in factories making elevator equipment.[5] What the IAM obviously wanted was the type of control held by the ITU, where the IAM could refuse to install or work on any equipment which had not been previously processed by IAM members. Not only were the employers in the elevator erection industry not afraid of the IAM (they could get their machines from the various manufacturers whom the IAM had been unable to organize), but they were fully aware of the risk of provoking the building trades unions by antagonizing the small, yet politically capable, elevator constructors' union. In any event, the IAM discounted the importance of the employers' attitude and tried to close in for the kill at the 1914 AFL convention, only to find that the victim had been rescued by the carpenters, who had made a deal with the smaller union to drive the IAM out of the construction industry. In addition to the development of cooperation between its two rivals, the IAM had also lost political strength in the councils of the AFL. As long as O'Connell led the IAM, the AFL leaders were sympathetic to IAM causes, and although they could not actually force amalgamation on the unwilling elevator constructors, they did whatever they could to help the IAM by applying such pressure as they could. Once O'Connell had been humiliated, the extent of their efforts seems to have lessened. Thus O'Connell's defeat ended one important phase of IAM jurisdictional development, one which stressed not only the importance of precedent in the resolution of disputes, and the use of tools or machine processes as criteria for jurisdiction definition, but also rested in part on the aid of friends in the councils of the AFL.

Johnston's reaction to the convention defeat was to pay back in kind for the treatment the IAM received. Consequently, he permitted the IAM to raid the job territory traditionally held by the flintglass workers' union, justifying this by explaining that the IAM was treating the flintglass workers in precisely the fashion in which the AFL permitted the carpenters to treat the IAM.[6] Because Johnston was personally unpopular with the leaders of the AFL, AFL censure resulted. In time the flintglass workers managed to recapture what had once been taken from them, and the whole venture did not net much of a gain for the IAM.

Wharton's approach was quite similar to O'Connell's. He repaired most of the broken relationships within the AFL by maintaining close personal ties with its leadership. He obtained a "cease-fire" agreement in 1931 with President Hutcheson of the carpenters, which was broadened the following year. It pledged the parties to cooperate with each other in the event of jurisdictional misunderstandings, and, pledged, if necessary, the two international presidents to intervene personally to settle the matter. Wharton's agreement failed to function because the carpenters, who at the time of the negotiations were on a periodic exodus from the Building Trades Department, decided that they wanted to join again and were unwilling to let this commitment (which, as may be recalled from Chapter VI, was rejected by the 1932 Cincinnati convention) stand in their way. Also, it is likely that there was no basic comprehension of the differences in the meaning of jurisdiction. In the face of these negative factors, it is little wonder that with Wharton's retirement (where at least both friendship with Hutcheson and a voice in the deliberations of the AFL executive council were factors) the old situation reappeared. The story of the Brown-Hutcheson-AFL war has already been told. President Hayes once again reestablished personal ties with the AFL hierarchy. He also recognized that the meaning of jurisdiction to the carpenters was so radically different that peace could only be obtained by abandoning the IAM's traditional tools or machine-process criteria. In 1954 he signed the agreement with the carpenters, which, while bringing to the IAM much millwright job opportunity and new membership, also admitted the "right" of the carpenters to work legally in an area which technically (albeit some four decades before), although observed in the breach, had been assigned to the IAM.

It would, however, be erroneous to assume that the 1954 agreement resulted only from the greater omniscience of President Hayes and his colleagues, although it should not be completely discounted. Three changes had occurred; one being the industrialization of the IAM. Not only did the craft-conscious railroad machinists no longer make up the majority of the membership, theirs was no longer an important voice in the formulation of policy. Instead the union swelled with aircraft and production workers, brought in after NLRB elections. The IAM was not a railroader-dominated institution, in the sense that it had been decades earlier. And the new membership was amenable to the abandonment of the old bench marks of craft, if the change netted a gain to the union. Secondly, while there is some evidence that Hayes had little faith in the efficacy of the AFL executive council as a jurisdictional-dispute settling body, he had a persuasive voice (as much or even more than O'Connell's or Wharton's) in the AFL executive council. And, finally, it should be added that by 1954 the political strength of the Building Trades Department was in eclipse, and the carpenters exercised a degree of autonomy which they had been unwilling to show twenty-one years before.

In retrospect, the fact that the government, principally the NLRB, was also involved in the handling of thorny jurisdictional relationships, may also have played a part. Putting all this together, the end result is that the IAM is more able to cope both with the differing concepts of jurisdictional sovereignty, and with relative political power relationships involved in the processing of disputes. The price paid by the IAM was the loss of its single-minded metal trades outlook; the price paid by the labor movement was relative freedom from governmental pressures. Probably the Building Trades Department paid the most; the power it exercised easily in 1932 could not be attained in 1954.

The experience with the carpenters' union has been analyzed at length because it shows the complex problems inherent in the meaning of jurisdiction. The IAM, it should be hardly necessary to add, has had disputes with many other unions. Some, like the one in 1925 with the United Association of Plumbers et al., were resolved by informal understandings, phrased in traditional metal trades language, between the leadership of the two organizations. Occasional flare-ups occurred on the local level where hunger for job-opportunity gained dominance over respect for precedent. On the whole, however, disputes of this type were resolvable because both parties had similar understandings of the meaning of jurisdiction.

Other disputes like the World War II fights with the UAW–CIO were outright competitive campaigns for members and contracts in previously unorganized areas.[7] They were resolved (in the form of the 1949 no-raiding pact) when it became obvious that the net costs of these fights far exceeded any possible net gains, particularly where there was little if any craft flavor involved.

The meaning of jurisdiction, then, is not a static thing nor does it affect all unions the same way at the same time. The history of the IAM affords a significant insight into the evolution of the meaning of jurisdiction to one union, because one can readily see the influence of the operative factors. In three and a half generations the IAM has passed from a definition that was railroad-shop-oriented, to one that was geared to the "realities" of rapid technological change, power bargaining, and the influence of employers as well as governmental intervention. Adaptability is said to be the secret of life; if so, the IAM should be adjudged to be a highly organic institution.

The IAM has had formal agreements with many unions; thus far we have analyzed two relationships in detail because their complexity and relative importance warranted somewhat more lengthy treatment. What now follows is a quick survey of the development of agreements with many other unions.

The airline pilots. Although talks with this union had been held since 1932, a formal understanding did not occur until 1957, when the two unions agreed to help each other in organizing.

The brewery workers.[8] In 1917 the IAM signed an agreement with the brewery workers union setting forth the respective jurisdictions of the two organizations. The IAM was to fabricate and erect brewery equipment; the brewery workers were to be taught how to operate the mechanical equipment. This agreement was, of course, affected by the economic vicissitudes associated with prohibition, as well as the efforts of the carpenters' union to take over the jobs of installing equipment. The Anheuser-Busch brewery in St. Louis was the scene of repeated carpenter–IAM fights; at times, the dispute going through arbitration and even the courts. In any event, the conflict was not between the brewery workers and the IAM.

The boilermakers. There has been a relatively long history of conflict with the boilermakers, much of which has stemmed from the technological innovation of acetylene and electric welding equipment in railroad shops. The conflict, apparent by 1916, led first to a threat by the IAM to leave the Railway Employees' Department in 1927, and then to a change in the voting technique within the department to accommodate the IAM. There is some evidence that General Vice-President Conlon worked out with President Franklin an understanding regarding the division of work involved in the installation of tubes in locomotives. After Conlon's death, the IAM professed to know nothing of Conlon's alleged agreement and took the unusual step of notifying all concerned parties that the "supposed agreement is . . . cancelled and declared null and void." In 1951 there were merger talks with the boilermakers, even reaching a point where the IAM executive council considered changing the name of the IAM to include "Blacksmiths and Drop Forgers." These talks eventually failed, and the IAM signed a full jurisdictional, no-raid, joint-organizing drive pact in 1956. It was dropped in 1959.

Bridge and structural iron workers.[9] Talks regarding a jurisdictional agreement with the bridge and structural iron workers were held in 1921, but no formal developments were subsequently noted.

The electrical workers.[10] The relationship with the electrical workers (International Brotherhood of Electrical Workers) is an old one. In 1918 the two unions signed a pact relating to materials. The IAM was given jurisdiction over machines used in shops except "lathes used for armatures, resistance coils, and field wiring and binding." Work on wire cable machines was to go to the IBEW, as was the handling of electric cranes. One aspect of this 1918 accord worthy of notice was the acknowledgment of grand lodge–local lodge friction; if any local broke the agreement, it was noted, the grand lodge (or the International Brotherhood of Electrical Workers on the other side) was to take immediate steps to secure enforcement. The IAM estimated that the work division thus defined, netted it almost seven hundred new members in Schenectady, New York alone. In 1929 there were more discussions with the IBEW about the IAM's taking in electrical workers where the IBEW had no locals; where the IBEW would eventually organize locals, the IAM would turn over the respective cards. During the Second World War (in 1943) a new general agreement was drafted, specifying in detail the machines and materials over which each union would exercise job control. The IAM executive council initialled one draft of this agreement. On the other hand, a subsequent proposal regarding work on diesel-electric railroad locomotives was rejected by the IAM. In 1954 new general negotiations were undertaken.

The marine engineers.[11] In 1916 and 1917 there were talks with the Marine Engineers' Benevolent Association; it appears from examination of the IAM's records that these were satisfactory, and although no formal pact was announced, the IAM agreed to withdraw its objections to the AFL's granting the marine engineers a charter. The new union agreed "that all machinist work, pipe fitting work, or any other mechanical work not imposed upon the marine engineers by maritime law, and the laws governing the licensing of marine engineers, shall at all times be done by the trades to which the work belongs on shore." The position, as therein expressed, was in accordance with a pact signed by IAM Local Lodge 68 (San Francisco) and the marine engineers in 1912, and was so noted in the 1916 convention proceedings. It may be recalled that difficulty regarding jurisdictional rights developed later over the same issue during the Second World War. In the latter instance, the conflict was with the operating engineers. This was discussed in Chapter V.

The jewelry workers.[12] There have been two times when the IAM and the jewelry workers have had discussions. The first was in 1917, when the IAM asserted its right to all tool and die makers' jobs in the jewelry industry. Whether this claim met with success is not clear; it can, however, be inferred that it did not, since general union strength in the industry was not great. In 1943 the IAM agreed to a jewelry worker demand that the IAM protect the vested right of its members working in plants that had turned from jewelry manufacturing to wartime general production work. This was less a jurisdictional pact than a no-raid agreement.

Maintenance of way workers[13] *and railway carmen.*[14] In 1919 the IAM agreed to accept gratis the cards of certain maintenance of way workers whose work had been reclassified by the Director General of Railroads. President A. E. Barker of the maintenance of way union made the request; Johnston replied "with thanks." It is worth adding that in 1922 a similar scheme was developed to accept railway carmen into IAM membership with full protection of their old seniority and benefits status. What was interesting here, however, was Johnston's insistence that retroactivity be granted to old railway carmen who had transferred on their own, prior to the agreement.

Metal polishers.[15] In 1918 the IAM took in all the brass workers from the metal polishers' union; at the same time it agreed to give up claim to all other metal polishing, buffing, or plating jobs. The brass workers were accepted with full seniority and benefits rights. In 1944 the metal polishers, after some negotiations, turned over some workers in the airframe industry, and the two unions worked out a plan for jointly handling collective bargaining problems as well as organizing campaigns.

The mine workers. The IAM and the mine workers agreed to form an alliance in 1922; the matter was also ratified by IAM referendum. Nothing appears to have come of the attempt, however. In 1930 John L. Lewis laid claim to machinists and other mechanics in and around collieries. Arthur O. Wharton discussed the matter, but again no positive outcome is apparent.

Motion picture operators.[16] A 1929 agreement with the International Alliance of Theatrical Stage Employees of North America gave the IAM the jurisdictional right of fabricating and making major repairs to movie projectors; the other union was to get the jobs of running projectors, setting up projectors, and making temporary repairs.

The pressmen, the operating engineers, the auto workers. We have already noted the agreements with the pressmen's union, the bitter dispute with the operating engineers, and the united auto workers.

The street railwaymen. The street railwaymen's union, which also played a role in the Brown AFL disaffiliation episode, had signed agreements with the IAM in 1928 and 1931, which gave the IAM the jobs disputed later when Brown was international president. In effect, the agreements had given the IAM the repairmen's jobs in the local transit field. The street railwaymen's anti-IAM activities in the forties seem to have been sheer opportunism.

The plumbers.[17] The United Association and its forerunner organizations consisting of plumbers, steam fitters, etc., have had several agreements with the IAM. A 1919 attempt to work out an understanding over jurisdiction with the plumbers failed largely because of an IAM unwillingness to compromise its marine work claims. Later in 1925 an agreement involving marine work was made, which specified the type of work each union was to claim. Local Lodges 441 (Portsmouth, Virginia) and 634 (Boston) repeatedly protested the terms of this accord. In 1937 the protests led the IAM to ask for a revision of terms, claiming that there was a verbal proviso which should be written out and signed. President Coefield of the United Association replied that no such proviso had existed (the IAM negotiators had died in the interim); nor would he consent to any modification. In 1938 the IAM issued a threat to cancel the 1925 pact but appears to have done nothing when the United Association was unintimidated. Talks were held starting the next year (1939), and an agreement was reached in 1941. It gave the IAM most of the work involving machinery; the United Association, most of the work involving pipes. The IAM was to machine, grind, and scrape all joints. It was also to repair all self-contained refrigerator and air conditioning units, as well as install tubes in end sheets of condensers. The UA was to install the refrigerator and air conditioning units, and to install and repair end coils in condensers. At the same time a supplementary agreement was made regarding steam fitters' work. Within two years the 1941 agreement was bilaterally abrogated, each party accusing the other of bad faith. The IAM chose to deal with naval yard officials to get its way through official channels. Much irritation resulted, and increasing bitterness was reported while the IAM was out of the AFL. In 1954 when the Hayes administration had reestablished good relationships with the AFL and some of the major AFL unions, a new accord was signed.

The teamsters.[18] Agreements with the teamsters were often concluded on a local basis; and in 1926 they agreed to give the IAM jurisdiction over mechanics in garages. This agreement was violated, according to IAM records in 1944. What ensued was a gradual deterioration of relations, reaching a nadir with the previously mentioned unsuccessful open raid in the Seattle Boeing plant in 1949. However, at the very time of the teamsters' raid, some factions within the IAM were trying to develop a rapprochement between the two organizations. Although talks were held, there was no prospect of resolution so long as the Boeing raid continued. The teamsters also started raids in New York City and Newark; they even made moves to organize the mechanics in the air transport industry. On the whole the teamsters' efforts were not successful. In 1952 David Kaplan, at that time economist for the teamsters, arranged a new set of discussions. These were successful and resulted almost immediately in joint teamster–IAM organizing drives. A formal pact was signed in 1953 and broadened in 1955. It was cancelled when the teamsters were expelled from the AFL–CIO.

CHAPTER X

The Iam and Employers

Sidney and Beatrice Webb discuss the methods of trade unionism in their book *Industrial Democracy*.[1] They claim that the earliest method of "mutual insurance" was the practice of working men helping each other by pooling their economic resources. The second was the "method of collective bargaining"; its important characteristic being the practice of workers' negotiating as a single unit with their employer. Unlike the method of mutual insurance, the method of collective bargaining emphasized the primacy of the relationship with the employer. The third, called the "method of legal enactment," was the technique of raising standards through parliamentary action. The Webbs favored the third because, as Fabian Socialists, they favored governmentalism and also because they believed that it was the best way for under-privileged workers to gain benefits.

The history of the IAM yields relatively little experience with the method of mutual insurance. True, at times the members pooled resources in order to pay strike as well as death benefits, but the purpose in both cases was to offer members a reason for continuing membership and faithful devotion to the union during periods of duress. On the other hand, the union, because it operated in the American environment, was generally unable to affect work standards materially through legislative intervention. Here it is worth recalling that the Fourteenth Amendment to the Constitution, as traditionally interpreted by the Supreme Court prior to the Wagner Act, seemed to offer reformers little hope of social intervention in matters concerning relationships between employers and employees. Furthermore, even after the implementation of the Wagner Act it was very difficult to get adequate economic reform measures through Congress. Congress is operated through seniority; and seniority in practice amounts to rural (rather than urban) domination. The new result has been a realization on the part of most American labor, including the IAM, that improved standards come most easily as a result of direct negotiation with employers. In other words, the method of collective bargaining is obviously preeminent.

However, in certain areas, political action has yielded significant improvements in working conditions. Obviously, where the government is the employer as in arsenals and shipyards, it is possible through pressure on Congress and administrative agencies to raise wages and improve working conditions. Furthermore, where the government has tended to play an important economic role in the development of industry, historically, or has been instrumental in the maintenance of a particular industrial product or service, Congress has been an excellent tool through which wages could be raised. Here, the most obvious example would be the railroads, particularly since the passage of the Adamson Act of 1916. One therefore can not conclude that the IAM and other American unions have completely eschewed political action and the method of legal enactment. Far from it; the IAM and other unions have maintained effective lobbies about Congress in order to protect the interests of their membership employed directly by the government, or employed on the railroads. But this situation has collective bargaining aspects and is, therefore, not the classic environment for applying the method of legal enactment.

It is important to add that the method of legal enactment has been used very successfully on the municipal and state levels, where the possibilities of getting favorable legislative treatment have been greater than in Congress. On the municipal level, where policy control is effectively determined, the unions, including the IAM, have lost no opportunity to exert whatever influence they could to improve the economic effectiveness of their policies. By this, we refer to the maintenance of sympathetic police attitudes during strikes and boycotts. It has often been observed by keen students of American unionism that a sympathetic police chief was the equivalent of a very large union treasury, when it came to winning strikes. While the IAM has not opposed the methods of legal enactment on the basis of any principle, the fact remains that the general business and industrial community in America has been relatively immune from governmental control, and it has been impossible to get adequate legislation passed by a rural-area-dominated Congress.

The natural result of all these factors has been to ensure close attention to the method of collective bargaining. The method of collective bargaining, as it was originally defined by the Webbs, carried no implication of subject matter; it simply implied a willingness on the part of an employer to negotiate with all his employees as an entity. What their negotiations were, was a matter of their own concern. At times the negotiations might deal with simple wage questions; at other times it might deal with insurance matters, questions of working conditions, or questions of dismissal and hiring. Each party was free to suggest whatever topics it wanted to discuss, and to see what it could secure in the way of concessions. In other words, collective bargaining was a method of carrying on a relationship, rather than a body of practices and customs of industry.

The Emergence of the Collective Agreement

How did the method of collective bargaining come into practical existence? Originally the IAM, like most unions, wished to have the employer recognize it as the appropriate representative of certain employees. The simplest way to secure this end, was to get the employer to make a joint statement with the union regarding the conditions of work which were to prevail. What follows is the earliest joint agreement on record involving the IAM: [2]

An agreement between Atchison, Topeka and Santa Fe Railroad Company and Officers of International Association of Machinists, National Brotherhood of Boiler Makers, and International Brotherhood of Blacksmiths of A.,T. and S.F. System, District No. 2. In effect August 1st, 1892.

Article 1. That the A.,T.&S.F.R.R.Co. adopt the Apprenticeship Agreement hereby presented by the International Association of Machinists, National Brotherhood of Boiler Makers, and International Brotherhood of Blacksmiths.

To prohibit Division Master Mechanics from advancing laborers, to the detriment of apprentice machinists, boiler makers, or blacksmiths.

Art. 2. Any boy hereafter engaging himself to learn the trade of machinist, boiler maker or blacksmith must serve four (4) years; three hundred (300) days to constitute a year.

The ratio of apprentices to be allowed: One (1) of each occupation to each shop, irrespective of the number of machinists, boiler makers or blacksmiths employed, and one (1) apprentice to every five (5) machinists, and every four (4) boiler makers, and every four (4) blacksmiths. This ratio shall be maintained in each shop.

No boy shall be eligible to be engaged as an apprentice until he is sixteen (16) years of age, or after he has reached the age of twenty-two (22) years. The applicant must be able to read and write a legible hand, and know the first five (5) rules of arithmetic; also, that he must be of good moral character.

That the company employ no more apprentices until such time as the number is reduced in accordance with the ratio, as mentioned above, in each shop.

Art. 3. That all back-shop men be paid one and one-half (1½) times for all overtime, and that round-house men get one and one-half (1½) time when called back after completing day's work; no overtime to be allowed until ten (10) hours have been worked in each daily period of twenty-four (24) hours.

Art. 4. That all men having charge of others, or responsible for work done by them, shall receive extra compensation consistent with such position. (The above relates to gang bosses in shops, only.)

Art. 5. That when vacancies occur, and promotions are necessary, in the mechanical department, boiler makers, blacksmiths and machinists in the service be given the preference in the line of promotion in their several departments — efficiency to govern.

Art. 6. That when reductions in force are necessary, seniority, proficiency and married men be given the preference of employment.

Art. 7. That when a grievance arises in any shop, the aggrieved shall have redress through the office of the Division Master Mechanic and Superintendent of Machinery.

Art. 8. That men be allowed their expenses when sent away from home to work for the company, and that the same be allowed in their pay-check for that month — expenses not to exceed one ($1.00) dollar per day.

Art. 9. The question of wages to be adjusted by the Superintendent of Machinery.

John Player,
Supt. of Machinery, A.T.&.S.F.R.R.

Wm. J. Wilson,
Chairman International Association of Machinists of A.T.&.S.F. System.

Lee Johnson,
Chairman National Brotherhood of Boiler Makers.

Henry Lewis,
Chairman International Brotherhood of Blacksmiths.

Note the sequence of the contract; first, the company accepted the apprenticeship program as proposed by the unions; second, the contract defined the working conditions for apprenticeships; third, it provided penalty rates for work in excess of ten hours in a twenty-four hour period; fourth, it provided extra compensation for extra responsibility; fifth, a modified seniority plan was accepted by the company both with regard to promotions and lay-offs; sixth, an elementary grievance system was organized; seventh, the wage question was left completely in the employer's hands. One can see that the contract was more concerned with status than it was with pay.

A supplementary agreement regarding the right to refuse overtime work was signed shortly afterwards. Again, it was a bilateral statement:

OFFICE SUPERINTENDENT OF MACHINERY,
TOPEKA, KANSAS

August 10, 1892.

To all Division Master Mechanics:

At a meeting at the Superintendent of Machinery's office on August 8, 1891, between the superintendent of machinery and committee representing the boiler makers, machinists and blacksmiths at Topeka and the various division shops, it was agreed that the working of overtime on engines undergoing general repair, or in the back-shop, would not be compulsory; that the men who were not disposed to work overtime were to be treated equally fair with those who were desirous of working — in other words, no discrimination against men who were not disposed to work extra time. It was also agreed that the engines in running service requiring necessary repairs to keep them running, such as flue work or any light boiler repairs; also, such as break-downs or necessary light running repairs, men should be required to work overtime on request of the company. They are expected to work overtime on such request, and the representatives of such divisions agreed in such cases all men would do so. Sunday not being a legal working day, to be regarded as extra or overtime, so far as back-shop work is concerned.

This agreement is not to interfere in any manner with any employee who is desirous of working extra time, when requested to do so for the company's convenience, and whenever it is necessary to do so, this agreement will be your authority to request such men, as are willing, to work extra time, paying them on the same basis that has been customary heretofore.

It may be necessary, at times, to work the men of the before mentioned branches — boiler makers, machinists and blacksmiths — night work. In this event, the working hours will commence at 7 o'clock P.M. and end at 6 o'clock A.M., one hour to be allowed for supper with eleven hours pay.

For A.T.&S.F.R.R. Co.:
John Player,
Supt. of Machinery.
For Boilermakers:
Lee Johnson.
For Blacksmiths:
L. Sheehan.
For Machinists:
A. Donaldson.

However, in many instances the union was unable to get the company to issue a joint statement. Instead, what emerged was a "passive agreement," in which the company unilaterally announced new working conditions, consistent with the union's voiced demands. At the same time that the Santa Fe signed its agreement with the three unions, the Union Pacific made its own statement. It is reproduced in full from the journal, where it was titled, "An Agreement":

Rules and Regulations for the Employment and Government of Machinists, Blacksmiths and Boilermakers, Helpers and Apprentices.

UNION PACIFIC SYSTEM,
OFFICE OF SUPERINTENDENT
MOTIVE POWER AND MACHINERY,
OMAHA, NEB., Sept. 1, 1892.

ARTICLE I.

SECTION 1. The standard working-time shall be nine (9) hours per day, except Saturdays, which shall be eight (8) hours with nine hours' pay.

SEC. 2. Should it become necessary to reduce expenses the time shall not be reduced to less than eight (8) hours for the regular day, with corresponding reduction on Saturday. Any further reduction in expenses shall be made by reducing the force, in which case senior and proficient married men shall be given the preference of employment, and the force shall not be increased while the time is reduced below the standard, except when absolutely necessary in order to carry on the work to advantage.

ARTICLE II.

SEC. 1. All time over the regular time that is in force, and on Sundays and legal holidays, shall be paid for at the rate of one and one-half (1½) time, monthly salaried men excepted.

ARTICLE III.

No first-class Machinist, Boilermaker or Blacksmith shall be employed for less than the standard wages at the place of employment.

ARTICLE IV.

It is not the intention to advance Helpers or Laborers to a Machinist's, Boilermaker's or Blacksmith's position, or to have them perform the duties properly belonging to those mechanics.

ARTICLE V.

The ratio of apprentices shall be one (1) of each occupation to every shop irrespective of the number of mechanics employed, and one (1) additional apprentice to every five (5) men employed in each class. This ratio shall be maintained in each shop, and the company shall employ no more apprentices until such time as the number is reduced in accordance with the ratio as mentioned above.

ARTICLE VI.

No Machinist, Boilermaker or Blacksmith shall be discharged or suspended without just and sufficient cause. If, after proper investigation, it shall be found that a man has been unjustly suspended or discharged he shall be reinstated with full pay for all time lost; ordinarily the investigation shall be within five (5) days from the time of suspension or dismissal.

ARTICLE VII.

It is agreed that the apprenticeship rules now in existence on the Union Pacific Railway System shall be enforced.

ARTICLE VIII.

It is agreed that the working of overtime be not compulsory, except in cases of running repairs.

ARTICLE IX.

When vacancies occur and promotions are to be made, Machinists, Boilermakers and Blacksmiths in the service will be given the preference, length of service and proficiency to govern.

ARTICLE X.

When a man is called at night to do work which does not exceed three hours and twenty minutes, he shall receive five hours' time; when the time exceeds three hours and twenty minutes, he shall receive one and one-half (1½) time from the time called.

ARTICLE XI.

Should a man be sent out on the road, he shall be allowed pay from the time he is called until he returns and necessary expenses.

F. Mertsheimer,
Asst. Supt., M.P. & M.

Approved: E. Dickinson,
Asst. Genl. Manager

Although the unilateral quality of its formal presentation appears less advanced than the Santa Fe agreement, the Union Pacific contact appears to contain the better conditions. The standard work day was shorter; apprenticeship ratios were more favorable to the union; the grievance system was more carefully designed; and the seniority clause was more explicit. This comparison is interesting because it shows differences of emphasis. The method of announcement of working conditions did not, as in this comparison, necessarily reflect the generosity of the terms.

In 1895 the journal provided an excellent *resumé* of the evolution of an "agreement." It is printed *verbatim* because it reflects so accurately both the procedural problems of getting a contract and the relative importance of the grand lodge in handling matters:

THE TOLEDO STRIKE. On the 18th of last month all the employees of the several bicycle works of Toledo, Ohio, in all about 6,000 were locked out. This act on the part of the manufacturers was caused by the machinists and die sinkers of the various factories making a demand for a ten per cent restoration of wages.

The trouble began in this way: About the eighth of last month, Toledo Lodge No. 105 submitted the following proposition to the various manufacturers of Toledo:

"PREAMBLE

"At the regular meeting of the Toledo Lodge 105, I.A. of M., held September 4, 1895, the following resolutions were unanimously adopted and it was decided to present the same to every manufactory employing tool makers and machinists, through their shop committee, for your favorable consideration.

"HALL OF TOLEDO LODGE 105, I. A. OF M.

To (name of firm) Gentlemen:

"Resolved, That tool makers and machinists are not paid in proportion to other trades, and as the success of any firm employing them is largely due to their ability to produce tools for the rapid production of duplicate parts cheaply and the skill required to produce such tools takes constant attention and study:

"Therefore, We deem it our privilege and duty to ask for a small advance in wages of 10 per cent to take effect October 1, 1895.

"Please give this your attention and answer at your earliest possible convenience.

Yours truly,

____

____

Shop Committee I. A. of M."

This was answered by the manufacturers requesting a little time to consider the proposition. This the men granted. In about eight days the shop committee made inquiry as to what decision the firms had arrived at. They were told emphatically that the advance would not be granted. During the interim between the submission of the demand by the men and their receipt of the above answer, the manufacturers — thirteen firms in all — formed themselves into the "Associated Manufacturers of Toledo." As soon as our men got the ultimatum of the newly formed association they dropped tools and walked out. The manufacturers' association met the same afternoon and the result of their deliberations was shown the following morning by this notice being stuck up on the main door of every factory interested:

"THIS FACTORY IS CLOSED DOWN BY ORDER OF THE ASSOCIATED MANUFACTURERS OF TOLEDO.

T. B. TERRY, SEC'Y."

This notice was put up on the morning of the 18th, and resulted on that date in about between five and six thousand employees being locked out. The situation remained unchanged until the morning of the 22d., when Brother O'Connell got a telegram, saying, "Come at once."

Hastening at once to the seat of the trouble, he arrived the following morning; held a consultation with the advisory board of the strikers and locked-out men, and had an interview in the afternoon with one of the firms implicated.

The result of this interview was that the men employed in the Gendron works would resume work that same afternoon, with the demands of 10 per cent granted. Other firms gradually followed suit, withdrawing from the manufacturers' association, until out of the original thirteen firms which composed the body only six remained.

Up to this period of the trouble the associated manufacturers refused most emphatically to recognize the International Association of Machinists in any way, but on the 23d Brother O'Connell received the following communication from the president of the Snell Cycle Co.:

"*Toledo, O.*, Oct. 23, 1895.

"*Mr. O'Connell, Jefferson House, Toledo:*

Dear Sir: — I have arranged the meeting as suggested this morning between yourself and manufacturers' association, who are now in room 121, Boody House.

"Kindly send word what time it will be convenient for you to meet us.

Yours truly,

(Dictated.) *S. Snell.*"

Taking advantage of this the G.M.M. met the manufacturers' association that afternoon. After a great deal of argument pro and con at the first meeting, in which Bro. O'Connell had to hold his own against the combined attacks of the manufacturers — ably augmented by an attorney whom they had employed to assist them — they asked Bro. O'Connell to submit a scale of prices, so that they would have some data to work upon. This he promised to do, and the following morning he submitted the following:

"*Toledo, O.*, Oct. 24, 1895.

"*T. B. Terry, Esq., Secretary Associated Manufacturers of Toledo:*

Dear Sir. As per request of your association, and in behalf of the employees, which I have the honor to represent, I beg to submit the following rates of wages, to take effect at once. If this proposition is accepted it is to be binding on the several manufacturers forming your association.

Very respectfully,

Jas. O'Connell, G.M.M."

Following is the rate of wages agreed upon by your employees:

The men who are receiving $3.50 per day if raised 10 per cent would be $3.85; we will accept $3.75 per day for the men at this rate.

Men receiving $3.25 per day if raised 10 per cent would be $3.57½; we will accept $3.50 per day for the men at this rate.

Men receiving $3 per day if raised 10 per cent would be $3.30; this rate will stand as it is even money.

Men receiving $2.75 per day if raised 10 per cent would be $3.02½; we will accept $3 per day for the men at this rate.

Men receiving $2.50 per day if raised 10 per cent would be $2.75; this rate will stand as it is even money.

Men receiving $2.25 per day if raised 10 per cent would be $2.47½; we add 2½ cents per day, making their rate $2.50 per day.

Men receiving $2 per day if raised 10 per cent would be $2.20; we believe, however, that they should be given an increase of 25 cents per day, making their rate $2.25 per day.

Men receiving $1.75 per day (if there be any) would receive $1.92½; we set their rate at $2."

Then began the tug of war, which culminated in the gentlemen forming the Associated Manufacturers of Toledo signing the document as follows:

"Office of the Associated Manufacturers,
Toledo, O., Oct. 26, 1895

"Mr. James O'Connell:
Dear Sir — We would confirm scale of wages herewith: $3.50 men not to be advanced; $3.25 to $3.50; $3 men to $3.25, $2.75 men to $3, $2.50 men to $2.75, $2.25 men to $2.50, $2 men to $2.25, $1.75 men to $2.

"Men who have been advanced within sixty days less than 10 per cent are to receive a further advance to make up ten percent.

"All men in our employ to remain.

"The Yost Mfg. Co., Ltd.
The Lozier Mfg. Co.
Baker Bros.
The Toledo Mach. & Tool Co.
The Snell Cycle Fittings Co.
The Dauntless Bicycle Co.
"Associated Manufacturers.

Jas. O'Connell, G.M.M., I. A. of M."

The greatest fight was over the last paragraph, "All men in our employ to remain," as they wished to tack on the words "at our option," but the G.M.M. stuck to the original, and it came out as shown above.

As there were only about four men who came under the $3.50 per day rate, and they had just got an advance, this part was conceded to the manufacturers.

The Toledo "agreement" is concerned with only two issues; wage rates and victimization. Tracing the bargaining on the former; it can easily be seen that the union modified its demands somewhat; in the cases of the four top-rated positions, the union actually abandoned its request. The "no victimization" statement with the deletion of "at our [the employers'] option" seems to have been the important victory. Yet, as a grievance system it was most elementary. Unionism had obviously secured greater recognition on the two western railroads then it had in Toledo.

Thus we have seen the emergence of two types of agreement; one, of which the Santa Fe statement is an example, was bilateral in form. The other, exemplified perhaps somewhat better because of the narrative statement of its development, was actually unilateral in its enunciation. Neither was in the true sense a contract; in the case of the former, the unions offered no consideration in return for the promise made by the Santa Fe management and, therefore, the terms were not enforceable by law. The Union Pacific and Toledo "agreements" did not even specify the names of the interested local union officials.

In Chapter II the history of the National Metal Trades Association experience is presented in detail. As a consequence of the 1901 rupture of relationships, all contacts between the IAM and the NMTA became limited to passive or informal understandings. In other words, the only way the IAM would "bargain" for its members was to send a business agent or a grand lodge official to discuss with individual member firms of the NMTA all matters of mutual concern.

This informal and lateral method of negotiation produced demands which did not in themselves require any outward or written acknowledgement of the union's existence as the representative of a firm's employees. From the union's viewpoint, the best that could emerge was an implicit agreement that all conditions of work would be discussed with a group of employees and any party whom these employees brought in as their adviser, and that no individual would be dismissed without a "fair" hearing. On occasions, this "fair" hearing involved the taking of a record and, possibly a decision by some disinterested party (frequently a local clergyman, judge, or university professor). In retrospect, what occurred in these cases was an informal recognition of the workingmen's union by the employer. The employer was not required to "lose face" before his fellow employers by giving the union a formal voice in the running of the plant. The employees, on the other hand, were given certain working rights, which greatly smoothed the relationship between them and the employer.

It is erroneous to assume either that the NMTA attitude was in all aspects antiworker, or that the union itself was rendered impotent by the outbreak of an employer's campaign of annihilation. In the first instance, the period, 1911–1914, saw the emergence of the nine-hour day; if not brought about by union demands alone, its institution was certainly aided by unionism. Employers generally could not afford to be brutally exploitive; there was far too much competition for labor, and worker mobility to permit the worst excesses of industrial feudalism to exist very long in a large number of production centers. Moreover good craftsmen were rare and their idiosyncrasies were frequently tolerated. If they did not want to work two machines (as the union's constitution forbade them to do, except under specified conditions), employers seldom tried to make them do so. It would have been inviting the men to quit. Other union rules were similarly respected; good workmen were not required to show unqualified men (helpers) how to perform skilled operations. The costs of training apprentices were usually so high (in terms of the long-run advantage to the employers providing the training) that there was relatively little reason why most employers would train the full number of apprentices to which they were "entitled" under union rules.

It would seem that good craftsmen were protected by the fact of scarcity. Many of the working rules which the union had promulgated to protect the craft were themselves actually enforceable by the economics of the labor market, even if they could not be enforced by the union, faced as it was by employers bent on annihilating it.

In some industries and areas the IAM actually was accepted by employers as a legitimate factor in the handling of industrial relations. Typical of such a relationship is a 1902 agreement signed in Baltimore giving the IAM a closed shop:

Baltimore, Md., Feb. 3, 1902.

AGREEMENT

Between firm of Wm. Mattheiss and My Maryland Lodge, No. 186, of the International Association of Machinists.

1. The said firm does agree that on and after Feb. 1, 1902, all machinists in their employ, or those they may thereafter employ, must be members of the International Association of Machinists; all machinists' work done by them or for them must be performed by members of the aforesaid Association of Machinists in good standing.

2. The firm further agrees that should they give out a contract the machinists' work must be done by members of the said Association in good standing.

3. Nine hours shall constitute a full day's work on and after Feb. 1, 1902, the same rate of wages per day shall be paid as at present.

4. All overtime up to twelve o'clock midnight shall be paid for at the rate of not less than time and one-half time, and all overtime after twelve o'clock midnight shall, the same as Sundays and legal holidays, be paid for at the rate of not less than double time; nevertheless in case of emergencies, where shop machinery breaks or runs down and it is absolutely necessary to repair the same so that the factory can run the following work day, this shall be paid for at the rate of time and one-half time. The repairs above referred to apply only to the machinery of the employer.

5. There may be employed one apprentice for the shop, and in addition not more than one apprentice to every five machinists.

6. The said firm has the right of discharging any machinist for incompetency, insobriety, insubordination or irregularities in attendance, providing, that this does not in any way abridge or destroy the right of appeal from any apparent or alleged unjust decision rendered by the said firm or their representative.

7. The members of My Maryland Lodge, No. 186, International Association of Machinists, shall see that the said firm shall receive all the benefits of a union shop, and their shop steward and committee shall insist on its members doing their duty and protect the said firm against loafing, or doing anything that may be detrimental to the success of their business or to the true intent of this agreement.

Wm. Mattheiss,
Firm.
Harry F. Vollmer,
Business Agent My Maryland Lodge, No. 186.

In 1903, for example, an agreement, somewhat legal in language, was negotiated by a Decatur, Illinois, firm with a group of five unions, collectively termed "parties of the second part." It covered union recognition, working times, wages, apprentices, lay-offs, physical working conditions, and grievance procedures. As a labor contract, it contains virtually all the types of clauses, except vacations and retirement, present in the bulk of modern agreements:

TEXT OF AGREEMENT.

This agreement, entered into by and between the H. Mueller Manufacturing Company, of Decatur, Ill., party of the first part, and the International Coremakers' Union, the International Association of Machinists, the International Brotherhood of Blacksmiths, the International Association of Allied Metal Mechanics, Metal Polishers, Buffers, Platers, Brass Molders and Brass Workers' International Union of North America, parties of the second part, witnesseth:

UNION EXCLUSIVELY.

Article 1. That the party of the first part agrees not to employ anyone in or about their offices and shops except members of the above named organizations.

LENGTH OF DAY.

Art. 2. It is agreed that nine (9) hours shall constitute a day's work. In instances where double shifts are employed, overtime shall be permitted under the overtime provision. In cases where there are no night shifts employed, not less than three (3) hours' overtime shall be worked, and same shall be paid for under the overtime clause.

Art. 3. Night gangs shall work fifty-four (54) hours per week on the regular night schedule posted in the shop, and any overtime worked outside of the schedule hours shall be paid for as overtime.

OVERTIME.

Art. 4. All overtime up to 12 o'clock midnight shall be paid for at the rate of time and one-half (1½ time), and that after midnight, and the following holidays, New Year's Day, Decoration Day, Fourth of July, Thanksgiving Day, Christmas Day and Sundays, shall be paid for at the rate of not less than double time. In cases of emergency, where the shop machinery breaks or runs down, and it is absolutely necessary to repair the same, or to erect new machinery, so that the factory can be run on the following day or Monday, this work shall be paid for at the rate of time and one-half (1½ time). The erections and repairs above referred to apply only to the machinery of the employers. Such rates of overtime shall not apply to men regularly employed on night gangs.

WAGES.

Art. 5. The minimum scale of wages for the different crafts shall be as follows:

Blacksmiths, 26½ cents per hour.
Coremakers, 22½ cents per hour.
Brass molders, 31 cents per hour.
Metal polishers, buffers and platers, 27 7/9 cents per hour.
Monitor lathe hands, 22½ cents per hour.
Speed lathe hands, 25 cents per hour.
Fox lathe hands, 27 7/9 cents per hour.
Metal patternmakers, 27 7/9 cents per hour.

Machinists, 27⅞ cents per hour.
Cock grinders, 25 cents per hour.
Brass molders' helpers, 18 cents per hour.

Allied metal mechanics, 5 per cent more than they are now receiving, same to go into effect at the time this agreement becomes effective, and an additional 5 per cent increase, to take effect six months from the time this agreement becomes effective.

Any employee receiving more than the foregoing scale shall not be subject to any reduction per hour on account of entering into this agreement.

It is understood that the above minimum rates of wages shall apply to men fully competent in their class.

APPRENTICES.

Art. 6. There shall be one apprentice at large for each department, regardless of the number of mechanics employed, and in addition such others as the constitutions of the various unions will allow.

It is hereby understood that this article shall not apply to apprentices now working; but it is further agreed that no more will be hired, except as above specified, until the ratio becomes as specified, by reason of expiration of apprenticeship contracts.

REDUCTIONS.

Art. 7. Should a reduction of expenses become necessary, it shall be made in a reduction of hours, unless otherwise agreed upon by both parties.

SANITATION.

Art. 8. It is agreed that the factory shall be kept in as clean and healthy a condition as the nature of the work will permit, and that, as far as is practicable, suitable pipes will be installed to take off all smoke and gases arising from furnaces, forges and molding rooms. It is further agreed to erect exhaust fans to connect to all polishing, buffing and grinding machines.

GRIEVANCES.

Art. 9. Should any grievance arise between the employees and the party of the first part that can not be settled amicably, the same shall be taken up by the shop representatives and the company for mediation and settlement. They failing to settle it, it shall be referred to the general officers of the organization involved for adjustment. Pending such adjustment, both parties shall continue business in the ordinary way.

DISCIPLINE.

Art. 10. In consideration of the foregoing articles, the party of the second part agrees to see to it that the members employed in this factory shall at all times be amenable to proper shop discipline, and will agree to any reasonable shop rules in operation in the plant.

LABELS.

Art. 11. It is agreed by the party of the second part to furnish the party of the first part with union labels for their product, and to disseminate as far as possible through their representative journals the fact that the firm is a strictly union house.

Art. 12. This agreement, when signed, shall be strictly adhered to by both parties, and no member of either the party of the first part or of the second part shall have a right to deviate therefrom, or to violate any of its provisions without an agreement between both parties.

LIFE OF AGREEMENT.

Art. 13. This agreement shall remain in force and effect beginning March 1, 1903, and ending December 1, 1904.

Whatever this Decatur agreement omitted, seems in part to have been included in a 1905 agreement between the IAM and the Milwaukee brewers. Note the eight-hour day, the incorporation of union rules regarding multiple machines assignments and apprenticeship ratios, the extent of the union security clauses giving the IAM the closed shop as well as permission to have its shop committeemen do relevant union business on company time, and the detailed nature of the arbitration clause. This agreement was termed a contract, presumably because the union also promised specific performance (clause 12):

CONTRACT BETWEEN MILWAUKEE BREWERS' ASSOCIATION AND INTERNATIONAL ASSOCIATION OF MACHINISTS.

This contract made between the Milwaukee Brewers' Association and the International Association of Machinists, to be and remain in force from the day of its date and until the 1st day of March, A.D. 1909, witnesseth:

1. All machinists employed must be members of the International Association of Machinists and shall control their trade exclusively under the following classification: A competent general hand, erecting hand, floor hand, vise hand, lathe hand, planer hand, shaper hand, milling machine hand, slotter hand, boring mill hand and toolmaker.

2. Eight hours (between 8 A.M. and 5 P.M.) shall constitute a day's work, but in occasional cases of necessity overtime not to exceed one hour on any day shall be worked with single pay.

3. Minimum wages shall be 35 cents per hour. Where over 32½ cents per hour is now being paid such higher wages shall not be reduced, but shall be increased 2½ cents per hour.

4. Overtime shall be paid at the rate of time and one-half. Work that continues after midnight shall be paid with double pay; also double time shall be paid for work done on legal holidays and Sundays. All overtime provisions in this contract not to apply where shifts are worked. Wages to be paid every two weeks after working hours.

5. New Year's Day, Washington's Birthday, Decoration Day, Fourth of July, Labor Day, Thanksgiving Day and Christmas Day shall be considered legal holidays.

6. No machinist shall be allowed to run more than one machine at one time or to do any other work while running one machine.

7. Foremen shall not do machinists' work, unless members of the International Association of Machinists.

8. One apprentice may be employed to every ten men, figuring on average men employed during year.

9. Men are not to be discharged or laid off for doing committee work for the International Association of Machinists.

10. Workmen shall not receive beer during working hours but shall receive two quarts after working hours.

11. Any difference of opinion arising in regard to the terms of this contract shall be decided by a board of arbitration, constituted in the following manner: Two shall be selected from the Milwaukee Brewers' Association and two from the International Association of Machinists, and in case these can not agree the members of the board shall elect a fifth member, whose decision shall be binding to both parties. Men shall not leave work while arbitration may be pending.

12. If at any time during the life of this contract any member of the International Association of Machinists declares the product of any one of the undersigned brewing firms boycotted or unfair notice of such action by said organization should be given by the Milwaukee Brewers' Association to the headquarters of the International Association of Machinists, and such body hereby promises to investigate such matter immediately, and if after investigation it is found that the respective brewer has not violated any existing contract, then a public declaration shall be issued by the headquarters of the International Association of Machinists, denouncing said boycott, and in case of refusal, then this contract to be null and void.

13. This contract shall continue in full force one year after March 1, 1909, unless either of the parties thereto, at least thirty days before said date, give to the other written notice to the contrary, designating any desired changes.

Dated April 15, A.D., 1905.

MILWAUKEE BREWERS' ASSOCIATION,

By *Joseph E. Uhlein,*
Chas. A. Miller,
S. Becherer,
Committee.

INTERNATIONAL ASSOCIATION OF MACHINISTS,

By *F. W. Wilson,*
J. J. Handley
Herman Manz.

The passage of the National Labor Relations Act in 1935 marked the end of this program of informal recognition. Afterward, whenever the union felt that it could successfully substantiate a claim to represent the employees hired by a given firm, it could force the employer to negotiate with it directly. The IAM, affected as it had been by the hostility of the NMTA, suddenly picked up a great many contracts in written form, where it had previously enjoyed informal understandings. Naturally, the more open the discussion, the easier it was for the union to bargain about wider and larger issues. The development of an interest in these extended issues, such as pension plans, vacations, hospitalization insurance, apprentice programs, and union security clauses, may have been the result of the institutionalization of the bargaining process. That is, when the employer became willing to negotiate directly with the union, it was possible for the union to raise many topics which it had only been able to do casually on the previous basis. And when the union came to realize that it could look forward to formal negotiations, it employed specialists to help prepare its case. Among these specialists were economists and lawyers. Consequently the range of issues which the employers then came to discuss with the union involved many technical matters, which previously could not be discussed for lack of technical knowledge on the part of the negotiators. Thus the modern labor agreement, characterized as it is by length, devotion to precise wording, and attention to minor details, may well be the result of the influence of technicians (bureaucrats) on both sides. Too frequently collective bargaining gets involved in these minor technicalities, or excessive attention to detail. Actually the method of collective bargaining is different from this type of thing and should be so understood.

The Grand Lodge and the Employer

The history of the IAM's attitude toward employers harks back to the personal philosophy of the IAM's first president, Talbot. He believed that the union should serve a moral, rather than a business, purpose, and was not particularly interested in developing relationships with employers except when doing so provided better opportunities for workers to lead sober lives. O'Connell was the next president to influence union history. His business orientation completely dominated the union's attitude during the next twenty years. He believed, as did his close friend and associate Samuel Gompers, that the leaders of labor unions should endeavor to establish a basic understanding (that is, recognition) with the leaders of big business. When recognition had been accorded, the leaders, or their subordinates could work out the necessary details of the actual agreement. O'Connell's belief in the efficacy of this system was somewhat shattered by the events marking the end of the Murray Hill agreement in 1901, and from that time on, his road was difficult. The union wrote into its constitution absolute prohibitions of negotiation over piecework, the operation of two machines, and motion and time studies. The ultimate point in the limitations imposed in the constitution was reached when IAM officials were prohibited from membership in the National Civic Federation, an organization whose avowed purpose was to facilitate employer–union felicity.

William Johnston, in contrast to O'Connell, favored the method of legal enactment for several reasons including his own preference for socially responsible government (i.e. Socialism). This personal conviction was strengthened by the observation of the failure of the Gompers and O'Connell approach. It was therefore entirely logical that Johnston put relatively less faith in the method of collective bargaining and somewhat more faith in the method of legal enactment. Johnston was eager to use collective bargaining, wherever he thought it could be used more successfully than legal enactment, but he started off with great doubts. Without question, the collapse of government intervention on the railroads in the early 1920's, plus the defeat of the La Follette–Wheeler ticket in 1924, emphasized once more the practical limitations of the method of legal enactment. This was realized by everyone, including Johnston's successor, Arthur O. Wharton, who was required to face the unpalatable truth that neither collective bargaining nor legal enactment worked very well.

In the chapter on the Wharton administration, the nature of Wharton's realism was stressed. It was based on the pre-Wagner Act conditions, which required that the employers voluntarily realize the advantages of recognizing the union. And in some instances, one example being the America La France strike in Elmira, New York, he was successful in using power bargaining to win over a recalcitrant employer. In this case his success resulted from use of both methods; at the same time that he was putting direct pressure on the company by keeping his members out on strike, he used whatever political means he had to keep local city councils from ordering the product of America La France (fire equipment). More generally, however, Wharton's successes were limited. As a result, he greatly resisted the union's spending its financial resources on industrial organizing drives. In that same chapter the additional point was made that after 1936 the Wharton approach was outmoded, because the government had agreed to help unions gain recognition from recalcitrant employers. No longer could employers effectively refuse to recognize the duly constituted representative of their employees. What had occurred in effect, was a shift of the type of major problem facing the IAM. The old question of recognition no longer loomed as large; instead, questions of contractual terms began to achieve a new importance. This situation continues until the present time. It marks the "maturation" of industrial relations in the United States; in other words, concentration on questions of substance, that is, on contractual terms rather than on questions of procedure (status problems).

During Harvey Brown's administration, the IAM sought to assure both workers and employers that the IAM was essentially a more reasonable and responsible union than any other. Here, it is worth emphasizing that this was the type of approach favored by O'Connell. Brown, like O'Connell, believed that the handling of industrial relations should be essentially a businesslike process, and he was of the opinion that a reasonable, responsible union would be the preferred choice of anyone with an alternative. It was entirely natural, therefore, that he recommended to employers that they sign contracts with the IAM, whenever possible. His conviction, based on some empirical experience, was that if the employers thus recognized the IAM, the employees would willingly accept the IAM as the legitimate bargaining agent, and the needless interunion industrial conflicts which affect employers would be eliminated. Many employers agreed. And partly as a result of this type of thinking, the IAM membership numbers swelled.

As we have already indicated, Brown increased the size of the grand lodge staff corps to aid the union's bargaining representatives. This corps included economic research workers, lawyers, and people skilled in navigating those shoals called governmental agencies. The grand lodge increasingly specialized in National Labor Relations Board and railroad work; [3] the legal staff was expanded and then unified under grand lodge direction. One general vice-president was detailed to handle all railroad shop matters and was assigned to Chicago, where the government's railroad (labor) adjustment board has conducted virtually all its business.[4] In brief, the IAM is wage-and-working-conditions-oriented. To carry out its program, it has had to develop a technical capacity for bargaining collectively both with employers and with governmental agencies. Bargaining with the latter may require some application of the method of legal enactment; that is, threatening to show its strength at the ballot box. But, on the whole, the IAM's relationships are still matters of direct and indirect bargaining, and it is fair to conclude that collective bargaining has remained by far the most frequently used (if not the most preferred) method of unionism.

Thus far we have described the institutionalization of the collective-bargaining process. It began as a method of conducting industrial relations. It developed into a concern over particular questions of working conditions. In other words, it lost its emphasis on recognition and gained a new emphasis on material matters. To paraphrase Sir Henry Maine, status taken from the worker by the industrialization of the manufacturing process was transferred to the union. Individual workers regained their status by membership in the union. The new status, however, required guarantees, or contractual meaning. The next development, therefore, was the enumeration of specific contractual clauses. Development was simply once again the substitution of precise contract for unarticulated status.

The Development of the Contract

Analysis of the development of the IAM contractual pattern is impeded because most contracts are negotiated on the local level, and at one time were not readily available to the grand lodge. Since 1948, however, the research department of the grand lodge has regularly analyzed the contents of virtually all the agreements to which any lodge is signatory.[5] Table 18, based on these agreements, indicates the development of certain contractual clauses.

Table 18. *Sample survey of IAM joint agreements.*

Topic	1948	1950	1952	1956
Number of agreements considered	3,937	5,125	4,633	4,719
Number of employees covered [a]	392,909	462,424	661,237	694,085
Average number of workers [b] per agreement	99.8	90.2	142.7	147.1
Agreements with paid vacations	99.1%	99.4%	99.4%	99.3%
Agreements with paid holidays	71.0%	83.6%	92.2%	96.3%
Agreements containing paid sick leave	4.7%	5.5%	6.6%	9.2%
Agreements with group medical/hospital plan	—	27.5%	42.1%	77.7%
Agreements with pension plans	—	4.6%	4.9%	17.2%
Agreements with check off	18.2%	21.7%	30.3%	42.8%
Agreements with top seniority for stewards	21.0%	25.3%	25.3%	32.7%
Agreements with shift differential	71.9%	75.6%	79.0%	81.2%
Agreements with percentage pay for vacations	11.5%	15.4%	12.8%	15.7%
Tool & Die Workers' average rates	$1.851	$2.025	$2.255	$2.722
Machinists' average rates	$1.657	$1.821	$2.063	$2.474
Auto mechanics' average rates	$1.600	$1.784	$1.934	$2.370
Helpers' average rates	$1.195	$1.352	$1.552	$1.890
Number of agreements over one year	9.9%	21.2%	19.1%	38.1%
Agreement signed after strike	.8%	1.6%	1.3%	2.8%
Strike threat used	8.8%	7.8%	7.2%	15.7%

Source: IAM Research Department.

[a] Not all of whom were IAM members.

[b] Derived by comparing number of workers and number of contracts.

Examination of the Sample survey is facilitated by separate consideration of several points. The first of these concerns the relationship between the number of agreements in the sample and the number of employees covered. Both the 1948 and 1950 figures reflect the decline in aircraft production. The 1950 figure also probably reflects the influence of an economic recession. The later figures, 1952 and 1956, with their marked increase in number of workers per agreement, is an indication of the effect of including the resuscitated airframe industry. The inclusion of these agreements, covering thousands of workers, has a very significant effect on other results of the survey.

Considering each agreement to be comparable, irrespective of the number of workers covered, certain patterns clearly emerge. For instance, by 1948 virtually all agreements contain references to paid vacations. Interest in guaranteeing holiday pay, that is, pay for a certain number of nonworking days per years, was great by 1948 and it became almost universally accepted within eight years thereafter. Interest in clauses guaranteeing a certain amount of pay for sick leave was fairly rare in 1948, and although it had doubled by 1956, it was not particularly widespread even at that later date. On the other hand, interest in group medical and hospitalization plans, generally not known in 1948, had become very widespread at the end of the subject period. Similarly, interest in pension plans, probably largely sparked by the UAW–CIO experience in the automobile industry, commenced in 1950 and increased by a factor of 200 per cent by 1956. Now these changes do not necessarily indicate that all the provisions contained new demands. It is entirely possible that many firms provided without contractual reference for holiday pay, New Year's Day, Memorial Day, Fourth of July, Labor Day, Thanksgiving, and Christmas. The point is that the union asked, and the employer agreed to specify that holiday pay would be granted for those not working on the days listed. Here is an example of what Maine had in mind when he said that as society became more civilized and institutionalized, there was a tendency to substitute contractual statements for what previously had been undersood as basic status rights.

Another set of changes worth considering relates to the much discussed topic of union security. Prior to 1947, it should be inferred that many contracts contained closed shop provisions. In 1948, the first year of the Taft-Hartley Act, less than one contract in five provided for a check-off; eight years later more than twice as many had such provisions. Another change relates to the granting of top seniority for elected shop stewards. These provisions, guaranteeing the union's duly elected shop officers with virtually complete job protection, probably indicate as clearly as anything can the employers' acceptance of the union as a full partner in the industrial relations process. In 1948 about one contract in five provided for this type of guarantee; half again as many contracts provided for it in 1956.

What about the length of agreements and the way in which they were negotiated? Less than one contract in ten in 1948 was negotiated for a period of more than twelve months. By 1950, again influenced by the UAW–CIO five-year agreement with General Motors, and perhaps influenced also by the stabilization of the rate of price changes, twice as many contracts were for a longer period. By 1956 almost two contracts in five were of a duration of more than one year. Another interesting statistical relationship is between the number of agreements signed after a strike, and the number of agreements where strike threats were used. In 1948, for example, for every agreement signed after the strike, there were about ten signed with the use of a strike threat. This ratio fell to about one in four in 1950; one in six in 1952 and in 1956. It is also worth noting that very few contracts required strike action on the part of the union. In fact, the remarkable thing is the very small number of instances where either strike threats or the use of a strike itself were required.

Table 19. *Relative annual changes in wage rates.*
(in per cent)

Category	1948–[a] 1956	1948– 1950	1950– 1952	1952– 1956
Tool & die makers	5.9	4.7	5.7	5.2
Machinists	6.2	5.0	6.7	5.0
Auto mechanics	6.0	5.7	4.2	5.6
Helpers	7.3	6.6	7.4	5.4

Source: Derived from Table 18.

[a] Straight-line average for the period.

The change in wage requirements seems to be the most obvious type of thing contained in new contracts. By 1948 it is evident that the principle of shift differentials had been well established. Of course, it does not follow that this change was the result of union pressure alone; often the need to recruit workers for the unpopular shift led to the payment of a special "bonus or differential." The size of vacation pay is again illustrative of the spelling-out in a contract of what probably had been established practice. In 1948 about one contract in eight provided that the vacation pay given to a worker should reflect in some way his normal wages.

Table 19, based on the same sample survey, indicates relative changes in wage rates. It is interesting to note for example that the wage rates of the most unskilled category, helpers, improved the most (58.2 per cent). Most of that improvement occurred during the period from 1948 through 1952; during the following four years the rate of improvement was considerably less. Conversely, the tool and die makers' rate of improvement was somewhat less; this group did relatively poorly in the period of 1948 and 1950 but have maintained a better, fairly constant rate of improvement during the latter years. In over-all terms, the machinists and the automobile mechanics have done about the same, having improved their wage rate about 48.5 per cent during the eight-year period. The machinists did best during the period of the Korean War, whereas the auto mechanics appear to have done best during the post-Korean War years. All the skilled groups, excluding the helpers, have done about the same, which amounts to doing 85 per cent as well as the unskilled helpers. In terms of relative standing, helpers were slightly better off compared to tool and die makers in 1956 than they had been in 1948. This advantage was probably further accentuated by the nature and structure of the federal income tax pattern. In other words, a tendency toward levelling wage rates has been accentuated by the progressive nature of American income taxation; a helper earning approximately $4000 a year (based on a forty-hour week, fifty-two-week year) pays relatively less in income taxes than does a tool and die maker earning about $5257 per year (based on similar hours and weeks of work). The point here is simply this; there has been a levelling influence in hourly rates, and because of progressive income tax rates, expendable income may be as much associated with the progressive nature of income taxation as with the decision taken at the bargaining table. Another factor to be considered in our examination of these changing differentials undoubtedly reflects the growing importance of aircraft production in the sample. The aircraft industry probably pays its helpers relatively well. They have to be recruited at short notice, and the effect on hourly rates in this situation is favorable to them.

In recent years the leadership of the IAM has become quite concerned about the relative scarcity of fully trained journeymen. Their interest in providing a reservoir of trained journeymen is not only the result of their concern with the national welfare, but it is also a legitimate consequence of the "industrialization" of the union. Traditionally, the leadership has come from the ranks of journeymen, but as time has gone on, the relative number of journeymen has diminished. To repair this loss, the leadership has been attempting to negotiate apprenticeship training programs with employers. The research department reported that in 1954 almost half the agreements negotiated during that year contained apprenticeship-training program clauses. Since then the picture has not materially changed. This represents something of a new approach in so far as the traditional notions of American unionism are concerned. Most students of industrial relations have long known that unions have not opposed apprenticeship programs, because they have not had to do so. It costs money to train apprentices, and most employers are unwilling to assume the obligation of training an apprentice at the risk of losing him when his training has been completed, and he goes to work for a competitor. Thus, it was common practice for unions not to worry about an excessive number of apprentices. Only since the Second World War has the extreme opposite case become common. Now unions are concerned about the lack of apprentices, because of a concern both for the national defense and welfare and their own future leadership problems.

The collective bargaining process in the United States has continued to change since 1936. The role of the government grows ever more important, and consequently the relative range of bilateral negotiation between the two parties, management and union, diminishes. But this change is essentially a relative one; so long as both management and union feel it desirable to spell out in ever increasing detail the precise nature of their relationship, new areas for their bilateral discussions will emerge. As the details become more numerous, the technical implications become more profound; with the result that specialists, generally employed on the grand lodge level, will play a more important role. In the long run it is entirely likely that the characteristic local lodge autonomy of the IAM will be further reduced. If that is to be so, it is probably to be regretted; but business and negotiation by large units seem to be one of the consequences of our current economic and political development. Another factor accentuating this same trend is the movement of the IAM into government-dominated industries, such as airplane, air transport, and rocketry.

CHAPTER XI

Unionism and Community Values

To what degree can a union be independent of the community to which it belongs? In other words, "can a union afford to ignore public opinion?" Or even, "should a union reflect the value systems of its members or the value systems of the community at large?" This chapter attempts to put a discussion of these questions in the context of the history of the IAM.

Before turning to the questions we have raised, it is desirable to consider two basic points. First, popular opinion, as the term is generally used, is frequently only a rhetorical phrase used by those who do not wish to identify the source of their views. When put to a test, the alleged popular opinion appears to be little more than the convictions of a few individuals. Second, union policy is usually more than the prejudice of a leader; it is generally the result of a serious conviction on the part of union leadership and its bureaucratic machine that some particular purpose is best served in a particular way. Because unions are made up of numerous individuals and factions, developed policies usually represent workable compromises. Consequently, in those instances where it can be said that a union has a consistent policy, what is meant is that either all factions are more or less content with the devised program, or that one faction within the union has managed to become dominant. Naturally, it does not follow that a union policy need be morally right or economically sound. It suffices simply that it represents, possibly, in the short run, the most practical approach in terms of the alternatives open to union leadership. Putting this matter in another way, most union policies generally require some degree of membership cooperation. No leader, irrespective of his moral failings, would try to implement an unpopular policy, if he could equally easily implement a popular one.

This chapter considers three aspects of the problem of the relationship of the IAM to the community at large. The first part considers the attitude of the grand lodge toward political activity on the national level; the second is concerned with the grand lodge's attitude toward certain "social menaces"; and the third is an estimate of the present position of the IAM in modern American community life.

The IAM and Political Action

In the previous chapter we discussed why the IAM concentrated on collective bargaining. In this chapter we are considering the obverse side of the same question, namely, why has the IAM changed its attitude from time to time toward political action. Generally the IAM's attitude has been based on three separate considerations: social, economic, and political. The social consideration is the desire to improve the social structure of the United States quickly and efficiently. No better way for this seems to exist than reform of some governmental policies and legislation. The second consideration, the economic, involves an estimate of the advantages to be gained by political activity as compared with collective bargaining activity. In other words, for a given amount of resources expended on political action, will the results be better, equal, or less than the results from collective bargaining? The cost of engaging in a political campaign can be relatively easily determined. And if the candidate is fully committed and will give you whatever you need or want, it might be worth calculating the odds. What we are suggesting is that when the cost of a political program is approximately the same as the cost of a collective bargaining program, the union will choose whichever produces better results; but, if the cost of a political program seems to be very, very small and the possible gains tremendously large, even though the calculated probability of victory is also small, the union may be willing to gamble. Finally, a union will engage in political activity up to the point where its return compared to its cost is about the same as a comparable input–output relationship would be in collective bargaining activity. We call this the economic analysis of political action, because it is based on a belief that the union will use political activity as an alternative, where it is economically feasible. Unlike the social approach, which assumes political action to be the *sine qua non* of progress, the economic approach makes the choice of a policy simply a question of the more satisfactory alternative.

The third or "political" reason for the IAM's engaging in political activity on the national level, relates to its own internal political process. So long as the national political arena is important, and only the grand lodge can cope with it, engaging in national political action may have the effect of increasing grand lodge authority and strength. No less important, of course, is the opportunity that engaging in national politics furnishes the personal ambitions of various grand lodge leaders. They become, in short order, national figures mentioned in the newspapers, and are consulted by other national leaders.

These three factors constitute the basis of our analysis of the reasons for IAM political activity. In citing them, we have indicated some of the ways in which political action can be used advantageously. For instance, with friends in the government it is possible to change the public policy with regard to collective bargaining. An example of this occurred during the Wilson administration, when support from the White House helped the IAM and other unions to gain such recognition as was contained in the Clayton Anti-Trust Act. Again the same thing occurred during the Roosevelt administration, at the time of the passage of the Wagner Act.

The disadvantages of this reliance upon politics for social engineering are of course legion. The government which passed the Clayton Act was unable to enforce the act; that is, an unsympathetic Supreme Court held the relevant clauses of the act to be meaningless and therefore invalid. The pro-union Congress that passed the Wagner Act later became antiunion and passed the Taft–Hartley Act. A third reason why resort to politics has not been successful relates to the "tarring" of the organization. For example, if the IAM chooses to support a Democratic candidate or a Democratic slate of candidates, and the Republican candidate or that slate of candidates wins the election, the IAM is "tarred" and can in the future only look forward to reaping the results of its miscalculation. For this reason, the IAM has frequently eschewed social reform by political action. The reasoning expressed at different times is discussed below.

The political disadvantages of involvement in national matters are fairly easy to comprehend. Frequently, engagement in national political life involves decision making that divides the IAM. For instance, how does the IAM feel about extending reciprocal trade powers to the President? On the one hand, national foreign relations require that imports into the United States be expanded and that tariff laws be softened, on the other hand, reductions in the tariffs on IAM-produced equipment will lead to short-term, if not long-run, unemployment for IAM members. It is no answer to say that the IAM need not have an official opinion in these matters; frequently engagement in political life requires that stands be taken even when it would be preferable to remain silent. This naturally leads to division within the IAM. Some members fear the effects of the given piece of legislation more than they fear the effects of no legislation; other members, motivated by a strong sense of public responsibility, wish their organization to come out categorically for a particular measure even if it means some loss to other IAM members.

It is apparent that each year the factors must be weighed anew. At one time it may be socially desirable to engage in political activity simply for an ideological reason. Regardless of the economic cost, it is the responsibility of free men to take a political stand in favor of issues, popular or otherwise. At the same time the economic costs must be clearly viewed, and the individual must compare the advantages gained with the costs incurred. It does not follow that if the advantages seem small and the costs great, that the union should refrain from political activity. To do so would be to say that the economic factor is all-important, which it is not; and it also disregards the element of chance in a great return on a very small investment. Free men because they value their freedom, may not look at short-run costs; instead, they will be concerned with larger issues which may, as in the case of the third factor, divide the union politically.

In reviewing the history of the IAM's attitude toward politics, it is useful to point out that the social approach was most popular during the early administrations and the Johnston administration. During the Talbot–Creamer–O'Day period the "Southern influence," with its dedication to moral improvement, implied an interest in national political questions. This influence, and that of the old "Knights of Labor," made the membership of the IAM particularly eager to discuss all sorts of social topics. For instance, in 1890 there was an editorial in the journal which said,[1] "We have always looked forward to the day when the working people of America would rise up in their own might and shake off the political yoke of all parties and place a representative from their number in the chair of Washington." This was not an isolated, Socialistic outburst; quite the contrary, it was the expression of the desire on the part of the "common men" for turning the government over to one of their own. From 1895 throught 1896, the journal discussed the important question of the day, the free coinage of silver.

Starting in the period, 1898–1899, the interest in Socialism grew rather rapidly. For instance, at the 1899 convention there was a proposal that the local lodges should educate their members in the problems of the "class struggle," so that it would be easier to combine to advance class interests, in order to take over the government of the country.[2] Instead, the law committee recommended that the IAM should stimulate the political education of its members to understand their political rights, and to use the ballot intelligently in their respective political parties, so that the government might be for and by the people and not simply exist as a tool to further the strength of management. At the 1901 convention, there was a resolution, rejected by the committee and by the convention itself, that the machinists' union declare itself for Socialism. The wording of the proposal concluded: "be it resolved that the machinists in international convention assembled, unqualifyingly declare themselves in favor of Socialism, the cooperative commonwealth, as being the means whereby the worker will ever obtain the full fruits of labor." The Resolutions Committee recommended that the motion be rejected because as it said, "the time [was] not quite opportune for the adoption of such a measure." However, by the 1903 convention the Socialists were beginning to develop more strength. Their increased prestige was undoubtedly associated with the falling prestige of the anti-Socialists, particularly O'Connell. The change was brought about first by the relative failure of the NMTA strike and by the change in the government attitude toward unionism. At the 1903 convention the preamble of the constitution was changed to stress the existence of a class struggle, and to encourage members' activities along the lines of restoring the control of the government to the people, and using the national resources for the common welfare of all the people.

Two years later, at the 1905 convention, the Socialists actually proposed that every union meeting should devote some time to the study of Socialist theory. This proposal, again perhaps reflecting an upward change in the fortunes of the O'Connell group, was not endorsed. During these years a considerable debate on the question of political activity, viewed as a social responsibility, raged in the journal, probably because it was popular in many other circles in the American community. Besides, D. D. Wilson, the popular editor of the journal, himself appears to have been actively sympathetic to the Socialist cause. Finally, in 1911 with the defeat of the O'Connell group, the IAM seemed to have embraced the doctrine that there was a basic social responsibility to participate in political action. At that time it seemed to most observers that the IAM was exhibiting its interest in Socialism; however, the election of President Wilson was to show that the interest in political activity and social reform contained within it an element of economic analysis. That is, the leadership of the IAM quickly turned from the support of Socialists to the support of the New Freedom and Wilson. This change was further developed during World War I when Wilson and his administration consciously furthered the interests of the IAM.

After World War I the leaders of the IAM were appalled by the possibility that American railroads would be turned back to their antiunion employers. They preferred to have the railroads remain in friendly governmental hands, as had been the case since the seizure in 1917. President Johnston became one of the leading officials of the Plumb Plan League and sought Congress' endorsement of the plan to nationalize ownership of the railroads. It would seem that Johnston's reason for advocating political control of the railroads was based as much on economic considerations as it was based on a belief in Socialism. By the time the Plumb Plan was debated, it was apparent that the government had made the life of unionists on the railroad relatively easy compared to what had transpired previously. Anyway, whatever Johnston's motivation, he took an active role in national politics. At the 1920 convention, he announced that all the evils facing unionism could be remedied without force, if the ballots were properly and intelligently used. At the same time, Johnston took care to disassociate his views from those of the political radicals of the hour. Also, in 1920 the IAM donated one cent per member to the AFL's national partisan political campaign fund, organized to elect prolabor members of Congress.[3]

The period, 1920–1924, when the railroads set out systematically to destroy their shopcraft unions, and the government stood idly by, served to convince Johnston that there was no hope in using either of the two established political parties. As a result he took an active part in the Progressive Party campaign of the La Follette–Wheeler ticket. It is possible that Johnston was convinced that political action was a public responsibility, regardless of the possibility of success. It is further possible that he actually believed that the La Follette–Wheeler ticket had a real chance of success, and for the amount of resources that the IAM devoted, its possible returns would have been tremendous. More likely, Johnston's position was the result of his personal belief that the leader of the IAM was a national figure, and that it was incumbent upon him to take a stand. In any event, he and the general executive board succeeded in getting the IAM to endorse the La Follette–Wheeler ticket. The resulting defeat did not strengthen Johnston's position within the union.[4]

Arthur Wharton succeeded to the presidency at a time when political action had been more or less thoroughly discredited. It is equally true that the method of collective bargaining had not proved to be very successful, but compared to political action, it was certainly superior. Wharton appeared to avoid all political activities. This does not mean that the IAM was indifferent to political questions. Quite the contrary, the IAM subscribed to *Labor*.[5] It also favored public unemployment insurance plans, despite the opposite stand of the AFL.[6] Emmet Davison, the general secretary–treasurer, was an active political figure in the Democratic Party of Virginia.[7] And there were many others who maintained active political careers. Our point is simply that Arthur Wharton, on the whole, felt neither the urge as a citizen to engage in a political career in a big way, nor did he believe that the method of legal enactment (that is, systematically engaging in politics to solve one's problems by enactment of laws) "paid off." That he himself may have had doubts, is contained in a memorandum he sent out in 1937. Noting that the Democratic

Party was trying to raise $200,000 to clear its debts, he informed the council members that he had personally contributed $200 and reminded them that the IAM itself had not contributed anything to Roosevelt's 1932 or 1936 campaigns. He concluded with the statement that "there are few of the larger labor organizations that have not made some contributions." He asked the council to reconsider its previous position.[8]

When General Vice-President Fechner was asked to become a member of the Roosevelt administration, Arthur Wharton saw no reason to dissuade him. However, Fechner was not allowed to function within the IAM while holding and carrying out the responsibilities of national office. Earlier, we indicated that in our judgment Arthur Wharton miscalculated the importance of governmental activity in shaping the development of American industrial relations after 1935. Fortunately, there were within the organization those who saw in the Roosevelt administration staunch support, and who were willing to engage in politics in order to maximize the IAM's position. Wharton managed to maintain nominal control of the organization, although it is apparent that his voice became less dominant in the private circles of leadership.

Both Harvey Brown and Albert Hayes realized that the day of relatively complete eschewal of political activity had passed. The government played far too great a role in the practice of American industrial relations, and the destiny of the grand lodge was far too dependent upon the role it played in the relationship with the government to permit the leaders of the IAM to be indifferent to general political questions. In other words, the political approach made it mandatory to engage in political activities, regardless of whether there was some ideological basis for so doing. It is entirely natural for the IAM to take a stand with regard to national political office and candidates, and, moreover, the IAM has even found it mandatory to have opinions on such diverse questions as pension rights, health plans, international trade issues, and foreign affairs. Whether in the long run IAM participation in political matters will prove divisive remains to be seen. It is highly probable that some negative effects will be observed.

The long-run consequences of the post-1935 developments have been to strengthen the grand lodge at the expense of local autonomy. Once the federal government chose to play a dominant role in the allocation of jurisdiction as well as the handling of certain grievances (i.e., unfair labor practices), it became almost certain that the grand lodge's powers would have to be augmented. The grand lodge, alone among the organizational units within the IAM, is equipped to handle the problems of federal government relationships. This is not to suggest that problems of state and local government relationship cannot exist, and that they are not best handled by state conferences or local lodges. But insofar as the national picture is concerned, grand lodge interest in political activity has certainly come to stay. The costs may be very great, the advantages may grow comparatively less, but as far as one can see, there is little likelihood of a return to the attitude expressed by Wharton during the latter part of the 1920's, when he in effect announced that political activity was an incubus sucking untold financial resources as well as considerable membership loyalty from the IAM.[9]

Whether in the long run the IAM can afford to be fully identified with one political party, namely, the Democrats, remains to be seen. Recently it is true that the Republican Party has leaned over backward to gain union support. Should at some time either major political party stop courting labor, as would be the case if certain segments within the Republican Party were to become dominant, then the IAM would have to reconsider its whole method of political participation.

In brief, the IAM's attitude toward political involvement has at different times reflected one or more of the three determinants. Generally, the economic approach (comparing the costs and the returns of using politics and other approaches) seems to have been the most important, although the roles of the other two, social reform, and national recognition, are far from negligible. In a market society, which to a great degree America is, it is natural that the economic approach should be the principal one. But one should not sell the idealism of social reform short; granted it has been dominant only at intervals, but its presence at other times may be strong enough to influence actions, if not to motivate them. The third approach, that concerning the union's concept of its own political importance as a national institution, has become, if anything, more, rather than less important as the union has become larger and as the grand lodge has achieved greater interorganizational importance. Considered analytically, however, it is the economics of using political means, which basically conditions the IAM's policies. So long as the important relationships remain the ones between employers and the union, the IAM will favor the direct collective bargaining approach over that of legal enactment.

Public Relations and Social Menaces

No problem has been harder for the IAM to master than that of handling dissident internal groups. Within the IAM there is a wide range of opinion regarding the desirability of extending union benefits to what are considered marginal or "inferior" groups. Facing this dilemma has been postponed on many occasions, when compromises have been found, as in the 1895 revision of the constitution, when the anti-Negro clause was technically deleted. Again, at the turn of the century the benefits of unionism were extended to specialists, but only after they had in fact been admitted. Even then, there were long debates prior to the formal action, and when the action was taken, it represented a compromise. Viewed from the inside, the lengthy arguments and the repeated ballots resulted in the optimum practical resolution, because by the time the "outsiders" were accepted, they came in with few, if any, complaints. Viewed from the outside, the delay in final action was both discriminatory and shortsighted.

To the members, the marginal group is a menace and has to be treated with suspicion. The burden of assimilation of an "inferior" group obviously rests upon the institution which competes with them. It is fairly easy for social reformers to urge that unions accept all individuals who apply for membership. However, if those who join the union are unwilling to adapt to the union's customs, the union will be weakened by their affiliation. A second point not to be overlooked is that the acceptance of an "inferior" group often results in the development of schisms in the union. For instance, it seemed reasonable to believe that accepting Negroes as members would have resulted in the secession of many southern white members. On the other hand, the union was forced to a choice; if it did not accept Negro members, the Negroes would have no alternative but to try to undersell the union and take jobs away from union members; if it did accept them, the disaffected white members would try to undercut the union's position and destroy it. The union could only select the lesser evil, realizing the while that this selection represented a very unsatisfactory resolution. Nothing better illustrates this point than the long series of debates between 1893 and 1948 on the subject of admitting Negroes to formal membership. The point was repeatedly made that unless the Negroes were admitted, the union would suffer economically. Yet, when the vote was taken, the majority of the convention delegates regularly voted to retain the discriminatory clause. They did so, not only because several of them sincerely objected to the inclusion of colored members, but because they feared even more the actions of the die-hard anti-Negro members.

In Chapter II we discussed how the anti-Negro clause was shifted from the constitution to the ritual in order to keep it from public view. We could have added that the clause was also used to keep out Orientals (Chinese), but the point was that the ritual had become the declaration of principle for the southern locals. O'Connell had little use for the ritual as it was practiced.[10]

To him its historical origins made it seem somewhat unnecessary, particularly since the IAM contained many Roman Catholics to whom the whole business was distasteful. O'Connell noted on several occasions that the ritual was greatly in need of revision and, more to the point, could be dispensed with entirely (as was actually the case in several lodges), without detrimental effect.

In November 1918, it may be recalled in another context from Chapter VII, District Lodge 46 (Toronto) sought to amend the ritual through referendum vote, in order to strike from it the offending whites-only clause. This use of the referendum instrument was challenged immediately, and the issue was put before the general executive board. President Johnston and all the members of the board, except General Secretary-Treasurer Davison, supported the Toronto proposal.[11] Nonetheless the issue was not voted upon. Instead, at the 1920 convention the matter was considered, and after considerable debate the IAM's position was left unchanged.[12]

No further move was taken to amend the ritual with regard to the race point until the 1936 convention, where the majority of the Committee on the Ritual recommended that the whole matter be turned over to the discretion of the executive council. The committee's minority report proposed the elimination of the offending clause in order to facilitate the organization of New York City transport workers. The convention was unwilling to authorize either line of action; instead, it tabled both reports. Thus by the 1930's the ritual had become more than anything else a racist declaration. Its original purpose of creating a sense of moral dedication seems to have been all but lost, although to be sure some aspects of the ritual, like the taking of the obligation (agreeing to abide by the customs and rules of the craft), were still presented with simple dignity.

At the 1940 convention the whole question was again raised, when it developed some legal overtones.[13] New York and Pennsylvania had passed Fair Employment Practices Acts, which many delegates felt made the retention of the offending clause illegal. Among these delegates, there was some division as to the most desirable course of action. Some, like Anthony Ballerini (San Francisco Local Lodge 1327), believed that the IAM ought to take Negroes in and say nothing about it. Others said that the Fair Employment Practice Commission laws were probably unconstitutional, and that the IAM should test them. Still others asked that the executive council determine the policies to be followed in the different state jurisdictions. General Secretary-Treasurer Davison, who was a southerner, told the convention that it did not really much matter what was voted; each local would probably do pretty much as it wanted anyway. The convention chose to retain the offending clause, and to authorize the executive council to make a test case of the Fair Employment Practice Commission laws, if thought wise.

Throughout the twenties, the thirties, and the mid-forties the IAM executive council piously announced that the IAM was not opposed to the employment of Negroes in industry; it merely did not want them as members. This position, of course, fooled no one and, when during World War II President Roosevelt appointed a President's Committee on Fair Employment Practices, it was inevitable that complaints would arise. They did. As early as 1941 Mark Ethridge, chairman of the President's Committee, wrote to the executive council citing reports about discriminatory treatment against Negroes in the San Francisco and Los Angeles areas. Davison replied for the council saying that it "is familiar with the general conditions throughout the country, and knows that there are many thousands of Negroes employed in defense industry, and that there have been for a number of years many thousands of Negroes employed in industry connected with the machine industry that are represented [*sic*] by the IAM. It is not now, and never has been the policy of the IAM to interfere with the employment of Negroes in industry." This answer, as might have been expected, satisfied neither Ethridge, nor those who had complained to him. The executive council then told the two locals in California against whom complaints had been filed (Local Lodge 68 and District Lodge 727) to act in accordance with the President's executive order. What that meant is not clear. From later records, it appears that District Lodge 727 accepted the Los Angeles Negroes as members, and that Local Lodge 1327 "saved the day" by admitting the San Francisco Negroes.[14] It is also clear that had Local Lodge 1327 not acted, there would probably have been a full discussion of the matter on the floor of the United States Senate.

During the war some Negro workers in St. Louis applied for membership. It was granted to them, but later withdrawn "as soon as it was discovered."[15]

The issue of dropping the whites-only clause was again fully debated at the 1945 convention, after the Committee on the Ritual voted 10 to 3 to recommend dropping the clause.[16] The matter was put to a roll call vote and was defeated 2173 to 1958. As the vote suggests, the debate was vigorous and bitter, with many speeches based completely on cultural atavisms.

Late in 1947 the executive council, on its own motion, moved to amend the ritual and to eradicate the race clause.[17] It did so, it explained to the membership, because the passage of the Taft–Hartley Act had made it necessary. Later it became clear at the 1948 convention that there were even more proximate causes.[18] At that convention, held in Grand Rapids, Indianapolis Local

Lodge 511 argued that the executive council was *ultra vires* in taking the previous action. General Vice-President Melton then explained why the council had been forced to act. In two cases before the National Labor Relations Board it had come out that the ritual barred Negroes.[19] In one case the employer argued that the bar was reason to decertify the IAM as the representative of his employees; in the other case the teamsters' union suggested that it, rather than the IAM, should be given the certification. Although these cases had been much earlier, the passage of the Taft–Hartley Act had left the executive council with no option; it had to remove the clause. The Committee on the Ritual rejected the Indianapolis lodge's contention and recommended that the convention uphold the action.[20] Several bitterly anti-Negro speeches were then made from the floor; but the convention upheld the committee.

For a while there were a few all-Negro lodges chartered. In 1954 the executive council ordered such practices to stop, even though several of the Negro lodges protested.[21] Nonetheless, the council thought that the good of the organization required the abandonment of any form of racial exclusion. In practice, it is necessary to add, many lodges even in 1958 were reluctant to give up the old practice, although some, even those in Georgia, have abided by the law and are admitting members irrespective of race. The executive council supported the application of the sleeping car porters' union, an overwhelmingly Negro organization, for affiliation with the Railway Labor Executives' Association.[22]

What caused this situation to change in 1948? We have recounted the exact incident which caused the executive council to change the union policy without recourse to convention vote, but an analysis reveals three factors emerging; one was the attitude of the country as exemplified by the policies of the National Labor Relations Board, which refused to permit the IAM to discriminate as it had done for the past sixty years. The second was a realization that the union's policy, based on an old premise that the IAM was a craft union and that there were few skilled Negroes, was outmoded, and that it was no longer possible to maintain it except at great cost to the union itself. The union leadership realized that not only the National Labor Relations Board but also many locals within the union found the policy to be distasteful and would either ignore it (thereby weakening the union's internal structure) or would actually seek affiliation elsewhere. The third reason for changing the policy, reflected growing confidence of the IAM leadership in the shaping of IAM policy unilaterally. Previously, leaders had been voted out of office for less. However, since 1926 no member of the administration had ever been successfully disciplined by the rank and file. Twenty-two years of such success gave the IAM leadership a type of confidence which it could not have had at any previous period.

What then did the IAM leadership do? First, it deleted the offending clause from the ritual. Second, it permitted the establishment of colored locals, giving to colored machinists of ability some opportunity for leadership recognition. Third, it later moved to incorporate these colored locals into the established "white" locals. Thus, it quickly engineered not only the *de jure* shift, but it set out to convert this shift to a *de facto* one as well. Within a few years the shift was complete; and what the leadership had been unable to do as late as the 1945 convention was accomplished, without reference to popular membership opinion, by executive council action within three years.

It is fair at this point to ask whether the method of accomplishing this reform was democratic. Quite obviously, the duly elected convention delegates had repeatedly refused to take the action which the executive council believed both right and necessary. Thus, in a very real sense the executive council's action was undemocratic because it did not meet with the type of formal membership approval which it traditionally required. On the other hand, the earlier refusal to take in members because of their racial antecedents was also in a very real sense undemocratic, as the term is used. The leadership's earlier refusal to take the type of action which it successfully carried through in 1948, may be considered under this line of reasoning to be nothing less than support for a basically immoral, as well as undemocratic, doctrine. Certainly, it was contrary to the established moral code of the land; that is, contrary to the federal Constitution, as amended. This type of argument, however, is useless because it fails to comprehend the dynamic forces which motivate our society as well as those forces which govern union decisions. The executive council acted because the social forces requiring its action had grown to a point where they could no longer be ignored; at the same time the executive council had previously failed to act because the social forces preventing it from acting were too strong. In other words, the IAM moved when it became mandatory for it to do so. Delay would have greatly weakened the organization. Conversely, an earlier decision by executive council action would have also weakened the organization.

To act or not to act, and if so, how, when, and action by whom, are the problems of every democratic society. One of the characteristic errors in popular thinking is to confuse representative democracy with a pure democracy. Virtually all civilized institutions, if they are democratic at all, are run through some system of representative government. It is important to recognize that a society is governed not by the will of the majority, but by the will of the majority of the representatives. Selection of the representatives should under optimum conditions reflect in some way or other the confidence of the rank and file. One is then left with the question of whether one group of representatives is better qualified than another to deal with specific questions. Of course, there is a legal answer; quite frequently one group of representatives is selected to handle policy questions, while another group is selected to administer the policy. So viewed, it is entirely reasonable to conclude that the convention should have amended the ritual, rather than turning the job over to the executive council. However, to pursue one legal argument further, it is necessary to realize that the executive council exercises the prerogative in matters of ritual between conventions. This point should be stressed; in most matters the referendum is the instrument for handling the prerogative. However, the ritual cannot be changed by referendum action. Therefore, it is incumbent upon the executive council to handle problems concerning the ritual between conventions. In any event, there is some legal basis for the executive council's acting as it did. Whether the executive council had full moral sanction to make the decision is a matter of opinion; those who believe that the original basic policy was immoral, may support the action taken by the executive council. Those who believe that the decision rested upon an analysis of its strengths and weaknesses, will conclude that taking the decision at the time it was taken, was wise because to have done so earlier, or not to have done so in 1948, would have been excessively costly in both instances. However, the point that does stand out is that the representative assembly (the convention) seemed unable to take a decision which was probably economically wise and certainly morally sound.

The "menace" of radicalism has also touched the IAM. Radicalism can be understood in two senses; one refers to the beliefs of those who harbor unpopular or heretical thoughts. The other, the type with which we are presently concerned, refers to a coordinated heresy. That is, it refers to a group of heretics sharing the common belief and conviction that the union should be converted, irrespective of the technique, to their basically different viewpoint. For many years, the IAM has had many highly individualistic members, each of whom felt entitled to his own view. At no time in the union's history has there been any real attempt made to make these individualistic heretics conform. On the other hand, from time to time, these heretics have "gotten together" and tried to shape IAM policy. On such occasions the IAM, in order to protect itself, has had to take steps against them. The IAM has not been opposed to radicalism, so much as it has been opposed to conspiratorial radicalism. Again, this would not present much of a problem, were it not for the fact that the conspiratorial radicalism which emerged in the IAM emerged in other sectors of society at the same time.

During World War I, American Socialism went into a major decline. Reasons for this are relatively clear. Wilson's New Freedom drew from the old Socialist ranks many of those interested in moderate social reform. On the other hand, the internationalism which characterized the old Socialist movement became swamped with patriotic fervor. Those who embraced the belief that all men were brothers, were accused of loving "Huns" as much as they loved good, red-blooded Americans. The Socialist movement was rent by this situation. The result was a super-patriotism on the part of many of those who had previously embraced Socialist doctrine. At the end of World War I, the United States, influenced by the specter of Communist success in Russia, became more sensitive than ever to conspiratorial radicalism of a left-wing variety. The raids, conducted by United States Attorney-General Palmer, are part of our national history. Within the labor movement, both in left-wing unions like the IAM and in right-wing circles like the one surrounding Gompers, great effort was made to stress the differences between nonconspiratorial (home-grown, individualistic) radicalism and the type which was killing authorities, confiscating all property, and destroying churches abroad. International President Johnston was swept along in this tide. He was not a great admirer of the Soviet Union, primarily because he had some knowledge of the brutality of its leaders.[23] On the other hand, he was regularly charged with having "un-American sympathies." This being the situation, he was particularly sensitive to developments within his own organization which seemed to betoken the growth of radical interests.

In earlier years the union had had to take steps against those members who sought to destroy the union by excessive factionalism. These were the groups who refused to abide by the majority decision when votes were taken. These were the groups who embraced dual unionism, in the eyes of unionists, the greatest of all sins. Johnston, influenced by the antiradical sentiment rampant in America, became convinced that any person who embraced the Soviet brand of Socialism (Communism) was for that reason alone a threat to the IAM. Consequently, he directed that those identified with Russian Socialism should be charged with insurrection. The history of the trial in Toledo and the subsequent appeal at the Detroit convention is referred to in Chapter IV. The outcome of the episode was a modification of the Johnston position. He was unable to discipline his "enemies," the Toledo "reds," successfully. When Johnston left the presidency, his successor, first by executive fiat, and then by regular convention and referendum action, outlawed Communism in the IAM. The IAM, in other words, declared that membership in any Communist organization was grounds for expulsion from the IAM. The reasons for its taking this action lie in two areas. One was a true fear that the Communists were trying to take over. The other reflected a public relations attitude.

Wharton, for reasons quite different from the ones developed by Johnston, concluded that it was socially desirable for the IAM to go on record as opposed to Communism. These were different from the ones developed by Johnston because they reflected an impersonal estimate of the situation. No one charged Wharton with being a radical; on the other hand, Johnston, because of his earlier political career, was believed to be one. Neither Wharton nor Johnston were political revolutionaries; in both cases they had had some Socialist interests, but these interests reflected a traditional American Populism. Wharton, however, had never played a significant role in the Socialist movement, as had Johnston; consequently, it was not necessary for him to be "more Catholic than the Pope" nor "more royalist than the King." Nonetheless, Wharton supported the executive decree outlawing Communism in the IAM, and at the 1928 convention that executive decree was incorporated into the basic IAM law through regular convention and referendum processing.[24]

As a result of the Wharton action and the steps taken by the convention, several individuals, who during the late 1920's and during the 1930's were charged with Communism, were convicted and suspended from membership.[25] Occasionally, after having assured either Wharton or the executive council or both of their true reform, they were readmitted to membership. In any case during the period, 1930–1935, there were a few instances of disciplinary action.

When the mass production industries were organized, in many cases by individuals against whom the charge of Communist affiliation could fairly be applied, the IAM was not overly squeamish in accepting their support. It was only when these same members, more true to their political affiliation than they were to their union membership, turned against IAM leadership, that the IAM leaders brought charges of Communist radicalism against them. In due course they were suspended, and their influence was eliminated. The Communist trials in Minneapolis in 1938 and in Seattle at the Boeing Plant during the period, 1940–1942, were held for different reasons. The Minneapolis situation reflected the development of an antiadministration cabal.[26] Action was taken against the leaders, Harry Mayville and William Mauseth, because they had set out to provoke a dispute. Mauseth sought to turn the Minneapolis machinist organization over to the CIO. The executive council brought him and twenty-nine others to trial, during which Mauseth and his associates sought a court order forbidding General Vice-President Nickerson and any other grand lodge personnel from issuing what were termed slanderous statements. Only three of those brought up on charges bothered to offer any defense at the trial, which was conducted in Minneapolis by the executive council. Those three were exonerated; the rest were found guilty and expelled. The record is replete with demonstrated arguments against the program advocated by the local leaders; the result was obvious, they were expelled.

The trials in Seattle were brought about because of war department pressure.[27] The military became quite concerned with evidence of subversion in the Boeing Plant. It is now fairly clear that the subversion came both from right-wing seditionists, particularly German *Bundists,* as well as from left-wing Communists. The IAM, because of its constitutional provisions barring subversives, agreed to the FBI request to bring charges against the ring leaders and expel them from the union. Once expelled from the union, they could easily be fired, and the danger of sabotage would be past. Parenthetically, it is worth adding that the company was also asked to get rid of the *Bundists.* The IAM administration made a thorough study of the situation, brought charges against sixty members, most of whom were convicted. In 1948, reflecting the emergence of a new fear, the convention denied membership to Nazis, Fascists, and any others who supported totalitarian forms of government.[28]

One other major example of radicalism is worth considering. This was the situation in San Francisco, where the leadership of Local 68, undoubtedly radical in its political views, had entrenched itself. The struggle to discipline the leadership is described in Chapter V.

One can well ask whether the IAM was "justified" in its antiradical measures. A truly democratic society generally permits a wide range of opinion. Were those who were expelled from the IAM merely exercising their citizens' prerogative? Or were they actually conspiratorial as charged? Again the answer rests upon some basic opinions. If the IAM were truly in jeopardy, it was probably justified in eliminating the "revolutionaries." If, on the other hand, the revolutionaries were merely sacrificed to provide a "clean record," there is some reason to doubt the justice of the action. The history of Communism in the American labor movement probably confirms the view that there was real danger to the IAM, and that the IAM's action was not taken simply to gratify some popular and prejudiced opinion. Whatever may be the criticism of the arbitrariness of the IAM action, it is worth pointing out that the union proceeded only after some form of a trial. Generally these trials were fairly run, and the defense was given every opportunity to be heard. At the same time that the IAM was taking these steps, other institutions in the country such as school systems, universities, and the government were facing similar problems. Those interested in comparative processes might point to the care which the IAM exercised to ensure fair hearings, and use the IAM's record as a basis for comparing the record established by the other institutions named. The general conclusion is that the IAM's attitude toward radicalism has a factual basis. Furthermore, the IAM is justified in establishing measures to protect itself. Finally, the IAM's record in trying subversives compares favorably with the record of society at large.

The Place of the IAM in Modern Community Life

As unionism has become more secure because of continued economic prosperity and the protective attitude taken by the federal government, many social leaders have come to recognize the importance of union cooperation in civic administration. Not only are union leaders asked to address civic functions, university seminars, and even public testimonial dinners, but they are asked also to lend their support to desirable public movements. During the two world wars, the IAM made gifts to agencies helping to entertain soldiers and sailors; it also publicized war bond drives.[29] For instance, some time during World War II and the years thereafter, many Community Drive leaders came to recognize that union cooperation often resulted in greater collections. Therefore the IAM, in common with many other unions, was frequently asked to endorse charitable drives. Sometimes the IAM responded for several reasons; for example, the March of Dimes was not only a worthy cause, but because of its association with President Roosevelt, it appeared politic to support it. In other cases, the IAM refused to lend support for similar reasons. In a few instances, the IAM was eager to give spot relief where it was needed; examples of this would be donations to the Red Cross for help in flood or disaster areas, contributions to help unionists abroad, or even contributions to deserving individuals. As the IAM became more established and wealthier, it agreed to play a larger role in community life. In the international foreign affairs field, the IAM was able to make a major contribution (discussed in Chapter V). Here it should be noted that the international president expanded the efforts which the IAM made overseas, extended its economic aid to sister organizations, and used the knowledge gained by its activities to advise political officials in Washington of developments in labor union fields.

The executive council took stands on several issues in which it felt that it had an interest. It initially opposed compulsory military training in 1945; it endorsed the Marshall Plan "with the understanding that it will not adversely affect our domestic economy"; and it directed local lodges to appoint committees to publicize cancer detection programs. In contrast, the council once declined to start a "College Scholarship Foundation" because "it was agreed that no matter how worthy it was, the fact remained that [such an effort] would not be [possible or] workable under the Association's laws and structure."

The executive council thus became more than the representative of machinists in industrial life; it became a voice in public affairs. Therefore it was natural that the council became "public-relations-conscious," and within a few years the public relations director became an important administrative aid to the international president and the executive council. This change is particularly significant, when it is realized that the traditional attitude toward the administration of the IAM policy had been internal; that is, the important opinion was that of the members, not what the public believed the policy to be. Increased dependence upon a public relations program indicated a significant shift in emphasis.

It is important to add that the development of an executive council public relations program caused some readjustments in the area of grand local lodge relationships. So long as the executive council eschewed public policy pronouncements, it could, and did, caution locals to refrain from speaking out on nonunion matters. But when the executive council switched its policy, not only was it harder to claim that only strictly union matters were to be considered on the local levels, it was hard to avoid friction over how issues were to be considered. If the executive council considered cancer detection to be a worthy cause for support, how could it claim that some other non-union-related drive, supported by local leaders, was not to be helped. The abandonment of the tradition harking back to Wharton's day of no involvement in nonvital questions, meant the opening of another area of conflict among the various levels of organization in the IAM.

Whether this shift in emphasis will continue, remains to be seen. So long as unions play an ever-increasing role in public life, it is hard to imagine the council abolishing its public relations interest. On the other hand, public relations emphasis, and attention to general public attitudes and problems, draw resources from other uses. It is important for an institution which must play both an internal or private role, and an external or public one, to strike a balance between the two. The strength of the IAM must rest upon the loyalty of its membership, but its influence will depend in good part on the wisdom of the executive council in the handling of its "public role."

APPENDIX I

Grand Lodge Major Office Holders, 1908–1953

(*see chart opposite*)

APPENDIX **II**

Report of the Grand Master Machinist of the I.A. of M.

Richmond, Va., April 1, 1895.

To the Delegates Assembled in the Sixth Convention of the I.A. of M.:

GREETING — The most trying and eventful two years of our Association have ended. We have assembled here to-day for the purpose of reviewing what has been done, correcting those things that are wrong, and legislating for the future. The past two years have been eventful ones in the history of the labor movement, and especially so for the men of our trade and calling.

During these two years we have witnessed success and defeats. We have seen former comrades as foes; we have heard cries of mistrust; we have felt the attack of the enemy, which being aided by former members has caused dissension in our ranks. The task of championing the cause of our craft has of necessity been an arduous one under those conditions, to say nothing of those who have remained indifferent when their principle as men were at stake. We have, however, felt the effect of those circumstances. We have even seen the wealth of the nations arrayed against us, and we were obliged to depend on a treasury that at times did not contain a dollar. This was not as encouraging as it might appear, especially when but few of those who were oppressed cared whether the fight was for or against them. I am satisfied, however, that the standard of our members who have been loyal to the cause during this great depression has been raised higher than ever, and that we have witnessed a general spreading of our organization until it has become as familiarly known as the oldest labor organization in America. We are as capable of defending our members against any unjust cause or condition as the oldest labor organization known, and much better than some who profess all the qualifications of the others combined, which spring up like a mushroom and go down as quickly. Unfortunately for us, however, we have not had the assistance of the men of our craft, and in many instances we have had the members of our organization arrayed against us.

At the very beginning of my term of office we had inroads made into our organization by sentimental efforts from other orders that made brilliant promises which were easily broken, and in a great many instances our members were made to feel the bitter consequences of catering to disgruntled labor men from other organizations. Time has proven the unwise steps taken — many of our members were compelled to leave their homes and become wanderers on the face of the earth, roaming from State to State in search of employment, put up with many inconveniences, that if we asked them to do, would appear like treason on our part. They have seen their families in want, and suffered untold misery in behalf of what appeared to be the best cause. I honor every man for his independence and the self-denial spirit shown in defence of his fellow workingman, but if this same spirit was displayed in behalf of our organization, there would be no limit to our success, and our craft would at once feel the results and benefits of the organization.

We have lived, however, to see a turn in the tide, and stand to-day with doubts dispelled and ranks unbroken, with a better understanding of the aims and objects of our order than ever before; for these two years have been the greatest educator that the members of our craft have ever experienced; in fact, we have all been attending school for two years in getting our first lessons in what thorough organization means. Our organization has passed through the most fiery ordeal. Having suffered in so doing is deserving more than ever of the consideration of the machinists of America. Great battles have been fought to strike down the chains that bound the negro in slavery and for the freedom of the American people, but a greater battle has been waged against us by men in our own ranks, who tried to pull down what it has taken years to build, who have no other purpose than they personally might be the gainer.

During my whole term as Grand Master Machinist the battle has not been against those who employ us, but against misrepresentation, and this of the most blackmailing character. When we lose confidence in those who have taken an obligation, the same as we have, what can we expect of those on the outside? No charge has ever been made against the Grand Master, nor those in connection with the affairs of the Grand Lodge but what could be successfully refuted; and if it has not been done in every case, it was not through fear, but because some court had sealed my lips or tied my hands. It would be useless on my part to deny that those things, with the great depression of business in the past two years, have reduced our membership. To expect anything else would be useless. I never expected that we would pull through so successfully and come out of this great struggle with the present record to our credit. I am as much surprised as any of you here to-day, for I was well aware of the great odds against which we had to contend. Knowing these facts, I felt that we were in danger of being annihilated in the great struggle. Those who entailed the greatest loss and expense to our organization and left us a legacy of debt as their monument, are not in the order now; some have passed to their eternal homes, and others from the order, but those debts had to be met by your present officers.

This was no light task, for when the convention at Indianapolis closed, the debt of about $12,000 was to be met by the present officers. The convention had taken steps whereby the debt would gradually be increased by ordering a strike at the Grant Locomotive Works in Chicago; also at the Ide Machine Works at Springfield, Ill. There were also a number of men placed on the pay-roll at intervals by the General Executive Board, which increased the debt very rapidly. It was impossible to administrate affairs of the order without money. To borrow it, would subject us to a storm of abuse and criticism. The greatest care was taken in regard to levying assessments, as we were well aware that a panic would be started very easily by those who regard dollars as mills when spent for amusements and pleasure, and mills as dollars if given in the cause of labor; by the greatest economy at headquarters, and patience of those with whom we were in debt, it has been necessary to assess our members only twenty-five cents each six months for the past two years. This would not have been necessary at all times had all our lodges paid their debts promptly to the Grand Lodge. The lodges that were promptly paying their per capita tax and the assessments were carrying along their sister lodges, who were unable, through a chain of circumstances, to pay their just debts to the Grand Lodge. There were other lodges, however, who were fully able to liquidate their debts, but who were poisoned against so doing by members of our Association; hence they have not stood the just share of the running expenses of the Association. Many times in the past two years I have become discouraged when I saw how easily the evil-minded could misconstrue our actions and create distrust; but having watched the order from its infancy, and knowing that we were more in need of organization than ever before, I would strike out with renewed energy to regain what had been lost.

MY STEWARDSHIP

The Grand Master Machinist, by the terms of the Constitution, is required to make a detailed report of his work during his term of office. If I was to comply with this provision of our law, it would be necessary for me to read every letter written, to repeat nearly two hundred speeches, to repeat every word spoken and every act done, for they have all been in the interest of our order. The duty of the Grand Master Machinist will not permit one moment's lost time. No matter who may occupy the position, the work is never done. While on the railroad train, on the steamboat, in the hotel, or on the street, and even upon retiring, he must keep continually before him the work of the order. It is therefore an impossibility to comply with this provision. I have reported all my official acts to the General Executive Board, and in their minutes will be found sixty-seven circulars, covering all the important transactions for the past two years, as I have kept them fully posted on all matters of interest and advised with them freely. I would refer you to the records of the General Executive Board for such information as you may desire, or for points not covered by me in this report.

OUR EX-TREASURER, JOHN J. LAMB

Previous to the close of the Indianapolis convention two years ago it was discovered that our ex-Treasurer, John J. Lamb, had fled with our fund. Upon this discovery I at once made it known to the convention, when a resolution was adopted authorizing me, at once, to proceed to have him captured. Telegrams were forwarded to all the principal cities, but we failed to discover his whereabouts until May 29, 1893, when he was caught in Scranton, Pa. We at once proceeded to bring suit against him. The Grand Secretary-Treasurer, Brother Dawley, was in New York at that time going over the accounts with the Association, in which Lamb was bonded. I wired him to go to Scranton at once, which he did and suit was entered against Lamb, which finally wound up on the 28th of June when he came before the court for trial. Brother Dawley and myself were present at this trial, as also were several members of No. 230, of Scranton. Lamb came before the court, pleaded guilty to the charges and was sentenced to one year in the county jail, a fine of $50 and the costs of court, which time he served in full.

Our ex-treasurer was bonded in the Co-operative Indemnity Union of New York to the amount of $5,000. This Association raises the amount of their losses by assessing those who carry bonds with them to the amount of one-tenth of one per cent of the amount of their bond. But one assessment can be levied on any one loss. This assessment on the loss of John J. Lamb amounted to $1,310.43, which amount has been received by us in two installments — one of $1,000, which was paid by my request, as we were very much in need of money, and the balance, $310.43, was paid a few months later. When the total collections had been made by that Association this relieved the Co-operative Indemnity Union from any further loss on this bond.

We then proceeded to bring about some arrangement with the personal bondsmen of our ex-Treasurer located in Bloomington, Ill., for another bond of $5,000, which was held by the Association. In company with a member of No. 81, of Bloomington, I called on the bondsmen and tried to adjust or settle the matter with them. They refused, however, to stand good for the loss. We finally procured assistance of Fifer & Philips, a law firm in Bloomington, Ill., to take up our case at 20 per cent of the amount collected. If they failed in the case they were to get no fees. The case has been argued before one court and decided against us. They now have the case argued before the Appellate Court, where a decision is pending. The great difficulty in collecting this bond has been the irregular way in which it was made out. I wish to call the attention of the convention to the duty of the Grand Secretary-Treasurer as to the amount of money he shall hold, and then requiring him to give a bond of $5,000 which is more than double the amount in his possession. No association, according to the law of our land, would be liable for more money than the laws of our organization allow the Treasurer to hold at any one time.

In the case of John J. Lamb, he was only allowed to retain $1,000 while he gave a bond for $10,000. This is one of the points of contention in the courts at the present time. In the personal bond of John J. Lamb, the word "grand" was omitted from the bond, simply reading "John J. Lamb, Treasurer of the International Association of Machinists," when it should have read, "John J. Lamb, Grand Treasurer of the Grand Lodge of the International Association of Machinists." You will find in the documents of the General Executive Board a full statement in regard to the case of our ex-Treasurer, but in order that you may know the exact position of affairs, I give you in full the last communication from our lawyers in this matter:

"BLOOMINGTON, ILL., March 28, 1895.

"JAS. O'CONNELL, RICHMOND, VA.:

"Dear Sir — We have your favor of the 19th instant, and noted its contents.

"The case of the International Association of Machinists against John J. Lamb and his bondsmen was tried in the Circuit Court of McLean county at the November term, 1894. There was an improper description of your organization in the bond, and the court held against us on this point, and we took an appeal to the Appellate Court, where the case is now pending. The case has been fully argued in the Appellate Court, and we are expecting a decision almost at any time. The result of the suit is somewhat doubtful, and yet we hope to succeed. If we do not succeed in this suit, which is one at law, we may be able to recover in a court of equity. We, of course, will exhaust every remedy in order to secure the amount due on the bond.

"The firm of Fifer & Philips has been dissolved, Mr. Philips having been appointed reporter for the Supreme Court of this State. The old firm has been succeeded by the firm of Fifer & Barry, who will look after the matter in question for your Association.

"Yours truly,
"Fifer & Barry."

ORGANIZERS AND ORGANIZATIONS

Amidst all the depression in business since our last convention and during my term of office, we have succeeded in organizing fifty-three new lodges and reorganizing seventeen that had died. When we consider the conditions surrounding the labor movement this appears to me to be an exceptionally good record. It has been absolutely impossible to make any great headway during the past year in organizing the men of our trade into new lodges, and I have deemed it wise to put forth our every energy to stimulate the lodges that were dying from the want of assistance. Therefore, with the consent of the General Executive Board, I have personally visited a large number of our lodges, addressed open meetings for them and lent my assistance to build their lodges up. This has proven to be a very wise move on the part of your officers, and I believe, to a certain extent, has saved the Association from becoming disrupted.

At our last convention it was decided to place a special organizer in Canada for six months. Brother Filmore, of Moncton, N.B., was selected for that position. Before the time came to place him in the field he decided to leave Canada and move to the States. This necessitated the selection of another man. In the mean time the finances of the organization became very low, and the General Executive Board decided, for the time being, we were unable to place a brother in the field in Canada. As soon as we became in a position to see our way clear, Brother John Reid, of Stratford, was selected, and has been for four months working among the machinists of Canada. While he has not organized any new lodges, he has done considerable work in visiting the old ones and adding new members to their rolls. He has been a faithful worker, for which the Association should feel gratefully indebted.

It became necessary to place a special organizer in the city of Philadelphia to carry on the work that was left unfinished by the removal of the Grand Foreman and Organizer from office by the General Executive Board. Considerable work was accomplished in Philadelphia by Brother Rockhill, for which the delegates here to-day from that city can speak.

A special organizer, Brother Frank N. Glaser, was also appointed for District 15, of New York and vicinity, to help carry on the work in that section. Much has been accomplished throughout New York and vicinity in spreading the seed of organization. The Association has been well repaid for the expenditures of the special organizer in this vicinity. He has proven himself to be a hardworking and energetic member of the I.A. of M.

Brother Glenn, of the General Executive Board, was sent over the Union Pacific and Santa Fe railroad; also through the western country, to revive the members in those sections, which work was well accomplished by him.

We have many local organizers throughout our jurisdiction who have given us unlimited assistance in the matter of spreading the seed of our Association. I have distributed upwards of fifty thousand circulars throughout the United States, Canada, and Mexico, besides distributing extra JOURNALS, which, with the revival of trade, will undoubtedly be felt by the Association in a general revival of organization. I have asked the assistance of our sister labor organizations to distribute our literature where we had no organization. We are indebted to all for the zealous manner in which they have carried out my requests.

The most important feature in connection with the organizers was the removal of the Grand Foreman and Organizer from office by the General Executive Board one year ago. This was found necessary, while it was to be regretted that at the time we were very much in need of an able organizer in the field, yet the dignity of the organization was at stake, and your executive officers found it necessary to up hold the organization at all hazards. You will find in the minutes of the General Executive Board a complete statement why the Grand Foreman and Organizer was removed from office; also in the hands of the Grand Secretary-Treasurer all the documentary evidence brought in this case. I therefore will not extend this part of my report by inserting any of this evidence. The Grand Foreman made an effort, by the assistance of the courts, to override the decisions of the General Executive Board and compel the Association to recognize him, though he violated every law within the covers of our Constitution. The courts, however, decided that the General Executive Board were in full power and authority, and upheld them in every action.

In a circular issued by me, I requested the local lodges to appoint a local organizer in order that we might make an effort in every locality to organize the towns in the close vicinity. Owing to the condition of trade, no particular success has come from this movement. However, I believe in the near future that this system of having the local lodges take hold of the matter of organizing the towns close by them can be made a success. It is an absolute impossibility for your Grand Master or your grand officers to do all this work. Unless the local lodges take an active part but little can be accomplished. Some law should be enacted stating what compensation the local organizer may be entitled to for organizing a lodge. I believe if this was the case it would be a stimulant to the local organizers to take hold of the work.

I would call your special attention to the great need of a good organizer being placed in the East for at least six months. My recent visit in that section leads me to believe that it would be a profitable investment for us to take earnest efforts to organize that section, as we have thousands of bright and intelligent craftsman there, men who would be a credit to our order, and it is our duty to consider if we need them.

The convention should leave nothing undone that would aid in spreading the growth of our organization.

STRIKES

The delegates at our last convention had not reached their several homes after the session had closed until strikes were reigning supreme all over the countries in which our order had sown its seed. At the Indianapolis session strikes were ordered in the Grant Locomotive Works at Chicago, also at the Ide Machine Works at Springfield, Ill., which placed a large number of men on the pay-roll at the start of my term of office. Following these strikes a reduction of wages was rapidly taking place, shops were closing down, and men being thrown out of employment right and left. Notwithstanding these conditions, it was almost impossible to keep our men from being involved in strikes, lockouts, and having their names placed on blacklists. We have had numerous small strikes during the past two years, but the most important ones, of which I find it necessary to mention, was the strike on the Louisville and Nashville Railroad System, involving the entire system from Cincinnati to New Orleans. The members of our organization were misled by the railroad organizations until they went on strike, when they were deserted by these bodies. Every effort was made to adjust the trouble between the railroad authorities and our men, but it appears that the machinists were held accountable for the actions of all, whether it was the freight handler, carpenter, blacksmith, or boiler maker, and the result was a total disorganization of our order on this system. This trouble could have been adjusted for the time being had our men not been dictated to or domineered over by those who refused to call in the officers of their organizations to try and adjust this trouble, believing that they could handle the matter independently of the grand officers. This resulted in a total failure of the strike.

Coming down to the late American Railway Union strike, which we were largely interested in, owing to our members' being involved all over the Western section in this trouble. You are all fully conversant with this struggle that took place between the American Railway Union and the railroad combinations of the West; it is hardly necessary for me to repeat here that with which you are well acquainted. It is well to consider, however, the result of our men being involved in that great struggle, which has been the cause of many of our lodges disbanding in the Western section, and the membership of others being driven from the locality entirely. Although we have lost a great number of our members through that struggle, yet we have the gratification of knowing that we are held in high esteem by all labor organizations for the stand our members took in behalf of their sister labor organization.

Our members on the Great Northern System were involved also in a strike with the American Railway Union, which strike was a success at that time. Whether it was the success of this strike or the belief that trades unions were a failure, I cannot say, but some of our members on that system were inflated to such an extent that they immediately began disorganizing our lodges and joining hands with another organization. Time has proven, however, the failure of this movement. During these strikes injunctions were the order of the day. The grand officers were being enjoined by the courts from breathing the air in some sections of our country; but we have survived it all and are here to-day in the full bloom of our manhood.

The great question for this convention to consider is whether it is wise for the delegates in session to order strikes. I have found, by careful investigation, had the Springfield (Ill.) strike been referred to the General Executive Board instead of endorsing it at that time, that it would never have occurred and the order would have been largely a gainer by this action. The cause of the strike was somewhat misrepresented at the convention, which was done for the purpose of infusing the delegates. It is a bad precedent to establish. No strike should be ordered without first being fully investigated by your Grand Lodge officers. Many small strikes during the past two years have resulted in some gain to the men of our craft, but, as a whole, strikes have been a failure. I earnestly trust, for the benefit of our craft and our organization, that the delegates here assembled will throw every measure of protection around our members that they may not be involved in unnecessary strikes. It has been almost impossible to have the laws of the Constitution carried out before our members involve themselves in trouble, and for this reason we have had but very few strictly legitimate strikes. You will find in the proceedings of the General Executive Board an account of all the disputes that our men have been involved in for the past two years.

SHORTER WORK-DAY

The sixth plank in our platform states that we should make an effort to reduce the hours of labor to eight, thus giving our members more opportunities for self-improvement and and social enjoyment. The question of reducing the hours of labor I consider to be one of the most important that the laboring people have to deal with in these trying times. We look around us, and on every hand we see other tradesmen enjoying the shorter work-day; yet we openly boast of being possessed of greater skill and knowledge, still we have not made that effort to reduce our hours which we should have done. At the Indianapolis convention considerable discussion took place on shortening our hours of labor. It was decided that an effort would be made to reduce the hours in Cleveland, Ohio. When this order went forth a general revival of organization took place at once in that city. When matters were about in shape to demand a reduction of hours the great depression in business set in that made it necessary to relinquish our claims at that time. This depression has been in force throughout the two years; consequently, we have been unable to make an attempt to carry out the instructions of the convention; but with the revival of trade in the near future no efforts should be spared to bring about the results of the sixth plank in our platform. The introduction of machinery to-day has made it possible for us to produce more in ten hours than could be accomplished a few years ago in fifteen; yet our hours have not been reduced nor our wages increased. This is solely due to the men of our craft failing to see the necessity of organization, refusing to join hands with those who are making an honest endeavor to reduce the hours of labor, increase their wages and make it possible for us to live in common respectability. This question of shorter hours is well worth your careful consideration. You should leave no stone unturned that will advance this movement. Our national eight-hour law should receive your careful consideration also. As the law reads to-day on our Statute books, it is being flagrantly violated by all manufacturers, and in some cases by the government itself. Your Grand Master Machinist should be instructed to make an effort to see that the eight-hour law is tested as to its constitutionality, then we will be in a position to force some of those who are to-day violating this law, to reduce the hours of their employees.

EXPENDITURES . OF . THE . GRAND LODGE

Much has been written in the columns of our JOURNAL and by the distribution of circulars throughout the local lodges on the question of expenses at the headquarters. In order that delegates here assembled may make themselves fully conversant with the expenditures of the Grand Lodge, and in order to satisfy yourself that the greatest economy has been in vogue, it will be necessary for you to compare the cost during this term and that of years gone by of each and every article that has been purchased by the officers. You will find in so doing that the expenses have been decreased from ten to twenty-five per cent. In the Grand Secretary-Treasurer's accounts you will find an itemized receipt or statement for all the expenditures during the term, which can be very readily compared with times gone by. Though it has been said by those who are willing to sow the seed of dissension that money was being lavishly expended, yet I challenge any of those to purchase work as cheap as we have done and have it done by strictly trades unionists. We have been to greater expense on account of your officers having to travel more in the past two years than was done by all your executive officers during the whole reign of our Association. This appears to have been lost sight of by those who were ever ready to criticise the grand officers for expenditures when they were not acquainted with the facts or causes that made them necessary. Your Constitution makes a provision that the Grand Master Machinist must pay his own hotel bills while travelling for the benefit of the organization. This is certainly an injustice to your executive officer. While it is a very delicate subject for me to touch upon, nevertheless, whether I or some other member will have to lead you in the future, you should not ask him to expend the greater portion of his salary for hotel bills; it is not expected that he will go begging from door to door in order that he may not have to pay for what he eats. It becomes the dignity of our order to have its representatives carry the organization to the front instead of going to the back alleys or in the slums to hide it. Every dollar has been expended with the most careful consideration, and not one dollar has gone astray.

OUR CONSTITUTION

Our present Constitution is very much in need of many changes being made, and in order that you may be in a position to judge well the best changes to be made, I suggest for your consideration the following: The laws in the Constitution now are not under their proper heads as a whole. As an illustration, I refer you to the duties of the General Executive Board, where you will find, mixed therein, duties of the Grand Secretary-Treasurer, also the qualification for a member of our organization being eligible to a grand lodge office. By this you will see that these laws are not under their proper heads; so you find through the Constitution generally.

Much has been written upon the referendum and initiative plan of adopting our laws through the organization. This is a plan that requires your careful attention.

A number of labor organizations have a plan in vogue of referring their laws adopted in convention to the local lodges for ratification. This plan, in my opinion, is a good one, but for the officers of the Association to be elected on the referendum plan, would, in my opinion, be an expensive way of selecting your leaders; it would also place the men who might be best acquainted far in the lead in the contest. Though some of our members might have far better qualifications for officers, yet they would be entirely unknown and would be lost sight of.

I recommend that the issuing of quarterly reports by the Grand Secretary-Treasurer be done away with, that monthly reports be made instead, and that the columns of the JOURNAL be used for this purpose. This would mean a saving of a large amount of money each year. It would also add to the interest of our JOURNAL.

I recommend that, instead of holding annual, we hold biennial conventions, that the matter of taking a referendum vote previous to holding the conventions be done away with, and that we hold stated meetings once every two years. This plan is adopted to-day by nearly all the older organizations, and some of them do not meet as often as this.

Each local lodge should pay for the JOURNAL sent their local secretary. This should be made plain in the law.

Some law should be adopted that local lodges would have to be governed by, before issuing circulars haphazard to the organization at large. This has a tendency to cause dissension in our ranks.

Our law now allows as a strike benefit eight ($8.00) dollars per week to married men and five ($5.00) dollars per week to single men. This is a higher rate of benefits than is paid by any other trades union in North America. I believe the amount should be reduced to not more than seven ($7.00) dollars and four ($4.00) dollars per week.

It should also state plainly the number of weeks that a man can remain on the pay-roll, and no benefits should be paid for the first week. This, in a measure, would have a tendency to avoid a great many strikes for trivial reasons. I have found it necessary at this time to force men on the pay-roll to look for work, as they seemed to be perfectly satisfied to live on the strike benefit for an unlimited time without looking for work.

The Constitution should provide that when a lodge surrenders its charter and is not reorganized for six months, that the number be given to the first new lodge organized, in order that the roster may be kept full at all times.

A great many of our lodges and brothers are desirous of having a label, to be used by manufacturers, bearing the emblem of our order. It would be well for the delegates to consider this matter, as I believe it could be used very readily by some who employ the men of our craft.

I am of the opinion that our requirements are too strong for applicants for membership. It seems to me that a man who is filling the position of a machinist and receiving average wages, should be eligible to membership regardless of what particular work he is employed at.

Strong laws should be made to protect the local lodges' funds. We have had many lodges in the past two years who have lost their funds through the dishonesty of their treasurers. I advise that a law be made compelling each lodge to bond its treasurer in a bond society of some repute, which can be done with but very little cost to the local lodge.

I am of the opinion that it would be much to the interest of the organization if the local lodge officers were elected annually instead of semi-annually. They do not become thoroughly familiar with the work under the present law until their term of office has expired.

There has been no law in our Constitution requiring a district lodge to pay for its charter. The Executive Board in its session one year ago authorized that the same charges be made as to local lodges. The convention should decide what should be the fee charged in cases of this kind.

It is required by the Constitution that each local lodge pay at least one ($1.00) dollar per week as sick benefits to members in good standing.

The great trouble has been in the sick benefits, that one lodge pays one ($1.00) dollar and another five ($5.00) dollars; a general fight has been in vogue between the local lodges on this question of sick benefits.

A law should be made setting forth very plainly the amounts that should be paid weekly, and the rights of one member who has been transferred from one lodge to another. In all the local by-laws that I have approved, which was one hundred and twenty-five (125), I have found a great diversity of opinion on this question. Each lodge construes the law to its own liking, and when the law is explained to them by your executive officer considerable ill-will is expressed.

The laws governing the district lodges at the present time are too meager to be of much assistance. Laws should be enacted setting forth the powers that the district lodge have, and especially should a law be made in regard to a lodge being in some manner able to withdraw its membership from the district. If a just cause can be shown, under our present law a lodge must continue its membership in the district regardless of the conditions that surround them; this in some cases has been the cause of disrupting our lodges.

Our ritual is more ornamental than useful. I dare say you will not find fifty members of our organization who can, without the use of the ritual, tell you the secret work correctly. I therefore advise that your secret work be reduced at least half of what it contains at present. It is better to give a man a few signs that he can remember than try to fill his head with a lot of nonsense that he forgets before he leaves your meeting-room.

There are many other laws and changes that I might suggest, but I believe these few will suffice to guide you onward to changing our laws for a more successful controlling of our membership, and the successful organization of those on the outside.

FEDERATION

Your executive officer was authorized by resolution adopted at the Fifth Annual Session to bring about, if possible, a federation between metal-working trades. After considerable correspondence a meeting was finally brought about, which was held at Indianapolis on October 22, 1894, when representatives from the boiler-makers, blacksmiths, brass-workers, moulders, and machinists put in an appearance. A constitution and preamble was adopted at that meeting to govern a federation between the bodies represented and such others as might attach themselves to it in time to come. You will find in the minutes of the General Executive Board the proceedings of the meeting, also the constitution and preamble in full. Mr. Lee Johnson, Grand President of the Boiler-makers, was elected president. I had the honor to be elected vice-president. Mr. William Anderson, of the Brass-Workers, was elected Secretary-Treasurer. The boiler-makers, blacksmiths, and brass-workers submitted the plan to their organizations, which was approved by all of them. The Iron-Moulders' Union are taking a vote on the matter at this time. It remains for the delegates at this session to ratify the constitution of the Federated Metal Trades of America in order that we may proceed to bring about the benefits of this federation. It is not the purpose of this body to in any way interfere with the American Federation of Labor, but to bring about a co-operation between the metal trades, that they may assist one another in organizing their various crafts and in many other ways be of great assistance to the labor movement.

The time has come for the International Association of Machinists to take its stand among the organized trades unions of North America, and join hands, if we possibly can do so, with the American Federation of Labor. It is unnecessary for me to tell you the great benefits that would be derived from such an affiliation. It means to us the spreading of our organization in every hamlet where to-day we have no foothold. We have had great assistance from the trades unions, affiliated with the American Federation of Labor, in the past two years, for which we are more than grateful. We would be ingrates did we not extend our right hand to all sons of honorable toil and join with them for the purpose of solidifying the ranks of organized labor. It becomes your duty, as the representatives from the various countries where our banner is floating, to think well on this question of federation. If by joining the federation, we find that a mistake has been made, there is no law that will make it impossible for us to relinquish our membership. Therefore I am more than heartily in favor of, at least, making the attempt in taking some advanced steps to advance our organization. We have the foundation for one of the strongest trades unions in North America. We are also held in high esteem by organized labor generally. See to it that no effort is lost to place us in the front rank.

LINOTYPE MACHINISTS

You are well aware of the fact that machinists are as necessary in a printing establishment in these days as are the printers. The use of machines for setting type in newspaper offices are rapidly replacing the printer. In all offices where these machines are used it is necessary to employ one or more machinists or men who are qualified to take care of the machines. This new industry has opened up a new channel to employ the men of our craft. In order that we may be able to bring about an understanding between the Typographical Union and our organization the question of an agreement should receive careful consideration at your hands. We should also endeavor to arrange our laws in order that we might be able to take care of all who are employed in this class of work. Our present laws do not admit of our taking some men who are fully qualified to handle the linotype machines into our organization. This has caused considerable friction during the past year. The printers are very desirous of co-operating with us on this matter, but they also demand that we organize all the linotype machinists, then the question of agreement can be readily brought about. I have, on several occasions, met Mr. Prescott, Grand President of the International Typographical Union, when this matter was thoroughly talked over. The great difficulty experienced, however, was that the International Machinists' Union were members of the American Federation of Labor, to which the International Typographical Union were also attached. They very seriously objected to an agreement, as it would debar their members from these positions. At the last convention of the International Typographical Union, held in Louisville, Ky., the members of Linotype Lodge, No. 355, made application for a charter under the International Typographical Union. Hearing of this, I at once telegraphed the following message:

"W. B. PRESCOTT, Grand President International Typographical Union,
"Louisville, Ky.:

"International Association of Machinists protests against granting charters to linotype machinists. We are fully capable of handling that part of the business. We stand ready to assist you always to build up your organization. No breach should come between us now.

"Accept fraternal greetings.

"JAS. O'CONNELL, G. M. M."

The convention left the whole matter in the hands of the executive officers to make the best arrangement possible in order to bring about an agreement. If, however, we do not, at this convention, arrange our laws so that we can organize these men, it is possible that the International Typographical Union may try the experiment of issuing a charter to the linotype machinists. This would cause considerable friction between the two organizations. We should by all means steer clear of these breakers, as we have, at the present time, about nine-tenths of these men in our organization. The positions are ones that pay nearly double what the average machinists receive, and are well worth throwing every protection around them by this convention.

ADDING MORE BENEFICIAL FEATURES

Now-a-days when a man joins a labor organization, the first question he asks is, "What benefits are attached?" and when you tell him that the local lodge pays a small sick benefit he will at once say he can procure that from a fraternal society. Nearly all the trades unions to-day have a death benefit attached to their organization. I am heartily in favor of the I. A. of M. paying a small death benefit. I believe this can be done if we make the proper attempt. In order to add greater benefits, however, it is necessary that our per capita tax be increased. All the older trades unions wonder how it is that we can, so successfully, continue the business of our organization on such a small tax, but it has been because we have not paid out-of-work or death benefits, and, consequently, we have kept our heads above water. If the per capita tax was increased we could pay fifty dollars on the death of a member who was in good standing in the Association for six months. This would add, in a great measure, to our members keeping themselves paid up in their dues. It would also be a starting point for a protective fund that could be used in behalf of our members when they were involved in trouble. A good bank account means a good labor organization, and no money means dissension on every side. Weigh this matter carefully over in your minds of adopting some method that we may raise a fund whereby our brothers may take more interest in the organization generally. You have the cigar-makers, carpenters, printers, moulders, and a number of others whose financial systems have proven successful. We might well be guided by their years of experience.

OUR TRAVELLING CARD

The travelling card during these hard times has been a source of great assistance to our members who have been forced to travel in search of employment. It has been the means of procuring for them employment, in many instances feeding them when they were hungry, providing a place to lay their heads at night, and providing them with money with which to travel on. I estimate that in the past two years there has changed hands between our local lodges, on account of loans given our travelling brothers, $5,000. Notwithstanding all the assistance given to our travelling brothers, our travelling card has been most unmercifully abused. It has been beaten in almost every manner by those who should have the highest regard for it. While we must concede that the travellers were very much in need of assistance, notwithstanding this, I do not believe it was necessary at any stage during this depression for a brother to forge the name of another, to erase the dates on the card, change the amounts that were loaned him, or in any manner deface the cards. This has been the cause of an unlimited number of disputes between our local lodges, as to the returning of borrowed money, and the transfer of brothers from one lodge to another. Some of our lodges have stepped outside the laws entirely and reissued cards for men not members of their lodge. This has caused considerable trouble as to who was justly entitled to pay debts that might be incurred by such a traveller. We must make laws in this session that will prevent, in the future, such violations of the principles of our card as have occurred in the past. I recommend that the card system be changed to a system whereby each member of the organization shall have a number, and a card be adopted that can be used only when punched by some style that shall be adopted by this body or their executive officers. There are many forms of cards in use, from which we can readly devise a card that cannot be counterfeited nor abused in No. 14 of my decisions. You will find a very important point that our laws should cover, in order that our members may be transferred when their lodges have disbanded.

MOVING HEADQUARTERS

It was decided at our last convention by a vote of the delegates that the headquarters of the Grand Lodge be moved to Indianapolis, Ind. On page 87 of the Proceedings of the Indianapolis Convention you will find a resolution offered by Brother Ashe, of the General Executive Board, which reads as follows: "Whereas the delegate from Lodge No. 64 stated to this convention that in the event of our headquarters being removed to this city, Indianapolis would furnish suitable premises for that purpose, with a lease of such premises, rent free, for a term of five years, and also pay the expense of removal of said headquarters; therefore,

Resolved, That it is the sense of this convention that the promises made by the delegate from No. 64 be fulfilled as a condition precedent to the removal of our headquarters." This resolution has never been carried out by the lodges in Indianapolis, consequently, the headquarters have never been removed. In my opinion, the moving of headquarters is a question that should receive the closest attention by the delegates assembled. I also believe that it would be unwise for the delegates to select, on the spur of the moment, a city to make their permanent headquarters without knowing the inducements that would be offered, or the conditions that would surround the Grand Lodge. This question is of such a vast importance I believe it should be left in the hands of the executive officers to select from the number of cities the one most suitable for our organization, and offering us the best inducements. Our organization has become a very prominent factor in the labor movement, and to say that we should move the headquarters at once would be an injustice to ourselves and the labor movement generally. It would be impossible to move our headquarters in a day, a week, or a month. It would take time. Therefore, in considering this question, consider well before you act, for in the future we might regret our actions.

RUNNING TWO MACHINES AND DOING PIECE-WORK

In the past two years an effort has been made by a large number of manufacturers to introduce the plan of running two machines by one man. Our Constitution is very plain on this question, we have been more than successful in combatting the introduction of this system. In fact, wherever our members have refused to run two machines we have unquestionably made a success of the test. I am satisfied that we can, very successfully, prevent the introduction of this system, providing we have anything like the assistance of the men of our trade, but the question of piece-work is one that requires your careful consideration, as it has become an established system in nearly every section under the jurisdiction of our order; in fact, our Constitution itself allows the members to refuse to do piece-work in one shop, then step across the street and do it in another. This appears to me to be very inconsistent on our part. We will take as an illustration a railroad system where piece-work is in vogue on part of the system, but not over the entire road. If a man refuses to do the work in one shop he can go to the next town and do it under the same company. We have had considerable complaints during these two years on this question, and it has been one that is more than difficult to settle. It would be well for the delegates here assembled to consider whether it might not be better to adopt some measures whereby we could control the system of piece-work by limiting the amount per day each man might make. A large number of labor organizations have adopted this system and it is proving a success.

THE WORD "WHITE"

By authority of our last convention we were authorized to take a referendum vote as to striking the word "white" out of the Constitution. On December 1st, '93, I issued to the Association a circular calling upon the members to vote on this question. The result of this vote showed that about one-third of our membership took interest enough in the matter to vote on it. The result of the vote, as forwarded to the lodges on June 1, 1894, was as follows: The total number of votes cast to retain the word "white" in the Constitution, 2,604; total number cast to take the word out, 1913. The majority in favor of retaining the word, 691. The word "white" in our Constitution has received considerable notoriety through the press and by the distribution of literature by the International Machinists' Union to do us injury. Considerable feeling exists between some of our lodges on this matter, but no real break in our ranks has appeared as yet, and I trust will not in the future. It is unnecessary for me to comment any further on this question, as you know full well my views in regard to it.

BOYCOTTS

Our laws make no provision as to how boycotts can be placed on any firm or corporation. Notwithstanding this fact, we have had several in the past two years, in which we have been more than successful. I must frankly acknowledge, however, that it has not been through the energy of the members of our Association that success has crowned our efforts. We are indebted, to a considerable extent, to the assistance given us by other labor organizations. The most noted of our struggles in this line was with the Armour Packing Company at Kansas City, Mo., and with the Schneider-Trenkamp Company of Cleveland, O. The Armour affair was a great success to our organization in the Western States, and was adjusted to the satisfaction of our organization. The Cleveland boycott, however, was of a longer duration, but was finally settled to the satisfaction of our Association, the firm paying the expenses of the boycott. It is well, however, for this convention to deal carefully with the question of boycotts, as it is a weapon that can be used on both sides. Laws should be framed plainly stating under what conditions boycotts should be levied, and no such action should be taken without the approval of the grand lodge officers.

THE TALBOT FUND

On page 57 of the Proceedings of the Indianapolis Convention, you will find a resolution presented by the Committee on Resolutions, which was adopted by the convention, authorizing the Grand Master Machinist to appoint three trustees in the State of South Carolina to invest this fund in behalf of Mrs. Talbot and her children, and that the fund should be increased from the funds of the Grand Treasurer to $2,000. You are well aware of the fact that our ex-Treasurer, John J. Lamb, stole this fund with the other money he had in his hands, which left us without a dollar of this fund to pay Mrs. Talbot. Previous to the Indianapolis convention we were paying Mrs. Talbot $20.00 per month out of the money collected for that fund. By authority of the General Executive Board we have continued paying the same amount out of the general funds of the organization, owing to our being unable during these very trying times to replace the money stolen by our ex-Treasurer, and I would advise that the convention authorize the continuance of this plan for the present. You will find in the report of the Grand Secretary-Treasurer an account of this fund; also of the fund for Mrs. Mathews.

THE EXECUTIVE BOARD

The Constitution makes no provision for having a report of the General Executive Board printed previous to the convention, as is ordered in the case of the Grand Master Machinist and the Grand Secretary-Treasurer. The work of the Board in the past two years has been something enormous, and would make a voluminous document, which would necessitate a large expenditure of money to print it in a form that it might be understood. By authority of the General Executive Board it was thought best that the report be not printed unless authorized by the convention. However, the minutes have been put in such a shape that they can easily be read for the convention or gone over by a committee.

I adopted a system of numbering each grievance that was laid before the General Executive Board, in order to facilitate the correspondence that might be more readily answered. One hundred and twenty-six (126) cases have been laid before the Executive Board during my term. I also adopted a system of numbering each circular that I sent to the Executive Board giving an account of my actions, and the information that would keep the Executive Board thoroughly posted on all the doings of the order. Sixty-seven (67) circulars of this character have been sent to the Executive Board.

The duties of the Executive Board have been more than arduous, although, at times, our local lodges may have felt that the Executive Board were not as prompt in rendering their decision as they should have been; nevertheless, the Executive Board are to be complimented in the very judicious manner in which they have looked to the interest of the organization. It has been due to their careful consideration of all subjects that our organization to-day is one that is pointed to with pride by the trades unionists generally, especially by our own members.

Owing to the number of members on the Executive Board, it has been slow work at times to reach a decision. The Executive Board, in my opinion, is too large; in fact, it is top-heavy, and I recommend that it be reduced to not more than five (5) members. No brother should accept a position on the Executive Board unless he is so situated that he can give the business of the Executive Board prompt attention, especially should he be in a position that he could be called upon in a moment's notice to leave home to look after the interest of the order. Some difficulty has been experienced in this matter in the past, as the members of the board at all times could not get away at the call of the Grand Master Machinist. The Constitution provides that no two members of the board can be elected from any one State. This, in my opinion, is a very bad feature. The best qualified men in our organization might all live in one State, and would not be eligible for the office; consequently we would be losing the benefit of good members, if this law was not changed.

I believe the title of the Executive Board should be changed to first, second, third, fourth and fifth vice president, in order that they might be in a position to step into the Grand Lodge office in case of the death, resignation, or removal from office of the Grand Master Machinist.

I am highly in favor of changing the title of Grand Master Machinist to Grand President, as I believe the title, as it is at present, is superfluous.

In selecting your board you should be guided at all times in having men whom you would have the highest respect for, and especially men who are qualified to fill these responsible positions.

OUR JOURNAL

At the Indianapolis Convention it was decided that an editor should be placed in charge of the JOURNAL. It was also left in the hands of the General Executive Board to select a brother to fill this position. A number of applications were laid before the General Executive Board, which resulted in the selection of Brother Creamer, who at once assumed management of the same. The editor was not selected for a few months after the convention, and it became necessary for your Grand Master Machinist to edit the JOURNAL, for the time being. I found upon assuming the duties of this office that the JOURNAL subscription list was very badly mixed up. I also found that the accounts between the subscribers and the editor of the JOURNAL, Brother O'Day, were in a very bad state. Letters were coming in daily making complaints for not receiving the JOURNAL, and claiming to have paid their subscriptions. In going over the subscribers' list, no record could be found of the names, nor the books of the ex-editor did not show any cash received; however, in going over the files of correspondence, in nearly every case a letter would be found stating that enclosed you will find a post-office order for such and such an amount, which was very near positive evidence that the money had been received. This at once aroused my suspicions that the JOURNAL fund was not reported at Indianapolis as it should have been. I at once proceeded to have an investigation made, which resulted in finding that $319.15 had been received for subscriptions which were not reported by Brother O'Day in his accounts.

I also found that $21.25 had been received for advertising, which was also not reported. It was impossible for us to charge Brother O'Day directly with having misplaced this amount of money. We assume on the letters that are in the office that this amount of money had been received and was not reported. I corresponded with Brother O'Day on the matter, and while in Indianapolis on business, I personally paid him a visit and talked this matter over. He promised me to make an effort to straighten the matter up, and acknowledge that the amount for advertising was received, but the other he would not acknowledge, making various excuses for how it appeared as it did. The whole matter was laid before the Executive Board, and they advised that the best settlement possible be made. I have written Brother O'Day on two occasions since, but could not receive a reply.

I found also that a large number of our local lodges were not paying for the JOURNAL that was sent to the Secretary each month.

At the Louisville Convention a resolution was adopted, which has never appeared only in one issue of the JOURNAL after that convention, authorizing each lodge to pay to the Grand Lodge one ($1.00) dollar per year. We sent out bills to all the local lodges for their amounts; a large number responded promptly, but a great number are still indebted and some refuse positively to pay the amount claiming that it is their right to receive the JOURNAL gratis. A very large number of our JOURNALS are used monthly for organizing purposes; in fact, it is one of the best educators that can be sent from the Grand Lodge office, and great credit should be given the JOURNAL account for this purpose.

In order that you may know the exact standing of the JOURNAL, I herewith attach Brother Creamer's report as editor and manager.

DECISIONS OF THE G. M M.

During my term of office many points have been referred to me for a decision. Failing to find in our laws anything that would cover these points or questions asked, I have found it necessary to make the following decisions, which have been approved by the General Executive Board while they were in session. Each one of these decisions have covered a large number of cases, and have been the means of settling a large number of disputes between our local lodges. It would be well for this convention to ingraft some of the ideas expressed in my decisions into our laws, or to amend the laws that govern these points, which are all very essential. Herewith is attached the decisions in full:

No. 1. — $5.00 is the full amount that can be loaned on any one card. No more money can be borrowed until a new card is taken out.

No. 2. — All money borrowed on the old card must be placed on the new card if not paid.

No. 3. — No lodge has a right to issue a card to a member of another lodge. Brothers must apply to the lodges they are members of for new cards.

No. 4. — Lodges loaning money on a card issued by a lodge which surrenders its charter while the card is in force, must look to the brother holding the card for payment of the borrowed money.

No. 5. — Lodges surrendering their charters, and having members travelling with cards, should notify the Grand Lodge at once, that the lodges may be notified not to loan money on said cards.

No. 6 — When a brother is initiated by request of a sister lodge, he is still a member of the lodge electing him, and must obtain a transfer card from the lodge electing him before he can become a member of the lodge in which he is initiated.

No. 7. — When a lodge's travelling card has been forged, the lodge concerned should make it known to the organization at once.

No. 8. — A member whose card has been accepted is entitled to sick benefits of the lodge the same as an old member, providing he is not sick when his card is accepted.

No. 9 — Lodges must not issue cards for a longer period than sixty days.

No. 10 — Where lodges have issued cards for longer than sixty days, they must transfer the amount over sixty days to the lodge accepting the card.

No. 11.— Lodges are not allowed to charge fee on any pretence when taking members in on travelling cards.

No. 12 — When a lodge accepts the card of a travelling brother, the secretary must send the card to the lodge issuing it, giving notice of the brother's election.

No. 13. — When a card is presented and money has been borrowed on it, and the lodge waits the fifteen days required by the Constitution for a reply, and receives none, they should collect the amount on the card before acting on it; then they can hold the money until the lodge is heard from of which the brother is a member.

No. 14. — A brother who was a member of a lapsed lodge can pay his back dues to the Grand Lodge and procure a transfer card from the same to another lodge, providing he can show he was a member of the order, and no charges were pending against him.

No. 15. — When a man is elected in one lodge and initiated in another lodge, he is a member of the one that elects him.

No. 16. — The lodge electing a man a member is entitled to the intiation fee.

No. 17. — When a man is initiated on the fifteenth day of the month, he must pay dues from the first of the same month.

No. 18. — Members in good standing against whom charges are pending are supposed to be innocent until found guilty, and their status remains unaffected until final trial, providing a travelling card shall not be granted the accused in the meantime.

No. 19. — A man can be proposed for membership though he is out of work temporarily. (The law on this point that a man cannot make application for membership who is engaged in other business, such as running a store.)

No. 20. — The local lodge is the judge of the qualifications of all applicants for membership, limited only by the general laws.

No. 21. — Apprentices taken in on the half-rate plan are only entitled to half benefits from the Grand Lodge.

No. 22. — The Grand Lodge pays benefits to members of the order only. Non-members cannot be taken care of by the Association.

No. 23. — Lodges must pay per capita tax on apprentices to the amount of 12½ cents per quarter.

No. 24. — When a member is suspended and then reinstated, all back per capita tax must be paid to the Grand Lodge for the time he was suspended. (This also applies to assessments as well.)

No. 25. — The master machinist and foreman are the only authorized persons that should be in possession of the travelling pass-word.

No. 26. — Each lodge must subscribe for one copy of the official journal for the use of the lodge.

No. 27. — Any member against whom charges are pending shall not be allowed to preside at a lodge meeting.

No. 28. — A lodge has no right to say in its by-laws that a member can only draw sick benefits for twelve weeks in any one twelve months; if a brother complies with all the laws covering sick benefits and is again taken sick in the same year he is entitled to benefits.

No. 29. — The seal of a local should not be attached to blank paper.

No. 30. — Cards can be granted to an apprentice, but should be marked apprentice.

No. 31. — When an ex-brother who has been expelled wishes to make application again and his lodge has disbanded, he should apply to the nearest lodge, who may act on his application, provided they are acquainted with the facts of his expulsion.

CONCLUSION

In closing my report I wish to extend my sincere thanks and to acknowledge the many courtesies that have been extended to me in my travels. I appreciate more than words can express the assistance given me by the local lodges and by our members generally.

Many hard tasks have been made light by the cheerful assistance given at all times, for all of which I am very grateful.

I would be more than ungrateful did I not acknowledge the assistance given me by my colleagues at headquarters — Brothers Dawley and Creamer. Though we have experienced many trying positions, we have at all times had the most pleasant relations. To the members of the General Executive Board, I am very grateful for the many words of kind advice so cheerfully given on all occasions. Though we have not agreed at all times on every subject that came before us, yet we have all agreed with the majority, and made an honest effort to carry out the decisions agreed upon. I have administered the law without fear or favor. I may have made mistakes, but they have been of the head and not of the heart. However, I do not recall any of my acts that I would not repeat, for I am satisfied that they have all been for the good of the Order.

To the delegates here assembled I wish to say a few words. You have been selected by your lodges to map out the future destiny of our order. See to it that you are not led from performing this duty by those who would disrupt our order. In selecting your officers for the ensuing term do not be guided by sentiment or sympathy, but at all times vote for the men whom you believe have the interest of our order at heart, and will carry out its principles. You have every reason to feel proud of the standing of our organization to-day. The finger of scorn has not as yet been pointed at us, but, on the contrary, we enjoy the highest respect from all. I return to you to-day that with which you entrusted me two years ago. I have guarded it as carefully as though it was my own child, and whether I or some other member be chosen as your executive head in the future, you will find me as hard a worker in the cause of unionism and in behalf our craft as I have ever been.

Wishing you all a hearty welcome, and trusting that from our visit here we will take away with us many fond recollections of our gathering, and hoping that your deliberations will lead to a thorough organization of our craft, I am,

Respectfully and fraternally yours,
/s/ Jas. O'Connell
Grand Master Machinist.

Notes

ABBREVIATIONS FREQUENTLY USED

AFLEC	American Federation of Labor Executive Council
EC	International Association of Machinists Executive Council
GEB	International Association of Machinists General Executive Board
MMJ	Machinists' Monthly Journal

CHAPTER I *The Early Years*

1. Norman J. Ware, *The Labor Movement in the United States, 1860–1895* (New York, 1929).

2. John R. Commons and Associates, *History of Labour in the United States* (New York, 1918), II, 157.

3. International Association of Machinists, *Machinists' Monthly Journal* (hereafter cited *MMJ*), 1892, pp. 65–6; 1889, p. 2.

4. International Association of Machinists, *Circular* (unnumbered), September 10, 1888.

5. *MMJ,* 1892. End of each issue contained directory of lodges.

6. American Federation of Labor, *Proceedings,* 1890, p. 9ff.

7. *MMJ,* 1890, p. 3; 1890, p. 2, "let us emphasize," said Talbot at the first convention, "that we are not advocates of strikes, nor foes to capital, nor do we desire to create a breach between our employers and ourselves," 1889, p. 9.

8. Creamer, born on May 1, 1861, in Richmond, received his craft training at the Richmond Locomotive Works. He joined the Knights of Labor when its first local assembly (3157) was organized in Richmond, becoming in time its secretary. He was elected a delegate of the Knights' District Assembly 84 to the Atlanta Convention, but did not attend. He was later instrumental in organizing IAM Local Lodge 10 and represented it as a delegate at the Atlanta convention in 1889.

9. Dawley came from upstate New York but moved to Atlanta as a young man, where he joined the Knights.

10. Miles, although a resident of Texas, was born in Baltimore in 1851. At eighteen he was apprenticed to the Baltimore and Ohio Railroad. He moved to Iowa in 1882, and to Marshall Texas, in 1883. He died in 1892. *MMJ,* 1892, p. 99.

11. *MMJ,* 1890, pp. 3, 34–37, 180–181.

12. IAM General Executive Board (hereafter cited GEB), Minutes, 1891, pp. 18–19 (typed).

13. They were Simon N. Dolan and George F. Kirk. Dolan, born in Ohio in 1867, learned his trade on the Baltimore and Ohio Railroad and spent three years traveling as a "boomer." He was active in the Knights from 1884 to 1886. He then tried to organize his own machinists' union, the National Organization of Machinists. The attempt failed and he turned to helping Talbot.

14. GEB, Minutes, 1891, pp. 2ff., 8ff, 10ff (typed).

15. *MMJ,* 1891, pp. 238–9; 1891, pp. 55–6.

16. GEB, Minutes, 1892, pp. 28–72. *MMJ,* 1892, pp. 130, 285.

17. GEB, Minutes, 1892, pp. 33–48. *MMJ,* 1891, pp. 65–6, 354–5.

18. GEB, Minutes, 1892, pp. 56–7.

19. *MMJ,* 1893, p. 2.

Chapter II *Toward Bargaining Unionism: The O'Connell Administration*

1. See Appendix II for a reprint of his report to the 1895 convention.

2. International Association of Machinists, *Proceedings,* 1895, pp. 62, 83, xxiii. International Association of Machinists, *Machinists' Monthly Journal,* 1893, pp. 58, 61, 521; 1894, pp. 209–10.

3. IAM, *Proceedings,* 1895, pp. x, 33–4. *MMJ,* 1895, pp. 234–5, 523–8. American Federation of Labor, *Proceedings,* 1895, pp. 7, 58–9.

4. *MMJ,* 1895, pp. 234–5.

5. IAM, *Proceedings,* 1897, p. 243. AFL Executive Council (hereafter cited AFLEC), Minutes, Jul. 23–8, 1918, pp. 37, 71.

6. *MMJ,* 1894, pp. 182, 224, 358.

7. IAM, *Proceedings,* 1893, p. 89; 1895, pp. iii–iv; 1897, pp. 216–17. *MMJ,* 1893, pp. 283–4; 1894, p. 360.

8. IAM, *Proceedings,* 1895, pp. v, 18–28, 29, 33. *MMJ,* 1894, pp. 97, 139; 1895, pp. 4–5, 53.

9. Lloyd Ulman, *The Rise of the National Union* (Cambridge, 1955), pp. 270–301. *MMJ,* 1894, pp. 94–5; 1895, pp. 185–7.

10. IAM, *Proceedings,* 1895, pp. 237–8, viii; 1897, pp. 220–1, 237–8.

11. *MMJ,* 1896, p. 527; 1895, pp. 277–80, 338–42, 375–6; 1896, pp. 51, 70–1, 108–10, 157–9, 503; 1897, pp. 10–11, 51–4, 61–3, 111–13; 1898, pp. 277, 414, 593–6; 1899, pp. 3–4, 68ff., 138, 146, 193; 1896, pp. 144–5, 248.

12. IAM, *Proceedings,* 1897, pp. 219–20, 273; 1899, pp. 331–4, 402; 1901, pp. 464–5, 649. International Association of Machinists, *Circular,* Aug. 22, 1895. *MMJ,* 1895, p. 359; 1896, pp. 93, 94, 98ff., 131, 384–5, 415–16, 431–2, 479; 1897, pp. 299–302; 1898, p. 2; 1899, pp. 43, 69, 125–6, 465, 493–4; 1900, pp. 13–14, 74, 80–1, 90–2, 97–9, 484; 1901, pp. 73, 76; 1902, p. 16.

13. IAM, *Proceedings,* 1893, pp. 66–73; 1895, pp. 43–7; 1897, pp. 213ff; 1899, pp. 337, 405. *MMJ,* 1893, pp. 135–6; 1894, pp. 359, 400; 1895, p. 436; 1896, pp. 245, 295, 338, 343.

14. IAM, *Proceedings,* 1897, p. 222.

15. See note 12.

16. IAM, *Proceedings,* 1895, p. xiii; 1899, pp. 335–6, 390–1, 403–4; 1901, p. 650; 1903, pp. 482, 599; 1905, pp. 78–9; 1907, pp. 68, 962ff (officers' report: hereafter cited o.r.); 1909, pp. 119–20, 929 (o.r.). *MMJ,* 1899, pp. 181–2; 1901, pp. 77, 130, 198, 378–80, 416, 439, 524–7, 536, 669–71, 690, 693; 1904, pp. 525, 778. *Circular* 21, May 12, 1904.

17. IAM, *Proceedings,* 1899, p. 391.

18. *MMJ,* 1900, pp. 195–9, 215, 249, 311, 347–8, 286, 438, 694.

19. Marguerite Green, *The National Civic Federation and the American Labor Movement, 1900–1925* (Washington, 1956), p. 31.

20. Clarence E. Bonnett, *Employers' Associations in the United States: A Study of Typical Associations* (New York, 1922), pp. 98–136.

21. *MMJ,* 1900, pp. 195–9, 249–55, 308, 347–9, 368–90, 438–40, 496–8, 555; 1901, pp. 3, 198, 378–80, 416, 439, 524–7, 436, 669–71, 690ff, 695, 753–4, 866–7; 1902, p. 254, 329–31. *Proceedings* 1901, p. 467 (o.r.).

22. Green, *The National Civic Federation . . .,* pp. 20–4.

23. Selig Perlman and Philip Taft, *History of Labor in the United States, 1896–1932* (New York, 1935), IV, 136.

24. Robert A. Hoxie, *Scientific Management and Labor* (New York and London, 1915).

25. One of the first uses of the term is in International Association of Machinists General Executive Board, Proposition 105 (April 3, 1907).

26. *MMJ*, 1902, p. 406; 1903, p. 352. IAM, *Proceedings*, 1903, pp. 607ff, 613. *Circular* 4, July 7, 1903.

27. IAM, *Proceedings*, 1909, pp. 918ff. *MMJ*, 1911, pp. 133–4, 151–2; 1910, p. 1044; 1904, p. 791; 1909, p. 928.

28. GEB, Proposition 37 (Feb. 26, 1906), 75 (Oct. 12, 1906), 114 (April 22, 1907).

29. *MMJ*, 1909, p. 947; 1911, pp. 1015–16; 1900, p. 409; 1901, p. 902; 1907, p. 981; 1909, p. 971.

30. IAM, *Proceedings*, 1905, pp. 35, 71, 79; 1907, pp. 41, 71; 1909, pp. 79, 94, 124. *Circular* 28, Nov. 24, 1904; 1, Jan. 1, 1908; 4, Mar. 27, 1908; 6, June 24, 1908; 8, Sept. 15, 1908; 9, Oct. 10, 1908; 11, Dec. 11, 1908, p. 481 (o.r.).

31. IAM, *Proceedings*, 1903, pp. 617, 635; 1899, pp. 337, 405; 1901, pp. 176, 468 (o.r.); 1903, p. 487 (o.r.).

32. *MMJ*, 1902, pp. 17, 509, 733; 1904, pp. 445, 489, 927.

33. AFLEC, Minutes, Sept. 20–25, 1915.

34. *MMJ*, 1904, p. 352. *Circular* 14, Jan. 15, 1904.

35. Earlier action is implied in numerous speeches at conventions.

36. IAM, *Proceedings*, 1916, p. 17.

37. *Circular* 32, Jan. 2, 1905.

38. IAM, *Proceedings*, 1901, p. 630; 1907, p. 963 (o.r.); 1909, pp. 136, 917 (o.r.). GEB, Minutes, Feb. 21–Mar. 3, 1921.

39. Mrs. J. Borden Harriman, *From Pinafores to Politics* (New York, 1923), pp. 137–8.

40. *MMJ*, 1900, pp. 347, 409; 1901, p. 902. *Circular* 28, Nov. 4, 1904; 1 Jan. 1, 1908; 4, March 27, 1908; 6, June 24, 1908; 8, Sept. 15, 1908; 9, Oct. 10, 1908; 11, Dec. 11, 1908. IAM, Proceedings, 1905, pp. 35, 71, 79; 1907, pp. 41, 71; 1909, pp. 79, 94, 124, 911 (o.r.).

41. *Circular* 6, Jan. 3, 1906. *MMJ*, 1906, pp. 163–4. GEB, Proposition 39 (Mar. 23, 1906).

42. *Circular* 7, Jan. 3, 1906; 12, April 4, 1906; 21, Feb. 13, 1907. GEB, Proposition 22 (Jan. 5, 1906), 130 (July 12, 1907).

43. *Circular* 51, July 7, 1908; 8, Sept. 15, 1908. *MMJ*, 1909, pp. 1044, 1075.

44. See Table 7, chapter VII.

45. GEB, Proposition 87 (Dec. 29, 1906); 28 (July 24, 1906).

46. James F. O'Connell, "Some Brief History," circular, June 15, 1911.

47. IAM, *Proceedings*, 1911, pp. 158–62.

CHAPTER III *The Declining Momentum of Reform: The Johnston Administration*

1. International Association of Machinists, *Machinists' Monthly Journal*, 1912, pp. 59–60.

2. *Circular* 5, Nov. 10, 1911.

3. For a general history of this strike, see Selig Perlman and Philip Taft, *History of Labor in the United States* (New York, 1935), IV, 368–73.

4. IAM, *Proceedings*, 1911, pp. 75ff. See *MMJ*, 1911, pp. 995, 969, 997–1001, 1006–7, 1010–11; 1916, pp. 15ff., 106–7. *Circular* 13, April 30, 1912; 17, June 25, 1912; 19, July 29, 1912; 26, Mar. 15, 1913; 29, May 9, 1913; 48, Oct. 31, 1914; 51, Dec. 12, 1914; 59, Mar. 15, 1915; 64, June 18, 1915.

5. It included the machinists, the boilermakers, sheet metal workers and pipe fitters, carmen, and electric workers.

6. *Circular* 64, June 18, 1915.

7. *MMJ*, 1916, 202–4. Railway Employees' Dept., *Proceedings*, 1916 (typed).

8. IAM, *Proceedings*, 1916, pp. 63, 142.

9. Carl Persons, *The Lizard's Trail* (Chicago, 1918), a study of the Illinois Central and Harriman strike from 1911 to 1915 inclusive.

10. For a discussion of the work of the United States Commission on Industrial Relations, see Mark Perlman, *Labor Union Theories in America: Background and Development* (Evanston, 1958), pp. 279–301. See also *Proceedings* of the conference of IAM officers, general organizers, and business agents in St. Louis, Mar. 9–14, 1914.

11. Milton J. Nadworny, *Scientific Management and the Unions, 1900–1932* (Cambridge, 1955), pp. 31–3.

12. AFLEC, Minutes, 1912–1925.

13. Unprinted *Circular* to general executive board, Nov. 19, 1915. See also correspondence between Johnston and Preston and the general executive board, dated Nov. 16, 1915.

14. GEB, Minutes, Feb. 14, 1916.

15. GEB, Proposition 9 (December 7, 1916).

16. IAM, *Proceedings,* 1911, p. 79; 1920, p. 919. See also GEB, Minutes, Jan. 14, 1913; Mar. 17, 1914; Sept. 14–22, 1917; June 15–21, 1918; Nov. 21 to Dec. 2, 1921.

17. IAM, *Proceedings,* 1911, pp. 112–14, 155; 1916, pp. 18–19, 87. GEB, Minutes, Jan. 3, 1912; Jan. 1913. *Circular* 50, Dec. 5, 1914. *MMJ,* 1916, pp. 112–13, 611ff.

18. IAM, *Proceedings,* 1903 pp. 487–8; 1909 pp. 935–8. GEB, Minutes, June 1912; Mar. 17, 1914; Sept. 17, 1914; Dec. 28, 1914–Jan. 3, 1915. *MMJ,* 1907, pp. 1177–85; 1911, 37ff.

19. *Circular* 16, June 20, 1912.

20. GEB, Minutes, Dec. 28, 1914. See also *Circular Letter,* Nov. 14, 1914 from Local Lodge 126 (Chicago).

21. IAM, *Proceedings,* 1916, pp. 64–5, 71–2, 111–12; see also *Proceedings* of Executive Session, June 29 to July 3, 1916. GEB, Minutes, Mar. 23, 1906; Feb. 9, 1912; Mar. 3, 1912; Mar. 8, 1912; Mar. 16, 1914; Mar. 22, 1916; May 9, 1916; Sept. 8, 1916; Jan. 17, 1917; May 28–June 28, 1917. *Circular* 74, May 19, 1916; 6, 1916; 7, 1917; 9, 1917; 11, 1917; 12, 1917. *MMJ,* 1916, p. 517; 1917, pp. 774–5.

22. He was given an exemption card in 1929 (letter from general secretary treasurer, Aug. 7, 1929).

23. *Proceedings* of the Executive Session, 1916, p. 98.

24. GEB, Proposition 8 (April 29, 1914). GEB, Minutes, Jan. 15, 1914.

25. *Circular* 41, April 25, 1914.

26. GEB, Minutes, June 16, 1916. IAM, *Proceedings,* 1916, pp. 63, 111.

27. GEB, Minutes, Jan. 4, 1912.

28. *Circular* 44, April 25, 1914.

29. *Circular* 35, July 30, 1913.

30. *Circular,* 33, 1918.

31. GEB, Minutes, May 28–June 28, 1917. See also IAM, *Proceedings,* 1916, p. 376.

32. Later the religious issue became important. Here it is useful to note that Conlon, Johnston's ally, was a Catholic.

33. *Circular* 54, 1919. *MMJ,* 1920, p. 323.

34. GEB, Minutes, Feb. 1917.

35. GEB, Proposition 216 (April 9, 1918).

36. GEB, Minutes, May 28–June 28, 1918; Oct. 13–23, 1919; Jan. 28–Mar. 8, 1920. GEB, Proposition 62 (April 28, 1917); 181 (Jan. 2, 1918); 243 (Aug. 19, 1919).

37. GEB, Minutes, Mar. 4–11, 1918; Nov. 14–17, 1918. *Circular* 19, 1918.

38. GEB, Minutes, June 15–22, 1918. Cellar File 7, folder 4, records of the IAM.

39. See Chapter VII for a discussion of this point.

40. GEB, Minutes, Oct. 13–23, 1919.

41. See S. Perlman and P. Taft, *History of Labor,* pp. 489–514.

42. IAM, *Proceedings*, 1920, pp. 111–14, 591. *Circular* 85, Feb. 10, 1921; 90, April 18, 1921. GEB, Minutes, Sept. 7–Oct. 6, 1920; Jan. 31–Feb. 8, 1922; May 15–24, 1922. GEB, Proposition 182 (Aug. 25, 1921); 224 (July 28, 1919).

43. S. Perlman and P. Taft, *History of Labor*, pp. 519–523.

44. GEB, Minutes, Nov. 4–16, 1922; July 29–Aug. 2, 1924; Feb. 11–14, 1925. Proposition 217 (July 3, 1922); 218 (July 13, 1922); 225 (Aug. 30, 1922); 260 (May 14, 1924). EC, Minutes, Feb. 3–Mar. 3, 1926; June 25–July 3, 1926. *Circular* 123, 1922; 128, 1922; 130, 1922; 133, Feb. 12, 1923; 185, Sept. 1, 1925; 198, June 1, 1926. *Proceedings*, 1924, pp. 225ff, 233ff. See also Railway Employees' Dept., *Proceedings*, 1922, pp. 52–151 *et passim;* 1926, pp. 1–61.

45. Sumner H. Slichter, *Union Policies and Industrial Management* (Washington, 1941), pp. 437–479. GEB, Minutes, July 9–12, 1923; Jan. 15–23, 1924; Aug. 29–Sept. 2, 1924. Also Cellar File 1, folder 4.

46. *Circular* 185, Sept. 1, 1925. Also EC, Minutes, Feb. 3–Mar. 3, 1926.

47. GEB, Minutes, August 29–Sept. 2, 1924.

48. IAM, *Proceedings*, 1924.

49. GEB, Minutes, April 5–16, 1921; May 15–24, 1922. EC, *Circular* 17, Jan. 12, 1926.

50. EC, Minutes, June 25–July 3, 1926. GEB, Minutes, June 15–21, 1918; Jan. 31–Feb. 8, 1919.

51. GEB, *Circular* 63, 1920. Minutes, Feb. 3–11, 1921; Sept. 8–27, 1924.

52. EC, *Circular* 9, Nov. 17, 1925. Proposition 8 (Nov. 23, 1925). Minutes, Feb. 3–Mar. 3, 1927; Feb. 20–27 1928; Mar. 8–17, 1937; May 23–27, 1938.

53. IAM, *Proceedings*, 1924, 41ff.

54. GEB, Minutes, July 18–29, 1921; Nov. 21–Dec. 2, 1921; Jan. 28–Mar. 8, 1920; Oct. 13–23, 1919; July 9–12, 1923; Sept. 1924. *Proceedings*, 1924, pp. 150ff. *Circular* 165, Oct. 20, 1924.

55. GEB, Minutes, Sept. 8–27, 1924. *Proceedings*, 1924, pp. 203ff, 206–213.

56. GEB, Proposition 102 (Aug. 2, 1910); 111 (Aug. 14, 1920), 194 (Oct. 14, 1921).

57. GEB, Minutes, May 15–24, 1922; April 20–25, 1923; Aug. 12–16, 1923; Nov. 21–27, 1923; April 2–6, 1924; Sept. 8–27, 1924. GEB, Proposition 252 (Mar. 10, 1924).

58. GEB, Minutes, Nov. 29–Dec. 15, 1919; May 10–28, 1920; Jan. 31–Feb. 8, 1922; May 15–24, 1922; Nov. 21–27, 1923. EC, Minutes, Feb. 3–Mar. 3, 1926; Feb. 20–27, 1928; Mar. 7–12, 1932; Nov. 12–17, 1934; Sept. 27–Oct. 7, 1944. *Circular* 72, 1920. *Proceedings*, 1920, pp. 513, 922, 928. EC, Proposition 674 (Aug. 29, 1938), 685 (Sept. 16, 1938).

59. IAM, *Proceedings*, 1920, pp. 41, 159, 512, 901 (o.r.); 1924, p. 73; 1928, pp. 131–2; 1948, pp. 63–4 (o.r.). GEB, Minutes, Jan. 28–Mar. 8, 1920. EC, Minutes, Feb. 3–Mar. 3, 1926; Aug. 8–13, 1932; June 12–16, 1933; Dec. 7–15, 1936; Dec. 3–12, 1940; Apr. 1–10, 1947; Mar. 6–16, 1950. *Circular* 215, Aug. 22, 1927. EC, Proposition 231 (Nov. 10, 1933); 349 (May 1, 1936); 1451 (Sept. 30, 1941).

60. IAM, *Proceedings*, 1920, pp. 43, 87, 168, 386–90. *Circular* 77, 1921; 96, 1921.

61. GEB, Minutes, Feb. 21–Mar. 3, 1921; July 18–29, 1921; Jan. 31–Feb. 8, 1922; Sept. 8–27, 1924. *Circular* 103, 1921.

62. *Circular* 78, 1921; 92, 1921.

63. GEB, Minutes, Jan. 28–Mar. 8, 1920; Apr. 18–26, 1920. GEB, Proposition, Feb. 21, 1920.

64. IAM, *Proceedings*, 1924, pp. 15ff, quotation is at p. 20. GEB, Minutes, July 29–Aug. 2, 1924. *Circular* 161, Aug. 9, 1924; 163, Oct. 16, 1924.

65. IAM, *Proceedings*, 1920, pp. 203–4, 227, 286, 327–36, 358–67, 460, also pp. 920–1 (o.r.). *Proceedings*, 1924, pp. 94ff.

66. *Circular* 183, Aug. 15, 1925.

67. EC, Minutes, July 1–12, 1925.

68. (Washington, 1925) privately printed.

69. GEB, Minutes, Feb. 11–15, 1925. EC, Minutes, July 1–12, 1925; Sept. 21–6, 1925; Feb. 3–Mar. 3, 1926. EC, *Circular* 9, Nov. 17, 1925; 174, Mar. 25, 1925; 180, July 20, 1925; 181 (no date); 182, Aug. 8, 1925; (unnumbered), Aug. 11, 1925; 186, Sept. 22, 1925; 187, Oct. 1, 1925; 189, Nov. 7, 1925; 193, Dec. 20, 1925; 194, Feb. 18, 1926; 210, Aug. 8, 1927.

70. EC, Minutes, Sept. 26, 1925; Feb. 2–Mar. 3, 1926. EC, *Circular* 11, Nov. 25, 1925; 13, Dec. 8, 1925. Proposition 1 (Nov. 19, 1925).

71. EC, *Circular* 4, Oct. 16, 1925.

72. EC, *Circular* 6, Nov. 2, 1925.

73. EC, Minutes, Feb. 3–Mar. 3, 1926; Feb. 3–Mar. 3, 1926.

74. *Circular* 197, May 21, 1926.

75. EC, Minutes, Dec. 4–Jan. 14, 1933; April 8–17, 1935. EC, Proposition 278 (Aug. 6, 1934).

Chapter IV *Stability: The Wharton Administration*

1. Wharton actually became international president on June 30, 1926; he formerly retired at the end of 1939, although he was on leave for some time prior to his actual retirement.

2. Leo Wolman, *Ebb and Flow of Unionism* (New York, 1936), pp. 21–75.

3. International Association of Machinists, *Machinists' Monthly Journal,* 1926, pp. 324–5.

4. *Circular* 198, June 1, 1926. EC, Minutes, Feb. 3–Mar. 3, 1926; June 25–July 3, 1926. *Proceedings,* 1928, pp. 77–9.

5. EC, Minutes, Feb. 3–Mar. 3, 1926.

6. IAM, *Proceedings,* 1928, pp. 91–101, 116–20.

7. EC, Minutes, May 17–26, 1926; June 25–July 3, 1926.

8. *Circular* 183, Aug. 15, 1925; 208, Mar. 1, 1927.

9. EC, Minutes, Feb. 14–22, 1927; July 14–19, 1930; Dec. 4–14, 1933; June 11–17, 1928; Sept. 10–29, 1928. *Proceedings,* 1928, pp. 76–80, 132, 256–7, 272.

10. EC, Minutes, June 27–July 2, 1927; April 6–11, 1931. *Circular* 248, Mar. 12, 1929. AFLEC, Minutes, May 10–17, 1927; Jan. 17–25, 1928; Apr. 4–May 2, 1928.

11. *Circular* 211, Apr. 9, 1927; 212, July 12, 1927; 218, Aug. 17, 1927. Quotation is from *Circular* 211.

12. EC, Minutes, Sept. 10–29, 1928; Feb. 4–11, 1929. *Circular* 244, Jan. 15, 1929.

13. *Proceedings,* 1928, pp. 250–52, 305–08, 461–2.

14. *MMJ,* 1928, pp. 691ff.

15. *Proceedings,* 1928, pp. 308–09.

16. EC, Proposition 91, July 13, 1928. *Proceedings,* 1928, pp. 193–8; 1929, pp. 323–4. See also *MMJ,* 1928, pp. 691ff.

17. IAM, *Proceedings,* 1928, pp. 120ff., 137ff.

18. *MMJ,* 1928, pp. 446, 465, 590; 1929, p. 671. *Circular* 232, June 19, 1928; 235, Aug. 29, 1928; 238 Nov. 1, 1928; 253 Apr. 27, 1929. EC, Minutes, Feb. 20–27, 1928; June 11–17, 1928.

19. IAM, *Proceedings,* 1928, pp. 68–75.

20. *Circular* 252, Mar. 25, 1929; 262, Jan. 6, 1930; 267, June 10, 1930; 273, Sept. 10, 1930. MMJ, 1930, pp. 528–9. EC, Minutes, June 24–July 1, 1929; Dec. 9–14, 1929; July 14–19, 1930.

21. *Circular* 257, July 10, 1929. EC, Minutes, June 24–July 1, 1929; Feb. 4–11, 1929; July 14–19, 1930; Mar. 3–12, 1932; Feb. 13–25, 1933; Mar. 8–13, 1937.

22. Proposition 100 (April 30, 1929). *Circular* 244, Jan. 15, 1929; 260, Dec. 15, 1929; 263, Jan. 6, 1930; 343, Mar. 5, 1937; 351, Dec. 1, 1937. MMJ, 1930, p. 42.

23. EC, Minutes, Feb. 4–11, 1929. Cellar File 2, folder 9 (1928). Quotation from folder 9.

24. EC, Minutes, Feb. 4–11, 1929.

25. *Circular* 270, July 29, 1930.

26. EC, Minutes, Dec. 9–14, 1929; Apr. 6–11, 1931; Nov. 16–24, 1931; Feb. 13–25, 1933. AFLEC, Minutes, Jan. 30–Feb. 14, 1939.

27. *Proceedings,* 1932, pp. 81–2, 122, 137–8, 409–22.

28. EC, Minutes, June 24–July 1, 1929; July 24–29, 1930. *Proceedings,* 1940, p. 407. *Circular* 269, May 28, 1930; 274, Sept. 30, 1930; 281, Apr. 23, 1930; 238, Oct. 21, 1931; 289, Mar. 25, 1932; 294, Nov. 1, 1932; 302, May 18, 1933; 308, Nov. 1, 1933; 313, June 8, 1934; 317, Oct. 22, 1934; 319, May 20, 1935; 323, Nov. 1, 1935; 329, Apr. 20, 1936, 336, Oct. 20, 1936; 344, Apr. 14, 1937; 354, Apr. 1, 1938; 356, June 21, 1938. Proposition 451 (May 14, 1937); 595 (Apr. 4, 1938).

29. EC, Minutes, Nov. 16–24, 1931; Aug. 8–13, 1932; Mar. 6–9, 1933. *Circular* 287, Aug. 11, 1931; 292, Aug. 15, 1932. *MMJ,* 1932, p. 128.

30. EC, Minutes, Mar. 6–9, 1933. EC, Proposition 216 (May 19, 1933).

31. EC, Minutes, Aug. 8–13, 1932; June 12–16, 1933; Dec. 7–15, 1936; Dec. 3–12, 1940; Apr. 1–10, 1947; Mar. 6–16, 1950. Proposition 231 (Nov. 10, 1933); 349 (May 1, 1936); 1451 (Sept. 30, 1941). *Proceedings,* 1948, pp. 63–4 (o.r.).

32. GEB, Proposition 77 (Mar. 12, 1919).

33. EC, Minutes, Aug. 8–13, 1932; Feb. 13–25, 1933; Sept. 9–14, 1935; Feb. 17–26, 1936.

34. EC, Proposition 336 (Jan. 11, 1936); 339 (Feb. 6, 1936).

35. EC, Minutes, Feb. 17–26, 1936; July 27–31, 1936; Dec. 7–15, 1936. Proposition 342 (April 8, 1936). *Circular* 334, 1936; 335, Aug. 28, 1936. *Proceedings,* 1936, pp. 316–355.

36. EC, Minutes, Dec. 7–15, 1936. *Circular* (unnumbered), Jan. 14, 1937.

37. EC, Minutes, Mar. 8–17, 1937; June 28–July 1, 1937; Apr. 11–18, 1943; Oct. 24–29, 1938.

38. *Proceedings,* 1936, pp. 296–306. EC, Minutes, Dec. 7–15, 1936.

39. EC, Proposition, July 21, 1938.

40. EC, Minutes, May 23–27, 1938.

41. EC, Proposition 507 (Aug. 11, 1937), 511 (Aug. 20, 1937), 516 (Aug. 30, 1937), 575 (Feb. 14, 1938). EC, Minutes, May 23–27, 1938; Sept. 14–Oct. 3, 1936; Mar. 8–13, 1937; Sept. 13–19, 1937.

42. EC, Proposition 578 (Feb. 18, 1938). Cellar File 2, folder 55 (1937).

43. Walter Galenson, *The CIO Challenge to the AFL: A History of the American Labor Movement 1935–1941* (Cambridge, 1960). Harry A. Millis and Emily Clark Brown, *From the Wagner Act to Taft Hartley* (Chicago, 1950).

44. *Circular* 278, Mar. 4, 1931. EC, Minutes, Feb. 13–25, 1933; Nov. 12–17, 1934; Apr. 8–17, 1935. AFLEC, Minutes, Aug. 22–Sept. 2, 1938; Nov. 12–17, 1934; Apr. 8–17, 1935; Sept. 9–14, 1935.

45. EC, Minutes, Feb. 17–26, 1936; Nov. 13–22, 1939. Proposition 298 (Dec. 7, 1934); 327 (Nov. 1, 1935). AFLEC, Minutes, Jan. 17–26, 1936; Aug. 4–13, 1941.

46. EC, Minutes, Sept. 9–14, 1935; Feb. 17–26, 1936. *MMJ,* 1935, p. 511. EC, Proposition 468 (June 2, 1932); 478 (June 9, 1937). *Circular* 345, June 14, 1937.

47. EC, Minutes, June 28–July 1, 1937.

48. EC, Proposition 416 (Feb. 25, 1937).

49. EC, Minutes, June 12–16, 1933; Nov. 16–24, 1931; Feb. 13–25, 1933.

50. See note 31.

51. EC, Minutes, Dec. 13–17, 1937; May 23–27, 1938; Oct. 24–29, 1938; May 3–13, 1939; Nov. 13–22, 1939; Sept. 14–Oct. 3, 1936; Sept. 6–30, 1940.

52. EC, Proposition 154 (Apr. 20, 1931); 160 (May 26, 1931); 359 (May 22, 1936); 438 (Apr. 26, 1937). *Proceedings* 1936, pp. 47–9; 1940, pp. 222–6. Galenson, *The CIO Challenge,* p. 501.

53. *Proceedings,* 1936 pp. 45–6.

54. *Duplex Printing Press Co.* vs. IAM, 252 Fed. 722; 254 U.S. 443 (1921).

55. *Proceedings,* 1940, pp. 3–44.

Chapter V *Midpassage: The Brown Administration*

1. American Federation of Labor, EC, Minutes, Jan. 24–Feb. 8, 1938; May 13–21, 1940.

2. IAM, *Proceedings,* 1945 (closed session).

3. EC, Minutes, Dec. 3–12, 1940; Mar. 3–12, 1941; Apr. 16–23, 1941. Proposition 1161 (Feb. 16, 1941).

4. EC, Minutes, Apr. 16–23, 1941. Letter is from Harvey W. Brown to Fred Laudeman, dated Mar. 28, 1941. See also letter from Laudeman to Brown, dated Apr. 7, 1941; AFLEC, Minutes, Jan. 30–Feb. 14, 1939; Aug. 4–13, 1941; Oct. 5, 1941; Jan. 12–17, 1942.

5. EC, Proposition 1161 (Feb. 15, 1941). AFLEC, Minutes, May 13–21, 1940; Oct. 1, 1940. AFL, *Proceedings,* 1941, p. 447.

6. *Circular* 400, Feb. 26, 1943. AFLEC, Minutes, Jan. 18–27, 1943; May 17–22, 1943. Minutes, Feb. 16–26, 1943; June 4–7, 1943; Aug. 11–18, 1943.

7. MMJ, 1943, p. 548. AFLEC, Minutes, Aug. 9–16, 1943. *Circular* 403, June 1, 1943; 407, Nov. 5, 1943.

8. AFLEC, Minutes, Aug. 9–16, 1943.

9. EC, Minutes, Jan. 26–31, 1942; May 14–June 7, 1943; Aug. 11–18, 1943; Dec. 9–17, 1943; Nov. 17–19; Dec. 7–9, 1944. AFLEC, Minutes, Aug. 9–16, 1943, Oct. 3, 5, 6, 13, 15, 1943.

10. *Circular* 410, Dec. 23, 1943. MMJ, 1944, p. 101; 1945, p. 73.

11. IAM, *Proceedings,* 1945, pp. 180–7; 1945 (closed session). See AFLEC, Minutes, Feb. 5–15, 1945; Aug. 6–14, 1945; Oct. 15–24, 1945. EC, Minutes, Sept. 27–Oct. 7, 1944; Nov. 17–19, 1944; Dec. 7–9, 1944; Feb. 20–March 6, 1940. *Circular* 425, Jan. 2, 1945; 428, Mar. 20, 1945.

12. The minority report of the convention *ad hoc* committee on disaffiliation was signed by five, including Don Burrows and A. H. Greener, whose political importance in Chicago was great. The other dissenters were C. C. Mitchell (Houston), A. Ballerini (San Francisco), and Ed. Schroedter (Richmond).

13. EC, Minutes, Feb. 5–Apr. 5, 1946. *Circular* 456A, Feb. 20, 1946; 478, Apr. 15, 1947; 481, June 9, 1947; 482, July 27, 1947. AFLEC, Minutes, Jan. 21–31, 1946.

14. *Circular* 455, Jan. 29, 1946; 456, Feb. 13, 1946. EC, Minutes, Feb. 5–Apr. 5, 1946. AFLEC, Minutes, Jan. 21–31, 1946; May 15–22, 1946.

15. It is clear that the decision to disaffiliate was taken with great reluctance. See *Circular* 481, June 9, 1947, as well as an open letter to General Vice-President Melton, dated July 9, 1947. Melton had objected to *Circular* 481, and had sent a letter to the membership on June 17, 1947. EC, Minutes, Apr. 1–10, 1947; Feb. 17–18, 1949.

16. AFLEC, Minutes, Aug. 12–20, 1946; Oct. 6–18, 1946; Jan. 29–Feb. 5, 1947; Apr. 21–25, 1947; Aug. 23–27, 1948; Jan. 31–Feb. 8, 1949; Aug. 12–20, 1946; Jan. 31–Feb. 8, 1949.

17. John T. Dunlop, "Structural Changes in the American Labor Movement and

Industrial Relations Systems," in Industrial Relations Research Association; *Proceedings,* 1956, pp. 12–32.

18. See Chapter XI for a full discussion of the problem.

19. Source material for this section includes some very rewarding interviews with General Vice-President Roy Brown as well as Grand Lodge Representatives A. C. McGraw, C. E. Lindsay, Thomas McNett, and Dale Reed.

20. EC, Proposition 419 (Mar. 16, 1937); 653 (July 15, 1938); 973 (June 13, 1940); 1154 (Feb. 5, 1941); 1011 (July 15, 1940); 1026 (July 29, 1940).

21. EC, Minutes, Mar. 3–12, 1941; Apr. 16–23, 1941; Apr. 29–May 18, 1941; June 12–13, 1941.

22. EC, Proposition 1625 (June 20, 1942); 1630 (June 26, 1942); 1802 (Sept. 4, 1943). EC, Minutes, Oct. 24, 1942; May 14–June 7, 1943; Aug. 11–18, 1943; Oct. 1–7, 1943; Dec. 9–17, 1943; Nov. 17–19, 1944.

23. *Circular* 401, Apr. 5, 1943; 411, Jan. 17, 1944. EC, Minutes, Dec. 9–17, 1943. EC, Proposition 3571 (Aug. 11, 1949).

24. *Circular* 430, Mar. 23, 1945.

25. Discussed in Chapter VI.

26. *Circular* 462, May 3, 1946. EC, Proposition 3524 (Jan. 18, 1949). EC, Minutes, Aug. 30–Sept. 25, 1948; Feb. 17–18, 1949; Apr. 21–May 6, 1949; Nov. 28–Dec. 9, 1949; Apr. 27–28, 1950. AFLEC, Minutes, Aug. 23–27, 1948.

27. EC, Minutes, Nov. 13–22, 1939; and July 18–24, 1941. Harvey Brown denied the allegation made by T. W. Howard, replying instead that Wharton's reasons were the nominal ones given; that is, he was uncooperative. There is some reason to believe that Brown may have underestimated in his reply Wharton's sensitivity to the Communism issue.

28. EC, Proposition 1196 (Mar. 27, 1941); 1315 (June 16, 1941); 1392 (Aug. 20, 1941). EC, Minutes, Apr. 29–May 18, 1941; June 12–13, 1941; July 18–24, 1941. AFLEC, Minutes, May 19–20, 1941.

29. EC, Minutes, May 17–26, 1944; June 24–25, 1944; Oct. 15–Nov. 14, 1945; Feb. 5–Apr. 5, 1946. *Circular* 460, Apr. 16, 1946.

30. Local Lodge 68 applied for return of local autonomy in 1948, but its request was denied. In the spring of 1949 the order of supervision was lifted, and some of the fines levied on the members were modified: EC, Minutes, Aug. 30–Sept. 25, 1948; Apr. 21–May 6, 1949.

31. Mark Perlman, *Labor Union Theories in America: Background and Development* (Evanston, 1958), pp. 31, 148–50, 235.

32. Charles C. Killingsworth, *State Labor Relations Acts: A Study of Public Policy* (Chicago, 1948).

33. EC, Minutes, Nov. 16–24, 1931; Apr. 3–13, 1939; May 17–26, 1944; Aug. 1–15, 1945; Sept. 26–Oct. 10, 1946; Apr. 1–10, 1947; July 14–26, 1947. *Circular* 440, Aug. 8, 1945; 467, Aug. 21, 1946; 439 (undated). *Proceedings,* 1945, 136–40, 207, 403–04.

34. EC, Minutes, Feb. 20–Mar. 6, 1945; Apr. 24–May 9, 1945; Apr. 1–10, 1947; Mar. 30–Apr. 8, June 24–July 10, 1948; Aug. 30–Sept. 25, 1948. Proposition 3812 (Feb. 5, 1952). *Circular* 496, May 3, 1948. *Proceedings,* 1948, pp. 35–48, 128–67.

35. EC, Minutes, Apr. 1–10, 1947; July 14–26, 1947; June 24–July 10, 1948; Aug. 30–Sept. 25, 1948.

36. *Proceedings,* 1948, pp. 340–1.

37. EC, Minutes, Apr. 3–13, 1939; Dec. 3–12, 1940; June 12–13, 1941; May 13–26, 1942; Apr. 24–May 9, 1945; Aug. 1–15, 1945. *Circular* 396, June 11, 1942.

38. EC, Minutes, Jan. 13–Feb. 6, 1947; July 14–26, 1947; July 30–Aug. 3, 1951. *Circular* 536, June 13, 1951. *Proceedings,* 1948, pp. 47–9 (o.r.); 1940, p. 408.

39. EC, Minutes, Mar. 3–12, 1941; Apr. 16–23, 1941; Jan. 26–31, 1942; Feb. 20–Mar. 6, 1945; Jan. 15–27, 1951; Apr. 15–May 1, 1952.

40. *Proceedings,* 1920, p. 180. GEB, Minutes, Feb. 21–Mar. 3, 1921. EC, Minutes, Sept. 9–14, 1935; Oct. 24–29, 1938; Apr. 24–May 9, 1945; June 6–12, 1946. EC, Proposition 1294 (May 29, 1941).

41. Letter from H. W. Brown to "all vice-presidents [*sic*] in the United States," dated June 11, 1943; letter from H. W. Brown 'to general vice-presidents in the United States," dated Sept. 1, 1943.

42. EC, Minutes, Jan. 26–31, 1942. *Circular* 472 Dec. 20, 1946.

43. EC, Minutes, Jan. 13–Feb. 6, 1947; Apr. 1–10, 1947; Nov. 17–Dec. 5, 1947; Mar. 30–Apr. 13, 1948; June 24–July 10, 1948.

44. *Circular* 473, Jan. 20, 1947.

45. *Circular* 501, July 3, 1948.

46. EC, Proposition 1079 (Oct. 10, 1940). EC, Minutes, Aug. 1–15, 1945; Oct. 15–Nov. 14, 1945; Feb. 5–Apr. 5, 1946; May 17–26, 1944; June 6–12, 1946; Sept. 26–Oct. 10, 1946; Jan. 13–Feb. 6, 1947; Nov. 15–22, 1948; Apr. 21–May 6, 1949; Jan. 15–27, 1951; Dec. 1–6, 1952.

47. EC, Proposition 1801 (Sept. 3, 1943). *Proceedings,* 1948, pp. 2630 (o.r.).

48. EC, Minutes, Feb. 20–Mar. 6, 1945; Apr. 24–May 9, 1945; Aug. 1–15, 1945; Feb. 5–Apr. 5, 1946; Apr. 1–10, 1947; Mar. 30–Apr. 13, 1948; Apr. 17–24, 1951. Proposition 2083 (Nov. 17, 1945). But cf. EC, Minutes, Feb. 14–22, 1927, when the cost of a public relations program was held to be uneconomic.

49. EC, Minutes, Apr. 24–May 9, 1945; Aug. 1–15, 1945; Oct. 15–Nov. 14, 1945. *Proceedings,* 1948, pp. 68–73 (o.r.).

50. EC, Minutes, Sept. 26–Oct. 10, 1946; July 14–26, 1947; Nov. 17–Dec. 5, 1947. *Circular* 492, Apr. 5, 1948; (unnumbered) June 21, 1948; 500, July 8, 1948; 506, Nov. 30, 1948; 511, Mar. 31, 1949; 519, Dec. 19, 1949; 523, June 15, 1950; 531, Jan. 9, 1951; 537, July 19, 1951; 542, May 23, 1952; (unnumbered) June 25, 1952.

51. EC, Minutes, July 14–26, 1947.

52. GEB, Minutes, Mar. 17, 1914; Dec. 28–Jan. 3, 1914–15; July 18–29, 1921. *Proceedings,* 1920, p. 587.

53. GEB, Minutes, July 9–12, 1923. EC, Minutes, Sept. 12–22, 1926; Feb. 20–27, 1928; Feb. 13–25, 1933. *Proceedings,* 1924; pp. 83–90; 1928, p. 81 (o.r.).

54. *Circular* 424, Jan. 2, 1945; 435, May 21, 1945. EC, Minutes, Feb. 20–Mar. 6, 1945; Aug. 1–15, 1945; Jan. 13–Feb. 6, 1947; Apr. 1–10, 1947; Nov. 17–Dec. 5, 1947; Mar. 30–Apr. 13, 1948; Aug. 30–Sept. 25, 1948; Apr. 21–May 6, 1949. EC, Proposition 1570 (Mar. 12, 1942); 977 (Mar. 16, 1945); 2717 (Apr. 30, 1947); 3041 (Dec. 16, 1947); 3064 (Jan. 14, 1948); 3099 (Feb. 11, 1948).

55. Interview with Fred Laudeman, Sept. 9, 1957. *Proceedings,* 1948, pp. 415–16.

56. EC, Minutes, July 14–26, 1947. *Proceedings,* 1948, pp. 412–36.

57. EC, Proposition 3569 (Aug. 8, 1949). EC, Minutes, Apr. 13–21, 1945.

CHAPTER VI *The Period of Reconciliation: The Start of the Hayes Administration*

1. AFLEC, Minutes, Aug. 12–20, 1946; Oct. 16–18, 1946; Aug. 23–7, 1948; Jan. 22–29, 1951.

2. There were talks almost immediately after the disaffiliation, but they provided no solutions. See AFLEC, Minutes, Oct. 6–18, 1946; Jan. 29–Feb. 5, 1947; Apr. 21–25, 1947.

3. EC, Proposition 3640 (June 27, 1950). AFLEC, Minutes, Jan. 30–Feb. 7, 1950; May 8–11, 1950.

4. EC, Minutes, Feb. 17–18, 1949; Mar. 6–16, 1950; Apr. 27–28, 1950; Sept. 25–

Oct. 5, 1950. Proposition 3640 (June 27, 1950). *Circular* 525, Oct. 25, 1950; 526, Oct. 25, 1950. *MMJ,* 1951, pp. 62–3. AFLEC, Minutes, Jan. 31–Feb. 8, 1949; Aug. 15–19, 1949.

5. Principally the carpenters and the teamsters.

6. EC, Proposition 3640 (June 27, 1950).

7. *Circular* 525, Oct. 25, 1950; 526, Oct. 25, 1950. AFLEC, Minutes, Aug. 8–11, 1950; Jan. 22–29, 1951.

8. EC, Minutes, Jan. 15–27, 1951. AFLEC, Minutes, Jan. 22–29, 1051; Jan. 28–Feb. 5, 1952; May 19–22, 1952.

9. EC, Minutes, Apr. 13–21, 1952; Aug. 25–29, 1953.

10. *New York Times,* Sept. 26, 1953.

11. EC, Minutes, Feb. 17–18, 1949; Apr. 27–28, 1950; Sept. 25–Oct. 5, 1950; Dec. 1–6, 1952. Proposition 4024 (July 7, 1953).

12. *Circular* 513, Sept. 30, 1949. EC, Minutes, Feb. 17–18, 1949; July 18–22, 1949; Mar. 6–16, 1950; Jan. 15–27, 1951; July 30–Aug. 3, 1951; Nov. 26–30, 1951; Aug. 28–Sept. 19, 1952; Dec. 1–6, 1952; Apr. 13–21, 1953; Nov. 30–Dec. 7, 1953. Proposition 4000 (May 20, 1953); 4124 (July 23, 1954).

13. EC, Minutes, Apr. 13–21, 1953. Proposition 4009 (June 4, 1953).

14. EC, Minutes, Aug. 25–29, 1953; Nov. 30–Dec. 7, 1953; Feb. 20–27, 1928; Mar. 8–17, 1937; May 23–27, 1938; Nov. 13–22, 1939; May 6–17, 1940; Mar. 3–12, 1941; July 18–24, 1941; Nov. 17–19, 1944; Feb. 5–Apr. 5, 1945; Jan. 13–Feb. 6, 1947; Mar. 9–16, 1954. *Circular* 392, July 30, 1941. Proposition 808 (July 10, 1939); 1143 (Jan. 21, 1941); 1739 (Mar. 18, 1943). *Proceedings,* 1940, p. 450.

15. EC, Minutes, Apr. 27–28, 1950; Apr. 17–24, 1951; Nov. 26–30, 1951; Mar. 9–16, 1954; Sept. 9–17, 1954. Proposition 4118 (June 25, 1954). *Circular* 571, Jan. 17, 1955.

16. Selig Perlman, *A Theory of the Labor Movement* (New York, 1949), pp. 169ff.

17. Mark Perlman, *Labor Union Theories in America: Background and Development* (Evanston, 1958), pp. 214–41.

Chapter VII *The Government of the Grand Lodge*

1. Since this chapter was written, William Leiserson's work, *American Trade Union Democracy* (New York, 1959), has been published posthumously. Coincidentally, the similarity of the author's terminology and that of Mr. Leiserson, makes for ready comparison of material.

2. *Constitution,* 1891: "Subordinate lodges," Art. 1, Sect. 1, p. 19.

3. IAM, *Proceedings,* 1897, p. 222. Italics added.

4. *Constitution,* 1901: "Subordinate lodges," Art. 1, Sect. 1, p. 20.

5. IAM, *Proceedings,* 1903, pp. 587–9.

6. *Constitution,* 1903: "Subordinate lodges," Art. 1, Sect. 1, p. 20; 1905: "Subordinate lodges," Art. 1, Sect. 1, p. 26.

7. Mrs. J. Borden Harriman, *From Pinafores to Politics* (New York, 1923), pp. 137–8.

8. *MMJ,* 1904, p. 201.

9. IAM, *Proceedings,* 1903, p. 489 (o.r.); 1907, pp. 5, 6. *MMJ,* 1899, pp. 149, 603; 1907, p. 963; 1909, p. 917; p. 991.

10. *Constitution,* 1921: Art. F, Sect. 9, p. 71.

11. EC, Minutes, Aug. 18–22, 1942.

12. *Constitution,* 1953: "Jurisdiction of the International Association of Machinists," p. iv; 1895: Art. 8, Sect. 1, p. 19.

13. EC, Minutes, Feb. 3–Mar. 3, 1926.

14. George E. Barnett, *The Printers, A Study in American Unionism* (Cambridge, 1909), pp. 58–9.

15. From 1912 until 1916 concurrent membership in the National Civic Federation rendered an individual ineligible for office in the IAM.

16. GEB, Minutes, May 15–24, 1922. Proposition 23 (Nov. 8, 1918).

17. *Circular* 209, Mar. 1, 1927.

18. GEB, Minutes (July 1891).

19. *MMJ,* 1892, p. 257.

20. IAM, *Proceedings,* 1893, p. 89; 1895, pp. iii–iv (o.r.); 1897, pp. 216–17. *MMJ,* 1893, pp. 283–4; 1894, p. 360.

21. IAM, *Proceedings,* 1895, pp. 38–41.

22. During 1950 it was discovered that a trusted senior employee of the general secretary-treasurer's department had embezzled no less than $215,000. Of this, the IAM recovered a bare $7300. Once again, as in 1893, the IAM discovered too late that its bond protection was inadequately drawn. Thus the net loss to the organization was in excess of $200,000. See EC, Minutes, Sept. 25–Oct. 5, 1950; Jan. 15–27, 1951; Nov. 26–30, 1951.

23. *Constitution,* 1901: Art. IV, Sect. 6, p. 11.

24. The practice antedated the formal authorization. For example, General Vice-President Carr was brought to headquarters by Wharton.

25. *MMJ,* 1900, p. 310; 1910, pp. 834–42.

26. *Constitution,* 1925: Art. VI, Sect. 1, p. 19.

27. EC, Minutes, April 16–23, 1941; July 18–24, 1941; Oct. 15–Nov. 14, 1941; Sept. 26–Oct. 10, 1946; Jan. 13–Feb. 6, 1947.

28. The *Machinists' Monthly Journal* was abolished in 1956.

29. *Proceedings,* 1911, pp. 121–3, 143–5. MMJ, 1911, pp. 976, 978, 993.

30. Lloyd G. Reynolds and Charles C. Killingsworth, *Trade Union Publications* (Baltimore, 1944), I, 182–6.

31. "Memories of the Past," *MMJ,* 1922, pp. 235–7, 307–09, 360–3, 457–61, 523–7, 588–92, 651–7, 725–30, 782–8; 1923, pp. 17–24, 80–3, 116–20, 135, 164–70, 191–3, 222, 236–239, 269, 282–4, 317, 373–5, 414, 428–30, 461–3, 523–6, 558–9, 570–3.

32. IAM, *Proceedings,* 1945, p. 276–8.

33. See Chapter IV.

34. Paraphrased from *Constitution,* 1946: Art. K, Sect. 5, pp. 85–6.

CHAPTER VIII *The Quantitative View of the IAM's Development*

1. In technical jargon, the dues elasticity of membership is probably very low during periods of labor shortage (and high wages), while it may grow to impressive proportions during periods of labor surplus (and low wages).

2. In 1956 the membership was distributed within industries as follows:

Airframe	23.3%	Mixed	7.8
Air Transportation	3.3	Production Worker	7.0
Auto	8.7	Railroad	7.8
Contract	40.8	Tool and Die	1.3

Airframe lodges constituted the largest type of headquarters in the southern Pacific coast, the northwest, the Canadian, and the southeastern, areas. Contract lodges dominated the northeastern, and both midwestern areas.

3. Figures are available starting in 1948 with 16,395; 1949, 13,939; 1950, 11,467; 1951, 10,817; 1952, 11,661.

4. The collection of much of this material as well as part of the analysis was done by Mr. Alan G. Wilner, while a student at The Johns Hopkins University.

CHAPTER IX *The Meaning of Jurisdiction*

1. John T. Dunlop, "Jurisdictional Disputes: 10 Types," *The Constructor,* July 1953, pp. 165–73.

2. IAM, *Proceedings,* 1897, pp. 219–20, 273; 1899, pp. 331ff., 402; 1901, pp. 464–5 (o.r.), 649; 1916, p. 108. *MMJ,* 1895, p. 359; 1896, pp. 93, 98ff., 131, 384–5, 415–16, 431–2, 479; 1897, pp. 279–302; 1898, p. 2; 1899, pp. 43, 69, 125–6, 223, 438–40, 441, 461, 493, 774; 1900, pp. 13, 71–4, 90–2, 97–9, 484; 1901, pp. 73ff.; 1902, p. 16.

3. IAM General Executive Board, Proposition 9 (Dec. 7, 1916). IAM Executive Council, Minutes, Aug. 25–29, 1953.

4. IAM, *Proceedings,* 1911, pp. 112–14, 155; 1916, pp. 18–19 (o.r.), 87, 112–13; 1920, pp. 176, 1917–19 (o.r.). *Circular* 50, 1914; 400, Feb. 26, 1943; 403, June 1, 1943; 407, Nov. 5, 1943; 419, Dec. 12, 1944; 571, Jan. 17, 1955. GEB, Minutes, Jan. 3, 1912; Jan. 1913; May–June, 1917; Apr. 18–26, 1920. GEB, Proposition 205 (Mar. 15, 1918); 243 (May 28, 1918). *MMJ,* 1916, pp. 611ff. EC, Minutes, July 14–19, 1930; Apr. 6–11, 1931; Nov. 16–24, 1931; Feb. 13–25, 1932; Dec. 13–17, 1937; May 23–7, 1938; Mar. 15–20, 1939; Dec. 3–12, 1940; Apr. 16–23, 1941; Mar. 3–12, 1941; Apr. 16–23, 1941 (includes letters from Brown to Landemann, dated Mar. 28, 1941 and from Landemann to Brown, dated April 2, 1941); Apr. 1–10, 1947; Apr. 27–28, 1950; Mar. 9–16, 1954; Sept. 9–17, 1954. Proposition 1161 (Feb. 15, 1941); 4118 (June 25, 1954).

5. *Proceedings,* 1903, pp. 487–8 (o.r.); 1905, pp. 23, 35; 1909, pp. 66, 81–93, 105–07; 1916, p. 20. *MMJ,* 1909, pp. 935–8, 946, 1177–85; 1911, pp. 37ff., 1003. GEB, Minutes, June 1912; Mar. 17, 1914; Sept. 17, 1914; Dec. 28, 1914–Jan. 3, 1915.

6. *Proceedings,* 1911, p. 79; 1916, p. 20 (o.r.); 1920, p. 919. GEB, Minutes, Jan. 14, 1913; Mar. 17, 1914; Sept. 14–22, 1917; June 15–21, 1918; Nov. 21–Dec. 2, 1921.

7. *Circular* 430, Mar. 23, 1945; 513, Sept. 30, 1949. EC, Proposition 3571 (Aug. 11, 1949); 4000 (May 20, 1953). Minutes, Feb. 17–18, 1949; July 18–22, 1949; Mar. 6–16, 1950; Jan. 15–27, 1951; July 30–Aug. 3, 1951; Nov. 26–30, 1951; Aug. 28–Sept. 19, 1952; Dec. 1–6, 1952; Apr. 13–21, 1953; Nov. 30–Dec. 7, 1953; Mar. 7–21, 1932.

8. GEB, Minutes, Nov. 12, 1917.

9. IAM, Proceedings, 1916, pp. 91ff., 101ff. *Circular* 211, April 9, 1927; 212, June 12, 1927; 218, Aug. 17, 1927. EC, Minutes, June 12–16, 1933; Apr. 17–24, 1951.

10. *Proceedings,* 1905, p. 26; 1909, p. 128. GEB, Minutes, Nov. 21–Dec. 2, 1921.

11. *Proceedings,* 1916, p. 111. *Circular* 21, 1918. GEB, Proposition 192 (Feb. 9, 1918). EC, Minutes, June 24–July 1, 1929; May 14–June 7, 1943; Mar. 30–Apr. 17, 1948; June 24–July 10, 1948; Mar. 9–16, 1954.

12. IAM, *Proceedings,* 1916, pp. 85–6, 147. GEB, Proposition 14 (Jan. 9, 1917). GEB, Minutes, July 10, 1916; Sept. 14–22, 1917; Nov. 12–27, 1917; Feb. 5–19, 1917.

13. EC, Minutes, May 14–June 7, 1943.

14. *Circular* 40, 1919.

15. GEB, Minutes, Jan. 28–Feb. 2, 1919; Jan. 31–Feb. 8, 1922; June 15–21, 1918. EC, Minutes, Sept. 27–Oct. 7, 1944. *MMJ,* 1922, p. 601.

16. GEB, Minutes, May 15–24, 1922. EC, Minutes, Nov. 10–14, 1930; Dec. 9–14, 1929.

17. *Circular* 248, Mar. 12, 1929. EC, Minutes, Nov. 10–14, 1930; Apr. 6–11, 1931; Jan. 26–31, 1942; Feb. 20–23, 1942.

18. *Proceedings,* 1916, p. 19 (o.r.); 1920, pp. 917ff. (o.r.), 220–24. *Circular* 49, 1919; 319, July 30, 1941; 9, Nov. 17, 1925. EC, Proposition 8 (Nov. 23, 1925); 808 (July 10, 1939); 1143 (Jan. 21, 1941); 1739 (Mar. 18, 1943). EC, Minutes, Feb. 3–Mar. 3, 1927; Feb. 20–27, 1928; Mar. 8–17, 1937; Feb. 23–27, 1938; Nov. 13–22, 1939; May 6–17, 1940; Mar. 3–12, 1941; July 18–24, 1941; Nov. 17–19, 1944; Jan. 13–Feb. 6, 1947; Mar. 9–16, 1954. *Circular* 462, May 3, 1946. EC, Minutes, Nov. 10–14, 1930; Sept. 27–Oct. 7,

1944; Feb. 17–18, 1949; Apr. 21–May 6, 1949; Nov. 28–Dec. 9, 1949; Mar. 6–16, 1950; Apr. 27–28, 1950; Sept. 25–Oct. 5, 1950; Dec. 1–6, 1952. EC, Proposition 727 (Jan. 31, 1939); 1049 (Aug. 15, 1940); 3524 (Jan. 18, 1949); 4024 (July 7, 1953).

CHAPTER X *The IAM and Employers*

1. Sidney and Beatrice Webb, *Industrial Democracy* (London, 1920 ed.).
2. IAM, *Machinists' Monthly Journal,* 1892, pp. 214–15, 280; 1895, pp. 442–3; 1902, p. 120; 1903, pp. 172–3; 1905, p. 492.
3. Lee Thomas, a grand lodge representative, organized a school to train IAM personnel in the technical surveys of the National Labor Relations Board.
4. *Circular* 468, Nov. 5, 1946. IAM Executive Council, Minutes, July 14–26, 1947; Mar. 30–Apr. 13, 1948; June 24–July 10, 1948. EC, Proposition 671 (Aug. 22, 1938).
5. EC, Minutes, Jan. 13–Feb. 6, 1947.

CHAPTER XI *Unionism and Community Values*

1. IAM, *Machinists' Monthly Journal,* 1890, pp. 194–5; 1896, pp. 414–15.
2. IAM, *Proceedings* 1899, pp. 350–1, 362, 1901; p. 653; 1903, pp. 434, 552, 570, 637; 1905, pp. 62–3; 1907, p. 14; 1920 pp. 6, 10–14, 37.
3. IAM General Executive Board, Proposition 299 (Feb. 21, 1920).
4. IAM, *Proceedings,* 1924, pp. 15ff.
5. See Chapter IV.
6. IAM Executive Council, Minutes, Nov. 16–24, 1931.
7. His candidacy was endorsed by the executive council when he ran for Congress in 1942; EC, Minutes, May 13–26, 1942.
8. IAM Executive Council, Proposition 441 (May 3, 1937).
9. EC, Minutes, Sept. 10–29, 1928.
10. *MMJ,* 1907, p. 969.
11. GEB, Proposition (Nov. 29, 1918).
12. IAM, *Proceedings,* 1920, pp. 207, 219, 385–6, 582; 1936, executive session (undated and not printed with regular proceedings); 1940, executive session, Sept. 27, 1940 (not printed with regular proceedings).
13. EC, Minutes, Dec. 3–12, 1940; July 18–24, 1941; Jan. 26–31, 1942.
14. IAM, *Proceedings,* 1948, closed session Sept. 21, 1948 (not printed with regular proceedings).
15. EC, Minutes, Dec. 9–17, 1943.
16. IAM, *Proceedings,* 1945, closed session Nov. 3, 5, 1945 (not printed).
17. *Circular* 487, Dec. 11, 1947.
18. IAM, *Proceedings,* 1948, closed session, Sept. 21, 1948 (not printed).
19. Norfolk and Southern Bus lines and Texas Motor Freight lines. NLRB Hearing, Case 16–R–2223, pp. 3232–3242 (Apr. 9, 1943).
20. See Note 18.
21. Letter to all grand lodge representatives and auditors, special representatives, business representatives railroad and airline general chairmen, from the general secretary-treasurer (Jan. 18, 1954).
22. EC, Minutes, July 30–Aug. 3, 1951.
23. GEB, Minutes, Apr. 5–16, 1921.
24. IAM, *Constitution,* 1929: Art. XXI, Sect. 2 and 3.
25. Case of Tim Buck: EC, Proposition 87 (Apr. 18, 1928); case of H. G. Price: EC, Proposition 84 (Mar. 5, 1928); 136 (June 5, 1930); case of William Simons: EC, Minutes, Feb. 4–11, 1929; case of C. E. Webber: EC, Proposition 102 (May 14, 1929).

26. EC, Minutes, Sept. 14–Oct. 3, 1936; Sept. 13–19, 1937; Dec. 13–17, 1937. See also Cellar File 2, folder 55, and EC, Proposition 578 (Feb. 18, 1938).

27. See chapter V.

28. IAM, Proceedings, 1940, closed session (not printed).

29. For instance, a gift to Father Flanagan's Boys' School was refused because such action was *ultra vires* of the council: EC, Minutes, Nov. 16–21, 1942; Nov. 17–Dec. 5, 1947; Jan. 15–27, 1951.

Index